TRAVELLE

TRAVELLERS IN EGYPT

Edited by
Paul & Janet Starkey

TAURIS PARKE PAPERBACKS
LONDON ● NEW YORK

Published in 2001 by Tauris Parke Paperbacks
an imprint of I.B.Tauris & Co Ltd
Victoria House, Bloomsbury Square, London WC1B 4DZ
175 Fifth Avenue, New York NY 10010
www.ibtauris.com

In the United States of America and in Canada distributed by St Martin's Press
175 Fifth Avenue, New York NY 10010

First published in 1998 by I.B.Tauris & Co Ltd

ISBN 1 86064 674 3

A full CIP record for this book is available from the British Library
A full CIP record for this book is available from the Library of Congress

Library of Congress catalog card: available

Printed and bound in Great Britain by MPG Books Ltd, Bodmin

Contents

Preface

The idea of a conference on Travellers in Egypt was first broached many years ago in the course of correspondence between myself and Neil Cooke, Michel Azim and Jason Thompson as we struggled to correlate conflicting data in the various letters and diaries on which we were engaged. 'Conference' was a rather grand word for what seemed likely to be the four of us meeting round a kitchen table but in the event it was easily justified as over eighty people finally arrived at the Oriental Museum in July 1995 for three days of papers, discussion and what might be best described as 'other conference activities'.

The conference brought together people from a variety of academic fields with so many contributions that it was necessary to run some sessions in parallel. It is therefore good to have this volume as a permanent record of the proceedings and in some cases as the first opportunity to see what our colleagues had to say.

Grateful thanks are due to all those who made the conference a success by their attendance and contributions and who have helped in the production of this volume.

John Ruffle
The Oriental Museum, University of Durham

Acknowledgements

Thanks and acknowledgement are due to the Oriental Museum for hosting the Conference in 1995, to the Centre for Middle Eastern and Islamic Studies, University of Durham for financial assistance and support in the preparation of this volume, and to the University of Durham Publications Board for generous subvention towards the cost of publication.

Paul and Janet Starkey
CMEIS, University of Durham, 1997

∾ Introduction

Paul and Janet Starkey

The subject of foreign travel – in particular, travel by Westerners to regions and countries further East – is one that has attracted an increasing amount of attention, both popular and scholarly, over recent years. This attention has been manifest not only in a growing number of conferences, books and articles devoted to the subject, but also in the establishment of an Association (ASTENE: Association for the Study of Travel in Egypt and the Near East), dedicated to encouraging research in this field.

Among the reasons for the growing attraction of the topic is the fact that the subject clearly has the potential to cross the boundaries between different scholarly disciplines and to overcome the sometimes rather artificial barriers between the professional academic and the enthusiastic amateur. Interdisciplinary by its very nature, it is a field, which brings together not only, Egyptologists, literary critics and historians, but also Arabists, architects and town-planners, archivists and a range of other specialists. The material that underpins this writing is vast and often diverse in its scope and extent, and much basic research remains to be done on it; but it also raises broader and more philosophical questions about the nature and scope of the cross-cultural contacts that are made through travel, and their impact on the cultures concerned.

The chapters in the present volume bring together contributions by experts who approach the subject from a wide variety of perspectives, often with different underlying assumptions. Behind many of these various approaches, however, lies the question which forms the theme of the first chapter by Hussein Fahim: to what extent did European travellers form a cultural image of modern Egypt as they wanted it to be rather than as it was in reality?

Most papers in the volume concentrate on the nineteenth century; for despite recent debate on the significance of this date for the socio-economic development of the country, it was the consequences of Napoleon's invasion in 1798 which raised European interest in Egypt to a new level and which added the country to the list of places to be visited by any well-travelled European. As the third and fourth chapters in the volume show, however nineteenth-century travellers were not without their historical antecedents. Peter Holt's account of Pietro Della Valle's visity to Ottoman Egypt in 1615–16 in an attempt to heal a broken heart conveys the sense of a less complex age, when preconceptions about the country were based mainly on classical authors and the Bible. Della Valle visited the Pyramids and Sinai; he was a careful observer and lively narrator, without prejudices, and his outlook may be regarded as a prototype for that of many later Western travellers. Rosemarie Said Zahlan's chapter looks at a traveller of a rather different sort: George Baldwin, a merchant and maverick, who in the course of his trading career amassed a vast knowledge of Egyptian affairs. After many years of almost constant dispute with rival European traders, British officials and the Sublime Porte his expertise was at last recognised by the British authorities and he returned to Egypt as consul-general between 1786 and 1793. Zahlan's chapter paints a vivid picture not only of the complex diplomatic manoeuvrings by Egyptian leaders and European diplomats but also of the repeated plagues which affected the whole community, Egyptian and non-Egyptian alike.

Many travellers to Egypt in the nineteenth century, as now, were motivated by an interest in the ancient civilisation of Egypt, which had received a boost with Champollion's decipherment of the hieroglyphic script in 1821–22. Any suggestion that this category of travellers was composed exclusively of dry-as-dust scholars is quickly dispelled by the accounts presented here, however; in many cases, passion for the new science of Egyptology was combined with other interests of a quite extraordinary variety. The flamboyant Belzoni, for example, discussed by Peter Clayton, actually began his career as a circus strongman; after travelling to Egypt in 1814, he worked on a hydraulic water-wheel for Muhammad 'Ali and when this venture failed was commissioned by Henry Salt, the British consul, to collect ancient Egyptian material—a pioneer of early exploratory Egyptology. Belzoni removed statues from Thebes and Karnak and excavated the temple at Abu Simbel; in 1817 he found the tomb of Seti I in the Valley of the Kings and the following year discovered the entrance to the Great Pyramid in Giza. Though no scholar, his account of his operations and excavations, published in 1820, is one of the most fascinating books in the whole of the literature about Egypt. Another brilliant and eccentric man was W. J. Bankes, who seems to have sought danger and excitement in travel in Egypt and Nubia. Patricia Usick describes his two journeys, one in 1815 and another in 1818–19, with Salt, Beechey, Ricci and Linant de Bellefonds; together, they drew and recorded all the then-known standing monuments along the Nile from Cairo to Sennar. Bankes was particularly interested in bilingual inscriptions, which he rightly regarded as the key to the decipherment of hieroglyphics and to dating the monuments. Linant de Bellefonds himself, a fine draughtsman and an acute observer, had begun his career by developing the irrigation system of Upper

Egypt, and eventually became Minister for Public Works and member of the viceroy's private council. The notebooks of his journey to Siwa Oasis in 1820 make delightful reading and, with newly transcribed manuscripts deposited at the Louvre at their disposal, Marcel Kurz and Pascale Linant de Bellefonds have had a wealth of interesting source material to draw on for their chapter.

Other Egyptologists discussed in the volume include Heinrich von Minutoli, whose collection formed the basis of the world-renowned collection of Berlin's Egyptian Museum, although many of the objects he collected were lost at sea. Joachim Karig describes how at the age of 48, in 1820, he realised his fondest dream to travel to the Orient with his newly-wedded wife, becoming the first European to enter the Step Pyramid in Saqqara. John Ruffle's paper uses archive material from Alnwick Castle to give an account of the travels of Lord Prudhoe and Major Orlando Felix in 1826-29. In Cairo Lord Prudhoe met E. W. Lane and supported the preparation and printing of his *Lexicon* over the next 23 years. His interest in hieroglyphs was matched by that of James Burton, who emerges from Neil Cooke's paper as a good-for-nothing philanderer, but who nonetheless produced the first fairly accurate collection of hieroglyphic inscriptions in 1825–28. On his return to Europe in 1822, Burton took with him a menagerie of animals and a slave-girl, whom he later married; he died in debt in Scotland, forgotten both by his family and Egyptian colleagues.

Not all travellers were as eccentric as Burton, or as single-minded as the emerging class of professional Egyptologists. As travel to Egypt became increasingly less hazardous, the country started to emerge as a destination for a wide variety of people seeking adventure, including women travellers. Deborah Manley's paper describes how Wolfradine von Minutoli and Mrs Colonel Elwood, both in their first year of marriage, travelled to Egypt in 1820–21. Both were enthusiastic observers who succeed in conveying a good idea of the physical conditions of travel; Anne Katherine emerges as a young woman full of enthusiasm for life, while Wolfradine appears as a gentle character eager to widen her horizons and full of compassion for the lives of ordinary Egyptians. Another delightful account of a honeymoon trip is provided by the Rowley-Conwy family, some of whose ancestors travelled to Egypt and the Sudan in 1835–36; their letters and diaries suggest that pure adventure was their main motivation, as none had a major interest in Egyptology. Their excitement as they venture south into Sudan and their descriptions of people they meet on their travels are full of a pleasurable naïve optimism.

For obvious reasons, travel to Egypt during the nineteenth century held particular attraction for artists and writers, who were often as concerned with the life of contemporary Egyptians as they were with the remains of ancient Egypt and whose work represents a vast treasure-trove for the historian of nineteenth-century Egypt. Diane Harlé's discusses the relatively little-known painter Nestor L'Hôte, a companion to Champollion, who twice visited Egypt on his own (1838–39 and 1840–41); Nestor L'Hôte was commissioned to paint a portrait of Muhammad 'Ali and left a large archive of unpublished and artistic material which is now lodged at the Louvre and the Bibliothèque nationale in Paris. Angela and Jason Thompson describe the Egyptian career of the artist and later Mayan scholar, Frederick Catherwood, who was trained by J. M. W. Turner; employed as a cartographer, he mapped many ancient Egyptian sites, but his attempts to publish a scholarly work on his Egyptian travels were rebuffed by publishers, and he subsequently made his name in Mesoamerican adventures. Another visitor to Egypt was Captain H. B. Martin, discussed by Sarah Searight; his subjects embraced a wide variety of material, including boats, Pharaonic ruins, Islamic buildings, landscapes and costume. Briony Llewellyn's contribution describes the legacy of J. F. Lewis and Frank Dillon, both trained architects, whose views of Islamic domestic architecture are of particular interest. Lewis sketched domestic interiors as well as street scenes with an intensity which derived from a close personal involvement with his subjects. Dillon's quick sketches formed the basis for more elaborate watercolours and oil paintings on his return to England and he was also active among a group committed to the preservation of Islamic buildings in Cairo. Attitudes towards the conservation of the Islamic architectural heritage are also discussed by Hossam Mahdy who notes that the political, economic, military and cultural hegemony of nineteenth-century European colonialism involved the notion that European attitudes to conservation were universally and eternally valid; the result, he suggests, might well have been the construction of an exotic theme park, a Disneyesque world designed to bring the 'Arabian Nights' fantasy to life.

Egypt also proved particularly attractive for practitioners of the new techniques of photography. One of the first British photographers to systematically record the ancient monuments was Francis Frith, discussed in Caroline Williams's. Frith was in Egypt between 1856 and 1860 and, inspired by David Roberts's drawings of the Islamic present and Pharaonic past, he established a reputation on his return from Egypt as Britain's first great photographer-publisher. He also provided a legacy of images which formed an important foundation on which subsequent 'Orientalist' artists relied to create their own visual records of Egypt.

The impact of Egyptian travel on European literature was also a considerable one. Already by the eighteenth century there was a growing interest in the Orient and its culture, and the increased opportunities for travel to Egypt in the nineteenth century produced a constant stream of writer travellers to Egypt. Disentangling the elements of fantasy from reality in their works is often far from straightforward, not least because some authors wrote lyrically about the Romantic Orient without having ventured there. Marianna Taymanova shows, for example, that although Alexandre Dumas travelled widely, he frequently relied on secondary sources to provide him with Oriental topological and cultural detail, and there is no evidence to prove that he ever actually visited Egypt himself.

Among those who certainly did set foot in Egypt were the French writers Flaubert and Gautier, discussed by Mary Orr and Peter Whyte respectively. Little attention has so far been given to Flaubert's travels to Egypt except as biographical background. Mary Orr demonstrates the folly of this neglect, both for a critical understanding of Flaubert's development as a writer and for his contribution to what is now known as 'Orientalism'—in which he has been held to have played a major part. Gautier's passion for Egypt was in part stimulated by the vogue of Orientalist painting in the 1830s. Having not yet travelled to Egypt, he paid particular attention to the work of writers and others who had—among them the composer Félicien David who had studied Oriental music in Egypt. Other sources of inspiration were the Egyptologist Champollion and Prisse d'Avennes. When Gautier finally visited Egypt in 1869, his mobility was affected by a dislocated shoulder. His last publication relating to Egypt was a book review of Lenoir's travels in Egypt and Arabia Petrea, an opportunity to blur the distinctions between the little he saw himself and the more extensive itinerary of the artist-writer Lenoir.

Among lesser-known writers visiting Egypt in the nineteenth century was the Polish poet, Juliusz Słowacki, discussed by Jan Weryho. Słowacki's early poems reflect his 'fiery dreams of the Orient' and he studied Arabic, Persian and Turkish in St Petersburg. He arrived in Alexandria in 1836 shortly after a close friend had committed suicide and his poems, coloured by his experiences in Egypt and the Levant, reflect his personal sadness. Other marginalised accounts of travel to Egypt include those by the French women travellers discussed in John David Ragan's paper: Suzanne Voilquin, a Saint-Simonian, wrote an account of her experiences in 1866, while Jehan d'Ivray became a novelist who used her experiences to provide an Egyptian perspective in her novels published in the 1910s.

A somewhat different perspective on travel to, and residence in, Egypt is provided by the career of the great ethnographer, translator and lexicographer E. W. Lane, discussed by Geoffrey Roper and John Rodenbeck. Lane's work and character have been sadly misrepresented by Edward Said, but as Roper and Rodenbeck show, he was a far more complex individual than the stereotyped 'Orientalist' presented to us by Said. John

Rodenbeck points out that Said's account of Lane's career, and his consequent judgments on his work, contain serious errors of fact and suggests that Said's claim to genuinely admire Lane is not only irrelevant but hypocritical. Geoffrey Roper discusses Lane's scholarly role as a purveyor of literary and linguistic knowledge from Egypt to Europe, noting how his depth of knowledge was praised by contemporary Arab scholars such as Dasuqi and Faris al-Shidyaq; indeed, every serious classical Arabic scholar has been indebted to Lane's great *Lexicon* since its publication.

The interplay of cultures in nineteenth-century Egypt was indeed considerably more complex then Said's simplistic 'Orientalist' paradigm would suggest. Philip Sadgrove's chapter on travellers' rendezvous and cultural institutions in Muhammad 'Ali's Egypt helps to illuminate one aspect of the processes by which the French occupation stimulated the emergence of new indigenous cultural institutions such as the Société Égyptienne, founded in 1836, and the Association Littéraire d'Égypte, founded in 1842. Michael Reimer provides a fascinating example of different cross-cultural perspectives in his chapter contrasting two nineteenth-century accounts of the Azhar by the Frenchman Gabriel Charmes and the Egyptian 'Ali Mubarak. Although the nineteenth century witnessed a vast number of European travellers to Egypt, few observers say much of significance about al-Azhar, the most important mosque and principal university in the city. Only Gabriel Charmes (1880) devotes a full chapter to al-Azhar, seeking to return through its history to the remote past of Islam; by contrast, 'Ali Mubarak—little interested in the picturesque aspects of the courtyard scenes—writes for an Egyptian audience, seeing in the glory of al-Azhar the glory of the nation's heritage as a whole. Finally, Paul Starkey's offers yet a further perspective, pointing out that the stream of Western visitors to Egypt was parallelled by an increasing number of Egyptians travelling to Europe, who in turn brought back observations and varied perceptions of the West. The writings of these Egyptian travellers provided their fellow countrymen with accounts of Western life that complemented and in some cases may have contradicted the impressions of European culture to be derived from Western travellers to Egypt itself.

The various chapters of this book provide a fascinating array of perspectives on a complex set of historical relationships—political, literary and cultural—which have considerable relevance for the present day. It is hoped that the volume, now reissued in paperback, will prove as enjoyable and stimulating to the reader as it was when it was published in 1998.

2 ～ European Travellers in Egypt: The Representation of the Host Culture

Hussein M. Fahim[1]

> Believe me, when the dullness of our cold nation enfeebles your heart, when you desire to enter into direct contact with nature and drink deeply from the source of things, then cross the Mediterranean, disembark on the ancient soil of Egypt, travel up and down the peaceful Nile, admire its ruins, grow drunk on its landscapes, listen to the wonderful song it murmurs into the ears of those who can understand it and wander bravely in the lonely deserts, and you will feel younger, stronger, more productive, more ardent and closer to God.[2]

In recent years travel literature has witnessed a new interest and vigour by a wider range of scholars than ever before. The great wealth of travel texts and documents has proved to be a prolific source of knowledge on lands, peoples and their cultures. As with other forms of literature, some travel accounts are neither scholarly nor academic; rather, they are intended to delight and inform the readers. Admittedly, travel accounts are found to be more influential than scholarly-oriented ethnographic works in shaping people's vision about one another and in fixing perceptual images of foreign peoples and cultures.[3]

This essay looks at the way Egypt's image was represented and publicised in most European travel accounts during the nineteenth century. Although travellers differ in their characters, motives for travel, interests and intellectual orientations, there were common themes among European travellers which influenced their perspective of modern Egypt and helped to form its cultural image. By way of introduction, a concise history of European travel to Egypt and its peak during the nineteenth century is provided. This is followed by an analysis of the nature of Egypt's cultural image as it was seen and perceived in the eyes and minds of most nineteenth-century European travellers. The assumption in this paper is that European travellers formed a cultural image of modern Egypt as they wanted it to be rather than as it was in reality. At the end of the paper, some remarks pertinent to the study of the biographies and works of Western travellers in Egypt in general are presented.

Travellers in Egypt: a historical note

A glance at the history of travellers in Egypt[4] indicates that it was not until the last decade of the eighteenth century that Egypt attracted many visitors from Europe. While the taste for ancient Egypt goes back to the spread of the cults of Isis throughout the Mediterranean in Roman times, accounts and drawings by travellers such as Richard Pococke and Frederick Norden fired Europeans' imagination. Bonaparte's expedition, followed by the publication of Vivant Denon's book in 1802[5] and of the *Description de l'Égypte* from 1809 to 1826, fuelled the fire to visit the antiquities of Egypt.

These publications and other travellers' accounts helped to maintain the momentum of Egypt's growing popularity in Europe. The opening of the Suez canal in 1869 and later the British occupation of Egypt (1882) boosted the influx of travellers from Europe to Egypt (most were tourists). Equally significant to the promotion of this trend was the active role of Thomas Cook & Son in initiating tours in the Upper Nile, a region rich in antiquities and a dry climate which was supposed to be good for pulmonary diseases, especially tuberculosis, a common Victorian complaint.[6]

The Egyptian revival in European public, intellectual and artistic circles became a fashion throughout the nineteenth century. But the volume of travel to Egypt from Europe during the first half of the twentieth century was reduced, mainly due to the two world wars and to the world-wide economic recession of the 1930s. Europeans at that time were perhaps more interested in reading emerging ethnographic studies on other cultures than travellers' accounts which seem to have lost most of their previous narrative charm and literary appeal. Following the Egyptian revolution of 1952, due to strained relations with the west, travel to Egypt came to be confined to specific purposes such as tourism, study and business. It is hard to find, to the best of my knowledge, travellers nowadays just wandering as they please in the country as did travellers of the past centuries.

Travellers in Modern Egypt: the formation of a cultural image

What seems to be striking and paradoxical in most writings of the nineteenth-century European travellers is what I characterise as 'a dual representation of a single culture'. This duality represents Egypt as a country with two contrasting cultures: an image that corresponded with, and also reflected Europe's common taste for the exotic nature of the Oriental world. This went side by side with its fascination with the antiquities of ancient Egyptian civilisation. This dual cultural image of modern Egypt which by and large filled most European travellers' accounts, seems, in my view, to have suited well the desire, if not the obsession, of both the public and intellectuals during the nineteenth century to seek knowledge of the exotic, the bizarre, of unfamiliar beliefs, customs and traditions of non-European cultures.

This knowledge was also required to provide evidence and support for an evolutionary scheme of human culture which ranked Europeans as superior and most civilised. In addition, this dual representation of Egyptian culture seemed to gain support in intellectual circles from the fact that the Oriental aspect of Egyptian culture constituted an intriguing subject of study for Orientalists, while the pharaonic domain of the ancient Egyptian civilisation was equally welcomed by the archaeologists, several of whom directed their studies to what came to be a distinct research field, namely Egyptology.

Subsequently, Europe's curiosity for the exotic Orient urged many travellers to visit Egypt to acquire a lively picture of medieval Cairo. Their travel accounts were meant to reconstruct the Oriental picture, and if reality was disappointing they patched it up from other places, such as Turkey, Persia or India. This view was clearly stated by the French anthropologist Claude-Lévi Strauss: 'I can understand the mad passion for travel books and their deceptiveness. They create the illusion of something which no longer exists but still should exist'.[7]

To illustrate how the 'Oriental image' of Egyptian culture was conceived and presented to the European public, Timothy Mitchell's article, 'The World as Exhibition', informs us of the experience of the Egyptian delegation who attended the Eighth International Congress of Orientalists that was held in Stockholm in the summer of 1889. He states that the Egyptians were viewed by Scandinavians as 'a collection of orientals, not orientalists'.[8] Perhaps the most disturbing experience for the Egyptian delegation had been in Paris where they stopped on their way to Sweden. In Paris, the delegation enjoyed their city tour but were astonished and disappointed, as one delegation member noted, when they visited the International Exhibition and saw the way the French portrayed Egypt's image.

The following passage recounts this incident as Timothy Mitchell translated it from its original Arabic version:

> The Egyptian exhibit had been built by the French to represent a street of medieval Cairo, made of houses with overhanging upper stories and a mosque like that of Qaitbay. It was intended to resemble the old aspect of Cairo. So carefully was this done that even the paint on the buildings was made dirty. The Egyptian Exhibit had also been made carefully chaotic. In contrast to the orderliness of the rest of the exhibition, the imitation street was arranged in the haphazard manner of the bazaar. The way was corded with shops and stalls where Frenchmen, dressed as Orientals, sold perfumes, pastries, and tarboushes. To complete the effect of the Orient, the French organizers had imported from Cairo fifty donkeys, together with their drivers and the requisite number of grooms,

farriers, and saddle-makers. The donkeys gave rides for the price of one franc up and down the street, resulting in a clamour and confusion so lifelike, the director of the exhibition was obliged to issue an order restricting the donkeys to a certain number at each hour of the day.

The Egyptian visitors were disgusted by all this and stayed away. Their final embarrassment had been to enter the door of the mosque and discover that, like the rest of the street, it had been erected as what the Europeans called a façade. Its external form was all that there was of the mosque. As for the interior, it had been set up as a coffee house, where Egyptian girls performed dances with young males, and dervishes whirled.[9]

This Oriental representation of Egyptian culture in general, and that of Cairo in particular, portrayed only one side of the cultural duality I referred to earlier. This side was conceived in the minds of travellers in Egypt as well as Europeans in general as mysterious, exotic, unchanging, and ultimately inferior.[10] The other side which relates to ancient Egyptian civilisation was described as fascinating, majestic and unmistakably civilised. In other words, for the Europeans modern Egypt had two contrasting cultures that co-existed side by side: one was ancient and great while the modern way of life was still medieval and backward.

Contrary to the 'Oriental' side which for Europeans constituted a subject of ridicule and amusement, the pharaonic aspect of Egyptian culture was highly regarded and widely adopted in European architecture and decorative arts.[11] In architecture the pharaonic Egyptian style spread over façades, fountains and funeral monuments. Sphinxes multiplied throughout Paris. If architecture made extensive use of Egyptian motifs, the decorative arts gave them pride of place: Egyptian-style decoration was a mass of lotus flowers and temple components.[12]

Paradoxically, the Oriental aspect of Egypt's modern culture that most European travellers were keen to record and publicise was in apparent conflict with the desire and efforts of Egyptian rulers to bring about change in Egyptian institutions and life-style. Muhammad 'Ali, the governor and viceroy of Egypt from 1811 to 1849, called upon the services of many Europeans to help in the modernisation of Egypt. He modelled the army on European lines, introduced new crops and encouraged commerce and industry. Europeans flooded into the country: merchants, soldiers, engineers, doctors, agronomists and teachers all came in the hope of participating in this development. Nonetheless, as Janet Abu-Lughod observed, guests and hosts sometimes operated at cross-purposes.[13] While Egyptians did their best to create a European image of Egypt in general, and of Cairo in particular, some Europeans wanted only the exotic.

It is ironic to observe that this dual presentation of Egypt's cultural image that dominated the writings of most nineteenth-century European travellers is still used by both European and Egyptian travel agencies to promote tourism and attract individuals and groups to visit Egypt today. I view this practice as alarmingly counter-productive because of the potential conflict of interest between the local and foreign tourist industries and the country's aspirations and efforts to present its image in the eyes and minds of its own people and the outside world as an integrated culture, rather than a polarised one with its potentially serious social and political implications.

Concluding Remarks

In conclusion, I wish to indicate that in order to undertake a comprehensive study of travellers in Egypt, foreign travel literature should be compared with that produced by Egyptian travellers abroad, especially in Western countries. From the beginning of the nineteenth century to the end of the Second World War, Egyptian travel to the western hemisphere had mainly been limited to Europe in general, and to England and France in particular. It was not until the late 1940s that Egyptian travellers acquired the urge to explore the other side of the Atlantic and became more closely acquainted with the people living in the New World. Those Egyptian travel pioneers have since provided their fellow Egyptians with varied perceptions of Western life and presented a diversity of interpretations of what they saw, heard and felt during their journeys.

Although there is no single line of thought which can be labelled 'Western', yet these different perspectives often have something in common, which may be significant in being able to identify how the West perceives both itself and the Other.[14] The image of the West in the Egyptian mind could be misconstrued if it is analysed in isolation from some of the basic foundations and themes in Western history and culture.[15]

It seems equally significant from an ethnographic perspective to find out how Egypt has perceived herself vis-à-vis the Other. As change in perception of a country's own self image and status occurs, its views toward the Other are expected to change accordingly. One may then assume that Egyptian travellers' accounts of the West in general, and Europe in particular, may have painted in the Egyptian mind different, if not contrasting, images. This is not solely attributed to the constantly changing political climates and types of relationships between Egypt and the West, but it also relates to the changing intellectual climates that Egypt has experienced, especially since the end of the Second World War.

Notes

1 I would like to thank my colleagues, Professors Dale Eickelman and Saad Gadallah, Dr Sulayman Khalaf and Mrs Barbara Hayward for reading and commenting on an earlier draft of this paper. Their remarks have been insightful and helpful.

2 Quoted from a letter addressed to Théophile Gautier (Maxime du Camp, *Le Nil: Égypte et Nubie*, 1855).

3 Hussein Fahim, *Travel Literature: An Ethnographic Perspective* (published in Arabic by Kuwait: National Council for Culture, Arts, and Letters, 1989), Introduction.

4 For information on the history of European travel to Egypt see Jean Vercoutter, *The Search for Ancient Egypt*, Series of New Horizons (London: Thames & Hudson, 1992), translated from Italian. See also Deborah Manley, *The Nile: A Traveller's Anthology* (London: Cassell, 1991).

5 Baron Dominique Vivant Denon (1747–1825), *Travel in Upper and Lower Egypt* (1902).

6 'Thomas Cook in Egypt', a draft paper, prepared by Thomas Cook Archive (London, 1995).

7 Eric Leed, *The Mind of the Traveller: From Gilgamesh to Global Tourism* (Basic Books, 1991), p. 285.

8 For detailed information see Timothy Mitchell's *Colonising Egypt* (Cambridge: Cambridge University Press, 1988) and his article 'The World as Exhibition', *Journal for Comparative Studies in Society and History* 1989.

9 Mitchell, *Colonising*, p. 217.

10 For detailed information see John M. MacKenzie, *Orientalism: History, Theory and the Arts* (Manchester: Manchester University Press, 1955).

11 It also influenced literature, such as Flaubert's work, and music, for example, Verdi's opera *Aida*.

12 Fernand Beaucour *et al*, *The Discovery of Egypt: Artists, Travellers and Scientists* (Paris: Flammarion, 1990), pp. 203–22.

13 Janet Abu-Lughod, *Cairo: 1001 Years of the City Victorious* (Princeton, New Jersey: Princeton University Press, 1971), p. 105.

14 See Talal Asad, 'Commentary' in *Indigenous Anthropology in Non-Western Countries* (Carolina Academic Press, 1981), (ed.) Hussein Fahim.

15 Some attempts to study these foundations and themes have been made by Edward Said in his book *Orientalism* (London: Routledge & Kegan Paul, 1978) and also by Talal Asad in his book *Anthropology and the Colonial Encounter* (New York: Humanities Press, 1975).

Part One

Early Travellers

3 ∾ Pietro Della Valle in Ottoman Egypt 1615–1616

Peter M. Holt

Pietro Della Valle was born on 11 April 1586. He came from an old Roman family, received an education appropriate to his rank, and acquired military training and experience. Meanwhile he had fallen in love with a young noblewoman, to whose service he devoted himself for twelve years in the hope of marriage. Unfortunately the young lady confided the secret to her mother, who had other ideas, and, in the words of Pietro's biographer, 'taking her from him, gave to another the destiny and name of husband'. Pietro was cast into intense despair, and contemplated suicide. He was, however, persuaded to seek relief in travel, and so, we are told, 'he chose to make the pilgrimage to the east, as a pious zeal to visit the Holy Land was aroused within him, ... trusting that he should yet one day heal that wound in his bosom which kept him mortally oppressed. That was the aim of his pilgrimage.'

So on 8 June 1614 this spiritual ancestor of Childe Harold set sail from Venice to Constantinople, whence he made his way to Egypt, and thence to the Holy Land. His pilgrimage was, however, to extend far beyond the countries of the eastern Mediterranean. In the following years he went to Isfahan, where he met Shah 'Abbas, and took part in one of his campaigns. Then he went on to spend a year in India, and made his return journey by the Persian Gulf and Basra to Aleppo. He finally reached Rome on 28 March 1626, accompanied by the remains of Sitti Maani, whom he had married on his travels. Troubled by his lack of offspring, he married a Georgian girl whom he had brought from Persia, and who in due course provided him with fourteen children. He passed the rest of his life in Rome, where he died on 21 April 1652.[1]

Della Valle recorded his travels in a series of letters to a friend, and these were published in three volumes between 1650 and 1663. His account of Egypt in the first volume is contained in two letters from Cairo, dated 25 January and 7 March 1616. He describes his departure from Constantinople on 25 September 1615, which coincided with the first day of Ramadan, 'the Turks' great Lent' as he calls it. He embarked in a galley belonging to the deputy in Constantinople of the grand vezir. His party consisted of seven

Christians and two Turks, and was provided with a Turkish escort, a *kapıcı* officer of the sultan's palace.

After a voyage which is described in some detail, the travellers made their landfall at Rosetta. This was not according to plan. They had intended to arrive in Alexandria, and Della Valle inveighs against 'the inexperience of the Turkish and Greek mariners, who do not understand charts, and hardly know how to use the compass.' After some unpleasantness the ship went on, reaching the port of Alexandria in the night of 25 October; and on the following morning the party disembarked. Della Valle was met by the dragoman and janissaries in the service of the French consul, with whom he lodged, and who showed him the sights of the town.[2]

Della Valle's ideas of Egypt had been formed almost entirely by the classical authors and the Bible, although he had read the writings of the Italian historian, Paolo Giovio (d. 1512), and the French traveller, Pierre Belon (d. 1564). Not surprisingly he found Ottoman Alexandria profoundly disappointing. 'I stayed but a little in Alexandria,' he says, 'because it is a malarial place, and there is very little to see.' It was sparsely inhabited except outside the ruined walls in the vicinity of the custom-house and the port. 'The Turks', he remarks sourly, 'take no care of old things. When one of their buildings falls into ruin, they do not construct another to supply the want. What is dilapidated is never repaired, even though that would be better, and could be done at little cost.'[3] He duly admired the relics of ancient times, notably the cisterns, on which it might be said that the whole city stood, and which provided the sole source of water for Alexandria, being fed by a seasonal branch of the Nile. He notes that the Arabs 'use exactly the costume of the apostles, as we are accustomed to depict it today in our paintings.' Among the plants of Egypt he describes the banana, which he knows by its Arabic name, *Mouz* (*mauz*), and says that 'the simple peasants argue that this was the fig-tree from the leaves of which Adam made himself breeches when he was ashamed to see himself naked.'[4]

On 1 November Della Valle set out with his party for Rosetta, whence they intended to go by river to Cairo. They travelled through the night, and reached Rosetta before dawn, where they were received by an Italian vice-consul. The town. although small, seemed active, being a port for goods coming from Cairo. Here Della Valle pointed out to his correspondent a difference between the classical and the contemporary geography of Egypt. 'I cannot today find the seven so-called mouths of the Nile, which existed in ancient times according to Strabo and all the other writers of the past; for two only [the Rosetta and Damietta branches] are navigable. Besides these, the only other I know is the branch which goes down to Alexandria to fill the cisterns, and another channel, also small, which are four in all.'[5]

The river-journey began on 3 November, when Della Valle and his companions went on board a boat which either sailed before the wind or was poled along. The nights were passed in riverside villages. He noted the agility with which the peasants, both men and women, would swim across the river with their cattle, stripping off their long, blue garments without shame, and carrying them on their heads to the other bank. At mid-day on 6 November they saw three great pyramids not far away, and in the evening they reached Bulaq, the port of Cairo, about two miles distant from the city itself. The next morning the baggage was loaded on camels, while the travellers mounted donkeys, horses being forbidden to all except cavalrymen and high officials. Della Valle comments on the beauty of the flood-plain, turning green after the retreat of the Nile waters. Beautiful above all was the Ezbekiya pool in the suburb outside the city-gate. Della Valle went on to the house of the French consul, where he was welcomed by the steward.

Cairo, unlike Alexandria, greatly impressed Della Valle. It was larger than Rome or Constantinople, and filled with houses both within and without the walls. He shows little interest in the urban architecture; the only mosques he mentions by name are those of 'Campsòn Gauro', (i.e. Qansawh al-Ghawri, the penultimate Mamluk sultan), and of Sultan Hasan, which he says is without doubt the most beautiful that he has seen. He visited the Christian churches of Old Cairo, and the legendary house of the Virgin Mary in al-Matariyya. He was interested by the narrow streets and alleys, and the painted inscriptions on the houses of pilgrims back from Mecca. About another house-painting he tells a curious story. He saw on the outer wall of many houses 'a circle in red and yellow or the like, divided by the middle into two parts. As if it were on an altar, there is painted a chalice with two candlesticks, one on each side, but barbarously done and ill-drawn. They told me that this was in memory of when St Louis, the king of France, came to the Levant for the war of the Holy Land, and was held prisoner in Egypt. Released by the sultan, he left the Most Holy Sacrament in Egypt as a pledge for his promised ransom. There it remained until, on his return to France, he sent the ransom, and got back the Sacrament—about which they tell no end of miraculous happenings.'[6] Della Valle, it is clear, was sceptical of this story, but what had he seen? It seems possible that the paintings were in fact the survival of a blazon from the time of the Mamluk sultanate, representing a cup and the insignia of the *futuwwa*, 'the trousers of nobility'. It has been suggested that the blazon 'forms a general symbol of nobility'.[7] From Della Valle's account it appears to have survived the fall of the Mamluk sultanate by over a century, perhaps distinguishing the houses of the neo-Mamluk beys.

On 12 November 1615 (20 Shawwal 1024), shortly after Della Valle's arrival in Cairo, there took place one of the great public observances inherited from the Mamluk sultanate. This was the departure to Mecca of the *kiswa*, i.e. the covering sent annually for the Ka'ba, which was accompanied by its escort and a throng of pilgrims under the command of the *amir al-hajj*.[8] Della Valle has left a full, and perhaps unique, account of the occasion.

I arrived in time to see another more curious solemnity, which was the departure of the caravan which goes to Mecca with a vast number of pilgrims, who go there to make their Mahometan devotions. This caravan leaves once a year, and the Pasha of Cairo sends a *sancak beshi* as its head. It carries to Mecca the gift of a very rich cover for the tomb and chapel of their hero, which is sent from Constantinople by the king. Each year the old one is removed, and dispersed in pieces among the leaders of the sect as relics. So many pilgrims gather from all their nations that the caravan is wont to be of forty, fifty and sixty thousand camels, and sometimes there have been ninety thousand. This year it was a very small caravan; there were forty-five thousand camels, apart from the horses, asses and mules, which were not lacking. Now to estimate the people, They amounted to more than two hundred thousand, because there is a very great number of indigent beggars, who go on foot without money or provisions. For them, however, there are many camels of the king, the Pasha, and others both living and dead, who as alms-giving charitably send them to supply water and victuals, and also to transport the weak and needy. The travellers need to carry food for all the journey, and even water to drink, because there is none in the greater part of the country through which they make their way. ...

Before leaving [the caravan] makes a solemn procession, so to speak, to which go all the pilgrims, camels, loads and baggage, to make a show through the city. They go from the Citadel, where the Pasha lives, as far as a certain open space outside the other part of the city, where they encamp, and remain for some days for everyone to assemble and get themselves organised. The camels pass, as I say, through the midst of the city, taking an entire day and more to pass. They are honoured by the company of a very great cavalcade of many troops of the soldiery, of officials and notables of Cairo, of their schools or seminaries, which are innumerable, and of all the dervishes and saints ... who act as is their custom in the oddest way in the world, and whoever of them goes the more uncovered and the more naked seems the more holy to the mad belief of these simpletons. Finally they carry the cover of Mahomet's tomb, which the Turks who stand watching in the streets touch with their head-coverings out of devotion.

The order in which this procession marched on the day when I saw it, the twelfth of November, was the following. First came many men on horseback, escorting the solemnity. Then began the caravan, in which were all the necessary trades, such as smiths, bakers, cooks, camp-followers of all kinds, and the like. Each of these trades had its throng of camels. The first to pass were those of the smiths. On their first camel under a fine silken canopy a boy went by, the young son of the chief of that trade—for every trade has a chief whom the others obey. When the tradesmen had passed, six falconets were brought along, each one drawn by two horses. Then there followed the camels of the bey who was the chief of the caravan, some loaded with waterskins, some with his belongings; then his litter, carried by two very large camels; then other camels, also his, in abundance, some with loads, and others without in order to carry poor people at need. Behind that a great number of camels was to be seen, some belonging to the people in the caravan and some belonging to other persons, living or dead, which were intended for the same purpose as alms-giving. Mixed with these from place to place there went a great number of men on horseback. Some of them were pilgrims making the journey; others their friends, who had come to accompany them; and others soldiers going to guard the caravan. Some of these were arquebusiers, and although they went on horseback, they nevertheless carried their arquebuses on their shoulders as the foot-soldiers do in our countries. Others had arrows and bows at their necks. There were also various troops of foot-archers, who as they passed below a roof which is across the street near the mosque called al-Ghawriyya, close to where I was standing to watch, shot arrows in the air at this roof.[9] They told me that from whether the arrow stayed there or fell down, they took some portent either good or bad. There was a good number of the foot-archers also.

Then there followed a numberless crowd of pilgrims on foot, accompanied by all the companies of those who profess a religious life in Cairo. Everyone had his flag, and they were endless. These falsely devout persons went two by two, singing in chorus, like our monks in their chanting. Among these was a handful of their santons of a more austere life. Variously habited, and with odd movements of their bodies they wearied themselves crying 'Hu!' in their manner. ... Others of them went naked, some on foot and some on horseback, liberally displaying the shameful parts for greater ostentation of sanctity, as their particular madness persuades them. One of those who was there on horseback had had a hand cut off for theft some years before, but then he devoted himself to hypocrisy. This sort of life being so much esteemed among Mahometans, he now also went in procession, venerated as a saint. Wherever he passed, the people kissed either his remaining hand or his arms.

Last there came a company of janissaries with their most formal head-dress fully plumed, and with their arquebuses. Behind them on horseback came the bey, the chief of the caravan, with many other high officials, and near them at the end was carried the drapery to cover the tomb of Mahomet. This was all made of silk, and very richly embroidered with gold. It came drawn along just as it would be in use, that is to say spread-out and extended on high upon a camel, which for this has henceforward the privilege of never carrying another burden. When it passed, there then followed all the rest of the camels, all decorated to the limit, and in such a number that neither in all that day nor in some more did they finish passing.

In short it was a curious sight which gave me much pleasure, the more so that I enjoyed another week of it in going outside the city to see the same caravan, which had not yet left, encamped in the open country with the pavilions. Certainly it was not a bad sight to see so many people and so many beasts gathered together.[10]

While he was staying in Cairo, Della Valle did not fail to visit the pyramids. With his head filled with memories of the classics, and guided by the writings of Belon, he crossed the Nile on 8 December. He had neither time nor patience, he says, to measure the Great Pyramid, but he gives a vivid account of his ascent of the interior passage to the burial chamber.

He also climbed to the top outside, and had the pleasure of carving his name with, as he obscurely hints, that of his lost love. He saw the Sphinx half covered in sand, and then went on to pass the night under canvas.

On the next morning he rode southwards to visit the Step Pyramid of Saqqara and the great necropolis. He was accompanied by a number of the local peasants, some soldiers, and many of his friends from Cairo, who had seized the opportunity to pay a visit to this dangerous locality. On reaching an area where the sand appeared undisturbed by previous tomb-robbers, he divided up his workmen to dig in different places, and set up his tent in the middle, determined not to leave before something was found. At this point a peasant came up, and whispered to the interpreter that he had a very fine mummy for sale nearby, if Della Valle would come quietly without alerting the others, who would want to share the price. When they arrived, the peasant unearthed the mummy of a man, 'which,' he says, 'being very well preserved, and curiously adorned and fitted out, appeared very fine and brave to me.'[11] This was followed by the disclosure of a female mummy, which was equally remunerative to the seller, and finally Della Valle himself was persuaded to descend into the mummy-pit. The descent was safely accomplished, and then Della Valle went back to his tent, paid off his labourers, and returned in triumph to Cairo with his finds. The mummies were placed on view in the consul's house, where, he tells us, they were visited by many Christians and not a few Turks, and the proud owner was assured that the like of them had never been seen. They were then boxed up, and sent to Alexandria for forwarding to Messina.

On 14 December Della Valle set out on a much longer expedition, intending to visit the monastery of St Catherine on Mount Sinai. He was provided with letters from the archbishop of Mount Sinai, who lived in Cairo, and took one of the monks with him as guide. The journey was to be made on camels, but Della Valle, finding it, as he says, unsuitable to ride exposed to the sun, the rain and the wind which he might encounter, obtained a kind of howdah, which he had seen used by travellers to Mecca.

The travellers took nine camels and several donkeys for use in the difficult mountain passes. The beasts were accompanied by their Bedouin drivers, armed with scimitars, lances, pikes, and shields of fish-skin. There were also two or three Arab guides, sent by special order of the archbishop, as men respected by their people, although Della Valle believed that if it came to a fight their authority would be worth little, and they would be the first to flee. He had his own ideas on ensuring a safe journey, and insisted that arms should be carried. This was deprecated by the monks, who feared the reaction of the Arabs, and he reluctantly agreed not to take arquebuses. He refused to join a caravan, which would restrict his free movement, and he calculated that his party was in itself sufficient to form a caravan. 'For two or three Greeks who accompanied me with their camels were worth at least as many Arabs, the *kapıcı* alone was worth not less than two, and we five Franks doubtless more than twenty-five.'[12] They took food and drink for a month, sufficient for the outward journey and the return. Della Valle specifies the provisions. 'I had them bring good coops full of live fowls, as is my custom, and a quantity of meal and rice. With this in particular, prepared with a good deal of sugar and spices, or cooked with almonds, or milk and butter as they do here, I am well satisfied when travelling by land or sea. We had also our cooking equipment, and every evening as night came on, the tent was pitched, and a fire was kindled from whatever woody vegetation we found on the way; and we ate and took our ease.'[13]

The party reached the monastery of St Catherine at midnight on Christmas Eve. Della Valle spent his Christmas Day (which, he notes, was ten days before the Christmas of the Greek monks) in going to all parts of the great walled monastery. On the following day he set out to climb the peak of Horeb. This, to his surprise, took the whole day 'because in fact it did not appear so high to me, and I did not deem it any greater than Santa Maria del Soccorso in Capri.'[14] The next day he intended to climb Mount Sinai (Jabal Musa), but there was a heavy snowfall during the night, and his friends sought to dissuade him. Della Valle, 'angry that a little snow should upset my plans, said that if an Arab could be found to come and show me the way, I would go with him, ... and let him who feared to come stay behind.'[15] These bold words roused his companions, and they set out led by Brother Manasses, a young monk, 'who ran over those mountains like a fallow deer.' Della Valle gives a vivid and detailed account of the party's perilous journey over snow and ice up to the rock in human form to which angels bore the body of St Catherine before it found its final resting-place in the monastery. The descent was even more dangerous, and once Della Valle ended up sitting in a small watercourse with his legs in the air above a precipice. However, before darkness fell they arrived, safe but drenched, at their night-lodgings in the small monastery of the Forty Fathers. The next day they returned to the great monastery. There the shrine of St Catherine was opened and they touched the body with their rosaries and the devotional rings which were given them. Della Valle took a considerable number of these—over five hundred made of bone for ordinary acquaintances but many made of gold and silver for persons of quality.

The next morning, 29 December, they started their return journey to Cairo, going this time by way of al-Tur, 'a city according to the Turks but a village according to us', which was the centre for trade with India. On New Year's Day of 1616, Della Valle went fishing for oysters and the fine corals of the Red Sea. His boat, he says, was extraordinary, 'for the timbers of its hull were not joined together by nails but by tarred cords. All the rest of the fittings were of leather, not boards, and the sail was of matting.'[16] It was like the boats which came to Cairo from Upper Egypt or beyond, the tiny timbers of which were joined by wooden pegs. When the goods were sold, these boats were broken up for sale as timber. The party left for Cairo the next day, and on 8 January, to avoid the detour around the head of the Gulf of Suez, they took a ferry-boat for the short crossing to the town of Suez itself. There Della Valle saw an Indian vessel with a sail made of palm-leaves, of which he disapproved, thinking it heavy, unmanageable, and liable to fire. On 8 January they left Suez accompanied by two caravans, which travelled, Della Valle asserts, 'safely in our shadow' for fear of highwaymen. The party reached Cairo in the evening of 12 January, and there Della Valle passed the next eight weeks before leaving for Jerusalem.

In the letters which describe this part of his travels, Della Valle shows himself to be a careful observer, and a clear and lively narrator of his experiences. He is not lacking in courage or self-esteem, and he presents himself as being very decidedly the leader of his little party in such matters as the organisation of the expedition to Sinai, and the ascent of the snow-covered mountain. Here and there he explicitly assumes the superiority of Western Europeans, in particular Italians, over the peoples of the East, but any religious animus against Muslims as such is notably absent. He himself appears to have been conventionally devout rather than deeply religious, and as a Catholic, he views with a cold eye his fellow-Christians of the Coptic and Orthodox Churches. In his outlook, attitudes and interests this seventeenth-century Roman nobleman is a prototype of later Western travellers in Egypt.

Notes

1 This account of Della Valle's life is summarised from the (unpaginated) biographical notice by G. P. Bellori in *Viaggi di Pietro Della Valle il Pellegrino, Parte Prima* (Rome, 1662); hereafter *Viaggi*, I.

2 The voyage from Constantinople to Alexandria is described in *Viaggi*, I, pp. 163–76.

3 Ibid., p. 176.

4 Ibid., pp. 178–9.

5 Ibid., pp. 180–1.

6 Ibid., pp. 260–1.

7 L. A. Mayer, *Saracenic Heraldry* (Oxford, 1933), 11, pp. 19–22.

8 The *amir al-hajj* was one of the great officers of state in Ottoman Egypt, and in the seventeenth and eighteenth centuries the position was invariably held by a Mamluk bey. For an account of the Pilgrimage and Mecca by an English pilgrim in the last quarter of the seventeenth century, see Joseph Pitts, *A Faithful Account of the Religion and Manners of the Mohametans*, 3rd edn. (London, 1731).

9 I am obliged to Dr Doris Behrens-Abouseif of the University of Freiburg for

the information that a roof over the street connected the mosque and
mausoleum of Qansawh al-Ghawri.

10 *Viaggi*, I, pp. 190–4.
11 Ibid., p. 204.
12 Ibid., p. 221.
13 Ibid., pp. 221–2.
14 Ibid., p. 229.
15 Ibid., p. 232.
16 Ibid., p. 239.

4 ∾ George Baldwin: Soldier of Fortune?

Rosemarie Said Zahlan

Since his first visit to Egypt in 1773, George Baldwin was convinced of its great economic and strategic potential. Determined to exploit its untapped wealth, he became deeply involved in its commercial and political affairs, and for the next twenty-five years became the only permanent English resident. A colourful character who enjoyed very little social, political and financial support, he relied on imagination, perseverance and wit, acting alone, often in splendid isolation from reality.

Baldwin was far ahead of his time, particularly when viewed from the perspective of the late twentieth century. Perhaps his most outstanding characteristic was his recognition of the importance of a reliable information system. Against many odds, he established a system to transfer English dispatches from Europe to India via the 'overland route', from Alexandria to Suez then through the Red Sea: this became the basis for imparting intelligence, and was of special significance in the Indian sub-continent during the Napoleonic wars.

Baldwin was also a strategist, able to recognise the difference between information and transportation, and the benefits of separating the two. A shrewd merchant who quickly grasped the earning potential of the Red Sea route, he almost single-handedly restored British trade with Egypt by promoting a novel and unusual permutation of established patterns which infuriated British, Indian and Ottoman officials.

The Early Years

George Baldwin was born in 1743, the son of a London hop merchant. In 1760 he sailed to Cyprus, and later moved to live in Acre, becoming a silk merchant. He became acquainted with the political structure of the area and recognised its commercial potential, especially as a possible link with the lucrative Indian market. To exchange the produce of Syria , Egypt and neighbouring countries for the wealth of Indian goods became so appealing to him that he resolved to settle in Egypt to promote that trade.[1]

Egyptian politics from the 1750s on were dominated by the ever-growing rift between the ruling Mamluk beys, and the Porte. The latter had started its inexorable decline, and its representative, the Pasha was often powerless to control the beys; factional opposition and sporadic *coups d'état* occurred with growing intensity.

Once the beys assumed complete control of Egypt, they were able to flout Ottoman authority. They surreptitiously allowed non-Muslims to sail the waters of the Red Sea, provided that they themselves derived a substantial profit from the resulting trade. In 1773, the *shaykh al-balad* (the supreme bey) encouraged Baldwin to use the Red Sea route, telling him, 'If you bring the India ships to Suez, I will lay an aqueduct from the Nile to Suez, and you shall drink of the Nile water.'[2]

The last quarter of the eighteenth century was dominated by a duumvirate of two Mamluk beys: Murad and Ibrahim. Both men were hated and feared, not least because of the immense and irrational extortions they made from all sectors of the population. Their ruthless *avanias* left English merchants powerless and unable to compete with the well-established and thriving French community of traders. Englishmen gradually left, and in 1757, the Levant Company closed the English consulate;[4] it remained strongly opposed to re-opening it despite Baldwin's frustrated appeals in later years.

Baldwin's First Period of Residence, 1775–79

When he arrived in Cairo in July 1775, Baldwin was the only English merchant living there. He had only tenuous links with the Levant Company and the East India Company, but used these fragile connections to promote himself, his ideas and his position. He took it upon himself, for example, to act as unofficial consul for Englishmen passing through Egypt; he also contacted merchants in Bombay, Istanbul, Izmir and London to sell Indian goods arriving in Suez. But his many involvements became entangled, leaving him vulnerable to a wide variety of enemies. His position as sole English merchant caused him much trouble with the rival European traders; the fact that he lacked any official title made him prey to the extortions of the Customs Master of Egypt; and the Red Sea trade brought on the anger in turn of the Porte, the British Ambassador in Istanbul, the Levant Company and the East India Company.

These problems clouded Baldwin's judgement. In attempting to avoid the pitfalls he encountered, he lost sight of his main objectives. His ambitions for personal gain overshadowed his efforts to encourage an efficient dispatch route from India to England; his far-reaching political insight was overlooked in the face of his determined trade. And his recognition of the strategic importance of Egypt was disregarded by Sir Robert Ainslie, the British Ambassador to the Porte.

The animosity between these two men was personal, commercial and political. It was also widely known, which only added to Baldwin's vulnerable position. As representative of the Levant Company, Ainslie regarded the Red Sea traders as adventurers who were damaging the firm's profits and jeopardising its factors around the Ottoman empire. He distrusted Baldwin, and addressed him in an aloof and patronising manner. Rather than appoint the obviously available Baldwin as an agent to keep him abreast of events in Egypt, Ainslie hired Brandi, an Italian tailor living in Alexandria who was also consul for Holland, Sweden, Denmark and Naples.

Despite the many rebuffs, Baldwin's spirit remained undaunted: 'I shall go on in the same prudential line that I have adopted from the beginning, and at my retreat give up the establishment to the most fallacious notion that ever was conceived: of the impossibility of establishing an advantageous commercial intercourse with Egypt.'[5]

Opposition to the Red Sea Route

The Ottoman authorities were appalled by the continued European use of the Red Sea trade route in defiance of their orders. In early 1779, they issued a strongly-worded *Hatti Sherif*, a copy of which was delivered in person to Ainslie. It was addressed to the Pasha in Cairo, to the Mamluk beys, to the judges, religious leaders, captains and officers in Egypt, and stated that: 'The Sea of Suez is destined for the noble pilgrimage of Mecca. To suffer Frank ships to navigate therein, or to neglect opposing it, is betraying your Sovereign, your religion, and every Mahometan.'[6] The edict made it clear that those who contravened it would risk having their vessels confiscated, and their crews imprisoned and 'condemned to perpetual slavery'.

The document was to play a decisive role in Baldwin's Egyptian career. It made him realise he could no longer remain there without some diplomatic standing. A short while later, he became involved in a harrowing experience which ultimately caused him to flee the country. Disaster struck in May 1779 when two commercial ships arrived at Suez. Both were English with Danish colours, and both carried substantial cargo: the *Nathalia* was commanded by a German, Captain van der Velden; and the *St Helena* by an Englishman, Captain Moore.[7]

Ten passengers of the *Nathalia* were tricked into believing that it would be safe to travel unescorted to Cairo; they were attacked *en route*, stripped of their clothes, robbed of their possessions and left in the desert without food, water, or camels. Seven died. John O'Donnell, one of the group, managed to escape; he had been a successful businessman in India and regarded the Red Sea trade route as the most efficient way to transfer his fortune home. The total value of his goods on the *Nathalia* was estimated at 150,000 dollars.

O'Donnell returned to Suez, intending to pursue the thieves, but was arrested before he could locate the stolen booty; again, he escaped, this time to Cairo where he joined Baldwin who was frantically seeking a solution. Carlo Rosetti, a politically influential Venetian merchant who had lived in Egypt for many years, suggested that O'Donnell appeal to Ibrahim Bey, the *shaykh al-balad*. The petition was written, translated and submitted.[8] Antun Pharaon, the powerful Syrian Christian Customs Master, brought back Ibrahim's answer verbally: the Englishmen were to return to Suez; the bey would send an armed force to accompany them and to seize the robbers.

An elaborate and confusing incident followed which Baldwin later realised had been a plot devised by Pharaon. It resulted in the arrest of Captain Moore of the *St Helena,* and in the seizure of the cargo by Ibrahim Bey's forces who arrested the remaining English passengers and sent them back to Cairo.

After a fruitless attempt to dupe Pharaon into releasing the men and cargo, Baldwin had to enter into a humiliating agreement in the Customs Master's house. This bound Baldwin and his companions never to claim damages for the theft of the cargo, and never to complain to the Porte; they would never return to Suez with a *firman* allowing them to trade; they would pay the expenses of any future commands from Istanbul concerning their welfare; and they would be held responsible for any ship coming to Suez to obtain redress for the incident.[9] As security for the bond, Baldwin and one of the Englishmen, Andrew Skiddy, were made hostages when the others were allowed to leave on 28 August for India.

In desperation, Baldwin appealed to Ainslie for help, asking for a command for his release from the Porte which would at the same time absolve the Egyptian government from any responsibility in the affair.[10]

Ainslie's fury knew no bounds. Baldwin had openly defied his orders about the Red Sea trade, and he had severely compromised his position vis-à-vis the Porte. Nevertheless, he exerted himself to obtain the release of Baldwin and Skiddy; he even referred to Baldwin as having been 'served with a royal order'.[11]

International Quest for Support

Rather than wait for what he knew would be only an ineffectual order from the Porte, Baldwin resolved to escape, leaving the unfortunate Skiddy behind. He was smuggled onto a French ship which took him to Izmir where he remained until the end of the year.

Baldwin's visit to Izmir marked an important milestone in his life: while there, he married Jane Maltass, the sixteen-year old daughter of his agent, Henry Maltass. Although the marriage was not to be happy, it proved extremely useful to Baldwin in his frenetic quest for connections in high places. Jane Maltass was an exceptionally beautiful woman with whom rich and powerful men in different parts of Europe would later be said to be in love, including Emperor Joseph of Austria, the Prince of Wales (later, the Regent), and Dr Samuel Johnson. Known in London as 'the fair Greek', she later became the darling of fashionable society and was immortalised by Sir Joshua Reynolds in two portraits.

From Izmir, the newly-weds went to Istanbul where Baldwin hoped to obtain Ainslie's help. When no help was forthcoming, it was Baldwin's turn to be angry: he blamed the Ambassador for his problems and publicly accused him of being incompetent. The relationship between the two men descended still further: they failed to greet each other on the street, and Baldwin made a point of insulting Ainslie whenever he could. The gap between them was never to be bridged.

Ainslie was particularly annoyed that Baldwin was spending much of his time with Saint Priest, the French Ambassador, an old enemy of his, something he saw as being 'audacious and troublesome to the last degree'.[12] Ainslie was incensed that Saint Priest treated Baldwin with the deference usually reserved for a government minister.

Ainslie might have suspected that Baldwin confided in the French Ambassador. He told him about the *Nathalia* episode, and spoke at length about the enormous potential of the Red Sea trade route. Saint Priest was so impressed with this information that he sent a memorial to Paris on the subject, strongly recommending that France promote its use.[13] The document was read with great interest in Paris, and was used by Napoleon when planning his invasion of Egypt. It is doubtful whether Baldwin realised that he had inadvertently contributed to France's strategic considerations.

After some time, the restless Baldwin could see no further reason to remain in Istanbul. He decided to go to India, so he departed, leaving his wife behind in the care of a British merchant. *En route*, however, he was attacked and robbed, so resolved to return to England instead, this time taking his young bride with him.

His first stop was Vienna where the British ambassador, Robert Murray Keith, had already received advance warnings from Ainslie. Keith, however, was warm and hospitable. He was impressed no doubt by Baldwin's connections and by the beauty of Jane Baldwin. Before long, the couple met the Emperor, who was also dazzled by Jane; as a result, they were eagerly received in Viennese aristocratic circles. Wherever they went, Baldwin spoke of the great potential of the Red Sea route, so much so that the East India Company considered him indiscreet and detrimental to its own interests.

Baldwin's indiscretion continued to grow. Hearing that the post of Ambassador at Istanbul was vacant, he tried to bribe R. B. Sheridan, the playwright, who was also Under-Secretary of Foreign Affairs to obtain the position for himself. Although Baldwin later denied it was attempted bribery, he only made matters worse by claiming that it was '... the importance of the object that led me to propose what I did, and my meaning was no more than to satisfy by some sort of compensation, the claims of a competitor.'[14]

Rekindling of Interest in Egypt

Unbeknown to Baldwin, two events occurred which were finally to convince the British government of Egypt's importance. Although Baldwin had no knowledge of the first event and was not directly involved in the second, their impact on his life was decisive.

The first event was the 1784 establishment by the British government of a new department, the Board of Control for India. Its main functions were the political, financial and military administration of the territorial possessions of the East India Company. The India Board was also responsible for the appointment of a Governor General as a representative of the Crown. The guiding force of the Board was Henry Dundas, later Viscount Melville.

The second was the signing of the Truguet agreements in 1785. An envoy of the French government, Chevalier de Truguet, was sent to Egypt to reach a formal agreement that would ensure France's right to navigate the Red Sea.

French awareness of the political importance of Egypt was not new; memorials and treatises on the subject had been written since the days of Louis XIV. But the renewed interest in the commercial navigation of the Red Sea had been directly brought about by knowledge of the lucrative trade carried on by the British. The departure of Baldwin in 1779, followed by that of Pharaon in 1783, left an opening which the French were eager to fill.

Truguet obtained the help of Charles Magallon, a French merchant who had lived in Egypt since 1775, and his wife. Through them he was able to conclude three separate agreements for French use of the route: the first was with Murad Bey; the second was with Yusuf Kassab, the Customs Master who had replaced Pharaon; and the third was with a Bedouin chieftain, Nasir Shadid. The agreements, signed in January 1785, gave France unprecedented use of the Red Sea route, with minimal interference by the Egyptian and Ottoman governments.[15]

When the India Board learned of the Truguet agreements, it quickly sought to establish an information base on Anglo–Egyptian relations to form their response to the French advances. It soon became clear that knowledge on Egyptian affairs was sadly lacking: nothing could be found on the British use of the Red Sea route, on the Ottoman response, or even on the *Hatti Sherif* of 1779.

Baldwin immediately became the only person who could explain the affairs of Egypt. He was probably introduced to Dundas by George Johnstone, who had been Governor of West Florida in 1763; in 1783, he became a Director of the East India Company and was a strong supporter of the Red Sea route, estimating that at least £25,000 a year could be saved if it were used for dispatches. He was personally close to Baldwin through his niece, a Miss Pulteney, who was a close friend of Jane Baldwin.

Baldwin was summoned to a meeting of the Board by Dundas who requested a memorial on the subject. As a result, Baldwin wrote *Speculations on the Situation and Resources of Egypt*, a pamphlet which he later published in two editions in 1801 and 1802 under the title of *Political Recollections Relative to Egypt containing Observations on its Government Under the Mamlukes*.

It was on the basis of this work that Dundas and his colleagues decided to establish a British consulate-general in Egypt, and to appoint Baldwin as consul. 'The great end of Mr. Baldwin's residence at Cairo is the opening of a communication to India through Egypt.'[16] His salary of £1,450 per annum was paid for by the government: £500 by the Secret Service, and £950 by the Treasury.[17]

The Board of Control for India

This sudden interest in Egypt was to prevent the French from gaining an important step over the English in India. To Baldwin was therefore provided the opportunity to single-handedly obtain equal rights for his country: he was to assert British prestige in Egypt, secure passage for dispatches of the East India Company, negotiate a trade treaty with the beys, and remain abreast of all matters French.[18]

Egypt was now firmly installed within the domain of the India Board. This alarmed the governors of the Levant Company who regarded it as being in their purview; in an attempt to stop Baldwin's appointment, they made strong appeals to the Attorney General and the East India Company.

Luckily for Baldwin, the Levant Company was overruled. In Istanbul, Ainslie was stunned, but quickly swallowed his anger.[19] But he could not help adding later that he was not alone in considering that the appointment was 'dangerous' and 'inimical' to the interests of the Porte.[20] He assured London that his disapproval was not personal and had little to do with Baldwin himself. Impressed with the Ambassador's new attitude, Dundas charged Baldwin to forget the past and refrain from any behaviour which would irritate his superior in Istanbul.

Lord Carmarthen (Francis Osborne, Marquis of Carmarthen), the Secretary of State for Foreign Affairs, delicately explained to Ainslie that Baldwin had been appointed to the consulate because of the great distance between Cairo and Istanbul, and not because of '... the smallest inattention to your rank and character.'[21] He did not mince his words when he referred to the conflict of interests between the Levant Company and the Crown: 'Your Excellency is to consider this instruction by the King's command with this express reservation, that it is only to be in force when neither the orders nor the interests of the Turkey Company shall be repugnant in any manner whatsoever to the superior interests of the nation at large.'[22]

Once his appointment was secure, Baldwin contacted the East India Company and offered to be their agent for correspondence between India and England. The Company decided to re-establish communications via Suez, and accepted the offer, but paid only half the salary Baldwin had asked for. Armed with the King's appointment, Baldwin left England in August 1786, and arrived in Naples on 29 September. He was accompanied by his wife, and possibly his daughter.[23] From Naples, they sailed to Izmir for a visit with his wife's family; he then sailed alone to Alexandria, intending to send for his family once he arranged lodgings. He took Thomas Turner, who was to be his vice-consul, with him.

Baldwin, British Consul-General, 1786–93

The political situation in Egypt had changed during his absence. When he left in 1779, Ibrahim had been the *shaykh al-balad* and Murad the co-ruler. The two men retained their hold over the country during the years that followed, except for the period 1783–84 when they quarrelled, and set up opposing camps. After their reconciliation in early 1785, Ibrahim, the older of the two, was proclaimed *shaykh al-balad* again, and Murad became *amir al-hajj*.[24]

Egypt had suffered from other problems besides political uncertainties. During 1783 and 1784, the Nile did not reach the required level during the flood season. Poor harvests ensued, causing prices—especially of wheat—to rise enormously. With regular extortions imposed by Murad on the merchants, poverty and famine struck. An inevitable outbreak of plague followed, causing many deaths.

The foreign community was not spared the misfortune of the Egyptians.

It was mercilessly taxed by the beys, and powerless to resist or refuse. The French community[25] was no exception: despite the enormous benefits accorded it by the Truguet agreements, its condition seemed to deteriorate rather than improve.

The Ottoman Expedition of 1786

In early 1786, as part of his annual collection of contributions, Murad sent his assistant to the foreign consuls in Alexandria, demanding a heavy fine from the Hospice de la Terre Sainte, the parish church of the Europeans; it was run by Franciscans who had repaired it without government permission. The consuls refused to pay the fine, claiming their rights under the capitulations. Murad's men then tore down the walls of the church. The foreigners were so frightened that they fled the city; only the consuls remained behind, in the house of Mure, the French consul.

They decided first to appeal to Ibrahim Bey, and then the Pasha, but the latter was a virtual prisoner in the Citadel, and Ibrahim's answer was long in coming. So they appealed directly to the Porte, sending two collective letters to their respective ambassadors in Istanbul.

When Murad and Ibrahim realised the seriousness of the situation, they hurriedly tried to defuse it, but they were too late. The Ottoman government reacted swiftly and seized the opportunity to re-establish their authority in Egypt. Ottoman forces under the command of Ghazi Hasan Pasha landed in Alexandria in July 1786, seized control of the city, then marched south to Cairo. Although the force which Ibrahim and Murad had mustered emerged victorious after the first battle, it was not able to maintain its power and was soundly defeated by the Ottoman army.[26]

Murad and Ibrahim retreated to Upper Egypt which remained under their control. Cairo and Lower Egypt were governed by the Ottomans who appointed a new *shaykh al- balad*, Isma'il Bey. This was the situation when Baldwin arrived back in Egypt. He noted, however, that Ghazi Hasan was very unpopular; he was rapacious, and intent on amassing a personal fortune.

Baldwin also learned of a new French company which had been established in Marseilles to trade with India via Suez and to sell Indian goods in Egypt and the rest of the Ottoman empire.[27] Magallon was the company's agent in Egypt, and as such had bought up half the houses and warehouses on one side of the European street in Alexandria. Antun Pharaon, the former Customs Master of Egypt, also had interests in the Marseilles company.

Return of the Duumvirate

Meanwhile, Ghazi Hasan Pasha was recalled to Istanbul in 1787 because of the Russo–Turkish war. He left a weak *shaykh al-balad* in charge. Before long, Murad and Ibrahim, who had been closely following events, began to move north. In early 1788, two of their party reached Cairo and contacted Baldwin. They explained the need of the two beys for foreign allies, and offered great commercial benefits—even a garrison in Alexandria—if England were to support the reinstatement of their duumvirate.[28]

Even the single-minded Baldwin, who would ordinarily have jumped at such an opportunity to promote Egyptian backing for his commercial schemes, was aware that this particular course was fraught with danger. This was heightened by a growing awareness of the Russian consul's complicity in attempts by the rebels to weaken Isma'il Bey; the consul was finally caught and executed in early 1790.

A year later, an outbreak of plague decimated the people of Egypt. Isma'il Bey himself suffered a fatal attack in March 1791. Murad and Ibrahim, however, managed to avoid the infection, devoting their energies to gaining strength as their enemies were immobilised by disease. In July 1791, they finally entered Cairo with their triumphant forces.

Baldwin was relieved at the return of the duumvirate. Isma'il Bey had shown a marked preference for the French, although he had given Baldwin permission for East India Company dispatches and passengers to land at Suez. But the route had gradually fallen into disuse. In order to keep it going for emergencies, Baldwin used it to keep the British in India informed of European affairs.

Although his instructions as consul-general explicitly forbade his involvement in trade or private business, there is little doubt that Baldwin discreetly continued his work as a merchant. His love of the good life was incompatible with his comparatively low salary.

In 1788, he reported that the French had started to export natron[29] from Egypt. He claimed to have discovered the mineral in 1776, but the caravan disaster of 1779 had cut short his plans to trade in it. It was available in great abundance at the eponymous Wadi Natrun, and during three months in 1788, the French had exported 5,000 tons to Marseilles.

Baldwin applied to London for permission to trade in natron, stressing that it would be in the national interest. He never received an answer, so went ahead and began to export it. But the high import duties in England cut his profits drastically. He appealed to London, but was unable to convince anyone. Undaunted, he continued the trade, reporting bitterly to Dundas that he had contributed to the revenue of England: the import duties he paid on natron apparently exceeded his salary as consul-general.[30]

His official work included preparing a report in 1789 for the Privy Council on the slave trade in Egypt: 'A Memorial Relating to the Trade in Slaves Carried on in Egypt'.[31] Of all his superiors in London, it was obvious that Dundas alone held him in high esteem. His relationship with Ainslie continued to be cold, and that with Carmarthen was difficult to assess. On the one hand, the Secretary of State would praise Baldwin; on the other, he would ignore his persistent pleas for a leave of absence. In July 1789, for example, Baldwin explained that his wife was not constitutionally able to withstand the weather and needed to go to England; Baldwin wanted to accompany her there, and find a place for her to live. But permission to leave Egypt was not granted. It was not until 1791 that Grenville,[32] who succeeded Carmarthen that year, granted him leave of absence to go to Cyprus. The unlucky Baldwin was unable to go, however, because an outbreak of the plague had made the island unsafe. The desperate man had lived in Egypt for seven years without a change of air, but his pleas for leave of absence had fallen on deaf ears.

Even more difficult were his entreaties to be reimbursed for the cost of arranging for East India Company dispatches to be sent on the overland route. The Company rarely answered his letters, and were clearly unimpressed with his efforts. But the indomitable Baldwin continued to work as though he were an established senior official of the Company. In early 1793, when he heard of France's declaration of war on Britain, he realised that the British and French in India would not have had the time to know about it. Aware of the strategic advantage of advance information, he quickly arranged to send a dispatch with the news to Bombay via the Red Sea route; the letter reached India well before the French there knew about the war. This gave the British a significant advantage, providing them with the intelligence required to expel the French from Pondicherry and save their own possessions there.[33]

Closure of the Consulate, 1793

Very few senior officials in London agreed with Baldwin about the strategic importance of Egypt, particularly during the 1790s. The directors of the East India Company apparently regarded the country and Baldwin's role in it as an inconvenience, and the government shared this view. In early 1792, for example, Grenville questioned Dundas about the usefulness of the consulate. Although Dundas was convinced that it was vital to British interests, he could find neither the time nor the funds to do anything about it. Baldwin thus lost his main backer in London, and it was not long before his position was terminated.

In February 1793 Grenville informed Baldwin that '... His Majesty had no further occasion for your services as Consul General in Egypt ... and gave him three months notice of final payment of services.'[34] For some reason, however, Grenville's dispatch did not reach Baldwin; it was not until early 1796 when the duplicate of the letter reached him that he learned of his dismissal. He continued therefore to act as British consul-general until 1796, and did not finally leave Egypt until 1798.

Ironically, those extra years proved the value of his position. In 1794, he finally announced the conclusion of a commercial agreement with the beys, signed on 28 February 1794, which had been delayed by the turbulent events of the past few years. The text of the treaty followed almost identically that of the French Truguet agreement and acknowledged the right of British subjects to navigate to all ports of the Ottoman empire.

The sanction of the Porte was vital to the implementation of the agreement. Baldwin sought the help of the new ambassador in Istanbul, but the government in London ignored the issue, since, to all intents and purposes, there was no longer a British consulate in Egypt.

The beys were anxious to have merchant ships arrive at Suez if the dispatch route was to be allowed to continue, so Baldwin sent an English emissary to Bombay to explain this to the presidencies in India; he also sent pleas to the directors of the East India Company in London, but no one there seemed interested.

Largely because of Baldwin's persistence and determination, however, the Red Sea route continued as a channel for British intelligence. Baldwin seemed to be alone in recognising the powerful edge it provided in war time. In 1795, he used it to score a significant gain, helping a British emissary, Hugh Cleghorn, to travel from Alexandria to Suez in pursuance of his clandestine mission designed to bring Ceylon under British domination in an easy and bloodless way.[35] In May 1796, Baldwin used the Red Sea once again to British advantage. He had heard from the British consul in Berne that a Dutch squadron was bound for the Cape of Good Hope. When Baldwin sent this information to Bengal, a British squadron was sent to the Cape where it captured the unsuspecting Dutch fleet.[36]

How Baldwin was able to survive in Egypt after his salary from London was discontinued in 1793 is a mystery. He was, of course, engaged in private trade. He exported natron in fairly large quantities, which must have provided some financial rewards. He was also involved in commercial relations with Jezzar Pasha of Acre as a defence against the French to whom he supplied arms and ammunition. Baldwin obtained the weaponry from London, but the Pasha paid for them in products, not money. When Napoleon entered Acre, he seized the arms which Baldwin had sent, and then sold them.

With increasing desperation, Baldwin informed Grenville in 1795 that there was a surplus of wheat in Egypt, and that he could supply England, which was suffering from a great shortage, particularly for the forces in the Mediterranean. Baldwin later claimed that if the Privy Council had taken up his suggestion at the time, the government could have saved £1 million.[37] The next year, he was anxious to prevent the French from buying the surplus wheat of Egypt. But Baldwin's interest in the trade came to nothing since the Privy Council decided it would not be expedient to send the grain from Egypt to Gibraltar because it would be impossible to grind and dress it there.[38]

Baldwin entreated Dundas to help him retain his position.[39] He reminded Dundas that the consulate was the 'creature of the India Board—the creature of Mr Dundas ... free it from ruin.'[40] But there was no response.

Triumphant Return

In March 1798, Baldwin finally left Egypt a sick, ageing and disillusioned man who in a childlike manner had never ceased to believe that Dundas would somehow save him from calamity. He left behind his property in Alexandria, estimated at £2,000, with no prospects of an income. From Alexandria, he travelled to Trieste where he heard of the French invasion of Egypt.

He had planned to continue to England, but when he heard that the French had confiscated his belongings in Egypt, he decided to 'retire from society in a corner of Italy and wait for a turn in the tide of affairs'.[41] He settled in Tuscany in an elegantly furnished palace for which he paid £20 per annum in rent. Ever the dramatist, he claimed that 'I clothed myself, amid this splendour, in perfect humility'.[42]

After the battle of Marengo in June 1800, Baldwin fled Florence, and travelled to Livorno where he boarded a British frigate crowded with British refugees fleeing the republican advances. The ship docked at Naples, where he received a letter from Admiral Keith Elphinstone, commander-in-chief of British forces in the Mediterranean who had led the British occupation of the Dutch colonies in the Cape of Good Hope and India from 1795 to 1799. Elphinstone invited Baldwin to Malta to join his fleet which was on its way to Egypt; his knowledge of the country was at last recognised as vital. Baldwin could not resist such a call: 'What answer could an honest Englishman ... make to so honourable a call—to so honourable a distinction, but command! I will shew the way.'[43] It was with irony that he noticed a captured vessel in Malta with a prisoner he knew well: Charles Magallon, his French counterpart in Egypt, who had seized his property after the Napoleonic invasion.

The fleet sailed for Egypt in late February and arrived in Abukir on 2 March 1801. Although Baldwin was there during the beginning of the battle, there is little evidence that he did anything specific. His own recollections of the British landings are filled with poetic outbursts of nationalistic expressions rather than details of military manœuvres. He did, however, help with provisions of all kinds, food, livestock and transportation. He was charged with organising the supplies of the soldiers, something he obviously did well, for Abercromby reputedly said 'The army, Gentlemen, are greatly indebted to Mr. Baldwin'.[44]

Baldwin did not remain for long in Egypt. He was back in England in May, having proudly brought back with him the standard of the Invincible Legion of Bonaparte which the British had captured. Little is known of his life after that date. He died in London in 1824.

Notes

1 George Baldwin, *Political Recollections Relative to Egypt, Containing Observations on its Government under the Mamlukes* (London, 1802).

2 Ibid., p. 4.

3 Demands for loans.

4 The Company ordered the consulate to be closed in 1754, but Richard Harris, the consul, did not depart until 1757. He left Robert Hughes, an Egyptian-born Englishman and the representative of Holland, in charge of British affairs. Alfred C. Wood, *A History of the Levant Company* (London, 1964), p. 166.

5 [Public Record Office, PRO], State Papers (SP) 97/53, Baldwin to Ainslie (copy), 24 June 1777. Unpublished Crown copyright material transcribed here appears by permission of HMSO.

6 Translation of *Hatti Sherif* to the Government of Egypt in ibid., SP 97/54.

7 An account of the caravan disaster is available in Eliza Fay, *Original Letters from India* (London: Hogarth Press, 1986), referred to in Anthony Sattin, *Lifting the Veil: British Society in Egypt 1768–1956* (London: Dent, 1988).

8 [India Office Records, IOR], Factory Records, Egypt and the Red Sea, vol. 5, O'Donnell to Ibrahim Bey, 8 July 1779.

9 [PRO] FO 78/1, 'Copy of a bond drawn up in Arabic by order of the Government of Egypt, obtained by violence from those who signed' (translation), n.d.

10 [PRO] SP 97/55, Baldwin to Ainslie, 31 August 1779 (copy).

11 Ibid., Ainslie's Memorial to the Porte (translation), 24 September 1779.

12 [PRO] FO 78/1, Ainslie to Hillsborough, 17 April 1780.

13 Archives des Affaires Etrangères (France), Correspondance Politique, Turquie, tome 166. 'Memoire contenant les details de ce que les anglois viennent s'eprouver en Egypte et de la traine odieuse dont les sujets du Roy été la victime'. Enclosed in a letter to Hennin, 3 February 1780.

14 British Museum, Additional Manuscripts 35118 f.37, Baldwin to Edward Monckton, a Member of Parliament, whom he asked to intercede with Sheridan on his behalf.

15 Archives des Affaires Etrangères (France), Correspondance Politique, Turquie, tome 162. 'Conventions preliminaires d'un traité de commerce et navigation de l'Inde par Suez, arretées et conclues au Caire le 10 Janvier 1785.'

16 [IOR] Factory Records, Egypt and the Red Sea, vol. 5a, Dundas *et al.* to Carmarthen, 19 May 1786.

17 Fortesque Mss., vol. II, Appendix V, Grenville to Dundas, 25 January 1793.

18 [PRO] FO 24/1, Heads of Instructions to Baldwin from the India Board, 19 May 1786.

19 [PRO] FO 78/7, Ainslie to Carmarthen, 10 October 1786.

20 Ibid., 25 October 1786.

21 [PRO] FO 78/7, Carmarthen to Ainslie, 1 September 1786.

22 Ibid.

23 Evidence of his having had at least one daughter is to be found in his book, *Mr. Baldwin's Legacy to His Daughter, or the Divinity of Truth* (London, 1811).

24 'Abd al-Rahman al-Jabarti, '*Aja'ib al-athar fi'l tarajim wa'l-akhbar*, in 4 vols (Bulaq, 1297/1879–1880), vol. 2, p. 92.

25 There were 61 Frenchmen in Egypt in 1786: 36 in Cairo, 15 in Alexandria, and 10 in Rosetta. [Les Archives Nationales] Affaires Etrangères, B I, Alexandria, Mure (French consul), n.d.

26 al-Jabarti, '*Aja'ib*, vol. 2, p. 113.

27 R. Clement. *Les Français d'Egypte au XVII et XVIII siècles* (Cairo, 1960), p. 264.

28 [PRO], FO 24/1, Baldwin to Carmarthen, 2 April 1788.

29 Natron is a cheaper form of saltpêtre and was then used to make soap, glass and bleach-linen. It was also used to make gunpowder.

30 [IOR] Factory Records, Egypt and the Red Sea, vol. 5a, 9 November 1793.

31 This was later incorporated in Baldwin's *Political Recollections*.

32 William Wyndham Grenville, 1759–1834. In 1789, he was successively Speaker of the House of Commons and Secretary of State for the Home Department. He became Secretary of State for the Foreign Office in 1791 and remained in office until 1801.

33 [PRO] FO 24/1, Baldwin to Grenville, 10 April 1793.

34 Ibid., Grenville to Dundas, 8 February 1793.

35 For the story of Cleghorn's mission, see Rev. William Neil (ed.), *The Cleghorn Papers: A Footnote to History* (London, 1927). See also [PRO] WO 1/361 (Ceylon), Cleghorn to Dundas, 10 June 1795.

36 Baldwin, *Political Recollections*, p. 29.

37 [PRO] FO 24/1, Baldwin to Grenville, 29 March 1796.

38 [PRO] Treasury, T.1 /759, Board Paper, 16 January 1796; and T.1 /760, 29 January 1796.

39 [PRO] FO 24/1, Baldwin to Dundas, 21 April 1796.

40 Ibid.

41 Baldwin, *Political Recollections*, p. 34.

42 Ibid., p. 36.

43 Ibid., p. 39.

44 Ibid., p. 124.

Part Two

Egyptological Travellers

5 ～ A Pioneer Egyptologist: Giovanni Baptista Belzoni, 1778–1823

Peter A. Clayton

Giovanni Belzoni was born in Padua on 5 November 1778, the son of a Roman barber. His early education destined him for the priesthood and he also appears to have acquired some knowledge of hydraulics before his student political activities and the French invasion forced him to leave his native Padua in 1798. Travelling across Europe selling religious baubles, he arrived in England from Holland about Christmas 1803. He was a man of immense size, two metres tall, often being later referred to as the 'Paduan Giant' or the 'Patagonian Sampson' when he began to earn a living as a strongman on the stage. A watercolour by R. H. Norman in the Percival Collection of material relating to the Sadler's Wells theatre[1] depicts him clad in a leopard skin and red gladiator boots, carrying eleven people on a special frame around the stage. R. H. Norman appeared with him at the same time as the character Pantaloon. Meanwhile, about 1805, he had married (some say in Ireland) a young girl of about twenty, Sarah (née Banne), who was to be a long-suffering wife in his travels and widow devoted to his memory, outliving him by forty-seven years (she died on 12 January 1870 in Jersey).

Belzoni tired of the circus-like life of the music halls and late in 1814 he, together with Sarah and a young Irish lad, James Curtin, who acted as their servant, was in Malta bound for Constantinople for a change of scene and, hopefully, fortune. In Malta they met a Captain Isma'il Gibraltar, an agent of Muhammad 'Ali, the Albanian Pasha of Egypt, who was seeking European engineers for work in Egypt, and Belzoni's hydraulic knowledge was obviously mentioned. The trio succumbed to the invitation and left Malta for Alexandria on 19 May 1815. Once arrived in Cairo an interview was arranged with Muhammad 'Ali who agreed a small sum for subsistence (£25 a month) whilst Belzoni worked on a hydraulic water-wheel to be used in the palace gardens. Suffice it to say that, when finished, the machine was effective but vested interests and prejudices, against a machine that with one man and an ox could do the work of four oxen, decreed its failure. Belzoni was left without any support for himself, and had his wife and James Curtin to feed. It was at this point that once again fate or fortune took a hand in the person of the recently appointed British consul, Henry Salt. Like so many British ambassadorial officials of the period Salt had been urged, by Sir Joseph Banks, to collect antiquities in his foreign posting. Salt's commissioning of Belzoni to collect was the turning point that changed him, literally and metaphorically, into one of the giants of the early days of exploratory Egyptology. It is fashionable nowadays to describe such characters as latter-day tomb robbers and vandals and many have applied this description to Belzoni, such as Professor Brian Fagan (who is also factually inaccurate). It is essential, however, to look at these characters, as best one may, in the context of their time and the then state of knowledge, not to judge by our present-day so-called 'politically correct' attitudes.

The Swiss explorer Jean Louis Burckhardt had noticed a large fine head of a king in a site in Western Thebes (that we now know to be of Rameses II, lying in his mortuary temple, the Ramesseum). Greatly impressed by it, and mentioning it to Salt, this discovery gave rise to Belzoni's first commission from Salt—to remove the head safely for transport to the British Museum. Belzoni specifically writes, 'It has been erroneously stated that I was regularly employed by Mr Salt, the consul-general of his Britannic majesty in Egypt, for the purpose of bringing the colossal head from Thebes to Alexandria. I positively deny that I was ever engaged by him in any shape whatever, either by words or writing; as I have proofs of the case being on the contrary.'[2] The French savants in Napoleon's expedition in 1798 had also noted the colossal head and, intending to remove it, had also engraved it in their immense work, the *Description de l'Égypte*. Belzoni sailed from Cairo to Luxor and made his way immediately to the Ramesseum. His instructions were quite definite:

> Having obtained the necessary permission to hire workmen, etc., Mr Belzoni will proceed direct to Thebes. He will find the head referred to on the western side of the river, opposite to Carnak [Karnak], in the vicinity of a village called Gournou, lying on the southern side of a ruined temple, called by the natives Kossar el Dekaki. To the head is still attached a portion of the shoulders, so that altogether it is of large dimensions, and will be recognised—1st, by the circumstances of its lying on its back with the face uppermost—2nd, by the face being quite perfect, and very beautiful—3rdly, by its having, on one of its shoulders, a hole bored artificially, supposed to have been made by the French for separating the fragment of the body—and 4thly, from its being a mixed blackish and reddish granite, and covered with hieroglyphs on its shoulders. It must not be mistaken for another, lying in the neighbourhood, which is *much mutilated*.[3]

The latter, a fallen seated statue of some one thousand tons, was to be the inspiration for P. B. Shelley's sonnet 'Osymandias'. Belzoni was not to move the bust, 'if he should judge there would be any serious risk of either injuring the head, of burying the face in the sand, or of losing it in the

Nile'. He found it, 'with its face upwards, and apparently smiling on me at the thought of being taken to England. I must say that my expectations were exceeded by its beauty, but not by its size.'[4]

A 'car', or raft, was made to take the colossus and the bust raised sufficiently to introduce the raft under it—the natives had said that it was impossible to move the bust at all. Once on the wooden raft and secured, rollers were slid underneath. This was on 27 July and, small wonder, Belzoni succumbed to heat-stroke for a few days after his exertions at this unfavourable time of year. Gradually the colossus was advanced towards the Nile;[5] on 30 July it was moved 150 metres and by 5 August it had reached the edge of the cultivation. Belzoni was most anxious to get past this before the inundation began. On 12 August the 'Younger Memnon' (as the colossus was known to distinguish it from the larger fallen statue left behind—Shelley's 'Osymandias') arrived at the river bank. It was to be mid-November before Belzoni would be able to embark the seven-ton head, and then only with difficulty by taking it down a six-metre drop from the bank to boat level. After several different locations in the British Museum, the head[6] now dominates the Egyptian Sculpture Gallery but, although the names of Burckhardt and Salt appear on the label, of Belzoni's contribution there is no mention.

Belzoni then made preparations to travel further south on the Nile. He visited Abu Simbel and began operations to open the great temple of Rameses II (but not then known as such), which Burckhardt had literally stumbled across in 1812. Unfortunately, having cleared several tons of sand away from the colossi in front of it, Belzoni ran out of money and made his way back to Thebes. There he inspected a large granite sarcophagus lid which Bernardino Drovetti (the Piedmontese French consul in Egypt, and Belzoni's rival in many collecting endeavours), had given to him if he could retrieve it from the tomb wherein it lay in the Valley of the Kings. Drovetti was none too pleased when, upon Belzoni managing to turn it over, the figure of the king in Osirid form flanked by two goddesses (Isis and Nephthys) was revealed, sculpted in high relief on the outside of the lid. It was the lid of the sarcophagus of Rameses III,[7] which Belzoni presented to the Fitzwilliam Museum, Cambridge, early in 1823 shortly before his death. The huge body of the sarcophagus was recovered by Salt and sold in his second collection to the King of France and is now in the Louvre, Paris.

He noted at Karnak that 'the place whence the French had taken their lion-headed statues [the goddess Sekhmet], at the time of the invasion, is where a temple stood, surrounded on three sides by a lake.'[8] This was the temple of Mut in Assher, just outside the south temenos wall of the Karnak temples, later excavated by the Misses Benson and Gourlay in 1895–97. The statues that the French found on the south side of the temple were subsequently captured at sea and came to the British Museum. Belzoni proceeded to dig on the west side, where he reasoned no one had previously excavated. 'In the course of a few days I discovered about eighteen statues, six of which were perfect, and among them a white statue as large as life, supposed to be Jupiter Ammon, which is now also in the British Museum.'[9] It is a magnificent seated light coloured quartzite statue of Seti II[10] holding a small ram's-head-topped shrine on his knees—it was this ram, the animal of Amun, that misled Belzoni in his identification of the statue. He also found a limestone slab with its inscription arranged in a series of small neat boxes. 'This piece in my opinion might be of much service to Dr Thomas Young in his undertaking of the discovery of the alphabet of the Egyptians.'[11] The seemingly crossword slab[12] is in fact inscribed with prayers to the goddess Mut and, by virtue of its arrangement, can be read from right to left, or top to bottom. However, it had to wait until 1971 for its definitive publication.[13] He also found a small painted limestone statue group of the priest and overseer of the Treasury, Athy, with his wife, Hentur, and their son, Nefer-Hebef.[14]

At Karnak Belzoni set 'several men to work on a spot of ground at the foot of a heap of earth, where part of a large colossus projected out', then he went over to Gourna. On his return he

> had the pleasure to find the discovery had been made of a colossal head, larger than that I had sent to England. It was of red granite, of beautiful workmanship, and uncommonly well preserved, except one ear, and part of the chin, which had been knocked off along with the beard. It is detached from the shoulder at the lower part of the neck, and has the usual corn measure or mitre[15] on its head. Though of larger proportion than the Young Memnon,[16] it is not so bulky or heavy, as it has no part of the shoulder attached to it. I had it moved to Luxor, which employed 8 days, though the distance is little more than a mile...Besides this head,[17] which is ten feet from the neck to the top of the mitre, I procured an arm[18] belonging to the same colossus, which measures also ten feet, and with the head, will give a just idea of the size of the statue. I brought also the famous altar, with the six divinities,[19] in alto relievo, which are amongst the most finished works of any I have seen in Egypt. It was thrown from its pedestal in a small temple in the north-east angle of the wall inclosing the great temple of Carnak.[20]

The statue is identified as Tuthmosis III, and on the flat surface of the dorsal plinth behind its right ear Belzoni carved his name and the date 1817. In this he was only following the norm of the times to identify his finds— inspection of the superb seated statue of Rameses II now in Turin reveals the name carved thereon of Belzoni's arch-rival, Bernardino Drovetti.

Belzoni then went south to Abu Simbel again and managed to clear away enough sand from the middle of the four great figures of the king to find the top of a doorway and slide down into the temple. 'We soon made the passage wider, and entered the finest and most extensive excavation in Nubia, one that can stand competition with any, except for the tomb recently discovered in Beban el Malook [the Valley of the Kings].'[21] Belzoni is writing here with hindsight as he entered the temple of Abu Simbel on 1 August 1817 and it was not until later that year, on 16 October, that he was to find the tomb of Seti I in the Valley of the Kings (KV 17). Belzoni and his fellow travellers (Henry Beechey, Charles Irby and James Mangles) were astounded by the temple's immense size and decoration. He realised immediately that the 'hero' seen on the walls in many actions was the same that he had seen at the Ramesseum and Luxor, that is, Rameses II. Belzoni records that it took twenty-two days to open the temple, besides the six days he had spent on his first trip there the previous year.

> The heat was so great in the interior of the temple, that it scarcely permitted us to take any drawings, as the perspiration from our hands soon rendered the paper quite wet. Accordingly, we left this operation to succeeding travellers, who may set about it with more convenience than we could, as the place will become cooler...I must not omit to mention that, in the temple, we found two lions with hawks' heads, the body as large as life;[22] a small sitting figure[23] and some copper work belonging to the doors.[24]

In 1817, Belzoni's success in the Valley of the Kings was such that on 9 October he found his first tomb, a second the same day, and another on 11 October, which has since proved to be that of Rameses I (KV 16). It contained two large standing wooden figures over two metres tall.[25]

On 16 October Belzoni found the entrance to the tomb of Seti I six metres below the then ground level. His account is full of his wonderment at the brightness of the painting and the fine work. He found fragments of wooden furniture, large standing wooden figures of the king (like those from Rameses I's tomb), and hundreds of wood and faience mummiform ushabti figures. The pièce de resistance, however, stood in the centre of the burial hall—the superb finely carved alabaster sarcophagus of Seti I,[26] empty and with only small fragments of the high relief lid scattered nearby. The whole of the sarcophagus is carved with texts from the Book of Gates in hieroglyphs on average only 5cm high, and its thickness is the same. The king's body was found in 1881 amongst the royal mummies in the great cache of forty mummies in Deir el-Bahari tomb 320.

Belzoni set to work to make drawings with his young Italian draughtsman Alessandro Ricci as assistant, and also to make wax impressions and casts—work which in all took him nearly a year. Sadly, in later years, some large portions of finely painted walls were removed by such as Champollion and Rosellini, and are now in the museums of Paris and Turin.

The sarcophagus was illustrated in John Britton's *Union of Architecture, Sculpture and Painting* in 1828 but was not properly published until 1864 when Joseph Bonomi and Samuel Sharpe produced their beautifully and carefully illustrated book on it. It is still a major reference for the

sarcophagus, although a new study by Dr John Taylor of the British
Museum is expected in 1998. Sir Wallis Budge published a short guide to
the sarcophagus in 1908, which has some curious errors in it.

After the work in the Valley, Belzoni left for Cairo. Early in 1818, whilst
visiting the Pyramids of Giza with two friends, he walked over to the Second
Pyramid: 'I observed that just under the centre of the face of the pyramid
the accumulation of materials, which had fallen from the coating of it, was
higher than the entrance could be expected to be, if compared with the
height of the entrance into the first pyramid measuring from the basis.'[27]
He returned the next day for some closer and more private investigations
and decided that he would apply for a *firman*, or permit, to dig.

The work went on for several days with little to show. Belzoni was upset
and laid the Arabs off work for a day and spent it closely observing the
pyramid. He noted that the entrance to the Great Pyramid was off-centre,
a factor he had not allowed for, and realised that he should excavate some
10 metres east of his present position. Belzoni found the first granite block
on 28 February, three blocks inclining inwards towards the centre on 1
March and, at noon the next day the right entrance, a passage 1 1/2 metres
high, a metre wide and 36 metres long, inclining downwards and filled with
large stones. At the bottom a granite portcullis half a metre thick blocked
the way. Gradually it was eased up a little at a time by putting stones beneath
it as short levers inched it upwards. Eventually it was raised high enough
for an Arab with a candle to enter and, when it had been raised some more,
the large Belzoni was able to squeeze through. After following the passage,
descending a shaft by means of a rope and following another passage,

> I reached the door at the centre of a large chamber.[28] I walked slowly two or
> three paces and then stood still to contemplate the place I was ... On my
> advancing towards the west end I was agreeably surprised to find that there was
> a sarcophagus buried on a level with the floor ... the lid had been broken at the
> side, so that the sarcophagus was half open. It is of the finest granite, but, like
> the other in the first pyramid, there is not a hieroglyphic on it.[29]

Belzoni was to leave his own name and the date writ large in lamp black
high on the southern wall of the burial chamber.

After this feat he left again for Thebes where he was tempted to excavate
at a spot he had had his eye on for some time—behind the colossi of
Memnon. On the second day, he found a large, seated black granite statue
of Amenophis III, and several lioness-headed Sekhmet figures like those
from Karnak, some seated, some standing. The statue had to go to Salt
since it was Salt's concession, but not before Belzoni had carved his name
in large letters on the plinth base of the Amenophis statue near its left foot.[30]

Belzoni next recorded his journeys to the Red Sea and to the Smaller
Oasis, and also the difficulty of recovering the obelisk from Philae that stood

before the entrance pylons to the temple of Isis. This monument, known as the Bankes Obelisk, which has an important place in the history of the decipherment of hieroglyphs (alongside the Rosetta Stone), now stands in the park at Kingston Lacy, Dorset.

Belzoni left Egypt in September 1819 for his native Padua, arriving just before Christmas. Previously he had sent two seated Sekhmet statues as a gift to the city. The city, wishing to honour him for his gift, commissioned a special medallion to be struck by Manfredini, the engraver of the mint of Milan. It was not finished until May 1821, when he received one for himself in gold, weighing almost three ounces, with a loop for suspension, which he used to wear on a blue ribbon. He was also given six examples in silver, which he presented variously to his patron the Duke of Sussex, the Universities of Oxford, Cambridge and Edinburgh, William Gifford (editor of *The Quarterly Review*), and Sir Walter Scott. Twenty-four medals in bronze he presented, according to a letter in the Museo Civico in Padua, to various 'professori di arti e scienze'. Some of the latter medallions have an inscription added around the edge, e.g. GIOV: BELZONI. TO T: MURDOCH. F:R:S: 18. JUNE 1821 (private collection). On the obverse of the medallion are shown the two Sekhmet statues and Belzoni noted with some pleasure the long inscription on the reverse which honoured him not so much for his gift but more for his greater discoveries: IOBAPT.BELZONI/PATAVINO/QVI.CEPHRENIS.PYRAMIDEM/ APIDISQ.THEB.SEPVLCRVM/PRIMVS.APERVIT/ ET.VRBEM.BERENICIS/NVBIAE.ET.LIBYAE.MON/ IMPAVIDE.DETEXIT.

His gold medal is now in the Department of Coins and Medals in the British Museum, with a note that it was presented in 1874 by Frederick William Collard, who styled himself a descendant of Belzoni. What his relationship was has, so far, been impossible to ascertain. The medal was given four years after Sarah Belzoni's death (on 12 January 1870), and her will leaves all her effects (and one would presume that the medal was amongst them) to her god-daughter Selina Belzoni Tucker residing in Cheltenham. There is no record of the Tuckers in the Cheltenham census for 1871 (the one closest to the relevant date), nor is there any record of her marriage with Collard, which could explain how he came by the medal. For that matter, there is no record of the birth, marriage or death of either of them in St Catherine's House, London, from 1837 (when the records began) down to 1900. The presumption is, therefore, that they must feature in some record abroad that has yet to be traced.

It was also in 1821, in June, that friends of Belzoni in Britain subscribed to produce a medallion in silver and also in bronze commemorating his opening of the Second Pyramid on 2 March 1818. The original sketches for the design by William Brockedon are in the National Portrait Gallery, London (2525/1) and, whilst the obverse portrait is an excellent likeness of Belzoni, the pyramid on the reverse is the wrong pyramid. Represented there is the Great Pyramid of Giza, obvious by its stunted shape in missing its upper 10 metres whilst the Second Pyramid is distinctive by being complete almost to its pyramidion with some of its original Tura limestone casing still surviving at the top.

Belzoni was anxious to get his book published and approached John Murray the publisher in Albemarle Street in March 1820, as soon as he arrived in London. It was published before the end of the year in two volumes: a quarto volume of text at two guineas (£2.10p), and a folio volume of plates at six guineas (£6.30p). It was well received by many serious publications and journals. Belzoni was also eager to exhibit his finds, casts, copies and models, and acquired the ideal premises—the Egyptian Hall in Piccadilly built in 1812 in the then extremely fashionable Egyptian style, heavily influenced by the temple of Dendera. Standing almost opposite the bottom of Old Bond Street, its memory is still preserved in 'Egyptian House', 170 Piccadilly, London W1.

The exhibition opened on Tuesday 1 May 1821 with a first day attendance of 1900 people paying 2s 6d (11.5p) a head for admission. The 1s (5p) catalogue sold extremely well, running to a further edition. One thing was missing, however—Seti I's alabaster sarcophagus. It arrived in England in the frigate *Diana* in August 1821 and then became the centrepiece not of Belzoni's exhibition but of one of the more sordid affairs in the history of British Egyptology. In the intrigues in the subsequent six years, the Trustees of the British Museum refused it and it was eventually bought by Sir John Soane for £2000, all of which went to Salt and not a penny to Belzoni or his, by that time, widow Sarah. It reposes today in the crypt of Sir John Soane's Museum in Lincoln's Inn Fields, one of the finest Egyptian antiquities in Britain. In June 1822, however, Belzoni needed to raise money and the contents of the Egyptian Hall were put up for public auction—two imperfect Sekhmet statues fetched £380; a perfect one, £300. The model of the Second Pyramid, cross-section and complete structure, made 34 guineas, and the façade of Abu Simbel, £24. A left-over relic of the sale, a small upper torso of a Sekhmet statue, may still be seen today in New Bond Street above the entrance to Sotheby's the auctioneers; presumably it was an unsold lot. A carved wooden Sekhmet upper torso is also incorporated into the decoration on the front of the auctioneer's rostrum.

Belzoni also had Masonic connections which are still fairly obscure. He was a member of Number 1 Lodge and had, presumably, been introduced by his patron, the Duke of Sussex, who was Grand Master. Two of his

Masonic jewels have survived (in the Freemasons' Hall Collection). One, incorporating a six-pointed star enclosing a sun's face, is dated 1821 on the obverse and, in the same design on the reverse, has his name on the cross-bar of the triangle. His second jewel, the Grand Arch with Compasses, is set with brilliants.

Belzoni was getting restless and he decided to set out, without Sarah, to seek the source of the River Niger, one of the last great quests. Shortly after his arrival in Benin he contracted dysentery and after several days of severe illness, he died shortly before 3pm on 3 December 1823 at Gwato near Benin. He was buried under an arasma tree on the outskirts of Gwato, and a salvo was fired over his grave. A carpenter made a wooden tablet recording his name and date of death, with an added sentence: 'The gentlemen who place this inscription over the grave of the celebrated and intrepid traveller, hope that every European visiting this spot will cause the ground to be cleared and the fence around repaired, if necessary.' The traveller Richard Burton visited the place some forty years later but the tablet was gone, only the tree remained.

Sarah Belzoni had a new engraving prepared of her husband showing him surrounded by all his principal discoveries. Even then she still had not lost hope that he might have survived but, in a letter dated 15 June 1825 addressed to the Victorian novelist Jane Porter, Sarah wrote: 'I have at last received the fatal ring—in my heart hope did linger till the fatal ring arrived' (private collection). It was Belzoni's signet ring. Sarah was to live on in semi-poverty first in Brussels and then in the Channel Islands for another forty-seven years, dying at the age of 87 on 12 January 1870, in Jersey.

Belzoni's memory is kept alive today in Padua by the society, Amici di Belzoni. On the occasion of his bicentenary in 1978 they commissioned a splendid bust of him from the sculptor Giancarlo Milano (and presented a second copy to the British Museum, now in the Students' Room of the Department of Egyptian Antiquities), together with a commemorative medallion by Mario Pinton. A second large and splendid medallion by Roberto Cremesini, showing Belzoni's discoveries on obverse and reverse, was struck in 1987.

Belzoni was certainly no scholar, but he was definitely a pioneer who made possible the work of many later scholars. The last, most fitting words about his work are surely those of Howard Carter, the most renowned excavator in the Valley of the Kings, who wrote that Belzoni's account (*Narrative of Operations...*) 'is one of the most fascinating books in the whole of Egyptian literature'. He went on to say:

> This was the first occasion on which excavations on a large scale had ever been made in The Valley [of the Kings], and we must give Belzoni full credit for the manner in which they were carried out. There are episodes which give the

modern excavator rather a shock, as, for example, when he describes his method of dealing with sealed doorways—by means of a battering ram—*but on the whole the work was extraordinarily good* [author's emphasis].[31]

Notes

1   British Library, Cmdl Tab 4b, vol. 3, fol. 106.
2   Giovanni Belzoni, *Narrative of Operations and Recent Discoveries within the Pyramids, Temples, Tombs...* (London, 1820), pp. 24–5.
3   Ibid., p. 27.
4   Ibid., p. 39.
5   Giovanni Belzoni, *Six New Plates* (London, 1822), hereinafter *Plates*.
6   British Museum, Egyptian Antiquities Department, No. EA 576.
7   Valley of the Kings tomb number KV11; Fitzwilliam Museum, Cambridge accession number E.1.1823.
8   *Narrative*, p. 113.
9   Ibid., p. 114.
10 BM No. EA 616.
11 *Narrative*, p. 162: the decipherment was achieved by Jean-François Champollion in 1822.
12 BM No. EA 194.
13 H. M. Stewart, *JEA* 57, pp. 87–104.
14 BM No. EA 31.
15 The corn measure or mitre represents the double crown of Upper and Lower Egypt.
16 Rameses II.
17 BM No. EA 15.
18 BM No. EA 55.
19 BM No. EA 12.
20 *Narrative*, p. 184.
21 Ibid., p. 211.
22 BM Nos. EA 11, 13.
23 BM No. EA 1376, 'a small sitting figure' of Pa-ser, Governor of Nubia under Rameses II.
24 *Narrative*, p. 214.
25 BM Nos. EA 854, 883.
26 Joseph Bonomi and Samuel Sharpe, *The Alabaster Sarcophagus of Oinemepthah I, King of Egypt, now in Sir John Soane's Museum* (London, 1864).
27 Ibid., pp. 256–8.
28 Giovanni Belzoni, *Forty-four Plates Illustrative of the Research and Operations of G. Belzoni in Egypt and Nubia* (London, 1820), pl. 6.
29 *Narrative*, pp. 270–1
30 BM No. EA 21.
31 Howard Carter, *The Tomb of Tut.Ankh.Amen*, p. 68.

6 ∽ William John Bankes' Collection of Drawings of Egypt and Nubia

Patricia Usick

William John Bankes (1786–1855) was a brilliant and eccentric man whose contemporaries feared he would dissipate his talent and very considerable scholarship by the breadth of his interests and his volatile personality. At Cambridge, rich, charming and good-looking, he may have outshone even Byron, who was to remain a lifelong friend, by his conscious adoption of immense style, his wit and his pretensions to grandeur. Extremely well read in the classics, including the classical writers on Egypt and Nubia, he made himself familiar with most of the later and contemporary works on this subject. He left a potential career in Parliament to follow in the steps of Byron and William Beckford to Spain and Portugal, to pursue a Bohemian lifestyle among the gypsies at Grenada, and then for the risk and adventure of travel in the Near East. He seems to have sought out danger and excitement, from clandestine trips to the forbidden mosque in Jerusalem to the perils attending early travellers in Egypt and Nubia, and he ended his life in exile in Italy fleeing a second court charge of indecent exposure with a guardsman in Green Park.

His fascination with ancient Egypt has left a collection of drawings and water-colours at Kingston Lacy, Dorset, a house which he inherited in 1834, and which, like Soughton, a house which came to him in 1820, he extensively redesigned and rebuilt with the help of Charles Barry, the architect. The existence of the drawings is known to Egyptologists but, with a few individual exceptions, they have never previously been studied or published. They were sent to the Griffith Institute, Oxford from around 1940 until 1961, and partially listed for the Porter and Moss *Topographical Bibliography*,[1] which identified where possible the sites and the specific subjects.

Bankes made two journeys in Egypt from Cairo up the Nile as far as the second cataract area, first on his own in 1815, accompanied only by servants and Giovanni Finati, his dragoman, and then in 1818–19 in a group including Henry Salt (1780–1827), the British consul-general in Egypt; Henry William Beechey (died c. 1870), Salt's secretary; Alessandro Ricci (died 1834), an Italian doctor and artist; and Louis Maurice-Adolphe Linant de Bellefonds (1799–1883), a young French draughtsman. They were joined between Thebes and Philae by Giovanni Belzoni (1778–1823), as an engineer and excavator. Bankes later commissioned Linant, accompanied by Ricci, to travel up the Nile between 1821 and 1822 to find Meroë, which had been spoken of by the classical writers and which was then a 'lost' city. Linant and Ricci also recorded the monuments of Sinai in 1820 and Siwa in 1821, and Bankes himself made a brief visit to Sinai in 1815 and the Delta in 1818. These men drew and recorded virtually all of the then known standing monuments along the Nile from Cairo to Sennar between 1815 and 1822. Weeks were spent at the major sites of Philae and Abu Simbel, considerable clearance and excavation was carried out, and they all went to great lengths to follow up any report of an ancient site. Until then, few writers had covered the area south of the first cataract, and very few travellers had passed beyond the second cataract.

The drawings are important as a source for information on ancient Egypt and for their place in the history of Egyptology, and of topographical and epigraphic drawing. Their great value lies in the meticulously detailed and accurate rendering of the architecture, reliefs, paintings and inscriptions of the major monuments, which was unusual for this period. Bankes was knowingly creating a study collection rather than artistic impressions and should be ranked among the earliest Egyptologists and above the majority of travellers of his day. As well as 'views', we find detailed site plans with orientations, measured sections and elevations, ground plans, architectural details and a fine epigraphic record of the reliefs and inscriptions. Bankes recognised the importance of the epigraphy, understanding how close they were to making the breakthrough in decipherment which would reveal the history of ancient Egypt, hitherto only known from the accounts of the classical writers. Champollion published his breakthrough *Lettre à M. Dacier* ... in 1823 and continued to build on his achievements in decipherment which followed early work by Thomas Young and Bankes.

The drawings are important for archaeology since so much that was recorded has now been lost or damaged, disappeared under Lake Nasser or been salvaged but moved from its original environment.

Of particular importance are the drawings in the collection relating to Nubia and the Sudan, areas which have tended to be studied previously from the point of view of their relationship to Egypt rather than in their own right. Bankes had hoped to reach Dongola and Meroë on his second journey, and subsequently talked of returning to Egypt and perhaps travelling to Meroë, and then on to investigate the sources of the Nile. [2] The sites of Napata and Meroë had not been securely identified in Bankes' time, and knowledge and particularly accurate mapping of the passage of the Nile through those regions was sketchy.

One motive behind the Bankes collection of drawings was to assemble as many accurate and, if possible, bilingual inscriptions toward the decipherment of the hieroglyphic script and the dating of the monuments. Thomas Young had discovered the name of Ptolemy, and Bankes, from his obelisk texts, that of Cleopatra, when the question of whether the hieroglyphs had any phonetic value was still undecided. In 1821, when Bankes printed and distributed the two copper engravings of his obelisk texts,[3] he annotated his discovery in the margin with the name of Cleopatra. Champollion, from a comparison of the two names, was able to prove that there was a phonetic element to the script—a proposition which he had previously denied.

In the Bankes collection at Kingston Lacy there are some 1,500 separate sheets of paper of varying sizes, qualities and colours relating to Egypt and Nubia. The work is unattributed (except for some work signed by Linant) and undated, but many drawings are numbered, and some of these relate to lists. They are mainly drawings and water-colours, ranging from very rough, sometimes faint, pencil sketches, often several to a sheet and on both sides of the paper, to very beautiful, highly finished ink drawings and water-colours. There are also some large sheets containing full-sized tracings. The watermarks on the paper are varied and sometimes dated, and the sketches are often accompanied by notes in various hands. Some of these are no more than a brief *aide-mémoire* for recording colours; others are more lengthy descriptions and comments almost in the format of a travel journal of the day, with full pages describing sites and monuments, the scenery, and the life-style and customs of the local people. The sheets of 'description' appear to be almost entirely in Bankes' own hand and contain many of his comments and speculations, based on his extensive reading and observation.

Far from merely being a traveller's romanticised image of the exotic for home consumption, we find the careful work of draughtsmen rather than artists, painstakingly copying inscriptions they were unable to read or understand, but the importance of which they recognised. This was perhaps the first serious attempt to make a comprehensive and accurate epigraphic record of ancient Egyptian monuments since the publication of the French savants' massive *Description l'Égypte* which appeared in twenty-four volumes from 1809 to 1828. Despite its scientific background, Bankes noted after inspecting the monument of 'Gau' [Qaw al-Kabir] that the *Description* was, 'as usual, highly inaccurate'.[4]

Remaining unpublished, the drawings have escaped the subtle Europeanising and distortions of the engraving and printing process, described by Beechey as often giving 'some fanciful effect destructive of the character of the drawings'.

Both Salt and Beechey were trained artists while Linant was an efficient draughtsman who developed as an artist. Banke carried in Syria two paint boxes and ' … all the apparatus necessary for drawing and planning, as a case of tin for very large sheets of paper, a portfolio for those of more moderate size, drawing instruments & implements of every description. ' He seems to have been a skilled draughtsman and familiar with the terms and techniques of architecture, and a large number of the measured plans are identifiable as his own work.

Some two hundred 'Miscellaneous' drawings and assorted papers remain unidentified, and these are now being put in place. All the papers had been arranged topographically, divided between large Manilla envelopes, marked in ink with their site names, apparently by or for Bankes, and originally stored in the library at Kingston Lacy in a pair of tin cabinets, grained to imitate wood, bearing the words 'Egyptian Drawings'.

The two 'albums' of Bankes manuscripts given to the British Museum in 1923 contain journals and notes which are helping to elucidate the drawings. In addition there are further drawings and writings relating to Egypt presently stored in the Dorset County Record Office, Dorchester. At the house are also fifty-six lithographic stones, mainly copies of inscriptions in Greek and various ancient Near Eastern scripts, which were clearly intended for a publication of which no other record has yet been discovered.

Many of the drawings have handwritten titles giving the site names. However, the nineteenth-century travellers generally recorded the unfamiliar Arabic names phonetically, and often variably, as they heard them, usually taking the nearest village name to identify the site. Phonetic recording is useful in that it can be a pointer to the native language of the artist, since spellings and accents can indicate a French, Italian or English speaker.

Language, handwriting and artistic style can aid in the attribution of the drawings, although Bankes often seems to have checked and annotated others' work. Ricci's work, often annotated in Italian, concentrates on reliefs and inscriptions which seem to have been his speciality, rather than views. Otherwise, the work of Bankes, Beechey and Linant can be identified, and there are copies of Salt's work which seem to be by Linant.

Charles Barry, who travelled in Egypt as artist to a Mr Baillie, and who spent the day with Bankes' flotilla in January 1819 noted:

> Mr Salt showed me the whole of the sketches that have been made since leaving Philae. They were all in pencil and very numerous. They are the work of himself, Mr Beechey (whom he called his Secretary) and a French artist named Linant. I looked over Mr Bankes' drawings, which, on account of their great number, he kept in a basket. They principally relate to details such as hieroglyphs, ornaments etc. and are executed by himself and an Italian doctor in his employ. All the drawings made by Mr Salt and his employee belong to Mr Bankes.[6]

Bankes and Salt enjoyed a relationship of friendship, perhaps overlaid with patronage. Salt effectively acted as an agent for Bankes after the latter's departure, directing the artists and organising the necessary financial arrangements, forwarding letters and the latest news, and arranging for items to be shipped back to England. In return, Bankes promoted Salt's interests in his negotiations with the British Museum, and passed on to the publishers journals collected by Salt. The relationship between Bankes and certainly Finati, Linant and Ricci was based on financial arrangements, with Bankes as employer of the artist and owner of the work produced. Issues of copyright and plagiarism were in the air, but most artists seem to have kept copies of their work as a future investment.

Since Bankes did not succeed in travelling further than Sai island on his journeys up the Nile, we can assume that any drawings made from that point southwards into the Sudan were made by Linant and Ricci on their journey upriver with Finati. We know that Linant was employed specifically by Bankes to make this journey and to explore and record the ancient sites, while Salt, fearful of Linant's rather precarious health, had insisted on his being accompanied by Dr Ricci, who at the same time contributed to the drawings. Ricci was also retained after Bankes' departure to do further recording, apparently never carried out.

Linant came to England in 1824 and his journal, Bankes' property, was written up in a fair copy. It remained unpublished until 1958.[7] There are two copies of the manuscript: one at Kingston Lacy and one, with other drawings and papers of Linant's, in the Louvre. A further manuscript by Linant at Kingston Lacy has not been published. Its title, 'General Notices upon the principal countries and peoples comprehended in the journey of A. Linant when sent by William John Bankes to seek for Meroë and to examine the course of the Nile', is handwritten by Bankes on the marbled paper of the bound notebook. The notebook contains some history of the area, largely contemporary, and the 'manners and customs' genre of writing which other contemporary travellers such as Burckhardt and Cailliaud incorporated within their journals to form one book for publication.

In 1815, while waiting for his hired boat to be equipped for his first journey, Bankes visited Mount Sinai, although the Sinai drawings are the ones made by Linant and Ricci which are referred to in Salt's letters.

The party which left Cairo by boat on 16 September 1815 consisted of Bankes, Finati his dragoman, general factotum, interpreter and guide, and three other servants. In a light-hearted letter to his father Bankes says that he is 'obliged to travel with a vast apparatus "en grand seigneur".' He has his brigades, like the French army, in case 'I choose to remove a Pyramid or the statue of Memnon'.

Finati notes that an attack of ophthalmia prevented Bankes from recording Thebes on the outward journey, 'depriving Mr Bankes totally of sight during that time'. They continued upriver, the local ruler at Derr sent them sheep and goats, and they were offered and ate crisply fried locusts. Travellers on the Nile invariably began in the north and made their way directly upriver, taking advantage of any north winds and only stopping when these were absent. Returning downstream they could rely on the current and so were able to plan their stops, and accordingly most investigation and recording was done then. On Bankes' return journey by boat they were 'landing almost continually, wherever there were tidings or expectation of any vestiges of antiquity.' At Abu Simbel the great temple had not yet been opened, and Bankes later regretted not having attempted to excavate the entrance. At Qasr Ibrim, his keenness not to miss anything led to him being hoisted up the rock with a rope around his body to reach 'some small painted chambers', the New Kingdom shrines. He spent some days at Philae, found a previously unknown inscription 'by the light of his candles at night' and made a first attempt to remove the obelisk, which had to be abandoned 'for want of proper tackle'. An attempt at Thebes to remove the colossal piece known as the head of Memnon from the Ramesseum was also abandoned although he had 'brought with him a proper rope with pullies and machinery, for the purpose'. At Giza, Bankes fainted in the sarcophagus chamber of the Great Pyramid while exploring the interior by torchlight, and had to be carried out into the air where he revived. They arrived back on 16 December 1815, just three months after their departure.

Barely a month later Bankes began a journey to Syria and Palestine and also travelled in Greece and Asia Minor. There is a substantial collection of drawings from these journeys.

According to Salt, Bankes returned to Egypt partly on account of the new discoveries. Abu Simbel was now open, the tomb of Seti I had been discovered at Thebes, and much excavation had taken place at Thebes and at Giza, the site of the great pyramids and the Sphinx. The second Nile journey began in October 1818. This time Bankes travelled with a large party consisting of Henry Salt, Baron Sack (according to Salt, chamberlain to the King of Prussia, an old Prussian nobleman, fond of natural history), Linant, and Ricci. They were accompanied by Finati, in his usual role, and 'two common servants'. They travelled in a flotilla of boats, with separate transports for Bankes, Salt and the baron, and a fourth for 'riding-asses, milch goats, sheep, fowls, and such conveniences'.[8] Belzoni later commented sarcastically on their luxurious mode of travel. Salt became ill in February 1819 while travelling, and left to return to Cairo, accompanied by Linant. 'All but the baron, who was chiefly engaged in killing frogs, snakes, beetles, and such like game, were enthusiastically fond of the arts, and really vied with each other who should produce the best sketches; being generally occupied hard at it, ... from nine o'clock in the morning till dark' was Salt's light-hearted version of the trip. [9] In a more serious vein he also comments in a letter to William Hamilton of 4 May 1819[10] that they think they can now identify the name Ptolemy in cartouches and therefore have deduced that Edfu, Esna, Denderah, Philae and Armant are Ptolemaic. 'All the drawings made to illustrate the above observations will be sent home with Mr. Bankes. '

Beechey and Ricci joined them at Thebes where they had been excavating and recording with Belzoni, who was now engaged by Bankes for the removal of the obelisk from Philae. Giovanni D'Athanasi, employed by Salt as an excavator, also joined the party from Thebes onward, according to his own record. At Thebes, Salt and Bankes rummaged through stacks of mummies in search of papyri.

Arriving at Philae, Bankes cleared the ground both inside and outside the ruins, revealing some unknown chambers in the temple. The granite obelisk and the pedestal which Bankes had been unable to remove on his first trip, 'for want of proper tackle', were now to be removed by Belzoni (see chapter 5), an expert in these matters. After much difficult manoeuvring the obelisk was removed to the Nile were it promptly sank. 'Mr Bankes said little but was evidently disgusted by the accident.' It was eventually refloated and began its long journey back to Kingston Lacy.

At Wadi es Sebua, the temple was cleared and the entrance opened. 'Very well preserved' Egyptian paintings were found which, according to Salt, 'had escaped all other travellers' and included 'some of the sacred boats with their colours entire' and the remains of a fresco of St Peter.

When they reached the great temple at Abu Simbel, stumbled on by Burckhardt in March 1813, and opened by Belzoni in August 1817, Bankes decided to excavate one of the colossal figures down to the feet, correctly guessing there might be further Greek graffiti on the statues next to the entrance. They also exposed the fourth colossal head and made drawings of the exterior.

> As for the interior, that, during all the time of our stay, was lighted every day, and almost all day long, with from twenty to fifty small wax candles, fixed upon clusters of palm branches, which were attached to long upright poles, and, spreading like the arms of a chandelier, more than half way to the ceiling, enabled Mr. Bankes, and the other draughtsmen, to copy all the paintings in detail, as they stood, almost naked, upon their ladders.[11]

Bankes notes of the graffiti: 'the inscription relates to the King Psammeticus, and is certainly among the very earliest extant in the Greek language. '[12]

Further extensive excavations were carried out at Wadi Halfa [Buhen]. Bankes had hoped to reach Dongola, and 'even upon penetrating to

Meroë'. Salt and Linant left the party at the beginning of March as they approached the second cataract area. On 9 March 1819 the rest of the party, now including Mr John Hyde, 'an English gentleman not previously known to Mr Bankes travelling with his Greek servant', were stranded 150 miles above the second cataract, when their servants ran off with the camels. Despite Bankes' strenuous efforts to continue the journey, they were unable to get either camels or a boat. They resorted to stealing pack animals as they found them, allocating Hyde, who was ill, the only camel, and beating up the local chief responsible for their robbery when they met him. On their return journey, at Maharraka, Bankes announced his intention of removing a great granite platform of steps to accommodate his obelisk— four blocks of red granite which were later removed by Linant in 1822 and brought to Kingston Lacy in 1829.

It was principally inscriptions and reliefs of a historical nature that excited Bankes. According to Finati, 'nothing that he found seemed to give him more pleasure, or to excite more interest' than the discovery of the Abydos king list which Bankes recognised as a find of major historical importance, a chronological list of pharaohs' names in cartouches. Bankes did not attempt its removal, 'but took a complete copy of all the sculpture upon it'. For Bankes, hieroglyphs are 'little worth the pains' if they are only used for 'hymns and homilies' rather than 'History and Chronology'. The Psalms of David were rumoured to have been found in Egypt: 'I had rather that he had found the annals of Sesostris'. Young, who had initiated an Egyptian Society by 1817 to publish all the existing hieroglyphic inscriptions, encouraged Bankes to publish his copies, 'with a few other select materials as pledges of your future intentions', and he continued to rely on Bankes' copies for his work.

Salt's letter to William Hamilton from Cairo, 1 July 1819, reiterates the importance of the Greek inscriptions in dating the monuments. The level of these inscriptions on the surface of the monuments showed the dates of many of the temples.

Every new discovery, in fact, confirms your first supposition of the value of the Greek and Latin inscriptions, and shows plainly that the greater part of the temples now standing are of late date. We have still the gratification of knowing that this derogates nothing from the great merit of the Egyptian artists, since the most ancient buildings which remain are undoubtedly superior in every point of view. Our inscription at Ipssambul [Abu Simbel], in the reign of Psammeticus, now becomes invaluable, giving us a most exact standard of the more ancient style.[13]

Linant de Bellefond's work, remaining unpublished, was immediately overshadowed by that of Cailliaud, who published his *Voyage à Méroé et au Fleuve blanc* to great acclaim in 1823 in four volumes together with a large and handsome atlas of plates. Linant made his career in Egypt, living in Oriental style, working as an engineer and hydrographer in the service of Muhammad 'Ali and becoming a Pasha. There is a large collection of his work in the Louvre Museum, Paris.

Ricci returned to Egypt in 1828–29 with Champollion and Rosellini's expedition, while Beechey, who remained in touch with Bankes after returning to England with him in 1819, later worked on ancient sites in North Africa. Salt died in 1827, leaving important collections of objects, and a large number of drawings, now mainly lost.

Bankes left Egypt for a stay in Italy in the winter of 1819. Egypt was never his sole passion and even his letters from there to his father at home are full of his other interests: the inscriptions and antiquities of Asia Minor, Syria and Palestine, the paintings he has collected, and matters of common concern at home. After the 1820s it seems that his architectural interests may have overtaken his interest in Egyptology. The second volume of Finati's *Adventures*, described as dictated by Finati is, from the evidence of Bankes' journals, virtually his own record of his travels. In a letter to Byron in 1822[14] he writes of publishing: 'I am always thinking of it, and from a strange mixture of indolence with industry always deferring it. I hate, and always did, method and arrangement, and this is what my materials want.'

In 1981 Kingston Lacy and its contents came into the possession of the National Trust. Thanks to their kind permission the Nubian drawings are now being catalogued and studied and have already produced much previously unknown information.[15] This, one hopes, would have pleased Bankes who wrote that, 'of all the parts of the world which I have visited, Egypt and Nubia are those which interested me, beyond all comparison, the most, and have made the deepest impression upon my mind.'

Notes

1 B. Porter and R. Moss, *Topographical Bibliography of Ancient Egyptian Hieroglyphic Texts, Reliefs, and Paintings*, I–VII (Oxford, 1951).

2 The journal of Mrs Arbuthnot for 1 August 1821, quoted by V. Bankes, *A Dorset Heritage* (London, 1986), p. 160.

3 W. J. Bankes, *Geometrical Elevation of an Obelisk from the Island of Philae* (London, 1821).

4 W. J. Bankes (ed.), *Narrative of the Life and Adventures of Giovanni Finati*, Vol. II (London, 1830), p. 100.

5 Bankes correspondence, Dorset County Record Office, D/BKL: HJ: 1/171.

6 C. Barry, manuscript diary of travels in the Drawings Collection, RIBA, London, quoted in P. Clayton, *The Rediscovery of Ancient Egypt* (London, 1984), p. 45.

7 M. Shinnie (ed.), *Linant de Bellefonds. Journal d'un voyage à Méroé dans les années 1821 et 1822*. Occasional Papers 4, Sudan Antiquities Service

(Khartoum, 1958).

8 Bankes, *Giovanni Finati*, II, p. 301.

9 J. J. Halls, *The Life and Correspondence of Henry Salt, Esq.* II (London, 1830), p. 132.

10 Ibid., p. 114.

11 Bankes, *Giovanni Finati*, II, p. 313.

12 The Greek Graffiti of the Foreign Mercenaries and Egyptian Soldiers of King Psammeticus II (595–589 BC) on his military expedition to Nubia.

13 Halls, *Henry Salt*.

14 Bankes to Byron, quoted in A. Mitchell (ed.), *Kingston Lacy, Dorset* (London: The National Trust, 1994), p. 25.

15 P. Usick, 'Excavating the Bankes Manuscripts and Drawings', Sudan Archaeological Research Society Newsletter 10 (June 1996), pp. 31–6.

7 ∾ Linant de Bellefonds: Travels in Egypt, Sudan and Arabia Petraea (1818–1828)

Marcel Kurz and Pascale Linant de Bellefonds

Among the numerous travellers exploring Egypt at the beginning of the nineteenth century was a young Frenchman, Linant de Bellefonds, who led an unusual life. He was just nineteen when William J. Bankes and the consul Henry Salt called upon his services, but he was already mature and experienced, a fine draughtsman and an acute observer. This brilliant character, whose career in Egypt was incredibly long and fruitful, left a large number of letters and many manuscripts, drawings and plans. In 1952, his descendants decided to donate to the Louvre Museum a series of documents concerning five important journeys made by Linant in Egypt and in Sudan between 1818 and 1828. In addition to his notebooks, this collection includes a portfolio comprising several hundred drawings, plans of various pharaonic monuments and many topographical maps of the Nile valley. The detailed inventory of the writings and drawings will soon be completed.[1]

Louis-Maurice-Adolphe Linant de Bellefonds was born in Lorient, Brittany, on 23 November 1799. His father, a naval officer, provided him with a thorough education, with the accent on mathematics, drawing and painting. At the age of fifteen, the young man became a midshipman cadet and, in 1817, as a naval trainee, he sailed on the royal frigate taking the Count of Forbin and a 'scholar society' to the Near East.[2] One of the expedition's artists died at the beginning of the journey and Linant, whose drawing talents had probably been noticed, was asked to replace him. The expedition arrived in Cairo in December 1817. At the end of his mission, Linant, fascinated by Egypt, decided to stay. The Louvre manuscripts reveal his travels over the following decade, his clever observations on the behaviour of the many foreigners with contradictory interests, and his sensitive approach to the locals. During his travels, Linant developed a growing interest in hydrographic matters and, in 1831, after a year spent in a Sinai hermitage to perfect his technical knowledge, he stopped travelling to work as an engineer for the viceroy, Muhammad 'Ali.

He started in the Sa'id, on the advice of an old acquaintance, Ibrahim Pasha. The Governor of Upper Egypt asked him to improve the irrigation system, and the skills he gained led him, over the years, to be associated with all major projects. Closest to his heart was the Suez canal, in which he played a significant role; he had been travelling all over the isthmus since 1821, and he was the first to draft a direct link between the two seas.

Linant rounded off his career as Minister for Public Works and as a member of the viceroy's private council. He received the title of Pasha in 1873. By the time he retired from affairs of state, he had already published a travel book on the Etbaye[3] and his *Mémoires sur les principaux travaux d'utilité publique exécutés en Égypte* ...[4] He died in Cairo on 9 July 1883, leaving a huge quantity of notes, including the notebooks documenting his early travels.

Journey through Lower Nubia (1818–1819)

The first series of documents relates to the journey through Lower Nubia from Aswan to the second cataract, between 12 December 1818 and 13 March 1819.[5]

When Linant wrote the first page of this notebook, he had been in Egypt for exactly one year. After contributing to the panoramas of Alexandria and Cairo, he left the entourage of the Count of Forbin who introduced him to Muhammad 'Ali. Six months of activities for the viceroy put him in touch with the many Europeans working in the country. One of them, William J. Bankes, who nurtured the ambitious project of publishing all the Egyptian monuments, organised an expedition in Nubia. He recruited Linant as a draughtsman.

The expedition left Luxor on 16 November 1818. Besides Bankes and Linant, the party included H. Salt, H.-W. Beechey, Baron Sack, A. Ricci and G. Belzoni. Linant makes no reference in his notebooks to his companions or their respective tasks, to the material conditions of the trip or its progress. Of all his diaries, it is the least colourful. It does, however, contain a long list of all the sites where he stopped. The architecture of each of these is described thoroughly, with observations on archaeological remains. When Linant describes a temple, he wonders about the possible existence of a town, of quarries, of a necropolis. He observes the area carefully, makes a few evaluations, while remaining aware of the limits of his knowledge.

Oddly enough, the descriptions and observations never refer to the drawings. And yet, Linant did draw, and for this journey, we have at our disposal a generous portfolio. A first series of eight drawings, compiled between 24 November and 11 December 1818, relates to Aswan and Philae. One drawing bears the mention: 'Vue d'un temple dans l'île d'Eléphantine brisé en 1821, disparu aujourd'hui', with a date: 'Le 30 novembre'. Of all the archives, this is the only drawing bearing a date and, as we can see, the caption was added later. About sixty other drawings illustrate the various sites, including Abu Simbel. These drawings were meticulously executed in pencil and show various stages of completion, down to rough sketches. Occasionally, Linant added a few shadows, or touches of watercolour to give a better feel.

Another document, a sketchbook containing about twenty plans and sections of monuments, also relates to this journey. It is the work of an architect, sometimes in ink, often highlighted in colour, with detailed explanatory notes. Finally, there is a topographical map of the Nile valley, executed over eight sheets.

The expedition stayed in Abu Simbel from 25 January to 18 February 1818, before making its way to the second cataract. There, its members split up: while Salt and Linant returned to Aswan in the shortest time, Bankes and the rest of the party, then joined by J. Hyde, carried on up the Nile valley. They did not go any further than Amarra.

Journey to the Siwa Oasis (2 March–10 April 1820)

Early in 1820, the Egyptian viceroy decided to send a military expedition to the west, in order to subject the Siwa oasis to his authority. This oasis enjoyed many commercial links with Cairo but, protected as it was by the vastness of the desert, it had retained an independence that its inhabitants defended jealously. The conquest was to be made by Hasan Bey.

B. Drovetti, who had lost his post of consul-general in 1814, had long been planning to search the oasis for the famous ruins of the temple of Zeus-Ammon. Making the most of his relationship with Muhammad 'Ali, he requested to be allowed to accompany the military campaign, and to take A. Ricci and D. Frediani with him. W. J. Bankes, for his part, asked the Pasha to include Linant in the Hasan Bey expedition. Authorisation was granted and Drovetti accepted, under one condition: Linant was to give him his notes and drawings, which Drovetti promised not to publish.

On 2 March, our travellers left the Hasan Bey camp, then stricken by the plague. They started by following the 'pilgrims' route'. Again, Linant does not bother to mention his companions or to describe the crew, concentrating on observing and taking notes.

The Louvre archives contain two notebooks concerning this expedition. However, while the other logbooks are scrupulously tidy, these two documents are in some disorder: the first is a set of notes on a variety of subjects, from basic references to whole articles.[6] None is dated. Certain pages are written one way, others in reverse. Some are in an ornate handwriting, without a single crossing-out, while others are full of alterations and deletions; the second, is a collection of well-written texts, again undated,[7] but obviously prepared for inclusion in a book.

Once merged and put in order, the two documents make for very pleasant reading. Apart from Linant's discretion over his fellow travellers, this is really a travel story. The journey is described at length. Then there is the meeting with the army, details of the battles and negotiations. After that, Linant depicts the oasis and its lifestyle. Monuments are described fully, with the greatest accuracy. All analyses are soundly argued. Linant explains, for example, the sorry state of the ruins of the Umm Beydah temple, at the foot of the Aghourmi rock: 'un vieux et respectable sheikh m'a dit qu'il y avait trente ans ce temple était plus grand de moitié et que tout était tombé par un tremblement de terre ... ' He also tells us of a temple called Deir Roum and of the trip to the lake of Arashyeh, where, according to Arab tradition, was situated the oracle of Ammon: 'les gens disaient ... qu'ils se feraient tous massacrer avant de conduire un Européen dans ce lieu ... nous fûmes étonnés de ne pas avoir trouvé aucune ruine de monument, pas même celle d'un village, ni une petite excavation dans la montagne ...' The journey back followed another route, taking the travellers to the Wadi Natrun. After praising Drovetti and Ricci and discreetly making fun of Frediani, Linant concludes: 'le point qui m'a paru le plus essentiel dans ce voyage a été de prouver positivement que le monument d'Omm Beydah est le temple de Jupiter-Ammon ... et pour moi, je n'ai plus aucun doute ...'

We must add that these stories, with their pleasant and lively style, contain a few tasty anecdotes and that, crucially, the author never forgot his role as a draughtsman. The Louvre keeps about fifteen drawings documenting this journey.[8] These line drawings are all executed in pencil and have become a little faint, but they retain all their elegance. In 1823, in Paris, E. F. Jomard published a book called *Voyage à l'Oasis de Syouah*. He had received either the originals or copies of Linant's drawings from Drovetti, who said nothing of his commitment not to publish them. Jomard had them all printed to illustrate his story.

Fourteen months went by before the next journey, the logbook of which is at the Louvre. We know that, in the meantime, Linant continued to criss-cross Egypt. From 1 September to 7 November 1820, he was joined by Ricci to explore the Sinai peninsula.[9] Then he went to al-Fayyum. He used his observations on the irrigation network to prepare a map published later, when the traveller gave way to the engineer.[10]

First Journey to Sudan (June 1821–July 1822)

Many travellers drew Muhammad 'Ali's attention to Sudan, a divided country ruled by four kings who shared about fifteen anarchic sovereignties.

This country was said to be rich in gold, in ivory and especially in men—slaves who could be recruited for the army. As a bonus, the viceroy would have the opportunity to get rid of the last Mamluks still ensconced around Dongola, and, as he went south, to discover ever more mysterious regions, even, perhaps, the sources of the Nile. By the spring of 1821, the army was progressing along the river. It was led by the Pasha's two sons, Ibrahim and Isma'il, and his son-in-law, and was accompanied by many Europeans—advisers, doctors and adventurers, notably F. Cailliaud.

W. Bankes decided to charge Linant and Ricci with a geographical and archaeological mission, outside the control of the war chiefs. Thus it was a small team of seven people, with no escort, that Linant led beyond Sennar. His courteous attitude was quite different from that of the soldiers, and his archaeological observations are complemented by a wealth of information gleaned not only from local people, but also from the conquerors' administrators, since he remained on friendly terms with both Ibrahim Pasha and Isma'il Pasha.

The Louvre manuscript appears to be the notebook leading to the document kept at Kingston Lacy. A large part of the latter concerns the journey from the second cataract to Sennar and back, between 27 August 1821 and 14 June 1822. This section was published in 1958 in Khartoum by Margaret Shinnie under the title *Journal d'un voyage à Méroé dans les années 1821 et 1822*. In her introduction, Mrs Shinnie notes: 'The book does not give the appearance of having been carried actually on the journey and was clearly copied out at a later date. The writing appears to be in Linant's hand.' A comparison with the Louvre notebooks reveals some discrepancies, which do not fundamentally alter the facts but give a different emphasis to the writing. Linant appears to have modified certain passages, deleted a few sentences, and left out a number of stories.

Two other sections of the journey have also been published, this time based on the Louvre document: the journey from Cairo to the second cataract, from 15 June to 30 August 1821, and the trip back to Cairo, from 11 June to 24 July 1822.[11]

In addition to the published documents, there is a series of about twenty substantial texts written later by Linant, then added to his travel diary.[12] These consist of geographical or historical observations: we find, for instance, the fabulous tale of the two battles between the invaders and the warriors of the Chaiquieh [Shayqiyya] tribes. These were the first and virtually the only people to oppose the Pasha's troops, later becoming his most faithful allies. Another long report tells of the plot leading to the murder of Isma'il Pasha in Shendi in November 1822, and of the following repression. This story is a model of economy and objectivity.

Then come a number of topographical charts of the Nile valley.[13] These contain a collection of toponyms giving a good idea of the population spread and of resources. When checking these charts four years later, during his second great journey, Linant noticed the depopulation and the desertification of the country, exhausted by the harshness of the conquerors.

Our traveller also added regularly to his portfolio with drawings of archaeological sites and relevant descriptive notes. The Louvre has around eighty good sketches concerning Semneh, Amara, Soleb, Sedeinga, Sessebi, Jabal Barkal, Tombos, Merowe, Mousaouwarat, Naga ...[14] Like all the others, these drawings are in pencil and show various degrees of completion. Finally, there are a number of landscapes and portraits, a few of which are included by Margaret Shinnie in her book.[15]

The last note of this trip is dated 24 July 1822; the traveller's pen only resumes on 12 March 1826. In the meantime, already fascinated by the idea of a maritime link between the Mediterranean and the Red Sea, Linant had set about studying the region in the greatest detail. In 1822 he made a first reconnaissance of the isthmus, and after returning from a trip to Europe in 1823, spent six months prospecting the Oriental desert, from the coast to the Saint Paul and Saint Anthony monasteries. It is doubtful whether he was still working for Salt and Bankes at that time. And yet it is in London that we find him, in 1825, together with his family. The Committee of the African Association accepted his offer to undertake a journey in North East Africa and, having signed an agreement with the Association on 24 May, he sailed from Liverpool in August.

The copy of the contract in the Louvre archives bears the number 4.[16] This eighteen-page bilingual document includes a series of instructions. The first and most important mission entrusted to Linant by the Association was to follow the course of the White Nile from its junction with the Blue Nile to its sources. The contract was signed by W. Bankes, Clive Hamilton and William Martin Leake, Secretary.

Second Journey to Sudan (March 1826–September 1827)

The relevant Louvre manuscript consists of three notebooks. The first two describe the author's peregrinations from the start to 31 March 1827,[17] the last from 5 May to 7 September 1827.[18] One notebook is obviously missing—the one relating to the White Nile expedition, the main objective of the journey.

Linant left Cairo on 12 March 1826. He reached Philae on 19 April and only crossed the second cataract on 13 July, when the flood subsided. He passed Dongola on 28 August, left Shendi on 21 November and reached Khartoum on 26 November. He used these eight months' sailing to gather a wealth of observations on a country he had already studied four years earlier, and which had been badly affected by the Egyptian occupation. In the meantime, Linant had acquired both experience and confidence: his diary is written in a lively and accessible style. Slowed by the flood, he wrote meticulously.

From Khartoum, the first expedition envisaged was a reconnaissance between the Nile and the Atbara, via Rera and Goz Regeb. On 16 December 1826, heading a party of 22, Linant left the point where the Rahad meets the Blue Nile. They advanced quickly, because this unsubdued region was also prey to plunderers. The information he had about the presence of antique remains proved inaccurate, and Linant confined himself to geographical observations. The journey finished in Shendi, where the traveller boarded his boat again. But his men were sick and he was himself laid low by fever from 8 January to 9 March. In addition, those in high places advised against a hazardous journey on the White Nile, and Salt informed him that the Pasha was officially concerned about the matter.

The notes written in March are laconic. The traveller was in Khartoum. The last message of this notebook was written on 31 March: 'je travaillai ...' And yet, he was about to set off on an expedition on the White Nile. The Louvre archives do not contain any document on this journey, which was nevertheless the object of a report.[19] We also know that, having met hostility from the Shilluk, Linant did not go beyond a latitude of 11 degrees north, and was forced to return to Khartoum.

The third notebook, entitled 'Troisième partie, suite du Journal', starts on 5 May: Linant left Khartoum and sailed on the Blue Nile. He went to Messalimie to meet a big trader of his acquaintance, named Chamboul, in the hope that he might accompany him on Shilluk territory. Unfortunately, Chamboul was called by the governor and so was unable to accept. Then Linant tried his luck with the *melk* Badi in Sennar ... in vain. The rains arrived and on 7 June he was back in Khartoum.

As Chamboul had given positive news about the Shilluk, Linant was prepared to wait for the end of the rainy season. He went to Shendi where he was involved in a major investigation by the Cairo administration, which he reported. But he preferred to return to the ruins of Mousaouwarat, and to see Meroë again. This was in mid-July:

> pour moi, je ne savais trop que faire, j'étais obligé de rester trois mois ici, à cause de l'hiver. Ensuite, j'avais besoin de plusieurs choses au Caire, mais comme je n'avais plus personne de confiance, mes domestiques étant morts, je ne savais trop qui mander. Enfin, en réfléchissant bien, je pensais qu'à l'avenir ma barque me devenait presque inutile ... Je pouvais aller au Caire en 45 jours, y rester 15 jours, revenir à Assouan en 15 autres. Là, j'envoyais mes dromadaires m'attendre, et d'Assouan à Berber, 20 jours ... Je me décidai donc à faire ainsi.

He left on 19 July. After Aswan, his diary is no more than a rough draft.

He arrived in Cairo on 27 September 1827. It is unlikely that he left again for Khartoum as he had planned, since we find him on 23 February 1828 *en route* for Petra, accompanied by Léon de Laborde. This is the fifth and last journey for which the Louvre has a notebook.

Journey through Arabia Petraea (February–April 1828)

Laborde and Linant had met in Cairo shortly before. After an archaeological mission in the Near East, Laborde was looking for someone to accompany him across the Sinai as far as Petra, which had been rediscovered and identified by Burckhardt in 1812. His meeting with Linant, who was more experienced and better acquainted with the country, was decisive for the organisation and progress of the journey.

Until then, the few occidental travellers to reach Petra had arrived from the north. To take advantage of the surprise effect upon the local people, the two Frenchmen opted for a new route via the south, across the Sinai valleys. Leaving Cairo on 23 February 1828, they reached Aqaba on 11 March, having taken time to draw several sites in the Sinai, particularly Sarbout el-Khadem. In Aqaba, they had to wait for emissaries from the Alaouis, a powerful Bedouin tribe which was to protect them on the road to Petra. They used these twelve days or so to explore the Aqaba region, especially the Island of Graie, known today as Jazirat Firaoun. Their caravan set off on 24 March and reached Petra on 27 March, via the Wadi 'Araba. They set to work immediately, devoting the next six days exclusively to drawing most of the monuments. Driven away by a plague epidemic, they left Petra on 3 April and got back to the Aqaba fortress on 10 April. They left again on 16 April and parted four days later. Before returning to Suez, Laborde wanted to stay a little longer in the Sinai to visit Saint Catherine's monastery, Wadi Mokatteb and the ancient mines of Maghara. Linant had to return to Cairo without delay: he took only three days to reach Suez and one and a half days to reach Cairo, where he arrived on 24 April.

As soon as they had met, Laborde and Linant had agreed to publish their journey separately, one year after their return. But Linant, by then completely immersed in his responsibilities as an engineer, never managed to do so. All we have are the Louvre documents: his logbook[20] and some twenty magnificent drawings.[21]

So in 1830, in Paris, Laborde was the only one to publish a glossy book entitled *Voyage de l'Arabie Pétrée par Léon de Laborde and Linant*, illustrated with 69 drawings, fourteen of which are by Linant. This book was re-edited in 1994, this time with ample excerpts from the unpublished Linant notebook.[22] The two texts complement and enrich each other, and present the journey in a dual light. Out of the 39 drawings reproduced from the original edition, eleven are by Linant. These are almost photographic in their accuracy a feature which can be appreciated even more on the Louvre originals.

As the transcription of Linant de Bellefond's manuscripts has only just been completed, we can only hope that our summary is accurate and that we have done justice to this courageous traveller: an attentive observer, discreet and modest, he depicts, with sensitivity and without complacency, the country he came to love and was about to serve. His observations of ancient remains are never isolated from those of contemporary people, whom he describes with warmth and often with amusement. He was also well liked by his fellow travellers, many of whom spoke of him in glowing terms.

Notes

1   Manuscripts and drawings are now kept in the Bibliothèque des Musées de France et du Musée du Louvre (Ms. 264–70).

2   Comte de Forbin, *Voyage dans le Levant* (1819).

3   Linant de Bellefonds Bey, *L'Etbaye. Pays habité par les Arabes Bicharieh. Géographie, Ethnologie, Mines d'or* (1868).

4   Linant de Bellefonds Bey, *Mémoires sur les principaux travaux d'utilité publique exécutés en Égypte depuis la plus haute antiquité jusqu'à nos jours* (1872–1873).

5   Ms. 267–1, 267–2, 267–3, 265, 268.

6   Ms. 264–4.

7   Ms. 267–5.

8   Ms. 268.

9   A. Sammarco (ed.), *Alessandro Ricci e il suo giornale dei viaggi* (Cairo: Soc. Royale Géogr., 1933), 2 vols, II.

10 Linant de Bellefonds, *Principaux travaux*, pp. 492–3.

11 These texts can be found in the *Bulletin de la Société française d'Égyptologie* 37–8 (Dec 1963), pp. 39–64; 41 (Nov 1964), pp. 23–32, with an introduction by J. Vercoutter.

12 Ms. 264–5 and 264–6.

13 Ms. 264–7.

14 Ms. 268 and 269.

15 Some others have been published by J. Mazuel, *L'Œuvre géographique de Linant de Bellefonds* (1937), pl. III–VI.

16 Ms. 267–7.

17 Ms. 264–8 and 264–9.

18 Ms. 267–8.

19 Written by Linant, this report was summarised in English. See the *Journal of the Royal Geographical Society of London* 2 (1832), pp. 171–89.

20 Ms. 266.

21 Ms. 268.

22 *Pétra retrouvée. Voyage de l'Arabie Pétrée, 1828. Léon de Laborde et Linant de Bellefonds* (1994), preface and notes by Ch. Augé and P. Linant de Bellefonds.

8 ᷎ A Prussian Expedition to Egypt in 1820: Heinrich von Minutoli

Joachim S. Karig

'Prussians in Egypt?' The phrase does not usually evoke immediate images for most people, and when it does, the first name that comes to mind is not necessarily Heinrich von Minutoli. More likely are Heinrich Brugsch,[1] who went to Egypt with Prince Friedrich Karl in the winter of 1882–83, or Richard Lepsius who from 1841 to 1845 led his expedition through Egypt and the Sudan.[2] Art connoisseurs would probably first think of Prince Pückler and Mahbuba, his dark-eyed beauty, whom he later brought to Brandenburg's chilly climes.

All of these pioneers in Egyptology, however, derived inspiration, either consciously or unconsciously, from a single source: Heinrich von Minutoli, who had pointed the way and often smoothed it for his successors to follow—a 'fatherly friend' as Pückler called him. It was Minutoli whose collection of Ægyptiaca King Friedrich Wilhelm III bought for the Prussian state, thus forming the basis and providing the impulse for the founding of Berlin's Egyptian Museum. It was Minutoli who as pedagogue to the princes exerted a strong influence on Friedrich Wilhelm IV, awakening and instilling in him a lasting interest in ancient Egypt and its culture, creating thereby an ear sympathetic to Minutoli's own wishes.

Minutoli was born in Ghent on 12 May 1772. Although of southern Italian parentage, he was Protestant by faith. By the age of fourteen he had entered the Prussian military service, eight years later suffering wounds which forced him to abandon active service. In 1794 he became a trainer of the aristocratic cadet corps, a position which apparently left him enough time to pursue the history and archaeology of both his own country and classical antiquity. It was probably Minutoli's expertise, along with his generally well-rounded education, that induced Friedrich Wilhelm III to appoint him as pedagogue to Prince Carl. However, at the prince's coming of age his teacher's responsibilities and duties came to an end. At this point forty-eight-year old Minutoli decided to fulfil his fondest dream and travel to the Orient. The king, caught up in Minutoli's euphoric plans, did everything in his power to support his undertaking. However, the king's enthusiasm was not entirely altruistic. He gave Minutoli explicit instructions to investigate the economically ever more interesting Near East—as well as seeking out objects suitable for enriching Prussian's growing collection of antiquities.

The Egypt expedition was primarily intended as a private trip. To everyone's utter surprise, on the way to the East in Trieste, Minutoli acquired a young bride[3] who would accompany him on this not entirely safe or comfortable journey. In the meantime in Berlin things had taken an unexpected turn, and a properly organised scientific expedition to Egypt was being planned. The Academy of Sciences appointed two scientists, Hemprich and Ehrenberg, to lead the expedition, putting all the means necessary for assuring its success at their disposal. King Friedrich Wilhelm III furthermore commissioned a member of the Royal School of Architecture, a certain Liman, to join the expedition as its architectural expert. From Bonn a philologist, August Scholz, volunteered his services. These were the stalwart and intrepid individuals who made up the first Prussian expedition. If the undertaking seems moderately staffed, it should be remembered that it was only at this time that Prussia was once again slowly beginning to recognise its individual national identity.

The expedition commenced with due fanfare and proper enthusiasm. However, from the very outset it seemed to be under an evil star. It soon became bogged down in difficulties of such massive proportions that the original plans eventually proved unfeasible. Untoward circumstances in Egypt—a general mistrust and misunderstanding on the part of the officials, suspicions of espionage, and mercenary and conniving guides (not to mention the plague)—predestined the expedition to an untimely finish and it all but ended in complete failure.

Minutoli stayed about a month in Alexandria, taking the opportunity to make important social contacts—especially with Khedive Muhammad 'Ali and his court but also with European diplomats such as Drovetti[4] and Salt.[5] He also bought his first antiquities, a collection of vases. On 5 October 1820 Minutoli's expedition set out with a caravan of forty-one camels and four horses. The route originally planned would have taken them westward along the coast of the Mediterranean, exploring the sites of ancient cities along the way until it reached Cyrenaica. But luck was not with them on their venture. Despite the friendly reception and support of the Viceroy Muhammad 'Ali, the caravan's progress was slow and difficult. Although sites were investigated and surveyed, the explorers had their eyes on the more alluring goal of Cyrenaica. However, this proved impossible, as the necessary entries and permits had apparently not been entered into their travel documents. After endless delays, Minutoli decided to abandon the expedition.

In early November Minutoli and a few companions rode to Siwa oasis, a locale particularly renowned if only because of Alexander the Great's expedition there 2,100 years before. His attempts at undertaking archaeological activities were hampered by unfriendly and suspicious local people, however, and Minutoli was able to conduct only superficial and incomplete investigations.

After his return to Cairo on 18 December, Minutoli rented a ship to take him and his wife, together with a certain Ricci,[6] an Italian doctor and artist, to Upper Egypt. His diaries, published and now available in numerous languages, give vivid descriptions of their journey and the sites visited along the way: Minya, Beni Hasan, Hermopolis, Malawi, Asyut, Gau el Kebir, Akhmim, Girgeh and Abydos.

Minutoli stayed about fourteen days in Luxor and visited the ancient sites on the east and west banks of the Nile. In contrast to today's mass tourist crowds, such a trip in the 1820s was no small or easy undertaking; in fact, it could be extremely dangerous. It is interesting to note Minutoli's candid observations on the damage already wrought at that time by grave robbers, tourists, and so-called 'scholars' whose predations were all taking their toll on Egypt's antique heritage.

From Luxor the little group made their way via Esna, Kom Ombo and Silsile to Aswan where the first Nile cataract prevented any further riverine navigation. Far more of an obstacle, however, were the bellicose actions of the viceroy of Dongola[7] which forced them to abandon their plans of continuing their journey into the Sudan. Thus they decided to turn back and set out on a precipitous homeward journey, arriving back in Cairo at the end of February 1821.

The news had already reached them in Aswan that, in accordance with instructions given before their departure, access to the interior of the so-called Step Pyramid had been granted. Minutoli was the first European to enter this ancient pyramid and view its rooms with their decorations and grave goods, preserving his impressions for posterity. Out of one of the Late Period graves came the large granite coffin which was to form the showpiece of his collection.

Contemporary newspaper reports tell of Minutoli's buying up three large collections in Egypt. In particular it included the collection bought from Drovetti who through his adjutant Lebolo had been able to acquire large and impressive collections of Ægyptiaca. Minutoli's newly acquired collection was packed away into boxes while he was still in Upper Egypt so that he was not even able to inspect it himself before it was despatched to Europe.

Minutoli, like other collectors and Orientalists of his day, was both layman and autodidact. Unfortunately, despite his deluxe publications *Reise zum Tempel des Jupiter Ammon in der libyschen Wüste und nach Oberägypten in den Jahren 1820 und 1821* (Berlin, 1824) and *Nachträge zu meinem Werke, betitelt: Reise zum Tempel des Jupiter Ammon etc.* (Berlin, 1827), the objects he bought along the way received little attention in these works.

Obliged to observe the twenty-seven-day quarantine upon arrival in Trieste on 25 August 1821, Minutoli and his collection later went their separate ways. Minutoli and his wife continued on to Venice and returned to Berlin only in the autumn of the following year. However, before leaving Trieste he divided his collection, sending about twenty crates of papyri, coffins, grave goods, musical instruments, objects of daily life, amulets and miniature figures by land to Berlin. With the help of the local Prussian consul of Brandenburg the main part of the collection, about one hundred crates, was loaded onto a Danish sailing ship named *Gottfried* for transport to Hamburg. Despite its apotropaic name, shortly before reaching Hamburg, at the mouth of the Elbe river, *Gottfried*, its crew and its cargo capsized during a storm and sank to the bottom of the sea.

For many years the Egyptian Museum in Berlin has been actively pursing the recovery of this collection. However, it has so far still proven impossible even to locate the site of the accident or the present location of the wreck.[8] Only the most scanty, summary references to the ship and its cargo can be found in contemporary reports which mention a large granite coffin as well as stone antiquities, stelae and vases, objects of daily life, animal and human mummies, coffin fragments and masks. A particularly unusual set of objects was a group of mummies in Greco–Roman coffins from the so-called grave of the Archon Soter. Of course, it is anyone's guess what the objects' condition might be after spending one hundred and seventy years under water.

Minutoli's stay in Egypt lasted ten months, a large part of which was spent in futile waiting and delays. The trip through the Delta towards the west via the Siwa oasis took only six weeks, and the trip to Upper Egypt two and a half months; but despite this relatively short time span the success of his journey is undisputed.

Three aspects deserve closer attention. First, there are Minutoli's eye-witness observations and descriptions of the country, noting its peoples, climate, economy and industry, including technological development, health measures, and of course, Egypt's military strength. Secondly, there are the archaeological gains: his descriptions of ancient sites and his estimation of their value, along with his recommendations for excavations. There are also his own excavations, especially those conducted on the Step Pyramid at Saqqara. Finally, there are his activities as a collector. The objects which Minutoli collected were bought up by the Prussian King and marked the beginning of a proper Egyptian museum in Berlin. Above all, and of inestimable value, was the influence he exerted on the Prussian royal house, especially Friedrich Wilhelm III and the crown prince, the future king Friedrich Wilhelm IV. It is due to Minutoli that the first chair in Egyptology in Germany was created in Berlin. It was also Minutoli who influenced the king to sponsor and finance Karl Richard Lepsius's extended expedition to Egypt. Finally, it was Minutoli who prepared the way for making Berlin's collection of pharaonic Egyptian art and culture one of the most important ones in the world and a centre of Egyptological research which still today enjoys worldwide renown.

Notes

1   Heinrich and Emile Brugsch also excavated the pyramid complex in south Saqqara.
2   Karl Richard Lepsius (1810–84) was appointed Keeper of the Egyptian collections in the Berlin Museum in 1865. The results of the Prussian expedition to Egypt were published in a twelve-volume work, *Denkmaeler aus Aegypten und Aethiopien* (Leipzig, 1849–59).
3   W. von Minutoli, *Reise der Frau Generalin von Minutoli nach Egypten. Deutsch herausgegeben von Wilhelmine von Gersdorf* (Leipzig, 1841). See Deborah Manley's contribution on his bride in this volume.
4   Bernardino Drovetti (1776–1852).
5   Sir Henry Salt (1780–1827), British consul-general in Alexandria.
6   Dr Alessandro Ricci.
7   Isma'il Kamil Pasha, Muhammad 'Ali's third son, commanded the expeditionary force against a Shayqiyya confederacy in the area from July 1820 until 1821.
8   J. S. Karig und R. Leive, *Auf der Suche nach der »Gottfried« und der Sammlung Minutoli* (Jahrbuch Preußischer Kulturbesitz XXX, Berlin, 1993), pp. 133–53.

9 ∾ The Journeys of Lord Prudhoe and Major Orlando Felix in Egypt, Nubia and the Levant 1826–1829

John Ruffle[1]

Algernon Percy was born in 1792, the second son of the second Duke of Northumberland. His name was a throwback to the nickname of the first recorded Percy of 1066, 'he of the moustaches'. He entered the Royal Navy in 1805 at the age of thirteen, and served with credit in various actions against the French: in 1815 he was made a captain at the age of twenty-three. A year later he was created peer in his own right as Lord Prudhoe, taking the name from a family estate on the border between Durham and Northumberland.

In 1826 Lord Prudhoe set out on his journey in Egypt and the Levant. His reasons for doing so are not recorded but it is consistent with what we know of him that he should wish to visit a part of the world where so many exciting new discoveries were in progress.

The records which he kept of this journey are preserved in the archive in the family seat at Alnwick in Northumberland but are unfortunately not complete. We have only some of his detailed notebooks which begin in 1827 with him already in Egypt. As second son he had no expectations of succeeding to the dukedom and maintained his own household at Stanwick in Yorkshire. His archive there was moved to Alnwick later but some items appear to have already been missing before the move and there seems little hope of recovering them.

What survives is eleven notebooks,[2] five of which are journals of Lord Prudhoe's travels, five more are copies of inscriptions and one contains notes on the history of Egypt and other Mediterranean countries. The journals cover his journey upstream by boat with Major Felix, beginning with their departure from Cairo on 27 February 1827 and ending at the first cataract on 4 April, and part of the return journey from the second cataract to Philae from 16 to 28 April 1827. Another journal chronicles his second journey from Cairo on 11 December 1828 to Sennar on 1 April 1829.

There are other journals which relate to his visit to Sinai in 1827, his travels in the Greek islands from 9 August 1827 to 20 April 1828 and yet another journal, describing a journey from Cairo, via Suez, Petra, Hebron and Jerusalem to Sidon. It starts on Tuesday 20 March, the date on which they left Cairo. The year could have been 1827 but the journals show they were in Luxor on that date, so this journey was evidently made several years later, probably in 1838. The exact dates of the various journeys have sometimes been confused because Lord Prudhoe did not usually mention the year and some of the documents have been incorrectly numbered and dated by a later hand (probably that of the seventh Duke). Fortunately there are instances when the day of the week is recorded against the date and this allows a check.

Lord Prudhoe was accompanied on his travels by Major Orlando Felix, who was formerly an officer in the Rifle Brigade but unattached after his promotion on 31 October 1826. It is possible to cross refer from Lord Prudhoe's notes to letters from Major Felix to his C/O Lt. Col. Brown in Malta. Eleven of Felix's letters are preserved in the National Library of Scotland but unfortunately they suffer from the same problems as Lord Prudhoe's journals in that only two have a full dateline (date, month, and year) and one more specifies the day of the week which means that the full date can be deduced. Eight of them carry two year dates, both apparently added some time later, one in what appears to be Felix's own hand (apparently inaccurately) and a second in a much later hand. From Felix's letters it appears that he had already made one journey up the Nile as far as the second cataract before December 1826.[3] If this is correct, he must have made three long Nile journeys in as many years, as well as the Aegean tour.

On the journeys with Lord Prudhoe, Felix made a number of sketches, now preserved in two albums in Alnwick. Other sketches and papers, which I have still to study, are in the British Museum.[4] Some of his drawings, for example of Luxor temple with both its obelisks and of Armant before it was reduced to building material, record views and monuments now lost. Thirty-nine of the fifty-four drawings in the Alnwick albums are precisely dated, apparently by the artist, and may therefore be used in conjunction with the notebooks and letters to reconstruct a dated itinerary for Prudhoe and Felix.[5]

There are also notebooks at Alnwick in which Lord Prudhoe copied inscriptions. Many of these copies have a note of the location and a few also record a date. Although they may not help with pinning down precise dates of his itineraries, the copies show a degree of care and observation which does him credit. Indeed, it is possible to compare some with the copies made by Peet in   nearly 100 years later.[6]

Lord Prudhoe had evidently prepared for his journey by learning what was then available of Jean-François Champollion's decipherment of the hieroglyphic script, even if he had some reservations about Champollion's conclusions. Felix claimed in a letter of December 1826 that he had 'learned Arabic and become a [?]clipper at hieroglyphics'. They evidently made efforts to keep abreast of Egyptological developments and on their first journey they 'met Mr [later Sir] Gardner Wilkinson at Assiut going to Aswan and got from him the Rosetta Stone inscription'.[7]

Their nine months in Cairo in 1828, before their second journey were spent, according to Major Felix,[8] 'bewildering myself with hieroglyphics and plunging into huge Latin folios' while 'Prudhoe is hard at Arabic'. Burton says in a letter of 28 July 1828[9] that 'Lord Prudhoe, Major Felix and Mr Wilkinson remain here [in Cairo] and strenuously second my labours.' Felix speaks of his 'long list of the Egyptian Pharaohs who are much more certain than the Kings of England'[10] and of how 'I differ very much from Monsr Champollion in the chronology of the kings and had a great triumph the other day, in finding that he is coming round·to my list.'[11] Felix also made some sketches in Cairo and Giza during this period.

They were evidently confident enough in their subject to discourse with the experts. Champollion wrote to his brother on 27 September 1828 that he had met Prudhoe and Felix, along with James Burton, and described them as 'Hieroglyphiseurs decidées et qui me comblent d'attentions'.[12] Later, on their second journey on Tuesday 20 January 1829, Lord Prudhoe recorded that:

> In the evening 6 boats with French and Tuscan flags came down the river, & remained with us fast to the shore at Korosko—it was Monsr Champollion & Signore Rosaline returning from their labors. Shewed us many drawings & Mons. C. said he had the names of the temples & people in Nubia—those he shewed for Derr & said for Ebsambul [Abu Simbel], we could neither make out or find on the temples. He has certainly much more knowledge on the subject of hieroglyphics than any man living, but I fear he is not entirely to be trusted. I require conviction where proofs to be obtained are [sic] that letters spell words— after five hours palaver he left us dead tired, & glad both of dinner & repose.[13]

However, Lord Prudhoe was evidently able to identify most of the cartouches which he found and made rather summary notes on the monuments. Here, for example, is his comment on his first visit to Luxor, after recording a morning at Karnak:

> From Carnac we walked two miles over a badly cultivated plain under a hot sun to Luxor. Here stand two still larger Obelisks & two Colossal Statues of granite beautifully carved, they bear the name of Sesostris[14] before & after his conquests—they are at the Portal of an immense temple of simple proportions— This temple is more ancient than the obelisks & contains [there follow the cartouches of Seti (Merenptah) II]; a name which with the present imperfect knowledge of hiergs is unknown.
>
> The Sculpture on the walls are [sic] tolerably well executed; the subjects are Battles, & offerings to the Gods. We remained in the boat for a couple of hours during the heat of the day, & then landed on the Western side intending to visit

Medinet Aboo 2 miles from Luxor but being tempted by the two Colossal Statues seated in the plain we lounged about them. They are of soft stone; one is like the other statues formed of a single block but the other is built, & this is Memnon. They stand on a pedestal 6 feet from the ground &, seated, are 50 feet high—The truth of Memnon is attested by Greek & Latin inscriptions of those who had heard his sounds. I copied the two following ... [15]

To visit Karnak, Luxor and the colossi on foot in one day would not leave much time for detailed observation, but, to be fair, this was on the upstream journey which was usually made as quickly as possible. They appear to have spent more time at those sites which were less frequently visited, for example in Sinai and Nubia, where they copied many more inscriptions and occasionally made more detailed verbal descriptions. A note in the journal of their second journey[16] speaks of an acquaintance whom they met 'last year, while living in the propylon of Karnak'. This would evidently have been on their return journey and it was then, presumably, that they made detailed copies and notes of the Chamber of Kings, which are referred to in a letter from James Burton to Henry Salt of 2 July 1827.[17]

On one of their visits to Thebes they had time to make a copy of the paintings in the tomb of Satea/Meryma'et [Merymaat]. Their record was valuable because this tomb (No. C4), in Shaykh 'Abd al-Qurna and vaguely located 'behind Yanni's house', was subsequently lost until rediscovered by a donkey in the early 1960s.[18]

Lord Prudhoe did not give long lyrical descriptions of the monuments and reveals little of his own feelings about them. His most revealing comment relates to Philae of which he says, on his second journey: 'This is certainly the prettiest if not the only pretty spot in Egypt. I look forward to pass a pleasant sejour here, if we are prevented in our journey to India.'[19]

Apart from describing the monuments, Lord Prudhoe makes only a few general comments which we might describe as Egyptological. On his first journey at Asyut he found a number of animal bones.

These are plundered from their burying place, & if the plunderers stopped here we might satisfy our curiosity without shocking our feelings, but the same plunder is carried on with human graves. Bodies are pulled out by dozens in their winding sheets, and not left to moulder, for in this climate they do not easily decompose, but whole bodies lie about the graves which held them.[20]

On the second journey he remarked how monuments had deteriorated.

The Temple of Commodus at Contra Latopolis which was in good preservation last year, is utterly destroyed ... The temple of Tothmes 2nd, a pretty one last year, is also entirely destroyed and the stones taken.[21]

The journals also record calls on local worthies, for example the kashif at Melawi, who received him with 'gentlemanly good-breeding' discoursed on Egyptian and Ottoman politics, and was magnificent in his presents including four Dongola horses. Lord Prudhoe was 'struck with his want of knowledge about geography, since he could not place Malta or Marseilles accurately, still less Dover and Calais'.[22] One wonders if the natives of Dover could correctly place Melawi!

As befits a country gentleman there are descriptions of the wildfowl and birds, including pelicans which '... have a remarkable character when sailing in the air, and are graceful in the water: they are indeed more to be admired at large, than on the table for it is coarse eating,'[23] and crocodiles: 'the unsteadiness of our boat would not give us much chance of hitting them.'[24] He also describes the state of various crops, the planting of sugar cane and so on.

Lord Prudhoe's references to other European travellers and residents in Egypt are not always favourable: 'we walked over to Philae to avoid dining with two French (or perhaps Greek) doctors who were on their way to Sennar'.[25]

There may have been other travelling companions who are not recorded in the existing volumes. On the first journey, for example, Lord Prudhoe records that they enjoyed a rest from 24 to 30 March 1827 at Elephantine 'principally for Francis' recovery but also much to our own satisfaction'. Francis was also ill earlier on the journey. It has been suggested that 'Francis' was Francis Arundale, who is frequently recorded in other letters and journals as being ill.[26] He gives a list of his companions on the second journey.[27]

On their second Nile journey they travelled on dromedaries, sending on their heavy supplies by a boat which kept pace with them. The convenience of this arrangement became evident when, having called on Dr Macara at Asyut, they were able to ride to the boat and send him two cases of claret before the boat and they parted company again.

At some point on these travels Lord Prudhoe acquired and removed the 'Prudhoe Lions'[28] which he gave to the British Museum in 1835. On his second journey upstream he records in detail his visit to Jabal Barkal and makes a brief mention of 'two beautiful lions'. There are drawings of them in the Felix album but there is no suggestion at that stage of their removal.[29]

After their Egyptian travels Lord Prudhoe and Major Felix appear to have gone their separate ways, although Felix did occasionally visit Alnwick. Felix published the lithographs he was working on as *Notes on Hieroglyphs* in 1830. He eventually reached India in 1841 as Deputy Quartermaster General, and died in Geneva on 5 April 1860.

Lord Prudhoe continued his interest in scientific matters. He went, for instance, with Sir John Herschel to the Cape of Good Hope in 1834 to observe the southern constellations. In 1847 his elder brother, the third Duke, died and Lord Prudhoe succeeded as Duke of Northumberland. He was then one of the greatest landowners in England and began an immense programme of work on the estates and the Castle itself, constructing and renovating cottages, bridges, roads, drainage and so on. He made various endowments to sailors' and fishermen's charities, supported the Royal National Lifeboat Institution—as one might expect, given that Grace Darling had carried out her famous rescue in his 'parish'—and was briefly involved in government as First Lord of the Admiralty in 1852.

In addition to all this activity the Duke found time to maintain his interest in Egypt by building up a collection of antiquities in the Castle. He had already bought extensively at sales in the 1830s, especially at the sale of the third collection made by Henry Salt in 1835.[30] He was undoubtedly encouraged and advised by Sir Gardner Wilkinson who made several visits to Alnwick and whose *Manners and Customs of the Ancient Egyptians*[31] was dedicated to the Third Duke, Hugh, Prudhoe's elder brother. The collection contains a number of fine and important items as well as many small but interesting pieces which reveal that the Duke had a discerning eye and discriminating taste. It includes an obelisk of red granite, 2.2 metres high, dedicated to Khnum by Amenhotep II (1427–1400 BC), which was presented to Lord Prudhoe by Muhammad 'Ali in 1838.[32] His Egyptian collection was published by Samuel Birch in 1880[33] and was eventually purchased by the University of Durham in 1950, where it became the founding collection of the Oriental Museum.

In Cairo in 1826, Lord Prudhoe met the Arabist Edward W. Lane and became enthusiastic about his proposed Arabic Lexicon.[34] For the next twenty-three years he paid for the cost of its preparation and subsequent printing (from 1863 onwards) with what Lane records in the Preface was 'a kindness and delicacy not to be surpassed'. The Lexicon is dedicated to the Duke as 'the originator of this work, its constant and major supporter'. A manuscript copies of this work, all 42 volumes, is preserved at Alnwick.

His learning was recognised by election as Fellow of the Royal Society, the Royal Astronomical Society, the Geological Society, and the Society of Antiquaries. He was made a Trustee of the British Museum, and died of gout on 12 February 1865.

Appendix: Lord Prudhoe's Notebooks.

These eleven notebooks are kept in 'the shoebox' in the archives at Alnwick Castle. They are listed here according to the present numbering in the Alnwick archive.

PN I'1828 Lord Prudhoe' (marked in ink, ?by Lord Prudhoe); '1828 Journal I to Sennar' (on a small paper label). This journal covers the second journey from Cairo, 11 December 1828 to Sennar, 1 April 1829.

PN II'Cooloo' (marked in ink, ?by Lord Prudhoe); '1828 Journal II return 2nd Cataract to Philae' (marked in pencil). This journal covers part of the return leg of the first Nile journey from 1827 from Wadi Halfa, 16 April 1827, to Gardass/Kerdassy, 28 April 1827.

PN III'1828 inscriptions III N. of 2nd Cataract' (small label on cover), contains copies of inscriptions noted at Beni Hassan, Dendera, Gournah and Aswan, together with some (earlier) notes in ink on towns in Spain.

PN IV'1828 inscriptions IV S of 2nd Cataract' (small label on cover), contains several good pencil copies of inscriptions, with locations.

PN V'date? journal V Cairo to Philae' (small label on cover). This journal covers the Cairo to Philae leg of the first journey upstream from 27 February to 4 April 1827.

PN VI'date? journal VI to Sidon various inscriptions' (small label on cover), contains copies of inscriptions located at Aaron's tomb, Mt. Hor, Wadi Musa and Nahr al-Kalb. A slip inside reads: 'Book of notes by Lord Prudhoe in Egypt—Greece? & the Holy Land contains an interesting journal of travel in the latter country—date doubtful ?1838'. This notebook begins with various notes of payments and some notes on the history of Greece and Egypt and the journal section begins on page 42 as follows: 'Tuesday March 20th [underlined] left Cairo at 4 o'clock by the Bab el Nasser—took the mountain road to Suez.' The date fits for 1827 but in that year Lord Prudhoe was in Upper Egypt in March; other years might be 1832, 1838 or 1849. On page 81 he notes: ' ... Samaria was destroyed by Abdallah Pasha ... [illegible] ... years ago in 1827.' The illegible word does not appear to be 'eleven' which would confirm the 1838 suggestion.

PN VII 'inscriptions Sinaitic and Egn VII Serabit el Khadim etc.' (small label on cover). This notebook also begins with three pages of journal entry written in pencil and subsequently erased. It begins tantalisingly: 'On Sunday [...] of July we left Cairo for [...]'. After the erased pages there are eight pages of copies of Thamudic, or similar, inscriptions with various locations as follows: 'Wadi Megara', 'Gebel Mohatteb', 'Between the convent of 40 Martyrs and Rock of Moses', 'Between St Catherine's and Moses Rock', 'Wadi Maggup', 'Wadi Barak', 'Nasby'. The first copy is marked: 'the first Hebrew [sic] inscription we met with in Wadi Saturday July 28th 1827.' At the end of the journal, used in reverse, are pencil notes and ink copies of hieroglyphic inscriptions marked: 'Wadi Genneh July 1827', 'Wadi Magarra', 'Serabit el Khadim'.

PN VIII'Inscriptions Sinaitic &c VIII Wadi Maghara &c' (small label on cover). This notebook contains 31 pages of Thamudic, or similar, and hieroglyphic inscriptions, some of which are marked: 'Wadi Ginnee', 'Wadi Magara Egreem'.

PN IX'Notes of inscriptions IX antiquities' (small label on cover). A few pages are taken up at each end of the notebook with copies of inscriptions on three objects: a sarcophagus on which Lord Prudhoe notes there was no name; 'a beautifully painted and inscribed mummy case'; parts of the inscription on a large Middle Kingdom stele in the Alnwick collection (N.1932).

No number, 'Greek Islands' (marked on cover). Journal of tour of the Aegean from Cairo 9 August 1827, returning to Cairo, 20 April 1828.

No number. Fourteen pages of notes on Egyptian history down to 1800. and no marking on cover.

Notes

1   I am indebted for much assistance and information to N. Cooke, M. Azim, C. Shrimpton and R. Cassidy.

2   For details of the numbering, dating and contents of the journals and other notebooks, see Appendix 1.

3   A transcript of Felix's letters is in preparation. They are cited in this article using the abbreviation FL with a provisional number. Bierbrier notes that Felix 'accompanied his colonel to Egypt on a political mission, visiting Upper Egypt and later joined Lord Prudhoe in his travels, (M. L. Bierbrier (ed.), *Who Was Who in Egypt* (London: Egypt Exploration Society, 1995), third revised edition, hereinafter *WWWE3*, p. 150). In fact Felix (in his FL 1 and 2) gives his companion as Col. Davison, probably Lt Colonel Hugh Percy Davison, the only colonel with that surname in the 1825 Army List. Davison was at that time on half-pay from the Fifth West India Regiment. He was the son of December Davison, who owned land near Alnwick, and may well have been the original link between Lord Prudhoe and Major Felix (information kindly provided by C. Shrimpton).

4   BM Add. Mss 25663, ff.42–1070. Other sketches, papers and letters by Felix are in the papers of James Burton, now in the British Museum (BM Add. Mss 25658, ff.79–83 and BM Add. Mss 25651), along with the papers of J. Bonomi.

5   This will be published separately in due course.

6   T. Eric Peet, *The Inscriptions of Sinai* (London: EEF, 1917).

7   PN V, 22. 11 March [1827].

8   FL 5, 20 June [1828].

9   Burton to Greenough, UCL 35/2. Information kindly provided by Neil Cooke.

10 FL 5, 20 June [1828].

11 FL 6, 18 December [1828].

12 J.-F. Champollion, *Lettres écrites d'Égypte et de Nubie en 1828 et 1829* (Paris, 1833).

13 PN I, 20 January [1829].

14 '...they bear the name of Sesostris'—making the mistake common since Classical times of confusing the Middle Kingdom Senusret (Sesostris), the 'birth name' taken by three kings of the 12th Dynasty (1985–1795 BC), with Rameses II (1279–1213 BC).

15 PN V, 16 March [1827].

16 PN I, 9 January [1829].

17 Prudhoe refers to the Chamber of Kings at Karnak in PN I, 9 January [1829].

18 The donkey put its foot through a hole in the roof of the tomb. The tomb was subsequently investigated by Dr Mohammed Saleh and entered again in 1985 by Dr Lisa Manniche (*City of the Dead, Thebes in Egypt* (London: BMP, 1987), pp. 109–10).

19 PN I, 16 January [1829].

20 PN V, 10 March [1827].

21 PN I, 13 January 1828. This is the site of Esna (Greek, Latopolis). The Temple of Commodus is probably that recorded by Napoleon's savants which did not survive, rather than the still standing temple of Khnum which has, at the foot of the north wall, a relief showing Horus, the Emperor Commodus (180–92 AD) and Khnum drawing a net of fishes and waterfowl. This was built on the site of a temple dating back to Thutmose III (1479–25 BC) at the time of Cleopatra Cocce and Ptolemy Lathyrus, but the sculptures were not completed until the reigns of Aurelius and Commodus. The Temple of Thutmose II (1492–79 BC) was subsequently partly excavated by Auguste Mariette (Editors' note).

22 PN V, 5 March [1827].

23 PN V, 3 March [1827].

24 PN V, 14 March [1827].

25 PN V, 30 March [1827].

26 Francis Vyvyan Jago Arundale (1807–53). Bierbrier, *WWWE3*, records that Arundale was in Egypt from 1831. It is possible that this is a slip for Felix who, we know, had been unwell before the journey, see first journal PN V, 27 February 1827, 'my companion was released from the doctors care' and FL 3, 'I have been … laid up in the house of a long-bearded doctor [Dr Dussaps] … '

27 Bierbrier, *WWWE3*, p. 150, notes that Giovanni Finati, Bankes' dragoman, claimed to have accompanied Lord Prudhoe on his travels in Egypt, Nubia and Syria but there is no reference to him in either Prudhoe's journals or his list of companions on his second journey.

28 British Museum, accession nos 1 & 2.

29 There are plans of the site in BM Add. Mss 25651, ff.2, drawings of the lions (4vs and 5rt), and descriptions of the site (21, 22 & 27, 57) at Jabal Barkal.

30 An annotated copy of the catalogue of that sale exists giving, against some lots, the name of the purchaser. Various items in the collection can be identified with more or less certainty.

31 Sir John Gardner Wilkinson, *Manners and Customs of the Ancient Egyptians* (London: John Murray, 1837).

32 The obelisk was first sent to Alnwick, where it was seen by Bonomi, then to Syon Park in London, and back. It was found not in a Thebaid village as described by Bonomi, but by Prisse d'Avennes who found it in use as the threshold of a house in Aswan. Part of its companion, found later in Aswan, is now in the Cairo Museum. They had presumably been moved to Aswan from the temple of Khnum on Elephantine island. See J. R. Harris, *Arts of Asia* 13: 6 (1983), 77.

33 Samuel Birch, *Catalogue of the Egyptian Antiquities at Alnwick Castle* (privately printed, 1880).
34 Edward W. Lane, *Madd al-Qamus. An Arabic-English Lexicon, Derived from the Best and the Most Copious Eastern Sources* (London, 1863–93). 8 vols. Parts 6–8 ed. Stanley Lane Poole. For further details see chapter 25.

10 ∾ The Forgotten Egyptologist: James Burton

Neil Cooke

In West Dean Cemetery, Edinburgh, a headstone remembers James Burton as 'a zealous investigator in Egypt of its language and antiquities', but he might have been better described as the 'Forgotten Egyptologist'. He was in Egypt from 1822 to 1834 and although a travelling companion to many discussed in this volume he alone has to be taken to task for failing to gain recognition during his lifetime. Although he was of a dilatory nature, he cannot be held totally responsible for not publishing an account of his investigations amongst the tombs and temples. Burton lived in times when the cost of publishing ventures was still financed by the author, his patron or by subscription. He returned to England at Christmas 1835 to find John Gardner Wilkinson and Edward William Lane ready to publish studies about both the ancient and the modern Egyptians. Burton, therefore, found himself with no time to sort out his journals and drawings, let alone put pen to paper and his two companions earned the credit and glory that could have been shared between them.

Burton did, however, manage to print in Cairo his *Excerpta Hieroglyphica*,[1] the first fairly accurate collection of hieroglyphic inscriptions for use by those who were trying to understand the ancient language. His book was printed as a series of plates and these were distributed to scholars and his friends throughout Europe, including Dr Thomas Young[2] and Champollion.[3]

Although Burton published nothing further of his own after returning from Egypt, his legacy is 'Collectanea Ægyptiaca' deposited with the British Museum.[4] However, the papers are not easy to use for useful facts are mixed in with weather records, compass bearings and calculations of camel speed. For the most part, the drawings and plans are unfinished but they do provide a record of monuments before the clearance of sand and the activities of later archaeologists made them more visible and accessible.

There exist three short accounts of Burton's life, the earliest in a journal kept by his father.[5] The brevity probably reflects a father's true feelings for his son.

James, born September 22nd 1788
Left school
Went to Mr Soanes, Architect
Went to Trinity College
Left College
Was in France to 1814
Was in France December 1815
Settled in Chambers Lincoln's Inn 1816
Went to the Continent July 11th 1819
Went to Egypt, in the service of the Pasha in the early part of
182–& arrived St Leonard's on Sea December 24th 1835 after
spending—months in the South of France

The second version of his life is a selective and sanitised account written from facts supplied by family members for the *Dictionary of National Biography*

HALIBURTON, formerly BURTON, James, Egyptologist, born 22 September 1788. His father, James Haliburton, of Mabledon, Tonbridge, Kent and afterwards of The Holme, Regent's Park (London), was a member of the family of Haliburton of Roxboroughshire, but changed his name in early life to Burton and devoted himself to the conduct of large building speculations, especially in London. James Burton the younger was educated at Trinity College, Cambridge. He was engaged by Mehemet Ali Pasha to take part in a geological survey of Egypt and sailed from Naples for that country in March 1822. During this and following years he made a journey into the eastern desert, in the course of which he decided the position of Myos Hormos or Aphrodite. In April 1824 he was with John Gardner Wilkinson, the famous Egyptologist, at Alexandria and was contemplating an expedition to the oasis and western desert. During 1825 and 1826 he made a journey up the Nile, and in the latter year met Edward W. Lane at Dendarah and afterwards travelled with him. Between 1825 and 1828 his *Excerpta Hieroglyphica* consisting of 64 lithographs without any letterpress, were published in Cairo. Shortly afterwards Burton returned to England where he spent the next two years. From April 1830 to February 1832 he was on a journey in the eastern desert. He came home about 1835 and does not appear to have again visited Egypt. In 1838 he resumed the name Haliburton and in the same year he was one of the committee for the White River Expedition. During the latter part of his life he devoted himself chiefly to the collection of particulars concerning his ancestors, the Haliburtons. For many years previously to 1841 he was a fellow of the Geological Society but after that date his name disappears from the societies lists. Haliburton died on 22 February 1862 and was buried at West Dean Cemetery, Edinburgh; his tombstone gives the dates of his birth and death and has the inscription, 'James Haliburton, a zealous investigator in Egypt of its Languages and Antiquities.'

Haliburton was a friend of Joseph Bonomi, and like him held an honourable place in the band of workers employed by Robert Hay to make sketches and drawings of Egyptian antiquities. His merits were rather those of an intelligent traveller and copyist than of a scholar but Sir John Gardner Wilkinson, in the preface of his *Manners and Customs of the Ancient Egyptians* speaks highly of the assistance which Burton rendered him. His *Collectanea Aegyptiaca* contained in 63 volumes were presented to the British Museum in 1864 by his younger brother Decimus Burton, the Architect. They include, besides carefully kept diaries, numerous drawings of hieroglyphic inscriptions, architectural sketches and notes on the history, geology, zoology and botany of the country together with his passports and correspondence. Many of Haliburton's other drawings and maps are contained in the collection of views, sketches etc. made for Robert Hay and now in the British Library.

Much of this is incorrect. Among the lesser errors are that Burton did not return to England between 1828 and 1830, nor did he have an honourable place in the band of workers employed by Robert Hay for he was independent. Perhaps the most serious omission, however, is that he was married.

The third version of his life is that given in Dawson and Uphill's *Who Was Who in Egyptology*,[6] which is a précis of the first two, with additional details taken from the diaries of his fellow travellers.

James Burton was born on 22 September 1788 at Crescent Place, London and christened with the family name Haleburton, the surname he began to use in 1838 having met in the street a man who had come to London in search of lost relatives. That man was Thomas Chandler Haliburton – better known as the Canadian author 'Sam Slick'– whose monthly serialisations in magazines out-sold those written by Dickens.

James was named after his father, who in a few years was to become a successful speculative builder—constructing many houses in Bloomsbury, including Crescent Place, as well as the terraces in the Regent's Park and parts of Regent's Street. Later, he established the town of St Leonard's on Sea. James junior was therefore born into what could be considered a wealthy family.

Reaching the age of eight he was sent to school with the Reverend Lewis Turner at Hammersmith but soon transferred to Dr Charles Burney's Academy in Greenwich. Dr Burney was brother to Fanny Burney, the novelist, and his day-school and boarding school catered for about a hundred boys. His object was to establish in pupils 'habits of regularity and principles of integrity'—with learning being of the last consideration.

James matriculated in 1805 and through the efforts of his father was taken on as an assistant or improver in the office of the architect Sir John Soane. But architecture was not for him. After a few months he left for Trinity College, Cambridge, to study for a degree in mathematics under the tuition of the Reverend George Tavel. He was not a good pupil and after graduation his father took him for an interview with a Captain Bush in the hope that the threat of a career in the Navy would change him. The desired effect being achieved, the young Burton was articled in 1810 to Mr Rouppell, a solicitor in Lincoln's Inn Square—bringing with him the benefit of most of his father's business.

It was only a matter of time before Burton's dilatory nature appeared, but the following year he met two men who gave him a new direction in life. The first was Sir Humphrey Davy. With the threat of a Napoleonic invasion still a reality, the Burton family had invested in a Gunpowder Manufacturing Mill at Tonbridge, Kent and employed Sir Humphrey Davy to experiment with explosives.

The second man was George Bellas Greenough, who had inherited a fortune while still at school and rather than work was able to pursue a diversity of interests. Greenough became a good friend to the whole Burton family. He was frequently their guest for dinner or they joined him at the theatre and he spent many Christmases with them at St Leonard's on Sea. Greenough also became a mentor to the young Burton and often acted as a go-between when relations between James and his father soured, which they did through gambling debts. A writ was finally served on James and his father threatened to disinherit him if he did not find some gainful employment.

Luckily, Greenough had learned from Sir Joseph Banks that Sir Humphrey Davy was in Italy, employed to find a safe method for unrolling carbonised papyrus rolls in the collection of the king of Naples. Greenough also learned that Davy required an assistant. Burton was recommended for the job and in July 1819 set off cross-country for Naples. When he met with Davy in October, however, he discovered William Gell and Peter Elmsley already at work with help from a locally-employed laboratory assistant. Burton was furious at having no job but he decided to stay in Italy and await Greenough, who arrived in May 1820. In the next few months, the two men saw all the sights Italy could offer.

It was always possible when travelling to meet interesting people from home and in June 1821 Burton and Greenough met and John Gardner Wilkinson in the company of Sir William Gell and learned of his intention to visit Egypt. Thus was formed in Burton's mind the idea of going there himself, although at that time he did not have the means to do so.

On his return to England, Greenough made enquiries of Briggs & Co, an import/export business with offices in London and Alexandria. Through them he found a salaried, expenses-paid position for Burton as a mineralogist in the employ of the Pasha, Muhammad 'Ali. On hearing this James prepared himself for the trip. With Wilkinson and Gell he went to classes in Arabic and trigonometry and to look the part of a Turk, he grew a moustache.

On 18 March 1822, Burton set sail for Alexandria with Charles Humphreys, the travelling companion-cum-secretary who had accompanied him from England, and with a newly employed Italian servant, Vicenzo.

Rather stupidly he chose a ship carrying arms for the Pasha: the Greeks were at war with the Sublime Porte and would have blown up the boat and all on board if they had found the shipment of arms. Eleven days later after a rough crossing they reached Alexandria on 8 April 1822.

Despite the demonic side to his character, the Pasha of Egypt was an astute man who could see the benefits of bringing his country into the modern world with European help. The Pasha had realised that if he could refuel the new steamships then able to reach Alexandria and if they could also be refuelled at Suez, he could halve both the cost and the journey time from England to India and earn revenue for his country. Employing Burton to find fuel was the first part of the Pasha's plan.

Following meetings with the Pasha, Burton set off for a first trip into the Eastern Desert in search of coal. Burton found no coal, but he became acquainted with the Eastern Desert. After a meandering journey found his way to Beni Suef and took a leisurely boat trip along the Nile back to Cairo.

Greenough, meanwhile, perceiving that James was not up to the job for which he was employed, sent him an assistant with experience as a mining engineer. Charles Sheffield arrived in Egypt at the end of 1822 in the company of a chemist, James Thornton. At their first meeting, Burton, who was drunk, fell off his chair and in celebration of Humphreys' birthday, offered Sheffield one of his slave girls for the night.

After some false starts, Burton set off with Wilkinson on a second foray into the Eastern Desert, together with a huge caravan of camels, servants and soldiers and his new mining assistants. Even though the right sort of rock formations were found and shafts dug, coal was still not discovered and it was left to a Frenchman some twenty years later to find it. The party, however, found the quarry that supplied the Romans with porphyry and on the coast of the Red Sea identified the ruins of Myos Hormos (although this identification is now being questioned).[7] They also visited the remaining Coptic monasteries and presented gifts of knives to the monks who gave them shelter.

Although they spent much time away from Cairo, Burton and his companions still managed to assimilate themselves into the ways of that city. On first arrival, Burton had met Osman, the former Scottish soldier who had become interpreter at the British consulate. With Osman's help he bought clothes to match his new and superior position. Osman also went to the slave market on Burton's behalf and purchased several girls. One was a dark-skinned Nubian and the others Greek. To complete the transformation and be fashionable, Burton sported a long moustache and had taken up smoking tobacco in pipes that were three feet long.

By April 1824, Burton had been in Egypt for two years, yet he had not visited the monuments. Having been in the desert talking with Wilkinson and looking through his notebooks, James decided to end his contract with the Pasha and spend some time studying the ancient remains—for that is how Burton accounted for his dismissal from the Pasha's service. Disappointed by this change of direction, Sheffield and Thornton departed for England and reported their version of events to Greenough—that the Pasha was not getting what he was paying for.

In January 1825 Burton set out with Humphreys and Vicenzo southwards down the Nile. For Burton it began as a leisurely tourist cruise, but on reaching ancient Thebes he stopped and set up camp in the Memnonium. At Medinet Habu he chiselled his name into the wall and commenced the first of his primitive excavations, exposing sections of wall to their full height. With the help of ladders and ropes, he climbed the colossi of Memnon and excavated to the bottom of their foundations. He then turned his attention to the Valley of the Kings and perceiving the effect of flash-floods on the future preservation of the tombs, built water channels to divert the rain. Following the experience of being beaten back by bad air when trying to clear debris from Hatshepsut's tomb, he turned to making measured drawings of those that were more easily accessible— including KV5.

Burton and his companions then continued their journey south on the Nile, calling at Kom Ombo, Aswan and Philae before reaching Abu Simbel in September 1825. On the return journey, the party again stopped in the area of Thebes where Burton transferred his attentions to the Eastern side of the Nile and set up camp on top of the first pylon of the temple of Amun-Ra at Karnak. Over a period of months he measured and drew plans of large parts of the temple. He also excavated in the area of the granite sanctuary and discovered and recorded a new List of Kings which helped fill gaps in that already discovered at Abydos. Back at Thebes, he called on Hay, Bonomi, Wilkinson and their various friends, helpers and servants who lived in and among the tombs on the opposite bank of the Nile.

His appetite for the antique satisfied, Burton slowly sailed back to Cairo where he set about acquiring a printing press. With the help of Humphreys, Bonomi and two new friends, Lord Prudhoe and Colonel Orlando Felix, he prepared the plates to illustrate his first printed work, the *Excerpta Hieroglyphica*.

In either 1827 or 1828, Burton began to search Cairo for a piece of stone. His attention had been drawn to it by Dr Thomas Young. One of the French savants, Mr Caristie, had first observed the stone in 1800 and it was thought to be supporting a window in a mosque near the French Institute. Like that found at Rosetta, the stone was carved with tri-lingual inscriptions and could be a further aid to the decipherment of hieroglyphics. After much searching, Burton found the stone—or one like it.

The stone is likely to be that now in the Louvre called the Caristie Stone, although this may not be the one Caristie first saw. One reason why the stone may have found its way to the Louvre, is through Champollion who had just then arrived in Cairo on his first visit to Egypt. When Burton, Bonomi, Felix and Lord Prudhoe met Champollion, they took an instant dislike to him and his companions—most of all a woman who worked her charms on anybody who would be useful to Champollion. As they later put it, Champollion presented as his discoveries everything they showed him and gave the real finders no credit at all.

In 1828, Burton decided to look at the Delta region and sailed northwards from Cairo along the various tributaries and canals of the Nile. By this date he had lost interest in making a record of anything he saw, apart from remarking on the dirt and filth and vermin. On his return to Cairo, he took a three-year lease on a house at Birket el Goornay. Edward Lane wrote to Robert Hay 'It has a small garden between it and the lake, where I suppose he will plant sycamores and wait for them to grow up. His father has received nothing from him lately but those short notes called drafts or bills of exchange.'

Here begins the strangest phase of Burton's time in Egypt for there are no clues from the letters and journals of what he did with the next four or five years. Even though he had leased the house in Cairo, Burton spent most of the time living with Humphreys and Vicenzo, servants and slave-girls in an encampment in the Eastern Desert. Occasionally he visited the monastery of St Anthony or moved his camp to the Red Sea coast. Hearing nothing from him, his father stopped paying the allowance that had enabled him to stay in Egypt. In desperation Burton turned to Greenough who loaned him enough money to stay.

Towards the end of 1833, Burton took the decision to return to England. Naturally, he set off with Charles Humphreys but he also took along the Egyptian servants, his remaining Greek slave girl, and a ménagerie of animals, including a giraffe, a dromedary, two antelopes, a hyena, an ibis, several hawks, owls, partridges and other animals.

Being the most valuable, his giraffe was well provided for on the voyage to Italy. It had special food and to prevent it falling over in the boat, it was suspended in a canvas sling with holes for each leg. He had a sheepskin coat made for it in case it did not take to the cold weather. After a few months' quarantine in Bordeaux, the whole ménagerie transferred to Marseilles. Sir William Gell wrote to Wilkinson that he had read in the newspaper of Burton exercising his giraffe around the outskirts of Marseilles.

Disaster struck in Paris when the hyena attacked one of the Egyptian servants, almost ripping off his arm. Burton immediately took the man to a surgeon and had the arm sewn together. The servant survived with his arm intact but without the use of a couple of fingers. To pay for the surgeon and the convalescence Burton sold his menagerie—except the giraffe—to the Jardin des Plantes.

In December 1835 Burton, Humphreys, the servants, the Greek slave and the giraffe made their way from Paris to Calais to board a ship for Dover. Unfortunately, the giraffe slipped on the ice just outside Calais, broke a leg and died.

Back in England, Burton had to think about repaying the money loaned to him by Greenough. The death of the giraffe had cost him dear for he could have sold it for up to £5,000.[8] To solve his financial problems, Burton decided to sell his collection of Egyptian antiquities and romantic books in Arabic through Sotheby's. The sale went well and the British Museum acquired and paid for many items which can still be seen on display, such as the carpenters' tools, and the bronze hinges from a door in the granite sanctuary at the Temple of Amun-Ra.[9]

Then Charles Humphreys died. Burton was devastated by the loss of this companion of nearly twenty years. To keep his mind occupied, he helped set up a committee to raise funds to send someone to find the source of the White Nile.

In July 1838 he met a man in the street who turned out to be his relative—the judge Thomas Chandler Haliburton ('Sam Slick'). Haliburton's grandfather had left Scotland for Boston, Massachusetts about a century before and the two branches of the family lost contact. Finding a new friend encouraged James Burton to revert to the old family surname of Haliburton for the remainder of his life.

To help Burton[10] earn some money, 'Sam Slick' persuaded him to edit his new book—much to Burton's horror, because he thought it was such rubbish. And, besides, he had another job in hand. Robert Hay had asked him to write the text for *Illustrations of Cairo*[11] and his uncredited descriptions of parts of the city make interesting reading.

The last third of Burton's life is something of a mystery. Greenough, his mentor and long-suffering friend, would have nothing more to do with him. Even his family turned against him and only Decimus maintained contact up until the day he died. In these remaining years, he researched and drew up a family tree—recently found in a box, in the attic of a house just outside New York.[12] Research for the family tree would have taken him all over England. Burton was related to Sir Walter Scott who from the sales of his novels had accumulated land and money. The suspicion is that Burton hoped to get his hands on some of Sir Walter Scott's wealth. However, he first had to prove the relationship.

In the collection of antiquities Burton sent back from Egypt was a mummy which was not included in the Sotheby's sale. It had spent the best part of twenty-five years in a room in Greenough's house in the Regent's Park. Greenough probably accepted it as part-payment for the long overdue loan. Just before Christmas 1848, Greenough held a raffle during a dinner party at Decimus Burton's house. Those taking part were Greenough, Decimus, and hid brother William and Edmund Hopkinson, the Burtons' brother-in-law and a partner in Hopkinson's Bank. Hopkinson was the winner and took the mummy to his home near Gloucester. Following the fashion, he organised an 'unwrapping' by a Dr Rumsey, the local physician. Curiosity satisfied, the mummy was given to the newly-formed Gloucester Museum. In 1953, it was transferred to Liverpool Museum to replace one lost during wartime bombing.

Apart from his will, the last reference for Burton is in a letter from 1855 written by John Knox of Tipperlinne, Scotland to Alexander Haliburton of Whitley, near Wigan and found in New York. Alexander Haliburton married 'Sam Slick''s daughter, Augusta. In the letter Knox says 'I occasionally hear of Mr James Haliburton at the antiquarian booksellers, Stevenson, in Princes Street, Edinburgh'. A recent find in a box of glass negatives in Hastings Museum is a last photograph of James Burton taken in the 1850s. In his old age he looks dejected and sad.

At the end of February 1861, The *Scotsman* newspaper contained the following notice: 'At 10 Hamilton Place, Newington, on the 22nd inst, James Haliburton Esq., a descendant of the ancient Scottish family of the Haliburtons, a branch of which Sir Walter Scott was connected on the maternal side; deeply regretted.' Burton had died, forgotten by his family and his London friends. Robert Hay, his old friend from the time in Egypt, was an executor to the will but Wilkinson refused to be involved. Hay paid off Burton's debt from the 1830s to Joseph Bonomi from his own pocket. A year later, Decimus gave the majority of his brother's Egyptian papers to the British Museum. His pictures have been found in a sketchbook kept in the Victoria & Albert Museum hidden away under the name of Joseph Bonomi. Adriana Garofalaki, the Greek slave he married, moved from the house in Hamilton Place to Stoneycroft Cottage, Morningside, and then to 9 Gladstone Terrace, Edinburgh. She probably died in 1883 aged about seventy, taking with her the last memories of Burton's time in Egypt.

Given recent publicity about the findings in Tomb KV5 it is possible that, again, credit and glory have passed Burton by. However, to put the new discoveries into context, some 170 years before the arrival of an archaeological team with hydraulic jacks, powerful electric floodlights and television cameras, Burton did what he could working alone and with candles as his only source of light. A sketch plan in his journals shows that he knew a passage extended further into the mountain. Just how much further, he was never to know.

Notes

1 Sir John Gardner Wilkinson, *Manners and Customs of the Ancient Egyptians* (London, 1837; rev. 1878); E. W. Lane, *An Account of the Manners and Customs of the Modern Egyptians, Written in Egypt during the years 1833, 34 and 35* (London, 1836). 5th rev. edition, (ed.) Edward Stanley Poole (London, John Murray, 1860).

2 James [Hali]Burton, *Excerpta Hieroglyphica*, in four parts (Cairo, 1825–28).

3 Thomas Young (1773–1829), the English physicist who identified the names of Cleopatra and Ptolemy in royal cartouches.

4 Jean-François Champollion, the Frenchman who succeeded in 1822 in discovering the long-sought alphabet by looking at royal cartouches.

5 *Collectanea Ægyptiaca*, British Museum Add. Mss 25613–25675.

6 In Hastings Museum.

7 Warren R. Dawson and Eric P. Uphill, *Who Was Who in Egyptology*, 2nd edition (London: Egypt Exploration Society, 1972); 3rd ed., (ed.) M.L. Bierbrier (London: EEF, 1995).

8 The ruins of Myos Hormos (or Aphrodite) were thought to be on the coast at latitude 27_ 24', and was the site of the principal port on the Red Sea at the time of Strabo, see *Handbook for Travellers in Egypt* by Sir John Gardner Wilkinson (London: John Murray, 1847), p. 271.

9 By coincidence, the first giraffe at the new London Zoo arrived in May 1836 only a few months later and took up residence in a building designed for it by James' younger brother Decimus Burton.

10 James' financial problems were still not solved. Having first lost his valuable giraffe, he then suffered as the famous Sotheby's went bankrupt.

11 For purposes of consistency the surname of Burton will continue to be used.

12 Robert Hay, *Illustrations of Cairo* (London, 1840).

13 In the Library of the University of Nova Scotia at Wolfsville.

Part Three

Women in Egypt

11 ∾ Two Brides: The Baroness Menu von Minutoli and Mrs Colonel Elwood

Deborah Manley

Baroness Wolfradine Menu von Minutoli, born Comptesse von Schulenberg, was a widow when she married the Prussian officer and scholar Heinrich von Minutoli. Her first husband, a Colonel in the Prussian army, had been killed at Waterloo. The Minutolis were both about twenty-eight when they set out from Trieste in 1820 for Egypt. Anne Katharine Curteis was twenty-six, and had married a man six years her senior: Colonel Charles Elwood of the Honourable East India Company whose return to India occasioned their journey. Both were brides in the then accepted sense of being in the first year of their marriages. Their reactions to their experiences—and those experiences themselves—were rather different from those of male travellers.

Wolfradine von Minutoli had always had 'an extreme desire to be acqainted with remote countries'. She had visited England. She spoke Italian and probably French. When her new husband, a lover of science and a student of antiquities, expressed 'a very natural desire' to visit Egypt, and was indeed commissioned to do so, she was 'happy to avoid a separation painful to her heart', so she packed her bags and followed. The Baron was far more knowledgeable than she, so she settled down aboard ship to make up for her deficiencies by wading through his library, diligently reading Herodotus, Volney, Denon, Hamilton and several other authors.[1]

On 7 September 1820 she hastened on deck to catch her first glimpse of Africa. They entered Alexandria harbour, and the former French consul-general Colonel Drovetti came aboard. He was already 'well known in Europe for his refined taste, his indefatigable researches, his fortunate discoveries and kind hospitality'.[2] They stayed with him, and Wolfradine was very glad to escape to his house from the 'extraordinary noise' of Egypt.

Alexandria was disappointing. She found it not only noisy but run-down, dirty and offering few resources except 'the gossiping of a little country-town'. Soon the Baron disappeared for a few months 'accompanied by several men of learning' on an excursion into the desert of Libya, leaving his bride in the care of the Prussian consul, Mr Charles Rossetti, who carried her off to his spacious house and his womenfolk in Cairo.

97

On 6 October 1825 Anne Katharine and Colonel Elwood set out from her family home at Windmill Hill near Hastings in Sussex, towards Dover— the first day of a journey that would last more than nine months until their ship eventually cast anchor in Bombay harbour on 29 July 1826. By then they had travelled through Europe, crossed the Mediterranean and spent weeks in Egypt, before traversing the desert to reach the ship that carried them and Napoleon's warder, Sir Hudson Lowe—a man she obviously disliked—to India.[3]

Anne Katharine described their journey with the kind of enthusiasm that encourages others to follow, and also provided much practical information for later travellers. She described herself as the first Englishwoman to have made this journey—apparently unaware of Eliza Fay who had visited Egypt and written about it long before her.

Had she read Eliza Fay's letters about her journey in 1797, she might have been more fearful, for Eliza met storms and thieves and heat that 'made the air of Cairo smell like hot bricks'.[4] The 'severe epidemical disease' which broke out while she was in Cairo would make anyone quail—and the remedy, to lie in bed and drink up to two gallons of Nile water a day, would keep most of us close to home.

Travellers had a great deal of advice and help from Marianna Starke (1762–1838) who, in 1820, had published her *Travels on the Continent written for the Use and Particular Information of Travellers*—the direct predecessor of Murray's Handbooks and of Baedeker's ubiquitous guides. Few people had been able to travel freely for the twenty years since the French Revolution and Mrs Starke realised that new guides were needed to bring information concerning roads, accommodations and even works of art up to date. She resolved, instead of updating her own very successful *Letters from Italy*, to produce a new work, and set off in May 1817—in her mid-fifties—to spend two years in the countries she planned to describe. Her research proved encouraging. In many ways matters had improved since her earlier travels in 1792, and the only real problem was that the great rush of tourists had pushed up prices. The Elwoods found her advice most useful. If they followed it on the contents of their medicine chest it would have carried such startling medications as sulphuric acid, pure opium, liquid laudanum and diluted vitriolic acid, alongside court-plaster and lint. The acids were a solution to the problem of impure drinking water: five drops of sulphuric acid in a large decanter would 'make any noxious particles drop to the bottom and render the water wholesome … '[5]

The Elwoods entered Valletta harbour on 1 January 1826—noting casually that several pirates were suspended near the entrance[6]—and settled in Malta for the winter. Despite being warned of the inadvisability of travelling to Egypt at all and the danger of piracy, they set sail on 5 April, bidding farewell to Europe and 'with a fair but strong breeze proceeded towards Alexandria'.[7]

Anne Katharine was of an imaginative turn of mind: she suspected each approaching ship of being manned by corsairs, and anticipated capture and slavery as several ships bore down on them, hailed them, and passed on. On 13 April they saw the coast of Africa for the first time and a swarm of flies came out to greet them. On the following day they could pick out Pompey's Pillar—tall and slender as a needle—with a glass and on 15 April 'Alexandria was the cry—we had reached our wished for haven'.[8]

The Elwoods were to stay with Henry Salt, His Majesty's consul-general in Egypt. But once ashore they faced an unexpected problem. Donkeys waited to transport them but Mrs Elwood's side-saddle had been left on the ship. However, with an umbrella held over her, and undaunted as usual, she contrived to seat herself sideways on a donkey with the servants holding her in place. The local Frankish ladies rode *en cavalier*, but not she. 'The camels along the way,' she shuddered, 'stretched out their ugly necks one way and they stretched them out the other, and looked half determined to eat me up as they stalked, stalked and stalked on so close to me that I could have touched them.'[9]

For once she wished herself back in England. But soon they were civilly received in the consul's house, drinking coffee from little cups which would have 'delighted many an old dowager in England' and discussing the latest English novels. On 19 April they sailed off into a Nile night, talking of Cleopatra as the moon shone brightly overhead. The boat's cabin was about six foot square and four feet high and Anne Katherine found herself too tall for the first time in her life.[10] When the lamp was lit it revealed swarms of cockroaches 'running about merrily in every direction' and during the night they were also visited 'repeatedly' by rats.

The water was low and one stage of the journey was made on land. After Anne Katharine's donkey tried to run under a camel, the Elwoods rode at the head of the procession, followed by the camels laden with their luggage. Their next vessel was a cargo boat that had carried sugar. The ceiling was encrusted with flies and the floor swarmed with fleas. In theory it should have taken only a day to reach Bulaq, but the low Nile delayed them. They were—after a glass of brandy on St George's Day (23 April)—regaled by their elderly dragoman Giovanni with stories of how, as *camérière* to Napoleon, he used to wake in the night to find the great man pacing up and down, sunk in thought. Giovanni had accompanied many travellers, including Sir Frederick Henniker and the Reverend Joseph Cook, an English clergyman, who in 1824 had ascended the Nile, carved his name at Abu Sir and then expired on his camel while riding to Sinai.

After five weary days they were met at Bulaq by the consulate's third dragoman—Osman, the Scotsman William Thompson—who took them to the consular house, as he took many other visitors over the years. Anne Katharine was delighted by this wonderful house with its carved window frames with painted glass and window seats, and its ever-changing array of people of all nations who visited all day long. She was less pleased with its insect life: 'every species of insect, crawling, creeping, jumping, flying, buzzing, and humming about one to a tormenting degree. Had we been disposed to study entomology, this would have been a glorious opportunity.'[11]

The Elwoods enjoyed their time in Cairo. Coffee was brought to their room at break of day; then they wiled away the hours, reading, writing, sleeping and receiving and making calls. At noon there was a buffet lunch and in the cool of the evening they rode out in the streets or walked in the public garden nearby. Anne Katharine found herself playing *quadrilles* and Irish melodies in the heart of Grand Cairo on the piano of Henry Salt's young wife who had died of puerperal fever two years before.[12] The Baroness, too, found the Rossetti's Viennese piano 'a frequent source of recreation'.[13]

When the Elwoods rode out, they sometimes encountered incivilities until it was noticed that there was a female in the party when attitudes changed to 'the most perfect courtesy and civility'. Although Christians might be held in abhorrence, she, as a woman, was always treated with deference and respect, and found the manners of the Turks 'towards our sex as far exceed those of our countrymen in courtesy as their graceful costume surpasses that of the Franks in magnificence and grandeur.'[14] She might gladly have put on Turkish dress, but Mr Salt had warned them against this 'as being a species of disguise which rendered it impossible for him to be responsible for the safety of those that wore it.' She did, however, cover her face with a veil, finding it both useful and courteous to local society, but found the combination of her white face and black boots most astonishing to local observers. When they visited the slave market—about which she seemed completely unconcerned—the Nubian women 'fell to laughing, grinning, and quizzing, and pointing at her in her strange English riding-habit.' Slaves, she opined, were often kindly treated except by European owners, and might even be better off than in their original state.

Five years earlier the Prussian consul had been kind enough to arrange for Baroness Minutoli to go out each afternoon, she riding on a mule, with a boy running alongside, 'over burning sand and uneven roads for many hours together.'[15] She rode side-saddle 'dressed in the French manner' into the most remote corners of the city without ever meeting anything disagreeable, although she could not forget that the daughter of Mr Bokty, the Swedish consul, had been killed some years earlier by a rampaging

Albanian soldier. Her guardians rebuked her when she got mixed up with the return of the caravan from Mecca, but she felt no fear, only fascination as she watched 'the strange medley of pilgrims of all ages, sexes and colours pass'.

Cairo's layout was unsuitable for carriages but Muhammad 'Ali had imported from France a pretty berlin drawn by six horses and had built a fine road to his country estate at Shubra to which the carriage, and his wives, could be driven. Rossetti asked if the Baroness could borrow it, and then Mrs Rossetti and her mother (both ladies of the Levant) and Wolfradine were driven furiously down the road by the Arab coachman. The trip was accompanied by cries from the populace, swearing from the coachman, and loud laughter from her companions. The Baroness was terrified that they would run somebody down and rode back beside the coach rather than in it.[16] Concern for the local people runs through her recollections; she was often saddened by the lives of ordinary Egyptians.

Of course both ladies visited the Pyramids. Anne Katharine portrayed this as high romance. They set off before day-break by the light of *flambeaux* in a great party with 'heavily-armed Janissaries, English friends in splendid Turkish costume rich in scarlet and crimson, green and gold' and Turkish, Indian and Arab attendants 'with dark countenances and fantastic dresses'. She was 'the only humdrum among the whole, and perhaps the only one who could have walked in London without being mobbed.'[17] At the Pyramids she failed. 'I can truly say that those ladies who have accomplished the arduous task without feeling alarm, and without encountering difficulty,' she wrote—probably thinking of Julianna, Lady Belmore who had reportedly climbed up easily in 1817[18]—'must have had very differently constituted nerves to mine, and their faculties, both physical and mental, must have been far stronger.' Halfway she settled down 'veiling her cowardice under the pretence of conjugal obedience', *tête-à-tête* with Osman 'suspended between heaven and earth … looking over the valley of the Nile on one side and the immense deserts of Africa on the other, surrounded by Pyramids and tombs, in the company of a Scottish Turk.'

The Minutolis visited the Pyramids in a great party including the ladies of their host, all in Mamluk dress. How envious Anne Katharine would have been, but the Baroness was embarrassed rather than excited by the disguise.[19] Only the Baroness, of all the women, dared to enter the Pyramid and found the effort of climbing and creeping along fatiguing. She suspected that, despite her Turkish clothes, the guides guessed who she was and were extra considerate. Anne Katharine too had ventured inside. With Osman holding her hand she went 'up and down through passages, dark, steep and narrow, and more gloomy than imagination can fancy' until they reached the King's chamber, but was only too glad to get out.[20]

In mid-December 1820 when the Minutolis set off up the Nile, the Baron did everything to make the journey comfortable for his bride. Their boat had two commodious rooms with an ante-chamber for their domestics; a smaller boat was towed behind. They were accompanied by Dr Alessandro Ricci who had copied the wall paintings in Seti's tomb for Belzoni in 1817 and acted as draughtsman to W. J. Bankes when he travelled to Nubia with Henry Salt and others in 1818.[21] He doubled as draughtsman and physician. Their unreliable dragoman was an Albanian renegade.

Meeting contrary winds, the Minutolis took three weary weeks to reach Minya—a distance which on their return took them two days. One day the Baron wished to excavate near Hermopolis, and sent his wife on, planning to follow in the small boat. She spent the day reading, then realised that he was long overdue and that a rising wind was pushing them along so rapidly that the Baron and Dr Ricci would not be able to catch them up. She entreated the *ra'is* to lower the sails, but he pretended not to understand and they swept on until he anchored at nightfall. She slept uneasily and was woken by 'loud and lively vociferations'. Her maid reported that some Arabs had approached with ill intent. The Baroness suspected that the Albanian was trying to intimidate her and told him 'in a pretty firm tone' that she was 'by no means afraid of the banditti without, and that for those *on* the boat, she would know how to make herself respected by them'. After that the Baron's valet, 'an honest German', slept at the door of her cabin with a brace of loaded pistols, and she ordered him to fire at anyone who tried to disturb her.[22]

The Elwoods had a much less impressive boat when they set out from Bulaq on 7 May 1826. After their earlier experiences they had taken the precaution of having the *cangia* thoroughly scrubbed and purefied by their servants. Anne Katharine was nervous about river pirates, but they were either imaginary or otherwise occupied and she saw none.

At Beni Hasan they scrambled up to look at the tombs and admire the wall paintings. Their dragoman tried to hurry them away with warnings of *banditti* and wild beasts as the sun set 'under a flood of golden radiance and liquid amber'. Keeping a watchful eye for hyenas and robbers, Anne Katharine suddenly espied a footprint on the ground—that of a boot 'as if some true London dandy or dashing dragoon had just passed that way'.[23]

Both ladies watched Nile life flow past: a buffalo 'lolling and awkwardly disporting itself in the water', half a dozen storks rising heavily into the air at their approach, or 'the sudden splash that proclaimed a creeping crocodile winding his unwieldy lizard-like form along' had plunged into the river.[24] January is a better month than May to be on the river, as the Minutolis found: 'All nature seemed attired in its festal robe; the air embalmed with the richest perfume ... from the fields of beans that were then in blossom.'[25]

While the men armed themselves with fowling pieces, the Baroness, accompanied by a little negro boy, walked about the country botanising and collecting cresses and aromatic herbs in her basket. Sometimes they rode their donkeys along the bank, 'exciting, in no small degree, the curiosity of the inhabitants.' They ate well and, having a small library aboard, passed their evenings agreeably reading. On one walk she disturbed a Nile monitor but the huge creature, as startled as she, leapt past her into the river rather than devour her as she first thought.[26]

Near Asyut the Elwoods were hailed from the shore by a person in Turkish costume riding a camel. It was Gardner Wilkinson 'amusing himself with making a survey of the Nile'. He came aboard and took refreshment with them.[27]

The Elwoods met a boat laden with a cargo of elephant's tusks, ostrich feathers, gold dust and parrots, and both parties met several boats filled with negro slaves. The pity the Baroness felt for these slaves would, she said, have been less had she then known the state of destitution in which the people lived in their own country. Before they left Egypt the Minutolis themselves purchased a boy and took him to Prussia with them—perhaps the little boy who carried her basket beside the Nile.[28]

On 17 January 1821 the Minutolis reached Thebes. In the great hall at Karnak the Baroness was 'struck with silent astonishment'[29] as Amelia Edwards would be half a century later.[30] She mounted some steps and looked out across the temple area in 'the magic hues of the setting sun'. They spent several days visiting sites on both sides of the river. With the aid of a ladder, she climbed one of the colossi and was told the meaning of the inscriptions; she witnessed a battle between the wild dogs of the ruins and the great hawks of Upper Egypt over the entrails of a sheep. With Dr Ricci, who knew 'Belzoni's tomb' so well, she visited the Valley of the Kings. She remarked on the comparative affluence of the people of Gournu, who then as now lived off the excavations and the sale of antiquities.[31]

Anne Katharine described their arrival at Thebes with all her usual drama. They anchored on the west bank near the tents of Messrs Robert Hay and Joseph Bonomi who had been residing there for some time, 'amusing themselves' making excavations and discoveries. These two gentlemen, like Gardner Wilkinson, may well have regarded their activities as more serious than amusing. However they found her irresistible, not only to themselves but also to their Arab staff. Hay noted when they left a few days later that 'it was no small pleasure for me to have enjoyed the society of an Englishwoman even for a day as their like is not seen in this city—the Arabs thought her very pretty for they admire a fair skin and were much surprised at the attention we paid her—so different from the custom of the country— and it was amusing to see the attention paid her by the donkey men who seemed to vie with us in gallantry.'[32]

Immediately the Elwoods moored they were set upon by wild-looking natives offering curiosities for sale, among them a cat which was poked through the window. Had she been alive, said Anne Katharine, she would have been invaluable on account of the rats which infested their *cangia*, but 'this was a staid old mouser, of the time of Pharoah perchance, looking as demure and wise, however, as are tabbies of the present day, though probably 3000 years had rolled over her head in mummy form.' Mrs Elwood was one of the few writers who admitted to buying antiquities, indeed noting that their value was lost by the profusion.[33]

When they crossed the Nile, they were invited to dine with the *kashif* of Luxor.[34] Charles made excuses, saying that it was not the custom for English ladies to dine where none of their own sex were there to meet them. This did not dissuade the *kashif* who instead accompanied Colonel Elwood to the *cangia* with various followers to meet the English lady, and this strange and motley party went to look at the temple. It was nearly choked with huts, heaps of sand, mounds of rubbish, dirt and filth; with pigeon lofts in the walls, and the colossal figures at the entrance half-embedded in sand. Such was the 'confusion that reigned around' that the Elwoods found it difficult to understand the structure of the building. Anne Katharine was invited to the *kashif*'s house within the temple, and—by now forgetting her excuses—she went. They were offered coffee in the usual pretty cups and then the *kashif*, having first smoked himself, offered his pipe to his guest. Repressing her giggles, she explained that Englishwomen did not smoke; it was then offered on to Charles and their Indian servant.

Visiting Karnak, Anne Katharine was happy to boast that she was the first Englishwoman to see the spirited battle scenes which had been hidden for centuries until Mr Hay had unearthed them.[35] Later that day, back across the Nile, they were lionised around the sites by Hay and Bonomi. The next day at Medinet Habu they saw the fresh marks of a wolf's foot. Their guide casually explained that the animal had probably slept there that night and was still in the neighbourhood. Anne Katharine feared the animal might spring out at her at any moment. Perhaps this was rather more exciting than a full diet of antiquities.[36] On the doorway of one tomb she was thrilled to find the name of her brother, Herbert Curteis, who had been in Egypt seven years before on his way back from India. Back at the house of Yanni d'Athanasi, Mr Salt's agent, where several mummies were lined up against the walls, her imagination took flight again at the possibility of these 'lack-lustre eyes rolling in their orbs' or one of the mummies opening 'leathern jaws'.

The Elwoods departed eastward across the desert from Qena on camels on their journey out of Egypt. Esconced in her litter with the Colonel riding nearby, Anne Katherine dreamed of new adventures in India.[37]

On 24 January 1821 the Minutolis continued south. At Esna they became involved in a local fair; they climbed high in the temple at Edfu, and eventually reached Aswan, only to find their way to the second cataract blocked. The Egyptian army was on the move against Dongola and Muhammad Pasha (son-in-law of Muhammad 'Ali) insisted that he could not answer for the discipline of his Albanian troops cooped up on Philae, and would allow them to go no further.[38] Wolfradine befriended the women of Elephantine Island with whom she chatted and laughed with mutual appreciation and admired their satin-soft skins and their courage in crossing the Nile oblivious to crocodiles.[39]

As they returned to Cairo they met boatloads of soldiers. On one occasion, seeing Wolfradine almost alone on the bank, one group fired their guns and uttered such insulting exclamations that she did not venture again to leave the boat 'preferring a voluntary imprisonment to exposing herself a second time to a similar encounter'.[40]

Near Minya they were overtaken by the dreaded *khamsin*. Their boat rushed forward 'with such rapidity that they seemed to cut the air';[41] the sky assumed a red and fiery tinge and then darkened. The air was hot and suffocating and a cloud of sand blew into their faces. There was no way they could put ashore and they were driven at such great speed that they reached Bulaq in two days.

Having been up river for two and a half months, they spent a further six weeks in Cairo before making an agreeable voyage to Damietta with Colonel Drovetti. There they stayed with consul Basil Faker, for their plans to go to the Levant had been disrupted by the Greek revolution. Wolfradine visited the ladies in the harems of the local dignitaries and considered that the life of Muslim women was not unacceptable. 'They are perfect mistresses at home' with exclusive command of their slaves who accompanied them on visits—so sometimes they would be absent for several weeks, allowing 'themselves incredible liberty'.[42]

On her travels Wolfradine had acquired a menagerie, a beautiful ostrich and three gazelles, and on the journey to Alexandria her animals mixed 'as in Noah's ark'[43] with the goats, sheep, five Arabian horses and the semi-tame hyena of the other passengers. This 'afforded a lively scene, and contributed to break the monotony of the voyage' especially when the hyena escaped and chased a gazelle overboard. Happily, it was rescued by a sailor.

By now it was the plague season, the Baroness had not been well and the Minutolis wanted to leave Egypt, but they could not. War preparations had stopped all ships leaving Alexandria. Lodged in Ibrahim Pasha's palace on the seashore, they were served by the Pasha's own kitchens and for much of the time were accompanied by Isma'il Gibraltar, the Pasha's admiral, who, sitting opposite Wolfradine 'in his rich and magnificent dress', further familiarised himself with European customs: he had lived in Sweden for six years and had also visited London. Like Sarah Belzoni before her, the Baroness entertained herself with pet chameleons, and in the evenings the Minutolis walked along the shore collecting shells which lay on the sand 'in the greatest variety of colour and form'.[44] At last the Pasha said they might leave and on 17 July 1821 they 'bade adieu to Egypt and its coast soon vanished from their view'.

Notes

1   Baroness Wolfradine Menu von Minutoli, *Recollections of Egypt 1820–21* (London, 1827), hereinafter *Recollections*, pp. vi–viii.

2   Ibid., p. 3.

3   Anne Katherine Elwood, *Narrative of a Journey Overland by the Continent of Europe, Egypt and the Red Sea to India, including a Residence There and a Voyage Home, Vol. 1, 1825–1828* (London, 1830), hereinafter *Narrative*, p. 4.

4   Eliza Fay, *Original Letters from India Containing a Narrative of a Journey Through Egypt, 1779–1815*, (ed.) E. M. Forster (reissued London: Hogarth Press, 1986).

5   Marianna Starke, *Travels on the Continent written for the Use and Particular Information of Travellers* (London, 1820).

6   Elwood, *Narrative*, p. 93.

7   Ibid., p. 105.

8   Ibid., p. 108.

9   Ibid., pp. 110–11.

10 Ibid., p. 125.

11 Ibid., p. 139.

12 Ibid., p. 140.

13 W. von Minutoli, *Recollections*, p. 38.

14 Elwood, *Narrative*, p. 150.

15 Minutoli, *Recollections*, p. 39.

16 Ibid., p. 48.

17 Elwood, *Narrative*, p. 153.

18 R. R. Richardson, *Travels Around the Mediterranean in 1816–17* (London, 1822).

19 Minutoli, *Recollections*, p. 75.

20 Elwood, *Narrative*, p. 157.

21 M. Bierbrier (ed.). *Who was Who in Egyptology* (London, Egypt Exploration Society, 1995), p. 356.

22 Minutoli, *Recollections*, p. 103.

23 Elwood, *Narrative*, p. 171.

24 Ibid., p. 175.

25 Minutoli, *Recollections*, p. 108.

26 Ibid., p. 109.

27 Elwood, *Narrative*, p. 180.

28 Minutoli, *Recollections*, p. 180.

29 Ibid., p. 125.
30 Amelia Edwards, *One Thousand Miles up the Nile* (London: Longmans Green, 1877).
31 Minutoli, *Recollections*, p. 130.
32 BM Add. Mss. 31054, Robert Hay's diary for 1826.
33 Elwood, *Narrative*, p. 184.
34 Ibid.
35 Ibid., p. 209.
36 Ibid., p. Select Bibliography
Ghassemlou, A. R. et al. *People without a Country: The Kurds and Kurdistan*, edited by Gérard Chaliand, translated from the French by Michael Pallis. London: Zed Press,1980.
Jawad, Saad, "The Kurdish Revolt in Iraq: An Assessment of its Failure", Inter State, (UCW-Aberystwyth, UK), vol. 1, no. 2, 1981.
Kutschera, Chris, *Le Mouvement national Kurde*. Paris: [n.pb.], 1979.
37 Ibid., p. 227.
38 Minutoli, *Recollections*, p. 155.
39 Ibid., p. 158.
40 Ibid., p. 164.
41 Ibid., p. 169.
42 Ibid., p. 215.
43 Ibid., p. 226.
44 Ibid., p. 250.

12 ⌒ A Honeymoon in Egypt and the Sudan: Charlotte Rowley, 1835–1836

Peter Rowley-Conwy,[1] John Rowley-Conwy, Deborah Rowley-Conwy

Introduction

Charlotte Shipley-Conwy was born on 3 April 1811, the second child of Colonel William Shipley of Bodrhyddan, North Wales. On 24 June 1835 she married at St George's Church, Hanover Square, Captain the Honourable Richard Rowley, second son of Baron Langford of Summerhill, County Meath, Ireland.[2] For their extended honeymoon, they spent three months travelling through Spain, then sailed via Tangier and Malta to Alexandria, arriving on 28 November 1835. They were in Egypt and the Sudan until July 1836, after which they moved on to Palestine.

Charlotte and Richard (of whom we have no likeness) were not alone. Charlotte's brother William travelled with the honeymoon pair, as did a Mr Seymer, evidently a close friend but of whom we know nothing further. They left a number of records of their journey. Richard wrote a diary in tiny pencil handwriting; Charlotte wrote lengthy letters home, and produced two volumes of watercolours and pencil drawings; William wrote a series of letters home; and Seymer left a long diary.

None of the four travellers had a major interest in Egyptology, although they all bought various antiquities. Seymer is the only one who describes the temples they visited. Charlotte has left two faint pencil drawings of Meroë and one of Philae; she never bothered to colour either, although her drawings of individuals are usually brightly coloured and well executed. This was clearly where her interest lay.

At no point does any of them record why they chose to visit Egypt. No reader of the letters of Charlotte and William, however, can avoid the conclusion that adventure was the main motivation. They had visited a Panorama of the Luxor temples before leaving Britain, and this may have stimulated the idea. The travel experience as a whole rather than particular monuments was what impressed them; 'adventure travel' is an entirely sufficient motive for the trip.

Arrival: Alexandria and Cairo

Richard describes their arrival at Alexandria, his Irish origins creeping into his prose:

> Its approach by sea is far different from anything I ever saw before. The land on which it stands is as flat as the sea; it is impossible to distinguish the town until you get within 6 miles of it. The only thing you see at the distance is the pillar of Pompey so greatly noted for its beauty and its oldness and the masts of the ships in the port you see at a great distance & looks like a fairy wood.

On 2 December they departed for Cairo in boats arranged by Colonel Campbell (the consul-general). The first boat belonged to a Mr Harris,[3] the second to a Mr Galloway. Seymer enumerates the party: in addition to the four principal travellers, there were an English servant and a French maid (neither of them named); 'Mahmoud our Arab servant', and a janissary called Salem, lent to them by the British consul in Alexandria. Charlotte was entranced by Cairo:

> There never was a place so delightful as Cairo or so full of curious Sights. We are not near the end of them yet, though we have worked like horses, and on such creatures too, belonging to the Pasha. Out of his stables consisting of 1,000 horses we (great people as we are) may have any we like and they are brought to us with velvet and gold saddles and the bridles covered with silver gilt ornaments and with gold tassels. Each horse is attended by its own groom who runs by our side, though we gallop most of the time, in the streets particularly it is the fashion to go this pace, much to the annoyance of the foot passengers ... Nothing can be kinder than the Natives are to us. They always ask us into their houses to drink coffee and smoke a pipe. Only the former is offered to me.

They visited the pyramids at Giza and Saqqara. 'It was not till we arrived quite close,' writes Seymer, 'that we were impressed with the immense size of the pyramids.' Charlotte notes that 'the ascent is perfectly easy', but was much more interested in Saqqara:

> Three hours more riding brought us to the small Pyramids of Sakara, too late to see them so we slept in a mud hut belonging to a Frenchman and tolerably clean. These Pyramids cannot be ascended but in spite of the great difficulty, we all contrived to go inside, and I am the first Lady that has done so. You begin by lying quite flat feet foremost in a hole just big enough for me, & work your way in the Dark, crawling on yr. stomach for ab't 10 minutes. The rest of the journey is almost all performed on one's knees over very rocky ground, which exercise joined to the very confined air of the Tomb made me hotter than I believed it possible to be. We were well repaid by the curious Hieroglyphics & the very going in was great fun, the coming out up the hill rather too hard work to be quite pleasant.

Clearly it was the fact that she believed herself to be the first woman to enter, rather than the archaeological interest, that made this memorable.

St Catherine's Monastery to Qasr Ibrim and the Sudan

On 15 December they left Cairo, riding to Suez on camelback and camping for the first time in the desert. They set sail on 20 December, taking 6 days to cover the short distance to El Tur due to contrary winds; the only disaster occurred when the sole surviving fowl, that they had been saving for Christmas day, was eaten by a cat. The boat was small, and William noted that the only covered space was just large enough for four mattresses; there is no mention of where the servants slept.

At St Catherine's monastery, Charlotte was again most concerned with boldly going where few ladies had gone before:

> There is no door and we were hoisted up by a rope 40 ft long into a window. I never was made so much of in my life as I was by the Greek Superior. I am the second Lady that ever has been there and in consequence he loaded me with all sorts of presents & though he was past 70, he always called me his *Mother*, the only term of endearment or distinction the poor man knew. He gave me a bit of the *real* burning bush and after taking off my shoes, led me as a great favour into the room where was the Ground on which the Bush grew, and also to see St Catherine's Body. He was very proud of its keeping so well, 'no stinking bad stink', as he said. Of course, I performed the whole Pilgrimage, even mounting the 12,000 steps to the top of Mount Sinai, to the Rock under which Moses stood when he received the Law, & have in consequence received a Silver Ring, and a Paper, to certify that I have done all the proper things.

They re-embarked from El Tur on 3 January 1836, arriving at Quseir on 9 January and travelling over the desert to Luxor, where they arrived on 17 January passing many pilgrims bound for Mecca on their way. They were beginning to regard themselves as seasoned travellers, and were all thoroughly enjoying themselves. William wrote:

> Remember me most kindly to all Friends and do not tell them how glad I am not to be in their Society in London ... I wish you could see what figures R. & I are, with our hair cut as short as scissors can go, & our Beards & Brown Faces.

Charlotte explains why everyone had cut their hair short except her:

> I cannot tell you how happy we all are; no drawback of any sort or kind. Quite our only bore is occasioned by the various Creatures that eat us up. The rest of the party catch their lice quite comfortably, thinking nothing of them, but the sight of them still makes me feel very sick. Luckily those that inhabit my head do not abound like the others and therefore I am not obliged to cut off my Hair.

Luxor was initially a disappointment. 'I was rather disappointed at first sight in Carnak for the Panorama had collected in one spot all the Ruins that are scattered about,' wrote William; while Charlotte states that 'that odious Panorama quite spoilt Thebes for us'. The panorama was probably that of Catherwood, believed to have been on display in London in 1834 or 1835.[4]

Charlotte and William refer only briefly to the antiquities, but Seymer gives fuller descriptions. On 19 and 20 January they visited Karnak, and Seymer was impressed:

> Carnac quite came up to our expectations, highly as they had been raised by Wilkinson's descriptions. We wandered over the ruins having succeeded at last in getting rid of our cicerone. These ruins are not disfigured like those of Luxor by modern buildings. A few palm trees are scattered among them and there are beautiful peeps of the mountains through the different gateways. These gates are I think the most striking and beautiful objects in Egyptian architecture.

On 24 January they set sail to the south. Seymer briefly describes visits to the temples of Edfu, Philae, Kalabsha, Dakka, Sebua and Derr. On 6 February he states that they reached Qasr Ibrim, Seymer's diary entry reading only 'landed at Ibreem where there are remains of an old fortress containing also the ruins of a Xtian church'. This entry is of particular interest to one of the writers (PR-C), who has worked at Qasr Ibrim recording animal bones and plant remains in an attempt to understand the agricultural history of Nubia.[5] The next morning they returned downstream to Korosko, where the trip took a new turn. Charlotte wrote:

> Our great excitement is the change in our plans, instead of being satisfied like sober minded Travellers, with the 2nd cataract, we are actually going into the interior of Africa. Does this not sound fine? We are really going a month's journey from the cataract to Senaar ... Very few Europeans have been where we are going and not one Lady I believe has been beyond the 2nd cataract though there is not more difficulty than going up the Rhine.

They departed on camels from Korosko on 9 February, taking nine days to Abu Hamed. On the second day, they discovered that their water skins had leaked, reducing the amount of available water from 26 skins to 8. Charlotte takes up the story:

> We held a Grand Council of War on the occasion and as we could not agree, the decision was left to me, and so of course we came on, sometimes riding 14 hours and always 12 each day, under a Sun much hotter than I ever felt, even in Spain last year. I was not at all tired with all this ... Camel riding is much less fatiguing for a conveyance than any other, as from the size of the saddle you may vary your position ... and you have not even the trouble of holding the Bridle, all the Camels following the Leader exactly.

On arrival at Abu Hamed, Seymer noted that they 'lost no time in drinking copiously' from the Nile. They acquired a boat and set off to the south, staying at Berber from 25 to 28 February.

Between Korosko and Abu Hamed they had 'made acquaintance with a Moorish slave merchant, who thought that Charlotte was a princess: at Abu

Hamed they were 'very well received by the Sheik of the Ababde who had been told by the Moor that Mrs. Rowley was the daughter of the King of England. ' This disinformation was to follow them for a long time; much later, in the desert between Wad Medani and the White Nile, William mentioned that:

> I am afraid we do not give a very high idea of the English Royal Family, for as such we pass. In all the Villages in which we halted between Waddy Medyn and the White River Charlotte had a regular Levee, the whole of the inhabitants coming to kiss her Hand.

After leaving Berber, Seymer describes a visit they made on 2 March to:

> ... some very curious pyramids. The first are about half an hour's distance from the river. The next group is another half hour further inland, and there is another group about ten minutes walk from these last. These pyramids are all built of stone, in other respects they are unlike any we have ever seen. They appear each to have had a small temple connected with them, the cellar of which joined one of the sides of the pyramid but apparently without communicating with its interior ... They are ornamented with hieroglyphics very much defaced. We traced on one or two of them the Egyptian emblem of the winged globe.

Charlotte provides two very faint pencil drawings of these pyramids, labelled on the back 'Meroe', which is clearly where they were.

Four days further on the party split for three days, as Seymer says showing off a little Arabic, 'for the first and (*inshallah*) only time'—and so it proved. William describes the circumstances:

> Seymer's servant had so violent a bilious attack, as to put his moving the next day quite out of the question. Charlotte, much as she wished to see the Ruins, would not hear of leaving him to be doctored by her Maid. Of course, R would not leave *her* so Seymer and I had to go on alone. The R's met us three days after, higher up the River bringing with them the poor man who was still far from well. The Doctor here said that all had been done quite right but thought it better to bleed him, and now he is quite well again. S and I had a most interesting ride through by far the wildest Country we have seen. No traces of Man, and plenty of wild beasts. We saw however nothing but Antelopes and Gazelles which managed to keep just out of Shot.

Seymer describes these 'ruins' in more detail, and with reference to the maps and descriptions in Adams' *Nubia: Corridor to Africa*[6] they can be identified as probably Musawwaret es-Sufra. After three and a half hours more riding, they came to more ruins. Seymer continues:

> These consist of four temples well situated on the side of a hill, besides other heaps of stone indicating other buildings of these temples. Three are in the Egyptian style, covered with sculpted figures and hieroglyphs. The fourth is Grecian, I should imagine from a very late date. The pillars are walled up which very much injures their effect. Between them are square and round windows

very much ornamented. The style of the round windows is so much that of the low ages that I should have been inclined to think this might have been a Xtian building had we not seen the Egyptian winged globe over the doorway. There are some quarries in the mountain above the temple and small caves frequented by wild beasts.

These appear to be the ruins of Naqa.

Khartoum and Sennar

The party reached Khartoum on 14 March. William describes the place:

It is really a very respectable Town, & improving every day under the Administration of Couschid Pasha. He has not yet returned from his annual slave hunt, which has been remarkably successful this year, he already having sent down 7,000. All the able bodied men are drilled for soldiers, which they like very well, so much so that in a couple of years they are sent to assist in catching their old friends, at which they are remarkably handy, and hardly ever desert. The Old Men, Boys, and Women are given to the soldiers as part of their pay, which is much in arrears. This makes slaves very cheap; our servant has bought a boy for less than £2 ...

They left Khartoum on 16 March, arriving in Sennar on 23 March after meeting Khurshid Pasha at Wad Medani. Charlotte writes:

We had not much to see at Senaar; it is not now as large a town as Khartoum, but the sail up to it was pretty enough & very interesting to a Beast lover like myself, the bank of the River being alive with monkeys and Green Parrots and the stream itself being full of Crocodiles and Hippopotomi.

They did not start their return journey without regret, being tempted to continue still further in various directions, including Abyssinia. Turn back they did, however, Charlotte lamenting 'we have at last turned our steps northwards, an act of no little merit on our part when only 12 days from the capital of Abyssinia'. But at Wad Medani she records that Khurshid Pasha had a further suggestion:

... we have had a very tempting offer from the Pasha, to see a Country which not only has never been visited by any European, but where the Turks even have never set a foot. It is the country a few days on the other side of the White River, and still unconquered. The Pasha sends an expedition into that Neighbourhood every year, to cut down wood, & catch slaves, & this time, they are going higher up into that Country than ever before, among the Cannibal Negroes—The Pasha ensures our safety, & would put a part of the Army, which consists of 3,000 men, under our Orders—The Negroes never think of shewing any fight, but run away at the 1st sight of a Gun; we should not certainly run any hint of risk, but we must give up all idea of the Scheme, on Account of the Heat ...

The heat had never daunted Charlotte before; perhaps even she now felt that they had travelled far enough.

From Khartoum to Cairo

They left Khartoum on 16 April and sailed to Shendi, then headed north west by camel to strike the Nile again on 30 April. On 1 May, Seymer mentions a visit to Jabal Barkal. They sailed on down the Nile, stopping at Argo on 12 May to see the recumbent statues, and visiting the temple at Soleb on 16 May. From here they took to camels again, riding now mostly at night to by-pass the cataracts. They experienced a violent sandstorm, graphically described by Charlotte:

> The time we roughed it was one night in the Desert when we fell in with the terrible Khamsyn Wind. We started from the Palm Trees where we had spent the heat of the Day at about six in the Evening, the wind then being what we should call in England tremendous, but an hour more shewed us what wind could be, the Dust so high that it was impossible to see half a yard before one of the Camels was unable to stand against it, so we got off and remained the Whole Night, lying on our stomachs, our faces buried in the Sand, and our Noses bleeding from the difficulty of breathing. All this was nothing to what we suffered from the want of Water, our Caravan somewhere with the Skins & we had with us only a bottle full, which we did not dare drink as there was more than a chance of the Caravan losing its way and not coming up to us the next Day. Our mouths were so parched that the Dust which got in could not turn to mud. The Wind fell when the Sun rose & thank God! Our guide returned with Water & this ended all our discomforts.

They then rejoined their original boat at Wadi Halfa, apparently with some relief; Seymer, using her Christian name for the only time in his entire diary, mentions that the previous night 'poor dear Charlotte suffered much from the neighbourhood of a dead camel and from her bed being made on a ledge of rocks'. He mentions also that they 'found our crew delighted to see us having expected us two months sooner'.

Sailing north, they visited Abu Simbel. Seymer felt that the temple was 'the finest remains we have seen on the Nile, always excepting Thebes'. They stopped at the temples they had not seen previously, namely Gerf Hussein, Dendoor, Kertassi and Dabod, arriving back at Philae on 30 May. On 1 June they sailed down the cataract and on past Kom Ombo and Edfu, arriving at Luxor on 7 June, from where Charlotte wrote:

> Here we are returned to Thebes (of which we got to talk as if it were a home spot) having performed our journey of 3,000 miles into the Interior of Africa, without a misfortune of any sort & excepting a little hard work in the violent Heat, no Hardship whatsoever.

So much, by then, for the sandstorm and the decomposing camel. On 14 June they left Luxor, visiting among others the temples at Dendera and

Abydos, reaching Cairo on 7 July, after an absence of nearly seven months.

A View of Ancient Egypt

The party's attitude towards the archaeological record was straightforward: it was to be enjoyed, and if possible purchased and taken home. Soon after arriving, Charlotte wrote:

> Nothing can exceed the kindness of Col Campbell ... getting us permission to carry out of the country any curiosity we buy, a thing which the Travellers here are not allowed to do as the Pasha is forming a museum. Think of my luck the other day, merely turning up the earth with a stone, near Cleopatra's Needle. I found three very old coins. With this encouragement I shall dig like a Lion at Thebes.

A couple of days later she mentions the prices of various everyday commodities:

> We mean to save a mint of money in this cheap country where eggs are 1/2d pr dozen, kids 1/0 and sheep 1/6. Boats and everything else in proportion. Of the antique green figures we have got 6 for 2d.

At Luxor she ran into a problem:

> We picked up a great many small and common antiquities, the only ones to be had. The Pasha's orders are so strictly obeyed that *even Money* will not induce these Arabs to excavate, or indeed sell any large object already above ground; we have got scent of three lovely Mummies & have begged Col Campbell to get us leave to take them away, & trust we shall find the order on our return.

Sure enough, on her return through Luxor she notes that: 'We have been detained here 4 or 5 days about the purchase of two Mummies. We got with great difficulty permission from the Pasha to buy them, not that he cares for Antiquities, but because he is making a Museum. '—An interesting distinction! Outward bound through Luxor, they sought to buy antiquities illegally; Seymer states that they camped in tents on the west bank: 'Our principal object in this move was to get the Arabs to bring us antiquities at night, and to ship them on board our boat at once, as there is difficulty now in carrying away any good bits of antiquity. '

The attitude of the party towards standing monuments was ambiguous. At Saqqara, Seymer mentions that 'there is also a great deal of mischief done by scribblers, among whom I did not perceive the usual proportion of English. ' At Medinet Habu, Richard and Charlotte joined the ranks of the scribblers, where the graffito 'R. Rowley Charlotte Rowley 1836' can be seen on a pillar in the second court immediately to the right of the entrance into the hypostyle hall. We have not seen their graffiti elsewhere in Egypt; but after leaving Egypt they travelled in the Levant, and the interior of the treasury in Petra bears all their names including Seymer's.

A View of Contemporary Egypt

The views of contemporary Egypt were much more complex, and it is interesting to see the changes that their perceptions (particularly Charlotte's) underwent. On 6 December, just a few days after their arrival in Egypt, Seymer's diary contains this entry:

> Went to the slave market, very well supplied, all negroes. Shown one woman who was considered a great beauty, magnificent eyes, but owing probably to our prejudice against her complexion we could not admire her altogether.

By the time they reached Sennar, this had changed completely; Charlotte describes how:

> An Italian medical man took us into his house … He has two black and one white wife, the former quite beautiful, you will hardly believe that we are all agreed in thinking black the prettiest colour & are rather disgusted at the sight of washy Europeans. I wish we could make others of the same opinion on our return.

Charlotte's attitude to the sight of naked children underwent a similar transformation, as did her reactions to her visits to harems. Her description of her visit to the Governor's harem in Quseir reflects a degree of nervousness; but by the time she visited Khurshid Pasha's harem at Wad Medani she was fully in command of the situation:

> I went yesterday to the Pasha's Harem and a most interesting visit it was. It consisted of one lawful Wife and 46 Circassians, Abyssinians etc etc. The first is an ugly Lady of high rank, whom he married for her money, the others are almost all beautiful, though of an unhealthy white colour. I stayed 3 Hours with them and thought I had thoroughly done the civil thing but all complained of the shortness of my visit & the Pasha who came in invited me to come and live with his Wives during my stay at Waddy Medyn, & upon my refusing to do so told me that I must stay with them from Sunrise to Sunset, or he and his women would be vexed.
>
> On his entrance to the Harem, all the women went out to receive him, *the* wife sat down at a distance from him. One who had a Child stood with her Arms crossed on the Divan & the others knelt, even the [Italian] Doctor's wife who went with me knelt the whole time, & they all seemed much astonished at my treating the Pasha like an Equal.
>
> The women were magnificently dressed, their heads covered with Skull Caps made of diamonds, notes of gold tissue and large cashmeer shawls round their waists. His favourite at present is a Georgian, whom he bought two months ago, at Cairo for £1,000. She has finer Eyes and more regular features than any Creature I ever saw. Her features are formed quite like those of a statue, but she has the same dead white complexion.

The gentlemen did not, of course, visit any harems and they make no mention of their views of the local womenfolk. Charlotte does record that the offer of emulating some of the Italian medical and military men was made: 'Nothing can be kinder than the Natives are to us, they have offered to the gentlemen as many Wives as they like, if they will but settle here. '

Retrospect

The long trip was clearly a remarkable—and hugely enjoyable—experience for Charlotte and her party. They were not particularly interested in Egyptology or archaeology; the monuments are usually described as a neutral backdrop, dutifully rather than eagerly visited. Although Seymer apparently had a genuine interest in the Sudanese Meroitic monuments, Charlotte's interest was most aroused when she believed herself to be among the first European ladies to visit a site. The descriptions of Charlotte and William, and Charlotte's drawings, however, testify to the impact that the foreign manners and customs of contemporary Egypt had on the party. The impact of early travellers upon the archaeological record of Egypt has been frequently discussed; perhaps the impact of travel in Egypt and the Sudan upon the manners, customs and perceptions of the nineteenth-century British is something worthy of further exploration.

Notes

1 We would like to thank Angela Tucker Thompson for information on Catherwood's Panorama, Deborah Manley for information about fellow travellers, and Gabrielle Rowley-Conwy for her photographic assistance.

2 N. Tucker, 'Bodrhyddan and the families of Conwy, Shipley-Conwy and Rowley-Conwy, part II', *Journal of the Flintshire Historical Society* 20 (1962), pp. 1–38.

3 Perhaps Anthony Charles Harris (1790–1869), merchant and dealer in Egyptian antiquities. (See W. R. Dawson and E. P. Uphill, *Who was Who in Egyptology* (London: Egypt Exploration Society, 1972), p. 133.) Thanks to Deborah Manley for this suggestion.

4 See paper in this volume on F. Catherwood.

5 P. Rowley-Conwy, 'Nubia AD 0–550 and the "Islamic" agricultural revolution: preliminary botanical evidence from Qasr Ibrim, Egyptian Nubia', *Archéologie du Nil moyen* 3 (1989), pp. 131–8.

6 W. Y. Adams, *Nubia: Corridor to Africa* (Princeton: Princeton University Press, 1977).

Part Four

Artists and Photographers

13 ∾ The Unknown Nestor L'Hôte

Diane Sarofim Harlé

The Artist

At Cologne[1] in August 1804[2] a boy was born to François Isidore L'Hôte, a Custom House officer and to Zoé Dequen, housewife. The infant was named Nestor. Both parents, of modest origin, could hardly imagine that one day their son would become one of the companions of Jean-François Champollion, the 'Father of Egyptology' and that three times he would travel to Egypt: once with Champollion (1828–30), and twice on his own (1838–39 and 1840–41). For those two trips he had been asked by the French Government to finish the recording of the Egyptian temples started by Champollion. Yet that bright, talented and industrious young man died in Paris on 24 March 1842, poor and forgotten.[3]

As a painter, Nestor L'Hôte is completely unknown despite having exhibited three paintings at the Salon in 1833.[4] He is mentioned by the authors of a book on the painter Jean-Baptiste Couvelet (1772–1830).[5] The interesting but brief monograph on Nestor L'Hôte by Mme J. Vandier d'Abbadie[6] reproduces mainly texts and drawings of the Department of Manuscripts of the Bibliothèque nationale but gives few examples of the watercolours and drawings of the Egyptian Antiquity Department of the Louvre Museum[7] or of the texts, drawings, watercolours and paintings in the Gréhant collection.

For the last eight years Jean Lefebvre, the Curator of the libraries of Laon, and myself have gone through over a thousand documents whether they be family archives (Gréhant-Dudeauville), the manuscripts of the Bibliothèque nationale or those in the Archives of the Institute. Our work has also brought to light, amongst the papers of Jean-François Champollion at the Bibliothèque nationale of Paris, the diary or logbook that L'Hôte kept whilst in Egypt (1828–30).[8] As to his artistic production we have worked on the two albums bought by the Egyptian Department in 1957 as well as on other drawings, watercolours and oil paintings belonging to the family and to collectors. We have already published many articles[9] and a book on the first voyage of Nestor L'Hôte to Egypt comprised of letters (mainly addressed to his parents as these are more spontaneous), diaries, drawings and watercolours of the same period (1828–30).[10] Whilst preparing this book we started working on the next which will correspond to the second and third trips to Egypt. This second book will bring to light L'Hôte as an adult in his own right, offer another dimension to the artist and, last but not least, show the work of the Egyptologist. It will also be an informal picture of Egypt during the reign of Muhammad 'Ali.

L'Hôte was not the only painter of the Franco–Tuscanian Expedition whose name has fallen into the depths of oblivion. Others include Alexandre Adolphe Duchesne (*b*.1797),[11] François-Edouard Bertin (1791–1871)[12] and Pierre-François Lehoux (1803–83).[13] It is with these three artists that L'Hôte became friendly in Egypt. L'Hôte had a complex which was unjustified: although his pictorial education was not as brilliant as that of the other three Parisian artists, nevertheless it was as thorough. His scholarship was done at Charleville-Mézières where his father had been appointed in 1815. At that time Jean-Marie Couvelet, who had been a student of David, was teaching drawing and painting at the College of Mézières. That artist had very rigorous precepts and he taught Nestor L'Hôte drawing and painting techniques; Couvelet encouraged him to copy the works of old masters as had been done throughout France since the creation of the Academy by Charles Lebrun in the seventeenth century. We know practically nothing of those youthful years, except that L'Hôte probably copied a lot of Denon's etchings. From the period between 1827 when he was appointed to the Paris Customs office and 1828, when he left for Egypt, we have catalogued two paintings: an excellent self-portrait kept in the family and a good copy of the portrait of an eighteenth-century artist Jean Baptiste Berthélémy (1743–1811) painted by Antoine Vincent (1746–1816). In Paris, L'Hôte probably wandered often through the Louvre Museum since he was living just on the other side of the Seine at 15, quai Malaquais. During his trip in Egypt, he spoke as a connoisseur when he wrote about Le Lorrain, Poussin, Cimabue, Giotto, Leonardo da Vinci, Raphaël and made pertinent analogies between their works and the landscape and the people he saw in Egypt.

When the Franco–Tuscanian Expedition left for Egypt, L'Hôte and the three artists faced extremely hard working conditions. One understands the excitement Champollion felt, and the pace at which he lived, so that every temple could be studied and drawn. For the young artists this imposition was a completely different matter, since they had volunteered on condition that they would have free time to do their own work and fill their own portfolios so as to exploit financially what work they had done once they were back in France. Nestor L'Hôte had joined under the same conditions as the others, for he had the intention of publishing the record of his trip with illustrations in *Un Voyage pittoresque*, as it is called, to which he added daily drawings and paintings of everything he saw.

Oil-colours are not the best medium to use when painting the vast skies of Egypt that change from one season to the other, from one hour to another, from one instant to another. The climatic conditions, with the merciless sun and devastating sand and wind, were not ideal. Watercolour has the double advantage of drying quickly, and lends itself to the haste with which our artists tried to paint during the little time Champollion had allotted them. Always rushed, they therefore worked either early in the morning just after sunrise or in the evening before sundown. Just by looking at L'Hôte's watercolours one can understand that he is a professional— little or no pencil tracing beforehand, little or no gouache. A transparency linked to the boldness of the colours demonstrates the mastery with which L'Hôte used this medium.

The drawings of L'Hôte kept at the Louvre show the same mastery as the watercolours. Drawn on all kinds of paper and in different scales, they are of a remarkable quality. The use of criss-crossed lines gives power as well as foreground framing to the views, and suggests the zoom of a camera. He always shows foreground, a very modern concept. In the few portraits or human studies that we still have, L'Hôte uses either a continuous line or shading to bring out not only the general aspect of his model but also the characteristics of each.

The Panorama

Upon arrival in Egypt, L'Hôte was completely dazzled by what he saw from inside the Citadel of Cairo; he wrote:[14]

Cairo, 23 September 1828

Before being admitted to the audience of the Habib Effendi,[15] we entered a large lobby, a kind of waiting-room, filled with people sitting on the floor, petitioners, cavas[16] and officers attached to the household. Large windows were open on the countryside and we discovered, when looking out with but little attention at first, the most magnificent panorama that exists in the world. Nothing that we know in Europe, either by description or by painting, could give an idea of that extraordinary view. Never had my admiration been so deeply excited. I thought I was dreaming Aladdin and the marvellous tales of A Thousand and One Nights, I thought I saw an ideal world, unknown. In front of me in a single frame, I had all that my imagination for ten years had imagined as most magical and sublime.

It was the time of the day when the sun, having lost its greatest power, still threw a bright light and enveloped the atmosphere with a vague hue, a luminous and speckled mist which appears in certain regions of the globe. Imagine, beyond this sparkling gauze, an unlimited plain crossed by a large river which, like a silver blade, appears out of the haze along the horizon and on your right bathes the walls of twenty palaces; beyond the river, on this side, are the Pyramids of Giza whose proud mass has braved centuries and survived destruction; in front and towards the background are the Pyramids of Sakkarah, much older; a girdle of sand surrounds them and cuts off the horizon on that side; beyond the Pyramids is a pleasant plain, intersected by numerous divisions of the river into so many ribbons, from which rise minarets, villages and thick woods. To the left, the Mokattam, an arid chain of mountains that separate the desert from Egypt. The desert crosses this dike and already spreads from the mountain to the river; at one time this sandy plain was fertile and inhabited, today it is deserted and dotted with ruins; not a tree, but tombs, minarets, factories and abandoned forts. Nearer to you, these ruins appear in their actual dimensions and form pleasant groupings detached in their semi-tints against the background. Nearer yet is the necropolis of the caliphs, the city of tombs, and an immense vaulted aqueduct; then minarets, domes, platforms and at last the town of Cairo at your feet, so elegant, its bold minarets, its thousands of terraces, and its enormous mosques of which a vivid colour brings out the entire picture and makes remote the immense perspective. That is a detail of the tableau we have before our eyes, but the general effect, the grandeur, the harmony of this magnificent tableau, is what strikes us with a kind of stupor; but to depict it words fail, and it would be necessary in order to render the magic of this marvel, to borrow the sun's rays and trace the painting with gold and azure.

This long and vivid description corresponds to the view one had from the height of the Citadel of Cairo. All along his voyage up to Nubia and back L'Hôte dreamed of painting (from this place) a Panorama that he could exhibit in Paris.

The Panorama had been invented by a Scotsman, Robert Barker, at the end of the eighteenth century and was first shown in Edinburgh. Nevertheless it was an American licence of Robert Fulton's that was used in France by Mr and Mrs James Thayer at the beginning of the nineteenth century: two domes were constructed on the edge of boulevard Montmartre, on the right of the new theatre Les Variétés. They were separated by a passage which even now bears the name of the Panorama Passage. The painter Pierre Prévost (1764–1823), who conceived the first Panorama, became Thayer's partner for the construction of a new hall between the rue de Neuve-Saint-Augustin and the boulevard des Capucines. But the taste for this kind of spectacle had abated and a perfected system replaced it, which was the Diorama. Created in 1822, a year before Prévost died, it was the invention of two Frenchmen, Daguerre and Bouton, with whom Prévost had previously worked. The Diorama permitted the artist to paint on a flat or slightly curved surface whilst the first Panoramas called for a circular painting.

L'Hôte wrote to his parents from Cairo on 20 January 1830:[17]

Think that we have worked practically non-stop; fogs, cloudy days, a nearly continuous north wind have delayed us; however we have nearly twenty oil studies of a good size, 12 or 15 sheets of drawings, and a great number of sketches; all this done with all the care of which we are capable of, and we have the most beautiful Panorama of the world in our pocket.

Further on in this letter Nestor L'Hôte is able to give a financial report to his father:

Our stay in Cairo, after the departure of Mr Champollion and our Panorama, will have cost us approximately 100 écus each. The advantages which we shall receive from those 100 écus, will apparently be very handsome. Some say that the Panorama can make our fortune, but I stick to the possibilities based on the population of Paris, according to which we could [...] on 300 or 400 [...] each, considering two years of life to the Panorama.

In the same letter, but written on 23 January, he writes:

Mr Mimaut[18] will come today to see our studies of the Panorama. I have told you, I think, that he was a passionate amateur of fine arts. He has, he tells us, made us known in France and has already informed the Minister ...

In the copy of the diary of Nestor L'Hôte done by his younger brother Edouard ca. 1870 we note these few lines:

The Panorama of Cairo has never been done on a large scale. It had been understood by MM. Bertin, Lehoux and l'Hôte that the project painted on a reduced scale, would belong to the last survivor. M. Lehoux, rue neuve des Mathurins, 12, was the last legitimate owner by right of survivorship. (I have learned that Mr Lehoux has since died, but I have no further word of the Panorama.)

At that very time Lehoux was still living at 7, rue Godot de Moroy in Paris, but Edouard L'Hôte was a provincial and did not know of Lehoux's change of address.

The Portrait of the Pasha

The story begins at the time when Champollion was in Alexandria waiting for a ship to take him back to France, whilst Bertin, Lehoux and L'Hôte, awaiting another ship, were in Cairo quietly at work on their Panorama.

A letter from Champollion written on 10 September 1829 excited them:[19]

Gentleman ... His Serene Highness the Pasha, has had the kindness of sending me on the feast of [...] a very nice State sword, and last night has shown the most eager desire to have his portrait, as well as that of Ibrahim, painted by your talented brushes. It occurs to me that you would be quite disappointed if you could not take back to Europe the faithful images of these two men on whom the eyes of the civilised world are fixed. I have thought, therefore, I might answer for your willingness, and of your zeal; it is understood that upon your arrival, His Highness agrees to pose for the necessary time. Distribute between you the roles, and perform the play quickly and well. Arrive therefore, grind your colours, wash your brushes and be prepared to receive the first homage a Pasha has paid to fine arts! It is a revolution in favour of painting. You have the honour of accomplishing it, etc, etc ...

On 23 September the three young artists, following Champollion's orders, left for Alexandria where Muhammad 'Ali was most often in residence. On their way, during a stop at Fouah, L'Hôte notes:

... at the separating point of the Alexandria canal and the Rosetta branch, a violent wind kept us tied up to the embankment; we saw the Pasha aboard his ship. He was en route for Cairo, sailing from Alexandria through Rosetta where he had spent a few days. I knew he was expected in Cairo, as we had seen the cannons of the Citadel being charged, but I did not think that he would arrive so soon. The letter of Champollion is dated of the 10th, we were expected on the 15th; he [Champollion] has probably offered our excuses to the Pasha who might have expected us; there will be time to make amends for all this, for I do want to paint the portrait of this personage. Ibrahim is in Alexandria and we shall see him there after our Panorama is finished.

Thus destiny and bad climatic conditions made them miss their appointment with the Pasha. A few months later, on 20 January 1830, meeting Mr Mimaut in Cairo, L'Hôte writes:[20]

He spoke of the Pasha's portrait, which had been in question, and we said that for us it was a great pleasure and much honour, but to expect the Pasha's return would probably take us too far out of our way and make us miss the frigate; it is then that he said that the Pasha would come specially for that.

But the Pasha never met them either in Cairo or in Alexandria and they were finally able to leave in February 1830 aboard the royal brig 'la Comète'.

In 1838 L'Hôte returned to Egypt on an official mission. He was to complete Champollion's work. He lived for a while in Thebes, but by mid-August, weakened by dysentery, he was obliged to return to Cairo where began the great adventure of Muhammad 'Ali's portraits, the project which had begun during the time of Champollion.

On 15 September, L'Hôte started to write a very long letter to his parents that continues to the beginning of November 1838.[21]

The Pasha being in Cairo, I paid him a visit accompanied by the consul; he remembered at the same time the voyage of Champollion and the proposition that had been made then to paint the portrait of His Highness; I thought I might put my little talent at his disposition, and it was agreed that I should start work immediately; a few days later I had my first sitting.

In the same letter he describes those sittings with a lot of humour. The half-length portrait that he did must have had a certain success for he continues: 'He now asks me for a portrait seated on a horse, life-size: an equestrian portrait of 12 feet ... !' On 15 October he notes:

The day before his departure and after the final sitting, the Pasha rode in front of me to give me an idea of his staying-power as a rider; in haste I made a sketch after which I shall do the portrait in large scale.

1st November

As for the equestrian portrait, I am preparing a frame 10 feet high and 8 feet wide, and have ordered that the dazzling saddle of velvet and gold be put at my disposition, and the favourite horse of His Highness. I am getting ready for the preliminary studies of the site, the accessories and finally the horse; the sketch or project on a small scale is nearly finished and I shall bring it to France as well as a copy of the bust portrait.

A small painting in the Gréhant family corresponds without doubt to the equestrian portrait, but we believed that both full-sized portraits were in Egypt. It was therefore with great interest that we saw in Gaston Wiet's book on Muhammad 'Ali, a text illustrated by a reproduction. The text indicated that this illustration was a lithograph of Muhammad 'Ali as a horseman, signed Léveillé, and that it had been acquired in 1840 by the Cabinet des Estampes of the Bibliothèque nationale. According to Gaston Wiet this lithograph had often been reproduced. In the correspondence between Gaston Wiet and Jean Schlumberger, a well-known French author and member of the Institute, we read that a painting that had surely been the model for the lithograph was kept at the castle of Guizot at Val-Richer (Calvados). There follows a description of the painting: 'It is a large painting of nearly three metres, remounted on one of the walls. A cartouche, today destroyed bore the mention: 'Given to Mr Guizot[22] by Mr de Lavalette.'[23] 'It is probable,' wrote Mr Schlumberger to Mr Wiet: 'that de Lavalette was at the time but an intermediary. My grandmother,' Schlumberger continued 'Mrs Witt-Guizot, used to tell us that Muhammad 'Ali had offered sumptuous presents, including magnificent riding horses at the Guizot residence in Paris. The Minister did not believe in accepting such gifts; nevertheless a beautiful embroidered saddle remains,[24] which is to-day at Val-Richer.'

There follows a reasonably precise description of the painting, of great importance. The painting appparently corresponded to the little oil that was in the Gréhant family (relatives of Nestor L'Hôte). We employed all the patience and the perseverance of Sherlock Holmes to find the present-day owners of the portrait to succeed in seeing the painting. It was indeed the equestrian portrait of Muhammad 'Ali, bearing the signature of Nestor L'Hôte with the date 1839 in the lower left-hand corner. The painting, although entirely glued to the wall, is of a rare quality. Considering the size and the conditions in which it was painted, this is one of the best portraits of the Pasha and attests to the great pictorial abilities of L'Hôte.

Conclusion

We know that our information is quite often full of historical gaps and also of contradictions, when it comes to French painter-travellers. In 1992, an exhibition was held in Paris, named 'Souvenirs de Voyage' and organised by the Department of Graphic Arts of the Louvre Museum,[25] which we hope has made the public conscious of those gaps in that particular field. In the near future we should be able to offer a more complete view of this first half of the nineteenth century, not only from the point of view of Egyptology,[26] but also from that of the story of art and the history of mankind.[27]

Notes

1   Cologne was within the boundaries of Napoleon's France.

2   The month of August is given by Hector Horeau in his excellent biography, *Notices biographiques: Nestor l'Hôte* in *La Revue de l'Orient* (1843–46), hereinafter *Notices biographiques*, pp. 225–8, and Madame Vandier d'Abbadie indicates the twenty-fourth day of the month. Cf. Note 6.

3   W. Dawson and E. Uphill, *Who Was Who in Egyptology* (London, 1972), pp. 177–8.

4   *Explications des ouvrages de Peintures, sculpture, architecture et lithographie des artistes vivans, exposées au Musée royal le 1er mars 1833* (1833), p. 115.
    — 'Une vue de la Citadelle du Caire et de la grande mosquée dite El-Soultan Hassan, prise du chemin de Boulaq.
    — Une rue du Caire.'
    — Un portrait étude.'

5   E. Baudson et H. Labaste, *Un artiste ardennais: le peintre J. B. Couvelet et son temps (1772–1830)* (Mézières-Charleville, 1934), pp. 59–62.

6   J. Vandier d'Abbadie, *Nestor L'Hôte (1804–1842) choix de documents conservés à la Bibliothèque Nationale et aux Archives du Louvre*, préface de Rosalind L. B. Moss (Leiden, 1963).

7   Acquired in 1957 and registered under the number E. 25423 a and b.

8   Bibliothèque Nationale. *Nouvelles acquisitions françaises* (20 377). Written between 1830 and 1833.

9   D. Harlé, 'Nestor L'Hôte, dessinateur de Champollion: deux albums inédits d'aquarelles et de dessins' in *La Revue du Louvre et des Musées de France* 4 (Oct 1990), pp. 272–4; J. Lefebvre, *Voyages sur le Nil avec Champollion*, Catalogue d'exposition (Laon, 13 Oct 1990–5 Jan 1991), pp. 92–7; D. Harlé, 'Aquarelles et dessins inédits de Nestor L'Hôte, dessinateur et compagnon de Champollion' in *Actes du Colloque international célébrant le bicentenaire de la naissance de Jean-François Champollion, l'Égyptologie et Champollion, Grenoble 29 novembre–1er décembre 1990* (Grenoble, 1994), pp. 149–59; 'Nestor L'Hôte ami et compagnon de Champollion' in *Atti VI Congresso internazionale di egittologia* (Turin, 1993), vol. II, pp. 167–77, tav. III, 1–2; *Le Ramesseum de Nestor L'Hôte* in *Memnonia, bulletin édité pour la sauvegarde du Ramesseum* (Cairo, 1990–91), Vol. 1, pp. 67–9.

10 D. Harlé et J. Lefebvre, *Sur le Nil avec Champollion. Lettres, journaux et dessins inédits de Nestor L'Hôte. Premier voyage en Égypte 1828–1830*, préface Christiane Ziegler (Caen-Orléans: Éditions Paradigme, 1993).

11 (1882), 464.

12 Chavignerie and Auvray, *Dictionnaire des artistes de l'Ecole française*, p. 80.

13 Ibid., pp. 983–4; *Dictionnaire des Contemporains* (1893), p. 962; E. Bénézit, *Dictionnaire des peintres, sculpteurs, dessinateurs et graveurs* (1976), p. 501; U. Thieme und F. Becker, *Allgemeines Lexikon der Bildender Künstler* (Leipzig, 1928), p. 586.

14 Cf. Note 8.

15 The Governor of Cairo.

16 Cavas: Originally 'archer', but their function became that of an usher as well as that of a guard.

17 Bibliothèque Nationale. Original letter (no. 19), *Nouvelles acquisitions françaises* (20395 ff, 133–8).

18 Jean-François Mimaut (1774–1837), French diplomat.

19 Bibliothèque Nationale. Original letter (no. 18.) *Nouvelles acquisitions françaises* (20395 ff, 125–31). Letter written between 29 October and 2 November and continued from 22 to 29 November.

20 Cf. Note 24.

21 This letter in the Gréhant collection has been published without commentary by Madame Vandier d'Abbadie in the *Bulletin de la Société française d'égyptologie* 34–5 (December 1962), pp. 35–42. We have used excerpts in a new reading by Jean Lefebvre.

22 G. Wiet, *Mohammed Ali et les Beaux-Arts* (Le Caire, 1949), pp. 382–3, no. 63, pl. XCV.

23 François-Pierre-Guillaume Guizot (1787–1874) became Minister of Foreign Affairs in 1841.

24 Charles-Jean-Marie-Félix, Marquis de la Valette (1806–81), was appointed consul-general at Alexandria in the same year.

25 The saddle that has recently been restored is a combination of two harnesses dating back to the time of the Pasha.

26 *Souvenirs de Voyages, Autographes et dessins français du XIXe siècle* (27 February–18 May 1992), which included texts and drawings of Nestor L'Hôte; cf. D. Harlé et J. Lefebvre, *Nestor L'Hôte*, pp. 81–7.

27 J. Leclant, 'Le voyage de Jean Nicolas Huyot en Egypte (1818–1819) et les manuscrits de Nestor L'Hôte', *Bulletin de la Société française d'égyptologie* 32 (December 1961), pp. 35–42.

28 My deepest gratitude goes to William Wiser, Professor Emeritus of English, University of Denver, USA, for his friendly checking of my translation.

14 ⌒ Between Two Lost Worlds: Frederick Catherwood

Jason Thompson and Angela T. Thompson

The British artist and architect Frederick Catherwood (1799–1854) is renowned for his contributions to the study of the Maya of Mexico and Central America. But his Mesoamerican accomplishments were rooted in his experiences as a pioneering scholar of ancient Egypt and the modern Middle East. His work in Egypt and the Holy Land, where he spent much more time and energy than in Mesoamerica, was an integral part of a creative process that attained its fullest flowering in his Mayan work. Catherwood must be understood not merely as a Maya scholar, albeit one of the greatest, but also as an explorer of old worlds and new, ancient and modern, Middle Eastern as well as Mesoamerican.

Details of Catherwood's life are distressingly sparse, moving his biographer to write, 'it was as if some spiteful poltergeist had followed in Catherwood's wake, destroying every page of his life's testimony.'[1] Nevertheless, enough is preserved to show that he received as good a preparation for his scholarly work as anyone in his place and time could have had. Early on, apprenticeship to the architect Michael Meredith provided a practical basis for his later study of monuments. Meredith's activities as a topographical antiquarian also gave Catherwood experience in placing monuments in their spatial and historical dimensions. In 1820, he enrolled in the Royal Academy where J. M. W. Turner was Professor of Perspective. From Turner, who often depicted classical and monumental scenes, Catherwood may have derived some of the romantic and mysterious elements that appear in many of his works, even detailed copies of antiquities. Another influence was the lecturer in architecture, Sir John Soane. Soane's rigorous insistence that students learn the principles of classical architecture heightened Catherwood's ability to sketch monuments knowledgeably. Soane also initiated Catherwood into the work of the incomparable artist of Roman ruins, Giovanni Battista Piranesi (1720–78), whose work he had largely discovered. Catherwood acquired Piranesi's remarkable talent for capturing a monument in meticulously accurate detail while conveying the emotions of viewing it. Catherwood was therefore a blend of classicism from Piranesi and romanticism from Turner.

After exhibiting at the Academy, Catherwood left on a tour of the Mediterranean in 1821 to develop his skills in the field. At Rome, living among the ruins that he already knew well from Piranesi's engravings, Catherwood sketched them himself, inspired by daily archaeological discoveries all around him. He travelled south to Naples where the excavations of the buried Roman cities of Pompeii and Herculaneum were just getting underway in earnest, then across to Sicily to wander among the little-known Greek temples there, sketching all the while. A particularly fine tempera work, 'Mt. Etna from the ruins of Tauramina', survives. Most of the others have been lost.

In the autumn of 1822 Catherwood and some of his architectural friends sailed for Greece, the study of which was considered essential for architectural training. They picked a thrilling moment to go, for the land was in the throes of the Greek War of Independence. It was also a thrilling moment for Greek archaeology, then in its first flush. We know that Catherwood exploited the opportunity fully, doing lots of sketching and making casts of monuments, but none of this work seems to have survived. Nevertheless, the experience provided further preparation for his great work in the Middle East and Mesoamerica.

Catherwood somehow slipped out of Greece in the midst of the fighting, experiencing unremembered adventures along the way, and passed through the Aegean to Syria. Dressed as an Arab he made his way south and entered Egypt in 1823. We can follow Catherwood's Egyptian itinerary in some detail because he travelled with an English tourist named Henry Westcar who kept a detailed diary. As often happens with Catherwood, however, Westcar's diary mentions him only occasionally and then in passing, although Catherwood was with Westcar nearly the entire time. Further consigning Catherwood to oblivion was the fact that Westcar's diary was never published, though it should have been.[2] During this Egyptian trip Catherwood ascended the Nile as far as Abu Simbel, compiling a large collection of sketches as he went. Some of these, contrary to the tendency of Catherwood documents, have survived.[3]

At Malta on his return voyage to England later in 1824, Catherwood met a young Scot named Robert Hay who was about to begin a long journey in Egypt.[4] Hay had inherited a substantial fortune that enabled him to realise a long-standing dream of travelling to Egypt and systematically studying the land, both ancient and modern. To that end he hired a team of talented artists. Nothing like Hay's project had been done since the great commission of French scholars accompanied Napoleon's expedition to Egypt, resulting in the magnificent multi-volumed *D escription de l'Égypte* (1809–22). Hay could not match the scale of the French operation, but in many details he surpassed it, and nothing equal to Hay's project would be seen again on the Nile for decades. During his conversations with

Catherwood, Hay examined Catherwood's sketches and was fascinated by their content and quality. The two men soon went their separate ways, Hay to begin his work in Egypt and Catherwood to make his way slowly back to England, but this encounter set the stage for Catherwood's participation in one of the most important yet least-known chapters in nineteenth-century Egyptology.

After his meeting with Catherwood, Hay spent several years in Egypt working on the initial stages of his project, inspired to higher standards by Catherwood's work. Although he accomplished much, he was still learning his way around Egypt; also, he had difficulty managing his temperamental team. When he returned to Britain in 1828, Hay was determined to mount an even more thorough expedition. Recognising that Catherwood was one of the best qualified archaeological draftsmen in the world, Hay offered him a place on the team. For Catherwood, whose artistic and architectural activities in London must have been anticlimactic to his experiences in the East, Hay's project was the perfect platform for his talents. He accepted Hay's offer and was soon on his way east again.[5]

Enormous possibilities awaited Catherwood in Egypt. Western awareness of ancient Egypt, previously slight, had exploded at the beginning of the nineteenth century in the aftermath of Napoleon's Egyptian expedition. A number of events over the next few years, including Champollion's announcement of the decipherment of the hieroglyphs in 1822, highlighted the mysteries of the ancient land. At the same time, the Egyptian political situation stabilised so as to allow virtually unrestricted internal travel. Catherwood and his colleagues were therefore in the very forefront of the development of modern Egyptology, a term that would not even be coined for decades.

In Egypt, Catherwood became part of a group of talented Egyptologists and Orientalists. Besides Hay and his team, it included Sir Gardner Wilkinson, the future founder of Egyptology in Great Britain. Another was Edward William Lane, whose accomplishments in Middle Eastern studies surpassed even those of Wilkinson in Egyptology. Others included Henry Salt, James Burton, and Joseph Bonomi.[6] Like most members of this informal group, Catherwood forsook European customs to live and dress in Eastern fashion, learn Arabic, and become, as one of his friends observed, 'well versed in Oriental manners'.[7] His cultural and linguistic facility served him many times by enabling him to penetrate deeply into local society to study things that otherwise would have been inaccessible.

Because of the complexity of Robert Hay's project, which sometimes included as many as six full-time members, its participants were often assigned specific responsibilities. Catherwood's specialities included cartography and panoramic views. As a cartographer he mapped some of the most important archaeological sites in Egypt, as in his dramatic 'Plan of Gizeh', rendered as an overhead view of the Great Pyramids and surrounding structures. His map of Tell el-Amarna, the capital of the heretic king Akhenaton, was one of the very first to be made; at Abydos he demonstrated his ability to cope with a difficult cartographical situation; and his map of the west bank of Thebes shows what was on the surface at that fabulous location in 1833. Although these maps were never published, they are important Egyptological documents, and they prefigure the excellent work that Catherwood later did with John Lloyd Stephens in Central America. Besides making maps for Hay, Catherwood also provided detailed critiques of the cartographical efforts of others, correcting them and moving them to a higher standard. As in so many aspects of his Middle Eastern scholarship, however, his hand frequently moved behind the scenes, bringing him little permanent recognition.

Catherwood was also Hay's panoramist. The objective was to render a 360° view from some advantageous centre point. Such a panorama would enable a reader to follow the scene all around the horizon. In preparing his panoramas, as well as in much of his other work, Catherwood used a portable instrument called the *camera lucida*, a new invention that enabled an artist to trace accurate outlines of subjects. Catherwood later used the *camera lucida* to great advantage in Mesoamerica. Little of Catherwood's panorama work has survived, but it was to play a major role in his career.

Just as the members of Hay's team were often assigned specific responsibilities, so too were they frequently put to work at different sites. One of those assigned to Catherwood was the so-called colossi of Memnon at Thebes. As Catherwood and his colleagues knew, these two enormous statues represented not the Homeric hero Memnon but Amenophis III, whose temple had once stood behind them. The statue on the right, known as the 'Vocal Statue', had been famous since classical antiquity because it uttered sounds at dawn, on days when it was so inclined. Catherwood's sketches of the colossi show his capacity for conveying the power and mystery of a monument while making an accurate copy of it, the quality that eventually became most striking in his Mesoamerican work. Catherwood also conducted excavations underneath the colossi, an unusually sophisticated approach for his time.[8]

Catherwood worked at many other sites at Thebes and elsewhere in Egypt. In Karnak Temple he drew the obelisk of Queen Hatshepsut— obelisks also being one of his specialities—as well as the interior of the Hypostyle Hall. Another of his surviving sketches is a general view of the Ramesseum. Still others show Giza, Dendera, Edfu, Philae, and Abu Simbel. In addition to views of monuments, Catherwood made detailed epigraphic studies of murals and inscriptions.

Ever adventurous, Catherwood eagerly seized opportunities for travel, as when Hay and the traveller G. A. Hoskins invited him to accompany them to the Western Oases of Egypt in 1832.[9] Before returning to the Nile valley, Catherwood passed through Libya to Tunisia where he documented the Carthaginian monument at Dugga. His account, published years later, is the only record of the monument, which was completely destroyed soon after he visited it.[10] That fourteen-page article is Catherwood's only published textual work about the Middle East.

In addition to his work for Hay on ancient Egyptian ruins, Catherwood worked for Egypt's ruler, Muhammad 'Ali, on several occasions, as a lecturer in architectural engineering at al-Azhar University and as an engineer to repair mosques in Cairo. By the close of his extended sojourn in Egypt, Catherwood's artistic and architectural experience encompassed ancient, classical, Islamic, and contemporary styles, a versatility that prepared him for even greater adventures, including those in Mesoamerica.

Catherwood left Egypt in 1833 to travel through Palestine and Syria.[11] A companion sketched him as he departed Cairo, but showed him riding away, his back to the viewer, elusive as always. Important though his Egyptian work was, Catherwood's work in the Holy Land, and especially in Jerusalem, surpassed it in both daring and originality, for despite the biblical associations that made Jerusalem a household word in the West, virtually no scholarly work had been done on the city. One reason for this was the difficulty of travel, which was much more arduous and dangerous in Palestine than in Egypt. Only someone with Catherwood's familiarity with Eastern life could have explored and recorded the town so thoroughly as he documented many major monuments and prepared a general map of the city, the first accurate one ever to be published.[12]

After some weeks in Jerusalem, Catherwood resolved to explore the Haram, the enclosed sanctuary containing the Dome of the Rock and the al-Aqsa Mosque, built upon the foundations of the Temple of Solomon. The Dome of the Rock, also known as the Mosque of 'Umar, reputedly incorporates some of the materials from Solomon's Temple. Constructed during AD 688–92, it is the earliest surviving Islamic commemorative building, and therefore of great interest to scholars of both Islam and the Bible. One of the holiest places in Islam, the Haram was carefully guarded against intrusion by infidels. Several Europeans were said to have lost their lives attempting to enter it. For Catherwood, dressed in Eastern clothes and speaking fluent Arabic, entry was easy. Trouble started when he began working inside the Dome of the Rock. In those days, simply sketching in holy places was looked upon as an impious act by Muslims; Catherwood's audacity in openly setting up his *camera lucida* could not fail to attract attention. As Catherwood later wrote,

At length, some [individuals] more fanatic than the rest, began to think all could not be right: they gathered at a distance in groups, suspiciously eyeing me, and comparing notes with one another; a storm was evidently gathering. They approached, broke into sudden clamour, and surrounding [me], uttered loud curses: their numbers increased most alarmingly, and with their numbers their menacing language and gestures. Escape was hopeless; I was completely surrounded by a mob of two hundred people, who seemed screwing up their courage for a sudden rush upon me—I need not tell you what would have been my fate … and, I believe, few moments would have passed ere [I] had been torn to pieces, … [13]

Catherwood averted disaster by convincing the angry crowd that he was a devout Muslim engaged in preparatory work for much-needed repairs to the monument. This not only saved the situation but even established Catherwood's right to work in the Haram at leisure. The result was a detailed, accurate study of the entire Haram, including its foundation. Nothing like it had ever been done before.

Besides Jerusalem, Catherwood worked at many other sites in the Holy Land. He travelled on to Syria where he was the first to make the splendid Roman ruins at Baalbek known to the general public, although his portrayals of them were published in the works of others. Passing through Damascus, Catherwood eventually made his way to Beirut, whence he departed for England. It was in Beirut that he married, but so sparse are facts about Catherwood's life that most of our knowledge about his marriage comes from court records ten years later when he brought suit against his wife's lover.[14]

When Catherwood returned to England in 1834 he confidently expected to publish a definitive book based on his unprecedented discoveries in Jerusalem, but he found London publishers unanimously uninterested. His work, the product of enormous talent, made at risk of his life, was unwanted. The main problem was Catherwood's attempt to present scholarly work at a moment when publishers preferred lively travel accounts. Scholarly material might be inserted in such books but in the course of a narrative of a journey. While sympathising with Catherwood's frustrations, one wonders why he did not just write a travelogue. Surviving fragments of his prose show more technical skill than most writers of his day possessed. He also had more travel experiences to draw on, and more adventurous experiences at that. His tales of Greece during its War of Independence, of sailing up the Nile, of travelling through the Holy Land, all would have made riveting reading. But Catherwood never worked within the travelogue form, the very genre that turned his friend John Lloyd Stephens into a wealthy, best-selling author. Perhaps Catherwood's natural reticence and retiring personality prevented him from expressing himself in that way.

Rebuffed by publishers, Catherwood put away his drawings and notes about Jerusalem. A few of the sketches were later recopied and published by others as incidental illustrations in their own works, for Catherwood was generous with his material after he had despaired of publishing it himself. One values the data that such publications preserved, but worries about the accuracy of the second-hand renditions. It certainly brought little renown to Catherwood, who was occasionally credited, but in small letters and with his name frequently misspelled. As for the bulk of Catherwood's Jerusalem papers, they have apparently been lost.[15]

Catherwood had also expected to be busy helping Robert Hay prepare his magnificent portfolio for publication, but here too he was disappointed. Hay did indeed set Catherwood to work on a book about Thebes. Magnificent in conception, it was intended to contain a map (the first accurate, volume-sized map of the area), twenty-two individual views of monuments, the panoramic view of Thebes, and a set of royal cartouches to identify the names on the monuments. Had it ever appeared, it would have been a landmark in Egyptology. As the work progressed, however, Hay began to act strangely, becoming increasingly difficult to work with and finally lapsing into the scholarly inactivity that marked the rest of his life. 'I am sorry to find that your Egyptian energy is giving way', Catherwood wrote to Hay.[16] He may well have been sorry, for Hay left his portfolio, along with some of Catherwood's best work, unpublished. The dozens of large volumes compiled by Hay's expeditions now sit in the manuscript collection of the British Library, a resource for the occasional scholar who consults them, their potential unrealised and Catherwood unrecognised as one of the pioneers of Egyptology.[17] As with Catherwood's work in the Holy Land, a few of his Egyptian sketches eventually came into the hands of others who redrew them for publication in their own works, with mixed results.

Frustrated in publication, Catherwood found a creative outlet for his Middle Eastern work in the great panorama shows that Robert Burford was staging in London's Leicester Square. These panoramas were among the most celebrated spectacles of their time. Vast painted canvases illuminated by backlights were so arranged around a large room to convey an illusion of the landscape. Where an expensive illustrated book could find only a small readership, Burford's panoramas reached the much wider audiences that flocked to see them. Burford, always on the lookout for travellers with useful material, instantly recognised Catherwood's potential. Altogether, Catherwood prepared four panoramas for Burford: Jerusalem, Thebes, Karnak, and Baalbek. He also lectured before them. Burford prepared a series of short pamphlets about each of the panoramic subjects; they are all that remain of Catherwood's panoramas, preserving nothing more than crude sketches.[18]

While he was lecturing at the panoramas, Catherwood met John Lloyd Stephens, just returned from extensive travels in Europe and the Middle East.[19] Stephens had heard of Catherwood in the East and used Catherwood's map of Jerusalem when he visited the city. Their conversations turned to the possibility of investigating the mysterious ruins in Central America, Chiapas, and the Yucatán in Mexico. Catherwood seems to have been contemplating such an adventure even before their meeting. He showed Stephens a book entitled *Description of the ruins of an ancient City discovered near Palenque in the kingdom of Guatemala* by Capitan Antonio del Rio and F. Cabrera (1822). It asserted that the Palenque ruins were of Egyptian, Carthaginian, or Phoenician origin, but Catherwood could see that the book's illustrations, though crude, represented something fundamentally different from anything in the Middle East or North Africa.[20] From these brief conversations between Catherwood and Stephens, plans for a joint Central American adventure began to take shape.

Catherwood's magnificent accomplishments in Mesoamerica are beyond the scope of this paper. It is, however, pertinent to point out how much they were based on his work in Egypt and the Middle East. There he developed his overall archaeological and artistic skills so as to enable him to sketch monuments and make maps quickly and accurately, even under distressing conditions. In Egypt, monuments might be covered by drifting sand and accumulated rubble; in Mesoamerica, dense vegetation often enveloped them. Catherwood's Middle Eastern experiences also gave him a number of particular insights into Mesoamerican archaeology that were altogether remarkable for his time. For example, he realised, in complete opposition to the scholarly consensus of the day, that the origin of the Central American, Chiapan, and Yucatán ruins was entirely indigenous, that they had been built by ancestors of the contemporary Maya who still inhabited the region, not by lost Egyptians or some other ancient Middle Eastern or Mediterranean people. Furthermore, Catherwood believed that the Mayan hieroglyphs, which no one at that time could read, were a key to understanding the people who built the monuments and that, like Egyptian hieroglyphs, they recorded historical information.[21] Recent success in deciphering the Mayan hieroglyphs has proved that Catherwood was correct.[22]

For Catherwood, one intellectual experience transposed to another as his genius achieved its fullest flowering in Mesoamerica before he was overtaken by the tragic obscurity that was somehow characteristic of this brilliant, yet self-effacing individual.

Notes

1 Victor W. von Hagen, *Frederick Catherwood Archt* (New York: Oxford University Press, 1950), p. vi.

2 The Westcar diary is now in the Library of the German Institute of Archaeology, Cairo. An inaccurate copy is among the Warren R. Dawson papers in the British Library, Department of Manuscripts, hereinafter BL.

3 These were located and preserved by the great collector of Middle Eastern manuscripts, Rodney Searight. They are now among the Searight Collection in the Victoria and Albert Museum.

4 Recorded in the manuscript diary of Robert Hay, BL Add. Ms. 31054, f. 41. For Hay, see Selwyn Tillett, *Egypt Itself: The Career of Robert Hay, Esquire of Linplum and Nunraw, 1799–1863* (London: SD Books, 1984).

5 This follows von Hagen's account of Catherwood's engagement with Hay's project. In fact, the initiation of their professional relationship may have been a good deal more complex.

6 For this group, see Jason Thompson, *Sir Gardner Wilkinson and His Circle* (Austin: University of Texas Press, 1992).

7 Von Hagen, *Frederick Catherwood Archt*, p. 30.

8 The results of his work at the colossi of Memnon are contained in BL Add. Ms. 29831, ff. 25 et seq.

9 See G. A. Hoskins, *Visit to the Great Oasis of the Libyan Desert* (London: Longman, 1837). Also pertinent is Hoskins' *A Winter in Upper and Lower Egypt* (London: Hurst and Blackett, 1863).

10 Frederick Catherwood, 'Account of the Punico–Libyan Monument at Dugga and the Remains of an Ancient Structure at Bless, near the site of Ancient Carthage', *Transactions of the American Ethnological Society* 1 (1845), pp. 477–91.

11 Although Catherwood's papers from the trip are not extant, some contextual information is available in Francis Arundale, *Illustrations of Jerusalem and Mt. Sinai, Including the Most Interesting Sites between Grand Cairo and Beyrout* (London: Henry Colburn, 1837), and in Joseph Bonomi's unpublished diary, a transcript of which is in the archives of the Griffith Institute of the Ashmolean Museum.

12 Frederick Catherwood, *Plan of Jerusalem* (London, 1835). Catherwood's map of Jerusalem was not surpassed until the results of an Admiralty ordnance survey were published in 1849 in the second edition of John M. Wilson's *Landscapes of Interesting Localities Mentioned in the Holy Scriptures* (Edinburgh: A. Fullarton and Co., n. d.). Even then, Catherwood's map remained more accurate for the Haram. See Yehosuah Ben-Arieh, 'The Catherwood Map of Jerusalem', *Quarterly Journal of the Library of Congress* (July 1974), pp. 150–60.

13 W. H. Bartlett, *Walks about the City and Environs of Jerusalem Summer 1842* (London: G. Virtue, 1844; reprint, Jerusalem: Canaan Publishing House, 1974), pp. 149–50.

14 Tillett, *Robert Hay*, p. 93.

15 That Catherwood's Jerusalem papers survived the general conflagration of his collections in New York in 1842 is documented by James Fergusson who used them after Catherwood's death. One hopes they may yet surface. See James

Fergusson, *The Temples of the Jews and the Other Buildings in the Haram Area of Jerusalem* (London: John Murray, 1878), pp. 4–5; see also Fergusson, *An Essay on the Ancient Topography of Jerusalem, with Restored Plans of the Temple, &c., and Plans, Sections, and Details of the Church Built by Constantine the Great over the Holy Sepulchre, Now Known as the Mosque of Omar, and Other Illustrations* (London: John Weale, 1847), pp. xii–xv.

16 Frederick Catherwood to Robert Hay, 2 May 1835, BL Add. Ms. 38094, ff. 81–2.

17 Hay's one publication was his *Illustrations of Cairo* (London: Tilt and Bogue, 1840). This contained only a few of his views of medieval Cairo, with which Catherwood was little involved. See Tillett, *Robert Hay*, p. 85. Hay's vast unpublished collection of sketches and notes is in the BL, Add. Mss 29812–29860.

18 See Robert Burford, *Description of a View of the Great Temple of Karnak, and the Surrounding City of Thebes, Now Exhibiting at the Panorama, Broadway, Corner of Prince and Mercer Streets, New York. Painted by Robert Burford, from Drawings Taken in 1834, by F. Catherwood* (London, 1839; reprint, San Antonio: Van Siclen Books, 1988). The title of this pamphlet indicates that Burford actually painted the canvases.

19 John Lloyd Stephens, *Incidents of Travel in Egypt, Arabia Petræa, and the Holy Land* 2 vols. (New York: Harper and Brothers, 1837).

20 Victor W. von Hagen, *Search for the Maya: The Story of Stephens and Catherwood* (Westmead, Farnborough: Saxon House, 1973), p. 62.

21 John Lloyd Stephens, *Incidents of Travel in Central America, Chiapas and Yucatan* (New York: Harper and Brothers, 1841; reprint, New York: Dover Publications, 1969), vol. 2, p. 347. Frederick Catherwood, *Views of Ancient Monuments in Central America, Chiapas, and Yucatán* (London: Vizetelly Bros., 1844), and Victor von Hagen, *Frederick Catherwood Archt.*, pp. 119–20.

22 See George E. Stuart, 'Breaking the Code', in Gene S. Stuart and George E. Stuart, *Lost Kingdoms of the Maya* (Washington: National Geographic Society, 1993), pp. 158–60.

15 ∾ A Naval Tourist 1834–1840: Captain Henry Byam Martin

Sarah Searight

Captain Henry Byam Martin was a young naval officer who had served in the Eastern Mediterranean from the mid-1820s, possibly at the battle of Navarino. In 1834, being on half pay, he decided to visit Egypt and the Levant.[1] Martin was typical of a mildly adventurous young man, involved in the Near East initially for political reasons and, like so many, attracted to travel there by the publicity surrounding its rediscovery in the wake of Napoleon's invasion of 1798–1801.[2] As a naval officer he was a well-trained draughtsman, but he was also naturally gifted with pen and brush. In due course he stuck his watercolours in albums which he left to a favoured niece. Some of these came on the market in the 1980s and are now either broken up or in private hands.[3]

Martin was born in June 1803, one of three sons of Sir Thomas Byam Martin, Controller of the British Navy from 1815 to 1831. He was educated at Harrow School but in 1816 was sent to the Royal Naval College at Dartmouth.[4] In 1825 he was commanding the sloop *Parthian* in the Mediterranean, giving him a taste for the ancient world whose ruins so often adjoined his ports of call. In 1827 he was promoted to the post of captain but soon after was placed on half pay, not going to sea again for another nine years. He spent this period travelling in North America, Europe and the Mediterranean, sketching landscapes, ancient sites, men and women of the countries through which he passed.[5] He arrived in Egypt in the autumn of 1834.

In Egypt the subjects he chose to paint are predictable. Many are of boats, as befits a naval officer, many of pharaonic ruins as befits someone likely to have been beguiled by their many publicists, some are of Islamic buildings, others of costume, already threatened with becoming exotic and soon to be in retreat before the European cultural invasion.[6] His travels are described in letters to his parents amongst the Martin papers in the British Library. His motives in visiting Egypt and the Levant at this juncture in Near Eastern affairs demonstrate the involvement of Europe in the region in the first half of the nineteenth century. Both Napoleon's invasion and political developments in the years following his final defeat in 1815 had highlighted its strategic position, astride the routes to India, as well as its vulnerability.[7]

Martin arrived in Egypt in September 1834, obliged, to his great frustration, to spend the first few weeks of his visit in quarantine, whiling away his time in sketching the Egyptian fleet in the harbour. 'Never have travellers been caught in such a trap', he wrote on 10 September, but plague and its contagion were much feared by the Mediterranean world.[8] The fleet had been decimated at the battle of Navarino but was being busily rebuilt by the governor of Egypt (and *de facto* ruler) Muhammad 'Ali, in order to defend the Egyptian occupation of Syria which had taken place the year before.[9] Coming out of quarantine Martin was able to stay with Colonel Campbell, British consul-general in Alexandria, who took him to call on Muhammad 'Ali; Campbell's support for Muhammad 'Ali and some of his expansionist policies was to put him in Palmerston's bad books and led to his recall in 1839.[10]

Martin's sketches of Alexandria include Pompey's Pillar and Cleopatra's 'obelisk', both already much painted;[11] Sultan Qayt-bay's fort built in 1479 on the site of the famous lighthouse; and the field of the battle of Alexandria as a result of which the British achieved the French withdrawal from Egypt, the sort of subject to appeal to a young man whose career had involved him in the aftermath of those campaigns.

Before long Martin was on his way up river, presumably starting along the 45-mile Mahmudiyya canal, cleared by Muhammad 'Ali to facilitate communications between Alexandria and the Nile which it joins at Atfah, depicted by Martin in a lively watercolour showing the *kanja*s and *dahabiyya*s lined up along the waterfront to take passengers up river to Cairo. In a few years' time they would be joined by uncomfortable but more reliable steamboats. A few of those hiring the vessels would be travellers on their way to India, using the newly developed overland route through Egypt rather than the much slower route via the Cape.[12]

Martin makes no comment in his letters home on the Islamic monuments of Cairo but was clearly impressed by their grandeur and abundance; his watercolours include a view of the courtyard of the mosque of Shaykh Mu'ayyad, built between 1415 and 1420; a panoramic view of Cairo from the citadel; another view from the entrance to the citadel that includes the Mahmudiyya mosque built in 1567 for the Ottoman governor of Cairo, Mahmud al-Maqtul, and directly behind it the grandest of Cairo's religious buildings, the mosque and *madrasa* of Sultan Hasan built between 1356 and 1360.[13]

Soon Martin was organising his tour up river, hiring a *kanja*, captain, cook, servant and a crew of ten sturdy Nubians. 'You would laugh at our menage,' he was to write later, 'the cabin with beds & mosquito nets, a fixed awning outside under which we dine & read & draw & smoke & abuse the whigs';[14] he sketches the captain and his young servant Hasan, 'infinitely better dressed than his master', according to Martin who rhapsodised on 16 November how 'I have not had a hat or a coat or a neck cloth or braces or shoes or boots since I left Cairo ... one pokes & prowls about half naked in one's night cap & slippers.'

Up river with a good following wind and the river at a standstill before the flood began its annual retreat, past the rock-cut tombs of Bani Hasan, the cliffs of Abu Fuda, depicted in a watercolour of the *kanja*'s sails being furled in a high wind, to Dendera and the temple of Hathor and then to Thebes and Luxor. On this first visit Martin was anxious to make the most of wind and flood to sail over the cataracts at Aswan and Wadi Halfa; a few sketches date from this first visit but the majority are from his second visit six weeks later. A curious omission from Martin's letters or watercolours is any reference to other Europeans in Thebes/Luxor at the same time, with one exception—Auguste Marmont, Duc de Raguse, with whom he watched a crocodile chase.[15]

One of the finest of Martin's watercolours is of the Colossi of Memnon staring across the flooded plain to the sunrise. Martin wrote lyrically to his parents: 'to jump up to see the sunrise without any intrusive recollection of the follies of the night before is a new life I find very enjoyable.'[16] Across the river he painted the Luxor temple: commenting on the French removal of one of a pair of obelisks at the entrance he wondered, 'why do we not put a small postscript to their story and take the other which is equally fine, and put it up in the Park to remind the world of the little circumstance that though they did conquer the country from the Arabs—they were speedily picked out by the English.'[17] And Karnak, in particular the hypostyle hall: 'if any of these huge temples had gates left, I am almost in a condition to do a bit of Sampson and carry them off', he wrote, referring no doubt to the removal of large numbers of substantial ancient Egyptian stones by the ex-circus strong man Giovanni Battista Belzoni and others.[18] On his second visit to Thebes he sketched the interior of the tomb of Seti I that Belzoni had so dramatically discovered and excavated in 1817. An exhibition of a model of the tomb, including copies of paintings from its walls, had been held in London's Egyptian Hall (in Piccadilly) in 1821, attracting great interest and perhaps viewed by the young Martin.[19]

Martin was disconcerted by the ruins—so impressive, so enigmatic. 'They want a history to make that interest which they deserve', he complained on 24 November, and his confusion may explain a wrong identification of Madinat Habu with the Ramasseum in titles to two of his paintings. But the wind called and he was on his way again up river. 'I was never better in my life', he wrote, at the end of his voyage, to his mother.

'The climate is delicious—still hot in the sun. I always see the sun rise, and still find the day too short by half; there is an elasticity, a lightness, a softness in the climate ... I wish I could send a cargo of pure Egyptian air home to my dear mother.'

Now to Aswan where he was as captivated by the ruins of Philae as so many others—Denon, Charles Barry, Owen Jones already, and later David Roberts and Edward Lear. Belzoni, in the *Narrative* which he wrote of his travels and discoveries in Egypt, wrote that the island of Philae 'is the most superb group of ruins I have ever beheld together in so small a space of ground'.[20] Martin painted a number of views at Aswan, including the interior of the temple, and some interesting portraits, one of them of a man probably of the Beja tribe from the Red Sea hills. Several of his figural sketches depict victims of the slave trade which had prompted Muhammad 'Ali's extension of his Egyptian empire into the Sudan. Martin was horrified by the trade—'perhaps 20,000 brought forth,' he wrote to his mother, 'excluding those who die en route.' They were cheap: 'a very tidy nigger from Darfur, about 4 to 7 guineas'.[21]

Despite wind and flood water Martin's boat still had to be dragged over the cataract by his Nubian crew before he could continue to Wadi Halfa. The album contains some fine landscapes—'the sad, uncompromising landscape' of Nubia.[22] At Wadi Halfa he sketched not only the cataract but also the great rock of Abusir on which every foreign passer-by liked to carve his or her name.

Martin's return voyage down river provides us with a valuable record of ancient structures, many of which have now disappeared beneath the waters of Lake Nasser or have been moved to escape them—Kalabshah, Derr, Dakkah, Gerf Husain and Korosko among them.[23] He painted a fine watercolour of Abu Simbel, unfortunately without comment in his correspondence; one would have liked something as pithy as Lear writing in 1867 to Emily Tennyson: 'I was absolutely too astonished and affected to draw ... As a whole the scene is overpowering from its beauty—colour—solitude—history—art—poetry—every sort of association ... all other things in this world seem to be as chips, or potato parings, or any nonsense in this world in comparison.'[24]

So on down river, calling at Edfu, staying longer at Thebes and reaching Cairo just before Christmas. 'Yesterday we smoked a pipe on top of the Great Pyramid', he wrote to his mother on 16 December. They 'fully answered all my expectations; how impossible it is for the mind to imagine their grandeur.'

On 2 January 1835 he sat down to write a long letter to his father, mostly concerned with the state of contemporary Egypt. He had noted the Pasha building up army and fleet, both with French help. The huge demand for military recruits to execute his expansionist policies in Syria and Arabia had depopulated Egypt: 'the villages up country seem to be inhabited only by old men, women and children. People injure themselves to avoid the Pasha's service.' 'The whole of Egypt may be called the Pasha's farm.' Martin himself was 'rashly' sceptical of Muhammad 'Ali: 'I am quite willing to admit that he is one of the most extraordinary characters of the age. I place him among the most successful of adventurers; the most illustrious of barbarians … though the ghosts of the Mamluks may rise to deny it, I am ready to believe that *for a Turk* he is a good and humane man *in his intentions* … [but] I should unhesitatingly appeal to the actual state of Egypt to support me in the assertion that he is a one-eyed man; neither an enlightened Prince or a sound Politician.'[25]

As for his sketches, 'I have of course as usual made a good many very bad [drawings] and you will easily believe that a boat is not the most favourable place for the production of finished works of art!—but they will serve me for reminiscences' and he hoped they would please his mother. 'One never sits down to a sketch but some curious object in the architecture or sculpture is sure to draw one's attention off.'

Part of a naval officer's training would have been draughtsmanship and several of Martin's contemporaries who visited Egypt showed how expertly they had learned the skill: Robert Hay and his companions whom Martin failed to meet in Thebes; Charles Irby who helped Belzoni excavate Abu Simbel; Robert Moresby who surveyed the Red Sea for Bombay Marine and a number of others.[26] While many of Martin's sketches are little more than that, occasionally he clearly had time to execute more considered studies of the places he visited—from which the modern viewer can capture some of the wonder felt by the nineteenth-century traveller. The attention to detail is that of the naval draughtsman but the texture, the harsh light of midday, the subtler colours of evening and early morning are those of a skilled and emotive artist.

Egypt was by no means the end of Martin's journeying. Plague in Alexandria and the cordoning off of the city was preventing him from continuing by boat but, tiring of Cairo, he planned to ride across the desert from Egypt to Palestine. 'Our camels are ready and all preparations made for a start,' he ended his diatribe against the Viceroy. The plague had already appeared in Cairo; a Maltese merchant from Alexandria had died after twelve days' illness. Martin planned to be in Jerusalem in two weeks' time, spend three weeks there and eventually reach Constantinople by mid-April. 'But there are rumours of war again in those parts which may impede our movements … '

The rumours which Martin picked up in Cairo had some substance: the Syrian population was finding the Egyptian occupation no more comfortable than the Ottoman had been. Intricate feuding between Maronite Christians and Druzes around Mount Lebanon, a Kurdish revolt in the north were stimulated by the activities of rival European powers, each backing one community against another. As far as Martin himself was concerned, travelling through the Levant from January to April 1835, the rumours proved no deterrent to his curiosity, but the upheavals which they heralded eventually led to his return to those parts in 1840.

In November 1836 Martin was appointed to the command of *HMS Carysfort* and he spent the next five years in the Eastern Mediterranean, part of a British fleet keeping an eye on Egyptian activity in Syria. Revolt broke out in Syria in the spring of 1840 and another 12,000 Egyptian troops were landed at Beirut to help suppress it. France, with greater commercial commitments in Egypt, was inclined to support Muhammad 'Ali in his stand against the Ottoman authorities but in July 1840 representatives of the other main European powers—Britain, Russia, Austria and Prussia—met in London to condemn the occupation, drafting the Convention for the Pacification of the Levant. Muhammad 'Ali refused to accept its terms and in September 1840 the allied fleets began a bombardment of coastal cities to re-establish Ottoman rule and force an Egyptian withdrawal.[27] With the *Carysfort* in action, Martin made the most of his opportunities, dodging on shore between bombardments to paint and sketch at Byblos, Tripoli and Tartus, for instance, and eventually participating in the bombardment of Acre in November. This finally forced the Egyptian withdrawal and the restoration of a reformed Ottoman regime, with the recognition of Muhammad 'Ali as the hereditary Pasha of Egypt.

After the bombardment of Acre, Martin was briefly in Egypt again in the winter of 1840–41, travelling up river from Alexandria and painting the riverside port of Bulaq, centre of the Pasha's modernisation programme, on this visit; it would have changed considerably since his previous visit, with the development of the overland route to India and the arrival of steamboats on both the Nile and the Mahmudiyya canal.

Martin was one among many Europeans whose visits to the Near East in the 1830s and 1840s resulted from the opening up of the region to European penetration in the aftermath of Napoleon's invasion of Egypt, reminders of which occur in a number of Martin's watercolours. The French expedition achieved little but its impact endured, both within Egypt and within the Ottoman empire whose lands lay astride links with India. The vulnerability of those communications lay behind the jostling of European powers over strategic areas of the Ottoman empire throughout much of the nineteenth century, labelled the 'Eastern question' by contemporaries. Martin's albums of fine, topographical watercolours and sketches, those of an observant and intrepid tourist in little known parts of the world, are a valuable insight into a region becoming strategically central to European diplomacy in the nineteenth century.

Notes

1 This chapter is based on the Martin papers in the British Library, BL Add. Mss. 41463, and on an album of watercolours painted by Martin during his visit to Egypt in 1834–35 and subsequently presented to his niece. It is now in private hands and I am extremely grateful to Bernard Quaritch & Co. for permission to research the album.

   Ottoman and Egyptian navies were destroyed by the British at the battle of Navarino, thus confirming Greek independence. Martin makes no mention of having been present but several watercolours by him, including one of Cape Sunion and a view from his Athens window, painted in 1827, make it likely he was there.

2 The main publicist for the expedition was Dominique Vivant Denon, who accompanied Napoleon, and journeyed as far south as Wadi Halfa, in 1802 publishing his *Voyage dans la basse et la haute Égypte*. The final scholarly compendium resulting from the expedition, *Déscription de l'Égypte*, ran to 24 volumes, published between 1809 and 1822.

3 At least four are known, of which that on Egypt and another mainly on Lebanon, Syria and Anatolia, are now in private hands. Contents of the others have been dispersed.

4 For details of Martin's naval career, see W. Laird Clowes, *The Royal Navy*, Vol. VI (1812–56).

5 His Canadian travels were published by the Public Archives of Canada in 1981, as *Friendly Spies on the Northern Tour, 1815–37*.

6 Thackeray's comment on the stimulation of Cairo streets is worth quoting: 'there is a picture in every street, and at every bazaar stall', noting that his friend, the painter J. F. Lewis who had been living in Cairo since 1841, 'has produced [some of these] with admirable truth and exceeding minuteness and beauty' (Thackeray, W. M. *From Cornhill to Grand Cairo* (London, 1845), p. 192).

7 These routes were being extensively explored and publicised at the time of Martin's visit, that through Egypt and the Red Sea by Thomas Waghorn and the alternative but more traditional route through Mesopotamia and the Persian Gulf by Francis Chesney. See H. Hoskins, *British Routes to India* (London, 1928) and S. Searight, *The British in the Middle East* (London, 1981).

8 The plague was a chronic hazard in Egypt until the latter half of the nineteenth century. Martin's later plans to move on to Syria by sea had to be changed because plague in Alexandria had led to the cordoning off of the city.

9 British official documents dealing with the Egyptian occupation of Syria 1832–40, under the leadership of Muhammad 'Ali's eldest son Ibrahim, to claim what Muhammad 'Ali considered his reward for coming to the assistance of the Ottoman Sultan in Greece, are in the FO 78 series in the Public Record Office.

10 [PRO] FO 78/472, 2.10.39.

11 The prone obelisk was requested by Sir Ralph Abercrombie from Muhammad 'Ali after the British defeat of the French in 1801 but it was only removed in 1877 when an English surgeon, Erasmus Wilson, offered £10,000 to remove

it. It was eventually erected on the Thames embankment in London, while its standing companion is now in New York's Central Park.

12 J. Sidebottom, *The Overland Mail* (London, 1948) cited in Searight, *Steaming East* (1991), pp. 30–50, 72–88.

13 A number of Europeans were beginning to draw attention to Cairo's Islamic monuments, among them Prisse d'Avennes, Pascal Coste and Owen Jones. See M. Darby, *The Islamic Perspective* (London, 1986).

14 16 December 1834.

15 Auguste Marmont (1774–1852) had fought with Napoleon in Egypt and elsewhere as a result of which he was created Duc de Raguse. He published 5 volumes of travels, *Voyages en Hongrie ... Egypte et en Sicilie*, in 1837 (M. Bierbrier, *Who was Who in Egyptology* (London, 1995), p. 277).

16 24 November 1834.

17 24 November 1834. There was once a pair of obelisks at the entrance but Muhammad 'Ali presented one to the French, now in the Place de la Concorde, removed in 1831. In return Louis Philippe gave Muhammad 'Ali a magnificently hideous clock for his mosque in Cairo.

18 Between 1817 and 1820 Belzoni was employed by the British consul-general, Henry Salt, to remove antiquities from Thebes, including a seven-ton block of granite known as the 'young Memnon', the 'shatter'd visage' of Percy Bysshe Shelley's *Ozymandias*. (See chapter 6 above for further details about Belzoni.)

19 'The mechanical ingenuity and indefatigable diligence by which Mr Belzoni has been enabled thus to transport to the arena of European controversy the otherwise immoveable excavations of Egypt reflect no less credit upon him as an artist than his sagacity and success in discovering the subject matter of this extraordinary exhibition' (*The Times*, 30 April 1821).

20 G. B. Belzoni, *Narrative of the operations and recent discoveries...in Egypt and Nubia* (London, 1820), p. 201.

21 In the 1820s Muhammad 'Ali despatched an Egyptian military expedition to Sudan to tap the reservoir of slaves held by local rulers and to gain access to the southern pagan areas, traditional fields for slave-raiding.

22 Lear to Lady Waldegrave, 9 March 1867, quoted in V. Noakes, *The Life of Edward Lear* (London, 1968), p. 216: 'dark ashy purple lines of hills, piles of granite rocks, fringes of palms, and ever and anon astonishing ruins of oldest temples.'

23 Kalabshah's temple is submerged; Derr's temple has been moved to al-Amada; Dakkah's temple has been moved to Sabu al-Gadid; Gerf Husain's temple has been submerged, as has Korosko's; Dabot/Dabud's temple is now in Madrid. For details, see P. Stocks, *The Blue Guide to Egypt* (London, 1994).

24 22 March 1867, see Noakes, *The Life of Edward Lear*, pp. 216–17.

25 For other contemporary views of Muhammad 'Ali see the [PRO] FO 78 series of Foreign Office papers, and comments by such contemporary residents as Dr R. R. Madden in *Egypt and Muhammad Ali* (London, 1841).

26 See Charles Irby and James Mangles, *Travels in Egypt and Nubia*, 1823. Drawings by Moresby are in the Searight Collection.

27 For details of the campaign see the account by its commander, Charles Napier, *The War in Syria* (London, 1842).

16 ∿ Two Interpretations of Islamic Domestic Interiors in Cairo: J. F. Lewis and Frank Dillon

Briony Llewellyn[1]

John Frederick Lewis and Frank Dillon[2] were professional British artists whose views of Islamic domestic architecture are of particular interest, both for their artistic quality and for their rarity value. Both were trained as artists rather than architects: Lewis was taught by his father, Frederick Christian Lewis, who was an engraver; Dillon studied at the Royal Academy Schools. Both were frequent exhibitors at the London artistic institutions—the Royal Academy and the watercolour societies. As a result their approach to architectural subjects was quite different from that of architect contemporaries such as James Wild and J. D. Crace who also drew Islamic houses in Cairo.[3] While Lewis and Dillon represented the decorative details of the rooms accurately—the *mashrabiyya* shutters, the carved and painted wooden ceilings, the stained glass windows, and so on—they were portraying them not as isolated architectural features, but as part of an atmospheric pictorial whole.

Lewis and Dillon are also unusual among their own artist contemporaries in that they appear to be the only two professional British artists at this time—roughly the 1840s to the 1870s—to have focused particularly on the private and secular buildings of Cairo rather than on its public and religious places. David Roberts, for example, represented many mosques and tombs in his volume of lithographs devoted to Cairo, published in 1849, but included only one generalised view of a private house.[4]

One reason for this must have been inaccessibility. In From *Cornhill to Grand Cairo*, published in 1846, William Thackeray made no mention of domestic architecture when he declared: 'There is a fortune to be made for painters in Cairo, and materials for a whole Academy of them. I never saw such a variety of architecture, of life, of picturesqueness, of brilliant colour, and light and shade. There is a picture in every street, and at every bazaar stall.' He continued: 'Some of these, our celebrated watercolour painter, Mr Lewis, has produced with admirable truth and exceeding minuteness and beauty; but there is room for a hundred to follow him.'[5] Indeed, many British, French and other European artists, from Roberts and Lewis onwards, did travel to Cairo and, deliberately or not, take up Thackeray's challenge to produce numerous lively and colourful street and bazaar scenes, as well as portraits of individuals to be seen there. Only a few—Lewis among them—had the opportunity to sketch inside private houses in Cairo.

Lewis was also one of the most remarkable and interesting of these artists, due to the qualities which Thackeray recognised in his sketches—his technical virtuosity and the accuracy and sensitivity of his observation.[6] These characteristics are evident in his street and bazaar scenes, and particularly in his scenes of domestic interiors, all, with one important exception (see below), executed at home in England, in the tranquillity of his own studio. His interiors are also notable because they display a particular intensity that derives not just from his direct, first-hand observation of his subjects, but also from a personal involvement with them. In other words his experience of them was subjective rather than objective.

In order to substantiate this claim, the source of Lewis's inspiration for these interiors—his life in Cairo—should be considered in more detail. He arrived there late in 1841, having sailed to Alexandria from Constantinople where he had spent the previous year making sketches of mosques and bazaars. He was thus not unfamiliar with the Eastern way of life, and the following year he extended his knowledge through a visit to Sinai. Until now his experience of the East does not appear to have been dissimilar to artists such as Roberts and William Müller who had preceded him as visitors there. Shortly afterwards, however, he found himself an old Mamluk-style house to live in, situated, according to a later English visitor, in 'the most Ottoman quarter of Cairo'[7]—the Esbekiyah district—and for the next nine years seems to have dressed and lived as a wealthy Turk, immersing himself in the local way of life. So determined was he to be a part of this Islamic culture that was so different from his own, that he seems deliberately to have held himself aloof from other Europeans resident in Cairo at the time, at least during the years before his marriage to an English girl, Marian Harper, in 1847.

He was apparently so unsociable that there is scant record of any communication with another famous Englishman who was at the same time living in the same manner, *à la Turque*, in a similar Mamluk house. This was E. W. Lane whose two recent publications, *Manners and Customs of the Modern Egyptians*[8] and his translation of the 'Arabian Nights',[9] both containing a detailed social commentary on the Muslim way of life, had been widely acclaimed. Lewis must have known Lane's work—he may even have been inspired by his example—but no mention of him has yet been discovered in any of the Lane documentation. It remains a puzzle that might yield to further research[10]. Lewis himself left no diaries, and no letters to friends or family at home—at least, none that survive. His presence there is mentioned in Murray's *Handbook*,[11] but no more than a handful of English visitors to Cairo seem to have communicated with him.

We have only one extensive source of information, Thackeray, whose travelogue, From *Cornhill to Grand Cairo*, has been quoted above. His brilliantly witty and acutely perceptive account of his visit to Lewis in October 1844 is, if one is prepared to read between the lines a little, most revealing. Approaching Lewis's house through a narrow crowded street, Thackeray 'passed the mysterious outer door' into a courtyard, full of animals, with a raised, covered area at one end of it. Opposite this 'rose up the walls of his long, queer, many-windowed, many-galleried house. There were wooden lattices to those arched windows, through the diamonds of one of which I saw two of the most beautiful, enormous, ogling, black eyes in the world, looking down upon the interesting stranger.' Conducted by a series of servants into an enormous 'hall of audience', Thackeray was left to contemplate its grandeur: 'All the ceiling is carved, gilt, painted and embroidered with arabesques, and choice sentences of Eastern writing ... Opposite the divan is a great bay-window, with a divan likewise round the niche. It looked out upon a garden ... surrounded by the tall houses of the quarter.'

If Thackeray's detailed account of this house is compared with Lewis's domestic scenes, close correspondences can be noted. In 'The Courtyard of the Painter's House'[10] can be seen the raised covered area at one end and the many windows with wooden lattices. This watercolour, painted on five pieces of joined paper, may have been executed towards the end of Lewis's stay in Cairo, perhaps with the intention of sending it or a version to London for exhibition. Further evidence that the courtyard is indeed that of the house in which Lewis lived is a drawing by Lewis entitled 'Courtyard of the Painter's House, Cairo'.[11]

A later oil painting is an example of the continuing use Lewis made of his courtyard. Despite the different title—'The Hósh [*hawsh*, courtyard] of the House of the Coptic Patriarch, Cairo' which Lewis gave it for the Royal Academy exhibition of 1864—it is a more elaborate version of the earlier composition.[12] The addition of the 'ogling, black eyes' peeping through the wooden lattices (*mashrabiyya*) and the extra animals—the 'happy pigeons ... no doubt fed with crumbs from the henna-tipped fingers of Zuleikah!'—prompt one to imagine that it was painted with Thackeray's text in mind. Another version, possibly a finished study for the exhibited oil, shows the same composition before it was cut down at the top.[13]

A further drawing in the Victoria and Albert Museum, inscribed by Lewis 'Mandarah in my House at Cairo', provides further proof that Lewis used his adopted Mamluk home for his compositions.[14] As late as 1873 the room with its great bay window and elaborate decoration is the setting for 'The Reception', which, except for the addition of the women, is exactly as

Thackeray describes.[15] More than twenty years after his residence in Cairo, Lewis has allowed himself some artistic licence in placing women in the *mandara*, the room on the ground floor, usually reserved only for men.

Lewis's two drawings of his *mandara* and his *hawsh* are among a handful of sketches of domestic interiors included in the various sales of the artist's work held after his death in 1876.[16] Another sketch that was included in the 1877 sale appears to be untraced but was certainly of great importance to him. Entitled 'Interior of Upper Room in a House, Esbekiah, Cairo, occupied by J. F. Lewis RA',[17] it was clearly the model for the setting of his most famous watercolour, 'The Hareem', which was painted towards the end of his stay in Cairo and sent to the 1850 Old Water-Colour Society exhibition. Until recently this watercolour was believed lost since its sale at Christie's in 1909, but some years ago it was noticed by an American businessman in the boardroom of a Japanese insurance company in Osaka.[18] Part of the composition was repeated by the artist in a version now in the Victoria and Albert Museum.[19] Once again the same scene reappeared in a later oil painting, 'The Intercepted Correspondence', exhibited at the Royal Academy in 1869 and now reinterpreted as a narrative centred upon the Oriental use of flowers to convey messages.[20]

Even though Lewis's sketch for this room appears to be lost, it is clear that it represented the upper apartments of his house since the large recessed window at the back of the composition corresponds exactly to the outside of the overhanging *mashrabiyya* shutters in the Victoria and Albert Museum drawing of the courtyard (see above).

If other Lewis interiors are carefully examined, architectural features from the same room can be recognised: for example, the carved wooden panel in the watercolour of 'Caged Doves' (1864) which reappears in the later oil 'The Harem' (1876) where the scene has been reversed.[21] Other sketches, no longer extant, may well have shown that background details from other paintings such as 'Life in the Harem' (1858) or 'The Siesta' (1876) were from other smaller rooms in Lewis's large house.[22]

At first sight it might seem curious that there seem to have been only a few sketches of domestic interiors among the several hundred that Lewis used for his other subjects. It is possible that more sketches of interiors were retained by his widow and have not survived, but possibly not many. This was a house in which he lived for several years—he knew it intimately. He also had a powerful visual memory. The house was so familiar to him that he could reproduce its details in his later paintings as often as he required, needing only the few drawings he had for reference.

Clearly the settings of Lewis's domestic scenes are convincing because they are real; he could portray them accurately and with assurance because he had lived within them. The costumes too are authentic since Lewis made numerous sketches of Oriental people, both men and women, and he also brought many garments back from the East to remind himself of their colour and texture. Despite this, the criticism has often been levelled against him that his domestic scenes showing women are imaginary because he would never have been able to witness an Oriental harem. It is certainly true that he would not have been able to enter the women's apartments of another man's house, but he was surely able to gain the information he needed by other means.

Thackeray described how Lewis lived and dressed as a Turk: at home he wore a long yellow gown, and on his head a red tarbush; when he went out his dark blue costume consisted of 'an embroidered jacket and gaiters, and a pair of trousers, which would make a set of dresses for an English family'. He employed several servants, including an Egyptian female cook who had 'done the pilaff and stuffed the cucumbers' that they ate for dinner—such as can be seen in 'The Mid-Day Meal' (1875).[23]

But was this Zuleikah with the black eyes more than just the cook? Lewis vehemently denied Thackeray's insinuations, but was he not protesting too much? It was one thing to cast off the conventions of his own society in order to live 'a dreamy, lazy, hazy, tobbacofied life', but quite another to be accepted by the society he had adopted.

Lewis was evidently the master of a substantial Oriental household, and as such he would have had to observe Muslim proprieties. Lane, in his compendium of Egyptian customs, had explained that it was considered disreputable for a man in such a position to remain unmarried, or without a female slave, and he himself had to move house because he had refused to take a wife. Subsequently he did take in a Greek girl, and later married her. It is unlikely that, living in his magnificent Mamluk house, in a respectable Ottoman district of Cairo, Lewis would have been able to resist these social pressures for the five years before he married Marian Harper, and it is probable that Zuleikah's status was as his female slave. Though unable himself to enter the harem of other houses in Cairo, she could go visiting with other women—as in 'The Reception'—and could bring him first-hand accounts of their customs. Lewis certainly seems to have been able to sketch Muslim men and women without the hindrances and suspicions usually encountered by foreign artists. His work displays the knowledge of Muslim manners and customs that he had had the opportunity and time to acquire, because he himself observed them.

This is especially evident in his first and finest harem picture, 'The Hareem'. The subject is the introduction of a new slave into the harem, and the detailed commentary that he provided for the picture when it was exhibited in 1853 at the Royal Scottish Academy[24] reveals how well he understood this event:

The scene is laid in an upper or women's apartment of a house in Cairo, the lower part of the house being always appropriated to the men. The master (a Bey or a Turk) is habited in the old Mameluke dress of Egypt, now not often worn. Immediately to his left is seated a Georgian, the 'sit el Gebir' or ruling lady of the Hhareem, having attained the privilege by being the mother of his eldest son, who is leaning against her knee. The lady stooping forward is a Greek, and the one reclining at the Bey's feet a Circassian. The laughing slave, an Abyssinian—an old inmate.

Could this be Zuleikah who had perhaps helped him to find the Oriental girls he needed as models?

Lewis continued:

The girl who is being unveiled by the black guardian is also an Abyssinian, but lately arrived from the upper country, and brought into the Hhareem by the wife of the slave owner, who is a fellah, and is seated in the middle distance, habited in the outdoor dress of the common people. The boy to the right is a Nubian, who is bringing in a sheetha or narghile. On the divan and near the boy are gazelles, the frequent indoor and outdoor pets of all classes. The windows, which are often of an enormous size, are all covered with the finest carved wood-work, at a distance resembling lace, and which does not prevent the inmates from seeing all that is passing, while it effectively precludes the possibility of being seen from without.

This wonderful representation of an Islamic custom totally alien to western society, carries conviction because Lewis had first-hand knowledge of the setting and the characters, and also because he knew as much as any foreigner could of the event taking place.

Frank Dillon was a younger contemporary of Lewis's, who must have seen and admired the older artist's highly successful Oriental interiors when they were exhibited in London during the 1850s and 1860s. He too had access to domestic houses in Cairo around this time and began exhibiting his own interiors in the 1870s. In some respects these are similar to Lewis's, but there are also many differences. They are not so ambitious in their iconography, nor are they so stunning in their effects; but they are worthy of consideration on their own merits.

Lewis's concern in many of his Oriental pictures was the portrayal of an aspect of Cairene society. Most contain a narrative, whether overt as in 'The Hhareem', or implied as in 'Caged Doves'. By contrast, Frank Dillon's interiors contain little or no narrative; his figures recline on divans, smoke pipes or serve coffee. They are not individually characterised but are adjuncts, together with the architectural decoration and the furnishings, in the re-creation of an authentic Cairene interior. They are suitably dressed props, placed to convey an idea of how the rooms were used, rather than of real people actually living in them. The different intentions of the two artists are apparent in the titles of their pictures: where Lewis describes the event, Dillon identifies the house and the room in it.

Frank Dillon visited Egypt four times between the 1850s and the 1870s. During his second visit in 1861–62 he lived with two fellow artists in an Arab house in Giza, and made several local contacts. It was probably these that on his third visit in 1869–70 enabled him to gain access to two old Mamluk-style houses: the mid-seventeenth-century house built by Raduan Bey, an influential emir, and the probably eighteenth-century 'House of the Mufti', which derived its name from the Shaykh al-'Abbasi al-Mahdi, the mufti or judge of Egypt, who owned the house between 1847 and 1886. Both these houses are notable examples of the large residences built in Cairo during the Mamluk period, containing airy reception rooms with painted tiled carved and stuccoed decoration. Many still survived in Cairo until the mid-nineteenth century, but then fell rapidly into disrepair. By the time Dillon visited these two, they were already in some decay, and his concern was to record them before they crumbled completely. They may even have been more or less empty, looked after only by caretakers. Five watercolours by Dillon show different parts of the house of Raduan Bey, including an exterior view of the *maq'ad*, or loggia, an interior of the same loggia, and the *mandara* or ground-floor reception room. Three further watercolours depict the 'House of the Mufti': one shows its large *mandara*, another a *liwan* or recess in the room, and another a prayer niche at the eastern end of the same room.

On his last visit to Cairo, in 1873–74, Dillon gained access to a third house, which he identified as that of the Shaykh Sadat. His four watercolours of it show the *hawsh* or courtyard, the *mandara*, the *qa'a* or largest room of the upper apartments for the women, and another smaller room on an upper floor.[25]

These watercolours may have been painted by Dillon in Cairo: some are quick sketches on rough, possibly local paper; others are more finished with architectural and decorative details more carefully delineated and the paint, a mixture of watercolour and body-colour, more thickly applied.

On his return to England, Dillon used these as the basis for more elaborate watercolours and oil paintings which he exhibited at the Royal Academy and elsewhere, notably 'Apartment in the Harem of the Sheikh Sadat' (c. 1875–76), in watercolour, and 'Recess in the Mandarah of the House of the Mufti' (1872), in oils.[26] In these the figures are slightly more substantial, but they are still generalised rather than real individuals. In the 'Sheikh Sadat' picture, Dillon has made an attempt to relate them to one another and to the viewer outside the picture space, but despite their undoubted charm, they retain an element of stiffness and artificiality.

The particular value of Dillon's Oriental interiors is as vivid and accomplished portrayals of real houses. He creates atmosphere through his carefully observed rendering of the effects of bright sunlight filtered through the *mashrabiyya* windows onto the richly decorated surfaces. Their interest lies in the depiction of the houses themselves, for their own sakes, rather than in events taking place within them or in the relationships between individuals who inhabited them.

By the 1870s the modernisation of the city meant that old houses were actually being destroyed and Dillon was aware that he was recording buildings and architectural decoration that would soon no longer exist. He later became active among a group of people committed to the preservation of Islamic buildings in Cairo, and displayed his watercolours during at least one meeting held at the RIBA to discuss Arab houses in Cairo.[27]

Notes

1 I would like to thank Charles Newton for his contribution to this paper, which has brought together some of the discussions we have had about Lewis and Dillon over many years, when I was working with him on the catalogue of the Searight Collection at the Victoria and Albert Museum, and also since. As ever, I would also like to pay tribute to the late Rodney Searight, whose collection and whose pioneering work on the artists in it has been the mainspring for much of the continuing research on travellers in Egypt and elsewhere in the Levant.

2 For further information, bibliographical references and illustrations for these two artists see: on Lewis, B. Llewellyn, 'Eastern Light', *FMR* (August 1984), pp. 131–53; on Dillon, B. Llewellyn, 'Frank Dillon and Victorian Pictures of old Cairo houses', *Ur: The International Magazine of Arab Culture* 3 (1984), pp. 2–10, hereinafter 'Frank Dillon'.

3 For examples of drawings by Wild, Crace and other British architects in Cairo, see Victoria and Albert Museum, London, Department of Designs, Prints and Drawings, and the Royal Institute of British Architects, London, Drawings Collection.

4 *Egypt and Nubia*, Vol. III (1849).

5 See W. A. Titmarsh [W. M. Thackeray], *Notes of a Journey from Cornhill to Grand Cairo* (London, 1846); reprinted with new introduction by S. Searight and illustrations compiled by B. Llewellyn (Heathfield: Cockbird Press, 1991), hereinafter *From Cornhill*.

6 The most detailed account of Lewis' life and work is by his collateral descendant Major-General J. M. Lewis, *John Frederick Lewis, R. A., 1805–1876* (Leigh-on-Sea, 1978).

7 Lord Elphinstone, Governor of Madras, to F. C. Lewis Jnr (brother of J. F. Lewis): letter dated 24 September 1845, quoted in Lewis, *John Frederick Lewis*, p. 21, note 6.

8 E. W. Lane, *An Account of the Manners and Customs of the Modern Egyptians, Written in Egypt During the Years 1833, 34 and 35* (London, 1836). 5th rev. edition, (ed.) Edward Stanley Poole (London: John Murray, 1860).

9 [Alf *Layla wa-Layla*.] *The Thousand and One Nights, Commonly Called, in*

England, the Arabian Nights' Entertainments. A New Translation from the Arabic, with Copious Notes, by E. W. Lane (London, 1839–41), 3 vols.

10 Jason Thompson, who is writing a biography of E. W. Lane, is working on this.

11 J. G. Wilkinson, *Handbook for Travellers in Egypt* (London: John Murray, 1847).

12 City Museums and Art Gallery, Birmingham, no. 44/48.

13 Victoria and Albert Museum, London, no. E5680–1910.

14 Private collection. See Royal Academy of Arts, London and National Gallery of Art, Washington, *The Orientalists: Delacroix to Matisse*, (ed.) MaryAnne Stevens (1984), hereinafter RA, *The Orientalists*, cat. no. 70, and Sotheby's, London, *Important Nineteenth-Century Pictures from a European Private Collection* (20 November 1996), lot no. 253.

15 Tate Gallery, London, no. 1688.

16 Victoria and Albert Museum, London, no. E5679–1910.

17 The Yale Center for British Art, Paul Mellon Collection.

18 The artist's sales were held at Christie's on 4–7 May 1877, 3 May 1897 and 24 May 1909.

19 Ibid. (1877), lot no. 176.

20 Illustrated in Thackeray, *From Cornhill* (1991 reprint), p. 146. Also in *The Independent Magazine* (4 January 1992), pp. 38–9.

21 Victoria and Albert Museum, London, no. P1–1949.

22 Private collection, see RA, *The Orientalists*, cat. no. 73.

23 Fitzwilliam Museum, Cambridge, no. PD.6–1959, and City Museums and Art Gallery, Birmingham, no. 14/49.

24 Victoria and Albert Museum, London, no. 679–1893; oil in Tate Gallery, London, no. 3594, watercolour in Fitzwilliam Museum, Cambridge, no. 2111.

25 Private collection.

26 Royal Scottish Academy, Edinburgh (1853), no. 494.

27 All these are in the Victoria and Albert Museum, nos 852–862–1900 and SD331.

28 Victoria and Albert Museum, Searight Collection, SD332; Private collection.

29 See B. Llewellyn, 'Frank Dillon', p. 8.

17 ∽ Travellers, Colonisers and Conservationists

Hossam M. Mahdy

In a Muslim society, as indeed in any traditional society, conservation is, and always has been, imbedded in a development equation (an equation of conservation and change). In other words, in any traditional society every minute there is a choice to be made. What should be changed and what merits conservation?[1] It is a fairly recent phenomenon to deal with conservation as a process of freezing or mummifying certain buildings, objects or aspects of cultural expression. After the industrial revolution, it became feasible to build in radically different materials, forms and scale. It also became feasible to erase complete urban or rural settlements and rebuild them differently. The supply of municipal services and the introduction of motor vehicles made it attractive to rearrange historic cities to offer modern standards of life. It is then that the concept of conservation changed to mean keeping parts of the past as museum pieces for future generations. Egypt was no exception.

Although modernisation reforms were initiated by Muhammad 'Ali (1805–48), it was in the era of Khedive Isma'il (1863–79) that the conservation issue was raised. Isma'il's notion of building 'an impressive image of modern Egypt' as an essential step towards modernising the country, is central to the study of attitudes. Isma'il's motivation for his grand modernisation projects was to impress European travellers in general, and those who were to participate in the opening of the Suez canal in particular. Public edifices were hurriedly constructed in European styles, Viennese and Italian in particular. Baron Haussmann's methods of urban arrangements were boldly implemented. 17 November 1869, the date of the opening of the Suez canal, was the deadline for the modern façade of Cairo to be completed. The Khedive was realistic enought to accept that he could not do much beyond the façade in the given span of time. The Cairo Opera House, for example, was built in elaborate rococo style and completed in five months, just in time for the premier performance during the canal celebrations.[2] Europeans of all ranks, professions and interests went up and down the country during the big celebrations of opening the Suez canal. However, Abu-Lughod[3] observed that: 'guests and hosts operated

157

somewhat at cross purpose. Isma'il did his best to create a European image of himself and his country; the Europeans wanted only the exotic.'

It was the Muhammad 'Ali Boulevard that shocked many and raised the question of conservation. The project was completed in 1873 by Isma'il's enthusiastic Minister of Public Works, 'Ali Mubarak. It sliced with uncompromising straightness[4] through 400 large houses, more than 300 smaller ones, bakeries, baths and many mosques for the distance of two kilometres[5] in the urban fabric of historic Cairo.

> These were all destroyed, or cut in half and left standing like dolls' houses with no outer wall, so that when the road was completed the scene resembled 'a city that has recently been shelled—houses in all stages of dilapidation, though still inhabited, giving most odd views of domestic interiors, frowning down upon you.[6]

The aim of constructing the boulevard was to connect the two palaces of al-Azbakiyya and the citadel. This aim, the once cherished dream of Muhammad 'Ali, became much less meaningful in the time of Isma'il after the completion of his enormous 'Abdin palace. The extent of demolition of historic buildings to open up the Boulevard Muhammad 'Ali was, therefore, hardly justifiable.[7]

> ... the rude hand of the modern street-improver, who within memory has cut a mosque in two or demolished a medieval palace for no better reason than the correct alignment of a hideous boulevard.[8]

The travellers' role was essential in both modernisation and conservation movements in Egypt. In the case of modernisation, Isma'il's approach to modernisation as an image-building exercise made the travellers' role crucial. Their approval and acknowledgement of Egypt as a 'modern state' was the aim of modernisation projects. Travellers were the spectators in a theatrical play. Though passive by definition, the spectators' existence was as important as the players'.

In the case of conservation, the travellers' role was an active one. They inspired and initiated the conservation of 'the exotic image of Egypt'. Egyptians, including Khedive Isma'il himself, were not aware of the existence of this image, let alone of its value. Edward Said convincingly argued[9] that 'the Orient', of which the 'exotic image of Egypt' is an essential part, was a Western colonial invention. In effect, the 'exotic image of Egypt' was needing to be built, rather than conserved. Thus travellers' attitudes to conservation were in essence similar to Isma'il's attitudes to modernisation. Both were image-building exercises. Their differences were not in attitudes but in the choice of the image to be built.

Conservation Within the Discourse of Colonialism

One may speak of colonial conservation, as we speak of the colonial city, where architectural and urban measures were taken to represent and enforce a colonial order. In the second half of the nineteenth century, architectural and urban policies of French colonialism in the Maghreb[10] changed course from modernisation to conservation. This was done by addressing three different questions:

1. What should be done to individual historic buildings? The answer was to conserve surviving historic buildings and reconstruct ruined ones.
2. What should be the style of new buildings? The answer was to build in neo-Arab style.
3. What should be done to the historic urban fabric? The answer was to preserve it.

These policies reflected the second phase of French colonisation which was based on co-operation between indigenous populations and European colonisers. Earlier practices of imposed urban modernisation and European architectural styles, which were characteristic of the first colonial phase of confrontation, came to a halt by 1865.

Conservation trends, which developed later in Egypt, addressed the same three questions. In the case of Egypt, however, unlike the Maghreb, neither modernisation schemes nor conservation measures were imposed by a colonial political power. Isma'il's Europeanisation of Egypt and Haussmannisation of Cairo were carried out voluntarily. Conservation measures, such as the establishment of the Committee of Conservation for Monuments of Arab Art in December 1881, were also adopted voluntarily by Khedive Tawfiq (1879–92). Even during the British colonisation of Egypt (1882–1954) architectural and urban policies were not reflecting a conscious colonial philosophy as was the case in India for the British, and in the Maghreb for the French.[11] Why, then, did national conservation tendencies in Egypt address similar concerns to those of European colonial policies in other regions?

Although Egypt was not colonised for most of the nineteenth century, the country was in a post-colonial era.[12] The French evacuation left Egypt with a conflict which resulted in a divided society. One section of the society belonged culturally to the West, whereas the other section remained loyal to the pre-colonial culture and value system. Both sections were Muslims, native Arabic-speaking and born-and-bred Egyptians. Their differences were limited to attitudes, a state of affairs which can be seen in most post-colonial societies.[13] The Egyptian ruling elite, after the French evacuation, formed a Westernised section of society. Consequently, government policies followed faithfully the footsteps of Europe as the model for scientific and modern development. Khedive Isma'il once boasted:[14] 'My country is no longer in Africa, for we are now part of Europe.' European travellers were therefore continuously needed for inspiration and assurance.

Nineteenth-century Egypt was, from a cultural point of view, in a typical post-colonial state. European architectural and urban policies were implemented. European policies in Muslim colonies were followed, even when these policies were meant to control and suppress the indigenous populations. Egyptian rulers enjoyed playing the 'European master' with their fellow Egyptians.

Travellers and the 'Arabian Nights': fact and fiction

In 1882, Stanley Lane Poole wrote[15] an advertisement for his great-uncle Edward William Lane's translation and commentary on *The Thousand and One Nights*. He started by describing 'the continued popularity of the work' since the first publication of Lane's translation in 1839. Lane Poole suggested that the success of his great-uncle was due to two factors. The first was his 'instinctive sympathy for the spirit of the East'. The second was 'the rich store of illustrations of oriental life and thought contained in his Notes'. He referred, now and then, to Lane's *Account of the Manners and Customs of the Modern Egyptians*. He reminded us that in the 'cheap versions based on Galland's French paraphrase ... the peculiarities of life and manners [of Muslims and Egyptians] ... were left unnoted and unexplained'. Then he projected the 'Arabian Nights' on reality. It is of Egypt, he claimed rightly, that the 'Arabian Nights' 'have most to tell'. Even if the place was Baghdad or India, and even if the people were Chinese or Hindus, 'it is in medieval Cairo, in the days of the Mamlooks, that the scene of the Arabian Nights was really laid'. His advertisement went on interlacing the wonders of both the 'Arabian Nights' and medieval Cairo. He promised the reader that he would see medieval Cairo in the 'Arabian Nights', and that he would meet Harun al-Rashid, Abu Nuwas, Kafur, Saladin or Qayt Bey in the streets of Cairo. Then Lane Poole reflected with remorse on the rapid change which was taking place in Egypt, so that Oriental buildings and lifestyles were 'fast becoming matter of history rather than of experience, a field for the antiquary instead of the traveller ... ' What is most interesting in his advertisement is his solution to the sad disappearance of the real world of the 'Arabian Nights' (i.e. medieval Cairo): ' ... it is well that we can 'reconstruct' it in the pages of the *Thousand and One Nights*, whose compiler saw it when it was still almost in its Golden Prime.'

Lane Poole's appreciation of the 'Arabian Nights' as a lively picture of the real exotic world of medieval Cairo, and as an aid in reconstructing this rapidly disappearing world, sheds light on the nature of European travellers' interest in medieval Egypt. European travellers went to Egypt to bring back a picture of the exotic—a nineteenth-century tradition which was initiated and inspired by Napoleon's expedition and its monumental work *Description de l'Égypte*. All talents and techniques which were available in Europe at the time were employed to record this picture, and everything brought back from Egypt to fulfil the European nostalgia for the exotic was extremely popular.

Exotic Pictures Recorded and Reconstructed by Travellers

After their travels during the first decade of the nineteenth century, David Roberts and Robert Ker Porter produced huge panoramic paintings of Egypt and other Oriental subjects with moving shadows and mechanical animations.[16] E. W. Lane's first journey to Egypt in 1825 was not as a writer but as an engraver. He took with him the new invention *camera lucida* which was a drawing device with a prism that projected the image of an object on the artist's paper.[17] In 1850 Gustave Flaubert and Maxime Du Camp went to Egypt on a photographic mission with a daguerreotype (see Chapter 20). They were by no means the only travellers in Egypt on a photographic mission at the time. In 1856 Francis Frith set out from Liverpool on his first journey to Egypt on a photographic mission with a 10 x 8 inch camera, stereoscopic camera, a dark tent, glass plates and chemicals. The result of Frith's missions came to be the most celebrated early photographs of Egypt and the Holy Land.[18] The very early application of photographic techniques in recording Egypt signifies the European desire to draw an accurate and lively picture of the country.

The emotional and sensual nature of travellers' motivations explains the sometimes bizzare mixture in their records of the painstaking attention to details of costumes, settings, facial types and buildings on the one hand, and the historical and contextual inaccuracy of the totality on the other. Like the 'Arabian Nights', travellers' reports were meant to reconstruct the exotic Oriental picture if the reality was too disappointing. Gérôme's famous painting 'The Snake and Charmer' is a precise example of such a carefree reconstruction. Like the 'Arabian Nights' the scene, people and objects in Gérôme's painting were from different places and times, but it was the picture of one exotic world. The painting is an art-historical pastiche of the following: figures with Ottoman faces, dressed in Balkan costumes, watching a naked boy as a snake charmer (a scene unknown in Ottoman popular culture); the boy is standing on a prayer mat (a most unlikely piece of behaviour at the time); the wall is decorated with Iznik tile panels, with Qajar Persian or Indian armour hung on the wall. The different parts of the painting were drawn in such accuracy that the tile panels and the inscription panel can be located today. They belonged, however, to two different buildings in Istanbul, and not to the portal of the Blue Mosque in Cairo, as it was meant to be, according to al-Sayyad.[19]

On the one hand, travellers were obsessed with the accurate recording of medieval life in Egypt but, on the other hand, what really mattered was to see and portray a lively exotic image, even if it needed to be patched up either from imagination or from images of other exotic places, such as Turkey, Persia or India. In effect, addressing travellers' desires, as far as the conservation of Islamic architectural heritage was concerned, meant that medieval buildings should be preserved, restored, reconstructed, patched up or even invented so as to fulfil the spectators' nostalgia for the exotic Oriental world. In other words, the aim of urban and architectural conservation is to transform medieval Egypt into a huge Oriental theme park, where the visitors can wander about and, as in Disneyland, can see their favourite buildings and characters. For a more serious traveller, whose intention is to study 'the Orient', medieval Egypt should be like a zoo, where the visitors can enjoy and examine their favourite animals to their pleasure, convenience and safety. The more wildlife is marginalised by modern human developments, the more the need for zoos becomes urgent.

> Zoos, realistic animal toys and the widespread commercial diffusion of animal imagery, all began as animals started to be withdrawn from daily life. One could suppose that such innovations were compensatory. Yet in reality the innovations themselves belonged to the same remorseless movement as was dispersing the animals. The zoos, with their theatrical decor for display, were in fact demonstrations of how animals had been rendered absolutely marginal.[20]

Like zoos, the Oriental theme park was becoming more urgent to the minds of European travellers as modernisation was spreading in Egypt. This might explain the timing of the European world exhibitions,[21] coinciding with the rapid urban modernisation in Europe on one hand, and the steadily marginalised non-Western world on the other. The 1867 Exposition universelle in Paris was no more than a theme park, where Khedive Isma'il was wildly inspired and strongly convinced to Europeanise Egypt. Meanwhile, many European travellers-to-be were as wildly inspired and as strongly convinced to Orientalise Egypt by travelling to Egypt hoping to be able to freeze its Oriental charm in time and space or, at least, to record the country's life-style before it ceased to be Oriental. At the time that Khedive Isma'il was hastily converting Egypt into a theme park of a European modern country, European travellers were arguing very strongly to convert the country into a theme park of the 'Arabian Nights'.

Conservation Trends in Modern Egypt

The concept of conserving medieval buildings for the sole reason of their historic merit was introduced, for the first time in Egypt, as a reaction to the urban, architectural and cultural modernisation schemes implemented by Isma'il. It was in Europe, however, that the conservation issue was raised and debated. The Society for the Protection of Ancient Buildings (SPAB) sent a letter to the Khedive[22] urging him to protect Arab art. Conservationists, Orientalists and travellers raised awareness in Britain and Europe of the dangers facing Egyptian medieval buildings.[23] Consequently, an Egyptian conservation movement started to gather momentum on different levels. Towards the last two decades of the nineteenth century, three major trends[24] were well established:

1. The conservation of individual historic buildings was carried out by the Committee for the Conservation of Monuments of Arab Art,[25] which was established in 1881;
2. The neo-Arab style for new buildings was conceived;
3. *Tanzim*[26] interventions in the historic urban fabric became more sympathetic to the existing urban fabric.

The Conservation of Individual Historic Buildings

Technically speaking, the Committee adopted the attitudes of the French school of conservation. Its conservation of Egyptian medieval buildings resembled that of Viollet-Le-Duc's conservation of medieval French buildings.[27] Not only the Committee's name and language were French, but also its technical practices. The Committee was not concerned with a building's function, nor with its religious, social or economic role and meaning within its urban surroundings. The *Saturday Review*[28] summarised the duties of the Committee as follows: 'to make an inventory of historic buildings, to draw plans for needed repairs and the inspection of carrying out the suggested repairs, to build and keep a library of plans, photographs and records of all conservation information and efforts, and finally to remove to the then newly opened Museum of Arab Art any object that could not have been safely kept in its original place.' The Committee's activities also included advice to individuals, the Ministry of Public Works and the Ministry of Waqfs on the execution of new buildings and schemes in the neo-Arab style.

The Birth of a neo-Arab Style for Buildings

The mosque of al-Rifa'i, the most monumental of neo-Arab buildings in Egypt, was designed and completed by European architects. The architectural vocabulary of its façades was 'Arab', whereas its plan was 'modern'.[29] Most other early neo-Arab buildings in Cairo were also designed by European architects. 'Ali Mubarak observed that building in the neo-Arab style was a foreign phenomenon, built by European architects for European clients. This was true until the turn of the century, when it became a part of the debate on the cultural and national identity of Egypt.[30] The neo-Arab style should, however, be placed within European contemporary trends. Neo-Mamluk, neo-Mughal and neo-Moorish styles were fashionable at the time, not only in the regions which produced them, but also in Europe. For example, a project proposed by Arnodin for the Hamidiya bridge at the gate of the Bosphorus in Istanbul had three pairs of mosque-like pylons. Each mosque had a central dome and four minarets of Cairene Mamluk style.[31] Other examples include a mosque-like tobacco factory in Dresden,[32] Chinese pagodas in Kew Gardens and Indian pavilions in Brighton.[33] Neo-Arab style was a compromise between the aesthetics of the Islamic architectural heritage on the one hand, and European modern concepts of hygiene and aesthetics on the other. It was a continuous effort to Europeanise the Arab, or to Arabise the European.

Nothing in the history of modern Egypt came nearer to the Oriental theme-park dream than the Heliopolis project initiated by the Belgian entrepreneur Baron Empain. A huge urban scheme on 7,000 hectares was designed in the neo-Arab style by Belgian, French and British architects. It was meant to be a recreation centre for European travellers in Egypt.[34] The importance of Heliopolis to the argument of conservation in modern Egypt, is not only because of its direct expression of the decades-long travellers' desire to construct an Oriental theme park,[35] but most importantly because of its direct indication of the strength of European impact on attitudes towards the conservation of the Islamic architectural heritage at the beginning of the twentieth century.

Tanzim Interventions Sympathetic to the Historic Urban Fabric

A compromise between the ideal geometry proposed by urban and municipal services projects on the one hand, and the existing urban fabric on the other, started in 1885 with the modification of article 10 of the 1882 *tanzim* laws:[36]

> Originally it read, 'If the alignment drawings require that new roads be built through private property, then those lands so designated can be expropriated from their owners by law.' By 28 February 1885, the text had been modified to

read, 'If the alignment drawings required that the new roads be built through private property, then those lands so designated should gradually be acquired from their owners.'

The shift in attitudes to accommodate both the old and the new is obvious in the planning of al-Hilmiyya. Khaled Asfour observes[37] that the same attitude, which he calls 'domestication', was applied on the smaller level of individual buildings. Modifications to both plans and façades of European-style buildings were made to suit the Egyptian life-style and value system.

Conclusion

European attitudes towards the conservation of Egyptian medieval buildings were most peculiar. They reflected local social and cultural moods. Like the Scottish quilt or the Bavarian clap dance, they were limited to their time and place. Any attempt to apply these attitudes out of the European nineteenth-century context would leave them meaningless and irrelevant. Unfortunately, however, the political, military and cultural hegemony of nineteenth-century European colonialism imposed the notion that these attitudes were universally and eternally valid, and perfectly justifiable.

The embedded aim of conservation trends in modern Egypt, though never stated openly, was to construct the Oriental theme park. Thus conservation was practised as a process of mummifying and visually preserving the architectural and urban medieval heritage. Like Gérôme's painting, breathtaking meticulous attention to detail was characteristic of the conservation projects for Egyptian medieval buildings. And also like Gérôme's painting, art-historical pastiche was widely practised. At the turn of the century, conserved, restored, reconstructed and newly constructed buildings with 'Arab' or 'Islamic' architectural vocabulary gave Egypt an 'Oriental atmosphere' so impressive that medieval buildings and attitudes towards their conservation became inseparable. It was possible to question the validity of conserving the Islamic architectural heritage altogether, but not how, why or for whom it should be conserved.

Notes

1 Stephen Owen, 'Change and Conservation in Settlements', *Planning Outlook* 18 (1976).
2 Janet Abu-Lughod, *Cairo, 1001 Years of the City Victorious* (New Jersey, 1971), pp. 105–8.
3 Ibid., p. 112.
4 Khaled Asfour, 'The domestication of knowledge: Cairo at the turn of the century' in *Muqarnas, An annual on Islamic art and architecture* Vol. 10, *Essays in honour of Oleg Grabar*, contributed by his students (Leiden, 1993), pp. 125–

37.

5   Abu-Lughod, *1001 Years*, p. 112.

6   Timothy Mitchell, *Colonising Egypt* (Cambridge, 1988), p. 65, quoting Edwin De Leon, *The Khedive's Egypt* (London: Sampson Low & Co., 1877), p. 139; André Raymond, *Grandes villes arabes à l'époque ottomane*, pp. 69–78, and Grecelius, *Roots of Modern Egypt*, pp. 15–24.

7   Abu-Lughod, *1001 Years*, p. 113.

8   'The Preservation of mediaeval Cairo' in *The Architect & Contract Reporter* (6 March 1896), p. 153.

9   Edward W. Said, *Orientalism* (London: Routledge & Kegan Paul, 1978), p. 3.

10 Shirine Hamadeh, 'Creating the traditional city, a French project' in *Forms of Dominance, on the architecture and urbanism of the colonial enterprise*, ed. Nezar Al-Sayyad, Ethnoscape, Current Challenges in the Environment Social Sciences (Hants, 1992), pp. 241–59.

11 Nezar Al-Sayyad (ed.), *Forms of Dominance, on the architecture and urbanism of the colonial enterprise*, Ethnoscape, Current Challenges in the Environment Social Sciences (Hants, 1992).

12 The term 'post-colonial' is strictly used to indicate the socio-cultural state of Egypt at the period from the French evacuation to the British colonisation. It should not be confused with the period of Egyptian independence, after British evacuation in 1954, which historians conventionally refer to by the term 'post-colonial Egypt'.

13 Munir Shafiq, *Qadaya al-tanmiya wa-al-istiqlal wa-al-sira' al-hadari* (Tunis, 1989), pp. 31–50. It was not until the 1940s–1960s that the Maghreb, India and other ex-European colonies were in a similar schizophrenic state.

14 'Abd al-Rahman al-Rifa'i, *'Asr Isma'il* (Cairo, 1932, reprinted 1972), quoted by Asfour, *Muqarnas*, Vol. 10, p. 129.

15 [*Alf Layla wa-Layla.*] *The Thousand and One Nights, commonly called, in England, the Arabian Nights' Entertainments. A new translation from the Arabic, with copious notes, by E. W. Lane* (London, 1839–41). 3 vols, a new edition, (ed.) Edward Stanley Poole (London, 1882), p. vi.

16 Kenneth P. Bendiner, 'The portrayal of the Middle East in British painting, 1825–1860', Ph.D. thesis, Columbia University (1979), pp. 13–18, quoted by Mitchell, *Colonising Egypt*, pp. 23–4.

17 Leila Ahmed, *Edward W. Lane: a study of his life and work, and of British ideas of the Middle East in the nineteenth century* (London: Longmans, 1978), quoted by Mitchell, *Colonising Egypt*, p. 23.

18 Julia Van Haaften, 'Introduction and Bibliography' in *Egypt and the Holy Land in Historic Photographs. 77 Views by Francis Frith*, selection and commentary by Jon D. Mandchip White (New York, 1980), pp. vii–xxiv. See also chapter 18.

19 Walter B. Denny, 'Quotations in and out of context: Ottoman Turkish art and European Orientalist painting' in *Muqarnas*, Vol. 10, pp. 220–30 and al-Sayyad, *Forms of Dominance*.

20 John Berger, *About Looking* (London, 1980), p. 24.

21 Mitchell, Colonising Egypt, pp. 1–21.

22 S. Tschudi-Madsen, Restoration and Anti-Restoration (Universitetsforlaget,

1976), p. 95.

23 K. A. C. Creswell, *A Bibliography of the Architecture, Arts and Crafts of Islam* (Cairo, 1960) lists many articles published in *The Academy, The Architect, The Saturday Review* and *The Architect & Contract Reporter* in the 1860s-80s propagating the conservation of Egyptian medieval buildings.

24 These three trends bear resemblances to French colonial policies in the Maghreb, and also to Lane Poole's concerns stated in his article quoted earlier (see 'Arab Art Monuments' above).

25 Henceforth referred to in this chapter as the Committee.

26 *Tanzim*: '... a word often translated as "modernisation" for this period [the era of Muhammad 'Ali] though it means something more like "organisation" or "regulation". In context it could mean simply "the laying out of streets", and it became the name of the Department of Public Works.' Mitchell, *Colonising Egypt*, p. 67.

27 Hossam M. Mahdy, 'Attitudes towards architectural conservation, the case of Cairo', unpublished Ph.D. thesis, Glasgow (1992), pp. 68–77.

28 'Ancient buildings at Cairo' in *The Saturday Review* (London, 3 September 1892), pp. 277–8.

29 Mohammed al-Asad, 'The Mosque of al-Rifa'i in Cairo' in *Muqarnas*, Vol 10, pp. 108–24.

30 Robert Ilbert and Mercedes Volait, 'Neo-Arabic Renaissance in Egypt, 1870–1930', *Mimar* 13 (1984), pp. 26–34; Hassan Fathy, *Architecture for the Poor* (Chicago, 1973), pp. 19–20.

31 Zaynep Celik, *The Remaking of Istanbul* (Washington, 1986), pp. 108–9.

32 Stefan Koppelkamm, *Der imaginaire Orient: Exotische Bauten des achtzehnten und neunzehnten Jahrhunderts in Europa* (Berlin, 1987), pp. 171–2.

33 Kamil Khan Mumtaz, 'Architecture in Pakistan', *Mimar* (Singapore, 1985), pp. 117–25.

34 Robert Ilbert, 'Heliopolis: colonial enterprise and town planning success?' in *The Expanding Metropolis coping with the Urban Growth of Cairo*, Proceedings of Seminar 9, 'Architectural Transformations in the Islamic World', held in Cairo, 11–15 November 1984, Aga Khan Award for Architecture (Singapore, 1985), pp. 36–42.

35 There is hardly any difference between a life-size Mickey Mouse strolling in the streets of Disneyland and a Nubian waiter dressed up in a pseudo-Arabian exotic costume serving in Groppi Heliopolis coffee-shop.

36 Asfour, *Muqarnas*, Vol 10.

37 Ibid., '... the traditional *salamlek*, that is, the reception room for men detached from the rest of the house, was retained in the otherwise European plan', p. 133; 'Typical was the treatment that involved the placement of a parapet of free-standing *mashrabiyyas* or shutters over the terrace balustrade to allow the women of the house to enjoy the openness of a terrace without being exposed to the public eye', p. 134.

Caroline Williams

Today, making a photographic record of where we have been and what we have seen is an almost instant, effortless, inexpensive process, so commonplace we hardly give it a thought. For this reason, the work of Francis Frith (1822–98) in Egypt around 1860 is worthy of note. His importance then, and now, is threefold. As a photographer, Frith was a pioneer in both a new art and a new process of that art. He was one of the first British photographers to record systematically the ancient monuments of a foreign land and to mass produce and distribute them. Furthermore, as Britain's first great photographer-publisher, his views defined the mid-nineteenth-century topographical image of Egypt, providing documents of a time and place which no longer exist. Finally, as a visual recorder, his legacy of images was an important foundation upon which subsequent 'Orientalist' artists relied to create their own visual records of Egypt.

In 1856, aged thirty-four, Francis Frith set sail for what he called 'the two most interesting lands of the globe—Egypt and Palestine'.[1] There is not much in his early decades to suggest his future success.[2] School, which he attended until he was sixteen, he found 'an insipid and mechanical portion of existence'. The next five years, an apprenticeship in a cutlery firm in Sheffield, taught him only 'the art of hard work', from which he departed with a nervous and physical breakdown. His early twenties were spent travelling in England and Wales, after which he entered the grocery business. Although he managed to corner the Greek raisin market, he left the retail world with 'a profound contempt for the commercial mind and a horror of having my soul murdered'. Frith had both a curious and reflective mind. He read poetry and philosophy; he was interested in religion, travel and biography. He was also a practical man. He enjoyed making mechanical models, and he had a good sense of detail. In 1850, at twenty-eight, he started a printing business. At the same time he took up photography, an interest which coincided with a new development in this new science.

The optical principles of photography had long been known, but it was only in 1839, when Louis Jacques Mande Daguerre developed a chemical way to affix an image to a light-sensitive surface, that a practical form of photography became possible.[3] The daguerreotype produced a direct positive image on a silver-coated copper plate, but the image could not be reproduced unless it was copied onto another surface. This disadvantage was overcome by H. Fox Talbot's invention of the calotype, the earliest practical negative process, in which one chemically-coated paper negative could yield an indefinite number of copies. But the paper negative was awkward to use in the field, the image it produced tended to be soft and grainy, and Fox Talbot restricted the use of his discovery through patents. The next photographic advance occurred in March 1851 when William Archer discovered a way to combine the clarity and the detail of the daguerreotype with the positive printing possibilities of the calotype. This was the collodion or wet-plate glass process, the fastest photographic method so far devised and the first to be free from patent restrictions in England. The potential for photography was instantly recognised. In the summer of 1851, at the Crystal Palace Exhibition, the first of the general exhibitions that celebrated the newest applications and achievements of industry and commerce, photography was one of the exhibits.

Of Francis Frith's early photographic training there is not much on record.[4] It is known that in 1853 he was one of seven who founded the Liverpool Photographic Society. He also photographed in the countryside around his home in Derbyshire. As an exhibitor at the London Photographic Society he was referred to as 'Mr. Frith, an amateur'. In 1856 he sold his printing business at a considerable and comfortable profit and set sail for Egypt with Francis Herbert Wenham, an optics and aviation researcher, as his companion.[5]

Egypt was a logical destination for Francis Frith, photographer, for several reasons. Egypt had been linked with photography from its very beginning.[6] When Daguerre's discovery of a way to make mechanical images was announced in August 1839, the instant copying of the millions of hieroglyphs covering the great Egyptian monuments was cited as an example of its potential use. Three months later, in November, the first known photograph taken in the Middle East was of the harem of Muhammad 'Ali's palace in Alexandria, Egypt. A number of books illustrated with daguerreotype and calotype images immediately followed.[7]

In the 1840s the growth of steamship travel and the development of the overland route from Alexandria to Suez as a stage in the trip to India made Egypt more accessible. Furthermore, as the knowledge about Egypt's pharaonic past and its Islamic present became more widespread, Egypt as an exotic destination became more attractive.[8] During the early 1850s a number of publications detailing the growing knowledge and observations about Egyptian culture were printed. Frith read these books, and he refers to them in the text he wrote for his photographs.[9]

For Frith, however, the most immediate impetus towards Egypt must have been its artistic presentation by David Roberts, the first professional British artist to go to Egypt and draw with the specific purpose of returning with a publishable portfolio of images. Roberts was in Egypt for three and a half months, and his drawings, of the Islamic present as well as the pharaonic past, afforded the most complete visual record of Egypt to date. They were published in six volumes between 1842 and 1849, and were reissued in 1855–56.[10] Frith was certainly acquainted with Roberts' images. Under his own photograph of the fallen colossus at the Ramesseum in Thebes Frith wrote: 'David Roberts in his splendid work,[11] has bestowed upon it a very respectable and recognisable profile; but my picture shows that the face is so mutilated as scarcely to leave a feature traceable ... '[12]

Frith wrote elsewhere, 'A truthful record is of more value than the most elaborately beautiful picture.'[13] Frith often photographed the same scene that David Roberts had drawn, as much because it was an important monument as to correct the artistic record. For example, under his view of the statues of Memnon, he wrote: 'As regards the shattered condition of these statues, I have only to refer to the Photograph, which will again, I fear, contradict some of the representations of previous artists.'[14] Frith's photograph deliberately makes this point.

Between September 1856 and the spring of 1860, Francis Frith made three trips to Egypt and the Holy Land. The first trip, from September 1856 to July 1857, was devoted to Egypt: to Cairo and its environs, and to the ancient monuments along the Nile. On the second trip, from November 1857 to May 1858, Egypt was an embarcation point for his photographing trip to Palestine and Syria. On the third trip, from the late summer of 1859 to the late spring of 1860, he went up the Nile as far as Sulb, between the second and third cataracts, the first photographer to travel that far and into what is today northern Ethiopia, and then via the 'long desert' overland from Suez down through Sinai, and on to Gaza. In all he spent over twenty-four months in Egypt and the Holy Land.

When Frith was not in the Middle East taking photographs, he was in England printing them for publication or preparing them for exhibition. Between 1858 and 1862 Frith published eight separate photographically illustrated books containing more than 400 images and supplied photographs for two different editions of the Bible.[15] Frith went to the Middle East as an amateur but the photographic views he brought back immediately established his reputation as Britain's first great photographer-publisher. His images also set the standard for published photographic views of foreign lands. Charmingly written, handsomely produced and full of exotic material, Frith's volumes were a wonderful addition to the drawing-room table. *Egypt and Palestine Photographed and Described by Francis Frith*

(1858–1860) had seventy-six photographs. Two thousand copies of it were made, for which over 150,000 prints were run off and hand-tipped onto the pages. It was the most ambitious photographic publication to date. *Egypt, Sinai, Jerusalem and the Pyramids of Egypt*, published in 1860, is the largest and most elaborate photographically illustrated book ever published. The photographs are roughly 19 by 15 inches on pages that measure 29 by 21 inches. The text was written by Mrs Sophia Lane-Poole, the sister of Edward W. Lane, and Reginald Stuart Poole, her younger son and assistant in the Department of Antiquities at the British Museum.

Early photographers in the Middle East rarely gave details about how their work was produced. Frith is an exception. He writes engagingly about the skill, resource, patience and speed required to produce at best six pictures a day.

Frith worked in the collodion or wet-plate glass process which produced the most reliable and sharpest negative, but it involved a very cumbersome and complex operation. First, the photographer cleaned and polished a sheet of glass. Then, with great manual dexterity, he would 'flow' the collodion— a viscous chemical liquid containing potassium iodide—over the plate; soak the coated plate in a bath of silver nitrate to make it light-sensitive; place it in a plate-holder, insert the plate-holder into the camera, make the exposure, remove the plate from the holder and treat it with pyrogallic acid or ferrous sulfate followed by hypo-sulphite of soda or potassium cyanide to fix the image, and finally wash, dry, varnish and store the plate. The entire exposing and processing operation had to be carried out while the collodion was wet, and therefore a darkroom or its equivalent had to be near.[16]

Frith carried three cameras with him: a standard studio camera, which used glass plates measuring 8 to 10 inches; a large format camera for glass plates measuring 16 by 20 inches (the only way to produce large prints since enlargements were not yet practical), and a third camera which had a dual lens for making three-dimensional stereoscopic views. The glass plates were packed in special boxes lined with India-rubber cushions. A crate of plates required two men to lift it. The necessary chemicals were stored in boxes lined with cork. Other supplies included: lenses; tripod; various dishes, scales, funnels, measures, pail and jars of distilled rinsing water—all of which could weigh upwards of 120 pounds or more and in the field had to be transported by animate energy. One French photographer observed: 'Learning photography is an easy matter, but transporting the equipment by mule, camel or human porters is more serious.'[17] Often a goodly part of each photo-opportunity was spent packing and unpacking the equipment. At one stop Frith writes:

> We were put ashore with our cumbrous loads of apparatus etc. and began our walk over the rough ground, and under the hot sun; ... mile after mile we went

until we began to regard our guides, our temple-mania, our stars, our photographic lumber, ourselves, as so many palpable mockeries and snares.[18]

Since the image, once taken, had to be fixed immediately upon the glass plate while still moist, the darkroom could not be more than a three-minute walk away from the camera. For this purpose, Frith writes:

> I had constructed in London a wicker work carriage on wheels ... which being entirely overspread with a loose cover of white sailcloth to protect it from the sun, was a most conspicuous and mysterious-looking vehicle, and excited ... a vast amount of ingenious speculation ... The idea which seemed the most reasonable ... was that therein ... I transported from place to place—my harem! ... and great was the respect and consideration which this view of the case procured for me!'[19]

Sometimes Francis Frith used tombs as darkrooms:

> Pushing myself backwards, upon my hands and knees, into a damp, slimy rock-tomb ... I prepared my pictures by candlelight in one of the interior chambers ... It was a most unpleasant apartment ... the hole in which I worked. The floor was covered to the depth of several inches with an impalpable, ill-flavoured dust, which rose in clouds as we moved; from the roof were suspended groups of fetid bats.[20]

But whether in tomb or tent, in Frith's words,

> I suffered a good deal through the journey from the severe labour rendered necessary by the rapidity with which every stage of the process must be conducted in climates such as these; at the Second Cataract with the thermometer at 110° in my tent, the collodion actually boiled when poured upon the glass plate ... and from the excessive perspiration, consequent on the suffocating heat of a small tent, from which every ray of light, and consequently every breath of air, was necessarily excluded.[21]

Composition also posed problems for the photographer. A comparison of David Roberts' and Francis Frith's differing views of the temple of Abu Simbel is illustrative. In the mid-nineteenth century the Great Temple was situated only twenty-five yards from the edge of the Nile. David Roberts paints the scene as a whole,[22] emphasising the visual and emotional impact of the site. In order to convey the stupendous magnificence of the statues of the façade, in the isolation of their setting, he paints the scene from a bird's-eye view and reduces the people to an ant-like procession in the untrodden sands. He uses artistic license to achieve dramatic effect. Frith cannot stand back, so he comes in as close as he can, with the tiny figure in the foreground outlined against Ramesses' beard to show the scale of the face, and by extension the size of the temple itself.[23] 'Only a photographer', he wrote, 'can appreciate the difficulty of getting a view satisfactorily into the camera: foregrounds are especially perverse; distance too near or too far; the falling away of the ground; the intervention of some brick wall or other commonplace object, which an artist would simply omit; some or all of these are the rule not the exception.'[24] Sometimes he found it hard even to position himself. 'Around [this obelisk at Karnak] is a perfect chaos of splendid ruin, amongst which I found it extremely difficult to fix my instruments so as to command a view.'[25]

How to suggest atmosphere, was another problem. In the hall of columns at Karnak, one of the marvels and triumphs of pharaonic architecture, Frith has concentrated on the interplay between the filtering light from the top and the dim and numinous shadows at ground level. But he chafes at the limitations of his medium: 'As for making you feel the witchcraft of the place, its oppressive grandeur, its dark mysterious interest, the thing is totally impossible ... the pillars are so strangely crowded together, and their height is so great, as to render it quite impossible to obtain a photograph within the hall itself ...'[26]

Working in Cairo, the compositional problems were aggravated by the technical limitations of the camera in portraying movement and colour. In the city, full of the bustle and curiosity of people where 'my camera was surrounded by scores of idlers, and innumerable half-naked children',[27] it was virtually impossible for Frith to choose his view or to work. The city-scapes that Frith captured are thus all taken from a high vantage point or in relatively deserted cemeteries. David Roberts' and Francis Frith's views of the *madrasa* of Sultan Hasan, a major Mamluk monument of Islamic Cairo located just below the citadel, offer another instructive comparison.[28] David Roberts shows the monument from its side, a clever way to highlight the height and the mass of the monument, and contrast it with the human figures milling about in the *maydan*. Francis Frith cannot use the human scale. He takes his view from the citadel. Sultan Hasan in its massiveness dominates the skyline, but the foreground is cluttered with wind scoops which he could not omit.

For the artist, Cairo was a great 'kaleidoscope' of people, colour, movement. In reproducing what he saw the artist was limited only by his originality and ability. The photographer, however, was also limited by the technical constraints of his craft. Long exposure times meant that people could be present in the composition only if they were posed or far away; if they moved they blurred. The slow exposure times also meant that the light inside buildings, such as homes, mosques, bazaars, was not adequate. The greatest limitation, however, and the one over which Frith fretted the most, was the lack of colour. 'Did but the sun paint *in colours* upon our bits of magic glass, what a delightful series of pictures would Eastern costume furnish.'[29]

Frith went to Egypt with an informed notion of what was important and noteworthy, as well as, thanks to the drawings of David Roberts, a sense of the places and monuments he would encounter. But Frith also had his own priorities and purposes. His photographs are informative and artistic documents.

Francis Frith took each photograph with a view to conveying as much information as possible. He often re-photographed the same monument at different times of the day, from different directions and in different formats. If possible he included visual information about the site and the landscape, and specifics about the geology and/or the vegetation. In the surreptitious placing of donkeys and porters he indicated scale, added contrast and focused interest. A figure in a black *gallabiya* in the white sand, or a white turban against dark shadows brought the scene to life. 'Pyramids of Geezeh from the Southwest',[30] for example, is a masterful arrangement and balance of elements: of contrasts between tiny figures and massive monuments; of light and dark; of solids and voids; of space and distance. Another admirable example of his style is the way he depicted the kiosk of the Emperor Trajan at Philae. The temple, on the river bank, dominates the upper half of the photograph. It is balanced and underscored by the *dhahabiya* or boat in the lower left corner, which also provides human scale as well as logistical information about Frith's travelling arrangements: '... the boat cost our party £30 per month, including the wages of the ra'is and ten men.'[31] The men, the tasselated palm trees, the boat's mast and the kiosk's columns provide visual rhythm and vertical counterpoints to the horizontal lines of the boat and the monument.[32]

Frith was keenly aware of the threat to the monuments from the accelerating changes in archaeology, tourism and political evolution, which he observed 'give[s] additional value to good Photographs of eastern antiquities ... '[33] About Cleopatra's temple at Erment [Armant], he writes: 'The photograph will give you some idea ... of the ruin into which the temple has fallen, which is due not so much to the ravages of time as to the vandalism of modern pashas and beys, who have broken up this precious relic of antiquity for the building of sugar factories.'[34]

In addition to the pharaonic monuments along the Nile, Frith also took views of the Islamic city of Cairo, not only of the major monuments, but of the urban landscape in its macro and micro forms. In his mammoth view of Cairo[35] looking west from the citadel, Frith has preserved a bird's-eye view of the city's past, present and future. The bottom third shows the medieval city: the barracks and windscoops in front of the adjoining, plastered houses contained by shari' Saliba along which stretch the Mamluk monuments from the mosque of Ibn Tulun (9th century AD) to the mosque of Qanibay al-Muhammadi (early 15th century AD). Next, in mid-section, the present: the grand palaces and gardens along the east bank of the Nile where the ruling family lived in the nineteenth century. Finally, top third, the future: the Nile's empty west bank, which would not be developed until the twentieth century. In Frith's photographs of the Islamic monuments the details are so vivid that it is easy to read the inscription bands around the domes.[36] As with his pharaonic series in which it is not only the monuments but the Nilotic landscape he indicates, so also with his Cairene views, which in addition to the monuments, include streets 'which [present] the general aspect of the city'[37] and 'give an idea of the repose of Eastern life in the Muslim quarters, undisturbed by association with the bustling, anxious, European [area]'.[38] While the artists concentrated on the colourful human kaleidoscope, Frith showed the city as it really was: crumbling, dirty, patched. In his 'View of Boolaq'[39] he captures photographically a description written in 1842 by Sophia Poole:

> The first impression received on entering this celebrated city [Cairo], is, that it has the appearance of having been deserted for perhaps a century, and suddenly repeopled by persons who had been unable, from poverty or some other cause, to repair it, and clear away the antiquated cobwebs.[40]

The 'infallible truthfulness' with which photographs captured a scene rendered them invaluable memory aids for later study, a true benefit for the generation of artists who followed Frith to Egypt.

> ... these faithful pictures have conveyed to ourselves more copious and correct ideas of detail than the inspection of the subjects themselves had supplied, for there appears to be a great[er] aptitude in the mind for careful and minute study *from paper, and at intervals of leisure,* than when the mind is occupied with the general impression suggested by a view of the objects themselves ...[41]

With speed and accuracy the photograph could faithfully capture complicated compositions. Frith writes of an encounter with a French artist: 'When, in a few minutes, I had possessed myself of more accuracy than his labour of perhaps days would yield, he exclaimed ... Ah, monsieur! que vous êtes vite, vite ... '[42]

With photographs it was no longer necessary for the late-nineteenth-century artist to be jostled in crowded thoroughfares to capture realistic and truthful views. These later artists did travel to Egypt. They saw. They sketched. They brought home costumes and artefacts. They used cameras and available photographs to verify and authenticate their compositions. But their main work was done in their studios at home.

To take one example, Jean-Léon Gérôme, a renowned French Orientalist painter, used Francis Frith's photograph 'Cairo from the East'[43] as a basis for his own view 'Looking East' painted in 1880.[44] Frith's view looks over the sixteenth-century domed complex of the Amir Khayrbak and other Mamluk monuments toward the *madrasa* of Sultan Hasan on the horizon. His vista emphasises the way this medieval area and architecture typifies Islamic Cairo. Gérôme's location is also identifiable by the Mamluk complex of the Amir Khayrbak, but he has added another dome, and moved the minaret to make the elements in his painting more interesting. With the literal scene already on record, the artist was free to interpret, or to concentrate on, other aspects of the culture which could not be photographed. In Gérôme's image it is the muezzin, not the architecture, which is the main focus of the composition. He stands on the uppermost balcony of the minaret, a tiny figure against the blue sky, whose call to faith and prayer floats down over the exotic city below.

'When I reflect upon the circumstances under which many of the photographs were taken,' wrote Francis Frith, 'I marvel greatly that they turned out so well.'[45] Today, in looking at his photographs, one also marvels at his work. As a pioneer he practised the art of photography as he wanted to, that is, and to quote him, with 'distinction';[46] as a professional he has left meaningful documents of a time and a place now forever changed; and as a recorder he left a foundation upon which subsequent generations of artists and photographers have based and developed their own work.

In the summer of 1860 Francis Frith settled down to marriage and family. He continued to photograph and publish, but the real adventure was over.

Notes

1 'Introduction', *Egypt and Palestine Photographed and Described by Francis Frith* (London, 1858–60), hereinafter *Egypt and Palestine*.

2 The following quotes are from B. Jay, *Victorian Cameraman: Francis Frith's Views of Rural England 1850–1898* (Newton Abbot, 1973), hereinafter *Cameraman*. For a biography on Frith see also *Egypt and the Holy Land in Historic Photographs: 77 Views by Francis Frith*, Introduction and Bibliography by Julia van Haaften; Selection and Commentary by Jon E. Manchip White (New York, 1980), hereinafter *77 Views*.

3 H. and A. Gernsheim, *The History of Photography from the Camera Obscura to the Beginning of the Modern Era* (New York, 1969), hereinafter *History*; B. Newhall, *The History of Photography: from 1839 to the Present* (New York, 1982); R. Flukinger, *The Formative Decades: Photography in Great Britain, 1839–1920* (Austin, 1985).

4 *77 Views*, p. viii.

5 van Haaften, 'Francis Frith's Grand Tour', *Portfolio* 2 (1980), pp. 56–61.

6 This relationship is detailed in D. Bull and D. Lorimer, *Up the Nile: A Photographic Excursion: Egypt 1839–1898* (New York, 1979); L. Vaczek and G. Buckland, *Travelers in Ancient Lands. A Portrait of the Middle East 1839–1919* (Boston, 1981); P. Chevedden, 'Making Light of Everything: Early Photography of the Middle East and Current Photomania', *MESA Bulletin* 18 (1984), pp. 151–74.

7 N. P. Lerebours, *Excursions daguérriennes: vues et monuments les plus remarquables du globe*, 2 vols. (Paris, 1842); Joseph-Philibert Girault de Prangey, *Monuments arabes d'Égypte, de Syrie et d'Asie Mineure* (Paris, 1842);

Maxime du Camp, *Égypte, Nubie, Palestine et Syrie* (Paris, 1852); Félix Teynard, *Calotypes of Egypt, a Catalogue Raisonné* with an essay by Kathleen Stewart Howe (New York & London, 1992).

8 S. Searight, *The British in the Middle East* (London, 1969, reprinted 1979); P. Clayton, *The Rediscovery of Ancient Egypt: Artists and Travellers in the Nineteenth Century* (London, 1982); P. Conner (ed.), *The Inspiration of Egypt* (Brighton, Exhibition Catalogue, 1983), pp. 55–161.

9 G. Belzoni, *Narrative of the Operations and Recent Discoveries within the Pyramids, Temples, Tombs, and Excavations, in Egypt and Nubia, etc.* (London, 1820); J. Irby and C. Mangles, *Travels in Nubia* (London, 1823); William Bartlett, *The Nile Boat* (London, 1850); J.G. Wilkinson, *The Architecture of the Ancient Egyptians* (London, 1850); and *Handbook for Travellers in Egypt* (London, 1847).

10 David Roberts, *The Holy Land, Syria, Idumea, Arabia, Egypt & Nubia* (London, 1842–49) vols I–III hereinafter *The Holy Land*; J. R. Abbey, *Travel in Aquatint and Lithography 1770–1860, Library of J. R. Abbey: a Bibliographical Catalogue*, Vol. II (Folkestone & London, 1972), pp. 334–41.

11 David Roberts, *The Holy Land*, II, No. 47 'Fragments of the Great Colossi at the Memnonium—Thebes'.

12 'Osiride Pillars', *Egypt and Palestine*, I.

13 'Introduction', *Cairo, Sinai, and Jerusalem: a Series of Twenty Photographic Views by Francis Frith. With Descriptions by Mrs. Poole and Reginald Stuart Poole* (London, 1860).

14 *Egypt and Palestine*, I; No. 27, *77 Views*; Cf. with Roberts, *The Holy Land* No. 11, 'Statues of Memnon. Thebes', I.

15 See list of Frith's publications in the bibliography.

16 Jay, *Cameraman*, pp. 22–23; Gernsheim, *History*, p. 16.

17 Maxime Du Camp, as quoted in J.-C. Lemagny and A. Rouille (eds), *A History of Photography* (Cambridge, 1987), p. 54.

18 'Cleopatra's Temple at Erment', *Egypt and Palestine*, II; No. 35 in *77 Views*.

19 'Doum Palm, and Ruined Mosque, Near Philae', *Egypt and Palestine*, II. The developing carriage is shown in 'Cairo from the East', *Lower Egypt, Thebes and the Pyramids*; its track marks in 'The Pyramids of Sakkarah, from the NE' in *Egypt, Sinai, and Jerusalem*; see also No. 9, *77 Views*.

20 'Portico Temple Gerf Husayn', *Egypt and Palestine*, II.

21 'Introduction', *Egypt and Palestine*, I.

22 No. 8, 'The Great Temple of Aboo-Simble, Nubia', I.

23 'Abou Simbel', *Egypt and Palestine*, I; No. 57, *77 Views*.

24 'Introduction', *Egypt and Palestine*, I.

25 'Obelisk and Granite Lotus Column, Karnac', *Egypt and Palestine*, I; No. 22, *77 Views*.

26 *Egypt and Palestine*, I; No. 20, *77 Views*.

27 'View at Girgeh, Upper Egypt', *Egypt and Palestine*, I.

28 Roberts, No. 124, 'Mosque of the Sultan Hassan, from the Great Square of the Rumeyleh', *The Holy Land* III; Frith: 'Cairo, from the Citadel (First View)', *Egypt, Sinai and Jerusalem*. Even at a height and from a distance the moving people are blurred.

29 'Introduction', *Egypt and Palestine*, I.

30 *Egypt, Sinai and Jerusalem*.

31 'Pharaoh's Bed—the Island of Philae', *Egypt and Palestine*, I.

32 Cf. with Roberts, No. 65, 'The Hypaethral Temple at Philae, called the Bed of the Pharaoh', *The Holy Land* II.

33 'Introduction', *Egypt and Palestine*.

34 *Egypt and Palestine*, II.

35 'View from the Citadel, Second View', Egypt, Sinai and Jerusalem.

36 'The Mosque of Emeer Akhor', *Egypt, Sinai and Jerusalem*.

37 'A Street in Cairo', *Egypt, Sinai and Jerusalem*.

38 'Street View in Cairo', *Lower Egypt and Thebes*.

39 *Egypt, Sinai and Palestine, Supplementary volume*.

40 Sophia Lane-Poole, *The Englishwoman in Egypt: Letters from Cairo. Written during a Residence there in 1842, 3 & 4*, 3 vols. (London, 1844–46), p. 42.

41 'Early morning at Wady Kardassy, Nubia', *Egypt and Palestine*, II.

42 'Osiride Pillar at Medinet-Haboo', *Lower Egypt, Thebes and the Pyramids*.

43 'Cairo from the East', *Lower Egypt & Thebes*.

44 'The Muezzin's call to Prayer', c.1880, in Gerald Ackerman, *The Life and Work of Jean-Léon Gérôme, with a Catalogue Raisonné* (London & Paris, 1986), No. 273 and p. 103; in M. A. Stevens, *The Orientalists: Delacroix to Matisse* (National Gallery of Art, Washington, Exhibition Catalogue, 1984), No. 36; Sotheby's, *Important Orientalist Paintings from the Collection of Coral Petroleum*, Sale Catalogue (22 May 1985), No. 18. C. Williams, 'Jean-Léon Gérôme: a case study of an Orientalist painter' in Sabra Webber (ed.), 'Fantasy or Ethnography?', *Papers in Comparative Studies* 8 (Ohio State University, 1995), pp. 119–48.

45 'Early Morning at Wadi Kardassy, Nubia', *Egypt and Palestine*, II.

46 Frith, 'The Art of Photography', *The Art Journal* 21 (1 March 1859), pp. 71–2, as quoted by van Haaften, *77 Views*, p. xvi.

Part Five

Literary Interaction:
Egyptian Influence on European Literature

19 ᔕ Alexandre Dumas in Egypt: Mystification or Truth?

Marianna Taymanova

Before discussing whether Alexandre Dumas really travelled in Egypt, it is necessary to establish the place which Orientalism (or Exoticism, as it is often called) occupied in European literature in general. First of all, it is necessary to note that the East/West opposition has little or no bearing on geographical concepts. It is rather related to distinctions and links within a single cultural tradition.

Allusions to the Orient began to appear in European literature in the Middle Ages in relation to the Crusades, when the Orient and its Muslim inhabitants, who were in possession of the Holy Sepulchre, were perceived as infidels and pagans who deserved to be exterminated. This hostile and disdainful attitude towards the Orient, and sublime confidence in the fundamental moral superiority of the West, prevailed until the nineteenth century. Hence the abundance of comical Turks, Chinese, Persians, e.g. in Molière's plays, the appearance of the term *turquerie* in French (barbarity), or the expression *'po-kitaiski'* [in a Chinese way] in Russian, in the meaning 'absurdly'. All this reflected an attitude towards the Orient, as something deeply different, and consequently, wicked. Yet Montaigne and Pascal compare the Qur'an and Muhammad to the Bible and Christ, and these are but the first indices of the growing interest in the Orient and its culture, which became even more distinct in the works of the philosophers of the Enlightenment—Voltaire, Diderot and Rousseau. In 1647 the Qur'an was translated into French, and in 1649 into English. Galland's French translation of the *Mille et une nuits* (1704–14) had given impetus to the translation of tales from the corpus of the *Arabian Nights* into other languages. In literature and the arts a pseudo-Oriental style was created, featuring a limited set of images and clichés.

A wave of scholarly interest in the Orient is apparent from the end of the eighteenth century. In 1795, the School of Oriental Languages was established in Paris and, following Napoleon's expeditions to Egypt, the Orient came into fashion. The beginning of the nineteenth century was the turning-point: the concept of the Orient as a deep and mysterious culture replaced that of a wild, barbaric and often hostile Orient which had

181

earlier dominated European consciousness, and became a source of inspiration.

This modification in the perception of the Orient became possible because of profound changes in social attitudes. The French Revolution, which brought about far-reaching changes in social structure, education and social behaviour, directly affected literature. The classical concept of Man gave way to new ideas which implied a multiplicity of racial types and different forms of national existence. The concept of national character and destiny was fundamental in a new literary movement, born at the turn of the eighteenth and nineteenth centuries—that of Romanticism. The Romantics, who believed in the unlimited potential of Man, were especially interested in distinguishing the features of different historical periods, as well as in the unique qualities of national cultures, which give individuals the opportunity to develop fully. As the Russian critic Terterian[1] stated: 'Romanticism became aware of itself in all that was alien, as if contemplating its own reflection in the mirror of an alien culture.' This interest in different cultures was also typical of later off-shoots of Romanticism, such as the Parnassians in France and the Symbolists in Russia. The Orient, its culture and its traditions completely revolutionised European concepts of intellectual life.

A veritable pilgrimage of Europeans to the Orient began during the first half of the nineteenth century. Some were looking for the classical past; others for Biblical traditions; yet others were attracted by Oriental exoticism. Several writers (such as Chateaubriand and Nerval) described their travels in diary form, others (like Hugo and Balzac) wrote about the Orient without having set foot there.[2] Hence, literary involvement with the Orient soon became a kind of 'internal dream'. In this respect one may speak about Romantic Orientalism and the intellectual assimilation of the Orient as a peculiar synthesis, where ancient Oriental wisdom fruitfully merged with European culture.

The French literary critic Jourda[3] distinguished several stages in this cultural assimilation: the Romantics concentrated mostly on the Levant, and were inspired by Byron's Greece and Turkey, the Realists turned towards North Africa, and the Parnassians were attracted by the Pacific islands. The next generation of writers was more interested in the Far East.

Alexandre Dumas (1802–70) belonged to the first category. He was primarily known as a novelist (*Les Trois mousquetaires, Le Comte de Monte-Cristo, La Reine Margot*)[4] but his vast literary output embraced other genres: plays, memoirs, diaries, literary criticism. Alexandre Dumas was the most prolific of writers: more than three hundred books were published under his name during his lifetime.[5]

Throughout his long literary career, Dumas remained faithful to the principles of Romantic literature. Wanting to show the limitless capacities of human nature, the Romantics preferred to place their heroes in new and unusual conditions: hence their interest in historical novels, and their preference for exotic, often Oriental, settings. Dumas had a clear preference for historical novels and dramas; in other words, he tended to displace his heroes in time. Spacial displacement was less frequent, yet, like many of his fellow-Romantics, he was attracted by exotic countries. His travels took him not only to numerous countries in Western Europe, but also to the Maghreb and in 1858–59 to Russia; he undertook the latter journey at the same time as Théophile Gautier, who described it in his *Voyage en Russie*.[6] Unlike Gautier, Dumas even reached the Caucasus, and wrote eight volumes about his adventures.[7] His dream, never fully realised, was to visit all the Mediterranean countries and to write a series of books describing them in both historical and artistic terms.

Like other Romantics, and particularly Gérard de Nerval, Dumas relied on scholarly sources. All his novels contain abundant information on geology, geography, ethnography and history. He also used Biblical texts and mythology. All these elements may be found in one of his most popular travel books *Quinze jours au Sinaï*,[8] which went through twenty-five editions in France and was translated into many languages. The present writer was privileged to translate this book into Russian.[9]

Quinze jours au Sinaï was published in Paris in two octavo volumes in 1839 under two names: Dumas and Dauzats. These names not being in alphabetical order, Dumas is tacitly acknowledged as the main author. The second author, Adrien Dauzats (1804–68), was not a professional writer but an artist who travelled widely in Europe and was particularly known for his water-colours. He contributed in 1828 to the *Voyages pittoresques et romantiques dans l'ancienne France 10* under the direction of Baron Taylor. In 1830 Dauzats and his fellow-artist Mayer were invited to accompany Baron Isidore-Justin-Sévérin Taylor (1789–1879), Commissaire des Arts, on his diplomatic mission to Egypt. The purpose of this visit was to negotiate with Muhammad 'Ali, the viceroy of Egypt, the transfer to France of the famous obelisks from the temple of Luxor in Thebes, the offer of which had been brought by Champollion in 1829 on his return to France: emperors of Rome and Byzantium traditionally marked their victory by erecting in their home countries obelisks taken from Egyptian temples.

Taylor came to Egypt bringing rich presents which included an important work by French Orientalists. His mission was a total success: he obtained for France not only confirmation of the gift of two obelisks from Luxor, but also the obelisk now known as Cleopatra's Needle which was granted to Louis XVIII. Due to political turmoil caused by the Revolution of 1830, only one of the three presents found its way to France in 1833. The western obelisk from Luxor, 'l'obelisque dépareillé' in the words of Théophile Gautier, was erected in the Place de la Concorde in 1836. The two Cleopatra's Needles were separated: one adorns the embankment of the Thames, the second stands in Central Park in New York City.

During his journey Adrien Dauzats wrote a detailed diary. Dumas learned about the existence of this diary from Taylor. The vast literary output of Alexandre Dumas is in part attributable to the assistance of anonymous co-writers, or 'slaves'. For this reason Carré[11] referred to Dumas with disdain as an 'entrepreneur en littérature'. But in this particular case Dumas did not try to hide his collaboration with Dauzats, although the name of the latter appears on the cover in second place and in smaller print.

Did Dumas really set foot in Egypt? It is well known that in *Les Compagnons de Jéhu* he affirmed that he could never describe the places which he had not seen. Before writing *Henri III* he had visited Blois and before working on *Le Comte de Monte-Cristo* he had been to the castle of If. Was Dumas then capable of describing a journey to the Orient *in absentia*?

The book is written in the first person. In the first paragraph the participants in the mission are named: as 'M. Taylor, M. Meyer and myself'. On the following pages the narrator, referred to as 'myself', makes drawings or, at the request of Baron Taylor, makes sketches of a mosque, thus implying that he is a professional artist. Yet neither the name of Dumas nor his literary profession is mentioned in the book. According to the Romantic tradition, he becomes the 'second self' of the main hero, who closely resembles Dauzats. As for the latter, in the words of Théophile Gautier: 'Aucune fatigue ne l'effrayait … Il aimait les âpres et féroces paysages, les horizons sauvages et grandioses, la mer implacablement bleue, la lumière blanche et crue du midi … .'[12] Jean-Marie Carré wrote that, had Dauzats published all his memoirs, he would be the equal of writer-artists like Delacroix and Fromentin.[13]

In *Quinze jours au Sinaï* the artistic vision of Dauzats is particularly strongly felt in the description of landscapes, and may be compared to the best poetic evocations of the Orient by the Romantics. In no other of Dumas' books can one find descriptions as poetic and authentic. Yet the literary skill of Dumas is equally apparent. Romantic writers like Chateaubriand and Lamartine, who began their literary exploration of the Orient in the early nineteenth century, usually wrote their travel books in the form of day-by-day itineraries, accurate but rather tedious. But Dumas, apparently using a similar type of account, was able to produce a fascinating novel, with emphasis not only on the description of the Orient, but on the adventures of his heroes in a new and exotic environment. It is significant that the real purpose of the mission is mentioned only occasionally. As the plot develops, the heroes sail up the Nile, travel into the desert accompanied by Bedouins, and visit the Monastery of St Catherine in the south of the Sinai.

While working on the translation of the book, with the assistance of Professor M. Piotrovsky, now the Director of the Hermitage Museum, the present writer had a rare opportunity to explore the museum's archives. There I had the good fortune to find a number of engravings made from the original drawings of Dauzats and Taylor, illustrating this particular journey. Some of these engravings have been published in the Russian edition of the book.

As is well known, the European perception of the Orient from the eighteenth century onwards, and particularly after the translation of *The Arabian Nights* into European languages, had created a pseudo-Oriental style, based on a limited set of Oriental stereotypes. In certain respects the book by Dumas still reflects this tradition, not in terms of description but in its general perception of the Orient. Europeans were particularly curious about certain aspects of Oriental life, such as marital habits, and especially harems, as well as Oriental baths, markets and physical punishments. All these are dealt with in the book, often through characteristic European clichés—the liberties, the restrictions and the role of the Qur'an being much exaggerated.

Irony is omnipresent in the novel. The use of irony, which creates a certain distance between the reader and the narrative, is characteristic of Romantic literary works. In using this technique, the Romantics were trying to overcome the limitations which were subjectively imposed on their perception of the universe. The irony and the self-criticism of Dumas enhance the humour of the situation, emphasising the ignorance and clumsiness of Europeans in their contact with Oriental culture. To his credit Dumas never suggested that European culture is superior and does his best to comprehend the culture and the way of life of the Orient.

Yet at no point can one find any evidence for Dumas' physical participation in Baron Taylor's Egyptian mission. Indeed J.-M. Carré[14] found 'indisputable' evidence to prove that Dumas had in reality never been there. He notes several factual errors and inaccuracies. For example, describing his journey up the Nile, Dumas wrongly indicates the location of Libyan mountains, confuses the lowlands with the uplands (the Embarah) and calls limestone 'granite rocks'. Carré argues that these mistakes demonstrate that Dumas had not seen these features with his own eyes ...

However, Carré was too harsh in his judgement. He affirms that Dumas had not even been in the Caucasus, although it is a well-established fact that he had been there. The inaccuracies noted by Carré are not numerous, and indeed they could easily be made by a not too observant tourist.

Even if Dumas had never been in Egypt, he was able skilfully to use the factual account he had at his disposal—that of Dauzats. Dumas' part in this joint work was sufficiently important to justify his name occupying the dominant position. As an experienced novelist, Dumas feels more at ease in history than in everyday life. Nine out of twenty-one chapters in the book deal with historical topics. Three lengthy historical novellas included in the book belong entirely to him. The first relates the Exodus: the Biblical account of the liberation of the people of Israel from Egyptian slavery under the guidance of Moses in the thirteenth century BC. The second and third deal with the two periods of French involvement in Egypt: the crusade of Louis IX in the thirteenth century, and Napoleon's expedition in the late eighteenth century. In these novellas Dumas is at his best: all three are based on historical and literary evidence: the Bible, the works of French medieval writers (the *Vie de St. Louis* by Joinville) and Arab historians (Abu'l-Fida, Ibn Iyas, al-Maqrizi). In the case of Napoleon's Egyptian expedition, it is well known that Dumas was working at that time on a book about the Emperor, and had at his disposal various historical documents and diaries, which he put to good use. This enabled him to give an objective assessment of events, although, in two later cases, his sympathies were obviously on the French side. But even in these novels one can find historical inaccuracies. As always, history served Dumas as a background: his aim was not to recreate historical events in their authenticity, but to choose those which served the purposes of literary imagination.

The book contains several paragraphs devoted to the history of architecture which are clearly out of place. They are dull and pretentious, full of insignificant technicalities, and clearly belong to Dauzats. It is possible that their inclusion was part of the agreement on co-operation. Nevertheless, the historical novellas are as vivid and colourful as the description of recent events. This may serve as further proof that Dumas' imagination could easily substitute for actual observations.

If there are any doubts left about the presence of Dumas in Egypt, they were finally dispelled by the writer himself. He wrote in a letter:[15] 'Le Sinaï? C'est vrai, je n'y suis guère allé, mais le pachah d'Egypte m'a felicité de mon livre; sans moi, ce pays-là serait inconnu de mes contemporains!' As in his historical novels, through which Dumas familiarised several generations of young people with the history of France, it is clear that in this particular book, where the Orient was presented in an entertaining way, Dumas opened up another exotic world to his contemporaries.

By the mid-nineteenth century, the Orient had ceased to be an object of literary exoticism, and provided a familiar setting for the action in works of prose fiction. One obvious consequence of this was the prevalence of a purely imaginary vision of the Orient shared by numerous Romantics, many of whom never went there. As Jourda[16] mentions, when such writers as Musset, Hugo and Balzac wrote about exotic countries which they had never seen, they based themselves on three elements: written documents, imagination and intuition. Exoticism creates literary form, and travel writings develop into a literary genre. In its turn, this led to the emergence of literary clichés, which occur repeatedly in Romantic works. The present writer noted when translating 'Oriental' works by Chateaubriand, Nerval and Dumas the recurrence of the same adjectives, synonyms and images in the works of all three. Several terms evoking Oriental features became common European usage through Romantic literature (e.g. *almée*—female dancer, *santon*—nomadic dervish and *soudan*—sultan). It is significant, as Piotrovsky[17] remarked, that none of these words would have been understood by those they purport to describe.

Dumas' book is sheer mystification: both the travel notes and the historical novellas are written in accordance with the same principles. The written sources on which Dumas based himself give his imagination free rein. Yet it is a brilliant work, in which he delineated the distinctive features of people, objects, landscapes and customs which he had never seen.

Notes

1 I. Terterian, 'Romantizm kak celostnoe yavlenie', *Voprosy literatury* 4 (1983), p. 155.

2 For example, F.-R. Chateaubriand, *Itinéraire de Paris à Jerusalem* (1811); Gérard de Nerval, *Voyage en Orient* (1851); Victor-Marie Hugo's collection of poems, *Les Orientales* (1829); Honoré de Balzac, *Voyage de Paris à Java* (1832).

3 P. Jourda, *Exotisme dans la littérature française depuis Chateaubriand* (Boivin, 1938), hereinafter *Exotisme dans la littérature*.

4 Alexandre Dumas [Dumas *père*], *Les Trois mousquetaires* (1844), *Le Comte de Monte-Cristo* (1844–45), *La Reine Margot* (1845).

5 C. Glinel, *Alexandre Dumas et son œuvre; notes biographiques et bibliographiques* (Geneva: Slatkine, 1967).

6 Théophile Gautier, *Voyage en Russie* (Charpentier, 1867).

7 Alexandre Dumas, *Le Caucase* (Librairie Théâtrale, 1859), 5 vols; *De Paris à Astrakhan* (Librairie Nouvelle, 1860), 3 vols; *Impressions de voyage: en Russie* (Lévy Frères, 1865), 4 vols.

8 Alexandre Dumas and Adrien Dauzats, *Quinze jours au Sinaï* (Dumont, 1839), 2 vols.

9 A. Dyuma & A. Doza (eds), *Puteshestvie v Egipet* (Moscow: Nauka, 1988), translated into Russian by M. Taymanova.

10 I. Taylor, *Voyages pittoresques et romantiques dans l'ancienne France* (Didot, 1820–1878), illustrated with lithographs by Vernet, Dauzats, Fragonard etc.

11 Jean-Marie Carré, *Voyageurs et écrivains français en Égypte* (Cairo, 1932), p.

20 ∽ Flaubert's Egypt: Crucible and Crux for Textual Identity

Mary Orr

It seems surprising, given the plethora of critical work on Flaubert, that his journey to Egypt has not evinced more interest. Tucked away in his early letters and before the 'big' novels, it has been sidelined except as biographical background for *Salammbô* (1862), *La Tentation de Saint Antoine* (1874) and 'Hérodias' (in *Trois Contes*, 1877). By concentrating on the *Correspondance* of the Egypt section of the 'Voyage en Orient', I hope to demonstrate the folly of this neglect, both for understanding Flaubert's development as a writer and for appreciating his contribution to what is now known as Orientalism.[1]

Said's much-quoted and influential book underlines persistent themes in Orientalist theory and Flaubert's responses are no less typical: his pilgrimage was to shake off the 'mustiness of the pre-existing Orientalist archive' but the project would resolve itself 'into the reductionism of the Orientalistic';[2] the Orient is synonymous with escapism and sexual fantasy;[3] the Orient is necessarily the Other, the alien, the exotic, the violent framed in the ethnocentric gaze of the imperialistic Occidental traveller.[4] While the simple Orient-Occident binaries of earlier Orientalist theory, including Said's, have undergone much revision, mainly through the work of feminist and post-colonial critics, treatment of Flaubert in these studies remains nonetheless largely unchanged. While Lowe, for example, justifiably argues that 'orientalism is not a single developmental tradition but is profoundly heterogeneous',[5] her reading in chapter three, 'Orient as Woman, Orientalism as Sentimentalism: Flaubert' reiterates the *lieu commun* of male desire and Oriental female sexuality and eroticism in a surprising fashion, given this critic's overtly feminist critical stance. Similar *idées reçues* emerge in the work of Kabbani and Behdad. Exemplary in her critique of Orientalism as a monolithic structure and essentialising movement, Kabbani, like Lowe, endorses the view that Egypt is a literary prop and authentication of European attitudes to the Oriental Woman,[6] while Behdad's sympathetic reading of Flaubert's more informed belatedness as an Orientalist nevertheless positions him squarely in the Self/Other split of recent continental critical theory (Freud, Lacan, Kristeva) that is, the

modern revision of Western metaphysics.[7] To tackle Orientalism or one of
its earlier proponents with modern critical spectacles is the fundamental
mistake Behdad makes in what is for the most part a largely well-informed
book—a mistake which MacKenzie largely avoids in his own critique of
Orientalisms.[8] It is his plea for maintaining a view of the complexities of
national and other identities which I want to apply to Flaubert, for it is in
the close reading of the letters from the 'Voyage en Égypte' that his
cognisance of cultural stereotypes, Occidental and Oriental, emerges.
Because even the best critics have failed to investigate the source letters
thoroughly enough, the influence of the Egypt experience on Flaubert's
understanding not only of his writing or of himself, but also of
contemporary French culture has not been properly appreciated. I will not
therefore be engaging with theories of *différance* and undecidability, or
Flaubert's 'uses of uncertainty' which evade the fixing of ideological
meanings.[9] Rather I will argue that it is the dynamic of experience of other
world views which enabled Flaubert to be such an adept critic of his own.
The 'crucible' in my title provides a place whereby Flaubert's Egyptian
experience can be read as a cultural and textual melting-pot for his own
œuvre out of which a real contribution to an understanding of contemporary
Orientalisms can be extracted.

Flaubert's visit to Egypt (1849–50) and the Middle East was his first
journey to non-European countries. He had been to Corsica and the
Pyrenees with Dr Cloquet after his *baccalauréat* in 1840 and to Italy with
his sister on her honeymoon in 1845. Moving outside France, its habits
and customs and undertaking the official mission with Maxime Du Camp
to collect information for the Ministère de l'Agriculture et du Commerce,
was the second phase of a pattern already tried and tested in their trip to
Brittany in 1847 and documented in *Par les champs et par les grèves* (1847).
Contrary to the view that Flaubert was a sedentary recluse, the Middle East
trip can be seen as a wider venture built on the familiar and meeting a
restlessness which Flaubert experienced many times in his life.[10] The need
to turn his back on what France, and particularly Rouen, represented cannot
be underestimated. And it is probably on the personal dimension that this
journey was such a point of re-orientation, not of dis-orientation as Richard
Terdiman has suggested.[11] While there must certainly have been motives
of escapism—both Flaubert's father and his beloved sister Caroline had died
in 1846—and the need to revivify creative impulses to cure writer's block—
the writing of the first version of *La Tentation de Saint Antoine* in 1848–
49 after his beloved friend Alfred Le Poittevin had also died was vociferously
rejected by Du Camp and Bouilhet—critics have only seen the Orient as a
clean break with the recent psychological past whereas I suggest it to be a
radical and direct extension and confrontation of it.

Reading closely between the lines of all Flaubert's correspondence and fictional *œuvre*, there is a constant and creatively regenerative interest in death and decay, the morbid and the grotesque which the actual family deaths only accentuate. Illness and cure concern Flaubert as physical states and metaphors for the body politic as well as for the personal. In the correspondence for the 'Voyage en Orient', for example, there are repeated and anxious letters to his mother to elicit news of her health and reassurances to her of his well-being and avoidance of various diseases.[12] There are also references to his health expressed as diet and his somewhat comic concern with his increasing girth.[13] Flaubert therefore reorientated his fixations on illness and political ills in France by confronting the disease and dis-ease of Egypt. It comes as no surprise then that, when the Egypt section of his 'Voyage en Orient' was completed, Flaubert wrote to Frédéric Baudry of his impressions in the cynical, figurative language of deformity and illness:

> La civilisation européo-orientale que l'on a voulu plaquer sur le musilmanisme est une monstruosité. Tous les beys éduqués en France n'en sont pas moins turcs dans le fond, ils portent des bottes vernies et dans l'intérieur du harem tuent leurs femmes à coups de sabre. ... À l'influence française, représentée si vous voulez auprès de la personne du maître par Clot-Bey, a succédé l'influence prussienne, autruchienne, russe, turque de Pruner-Bey, médecin actuel du vice-roi. Je crois que l'Orient est encore plus malade que l'Occident.[14]

Flaubert constantly observes with such cultural bi-focalism. It seems in fact that the terms Occidental and Oriental change hands at various moments before, during, and after the Nile experience. Alexandria, that point of entry and departure, is for Flaubert European.[15] However, time and motion are Oriental for not being European: Flaubert's letter to his mother of 5 January 1850 exemplifies the frustrations of not receiving his post speedily while at the same time accepting that to rush round Egypt 'à l'européenne, c'est-à-dire vite et avec nos usages, c'est vouloir se faire crever.' Whether by camel or by Nile riverboat, indigenous modes of journeying are the only viable and comfortable alternatives, the slow-moving armchair approach to covering large distances.[16] It is on board these Oriental vehicles that Flaubert's requests for news from home, for reconnectedness with his French cultural roots, become more sharply defined yet also provoke his venomous hatred of mediocrity, French or Oriental.[17] Flaubert's floating craft, between two destinations and two banks, mirrors his unusually intercultural Franco-Oriental optic which registers the best and worst of each culture and records, not with objectivity, but with the kind of sharply observed disinterest rare among his fellow traveller-compatriots.

Another aspect of continuity before, during and after the 'Voyage en Orient' is *La Tentation de Saint Antoine*. St Anthony was of Nubian origin.

It is to this region that Flaubert makes his pilgrimage as well as to the other great sites of learning, archaeology and civilisation. Mythic time, the Egypt of Coptic and Ptolemaic history experienced directly by Flaubert within nineteenth-century time, only seems to corroborate his research and knowledge via Creuzer, among others, of the life and times of St Anthony. However, Flaubert moves beyond the Orientalist critic's stance whereby he can only see 'an East he had transported with him; one that he would transport back, in piecemeal'.[18] Quiet evolution and transformation of understanding renews acquaintance with his written saint. Recurrent mention of him in the 'Egypt Letters' forms almost a litany or prayer to the saint himself to make good Flaubert's previous, failed, Occidental attempt at recreating him. The period of writer's block Flaubert experiences in Egypt at this crucial point in his journey is then creative.[19] Flaubert's inability to write the Orient directly means that he can then write *with* the Orient, that is, he does not colonise it by writing over it, but allows it to infuse his Occidentalism.[20] It took two versions and much personal development before Flaubert achieved his *La Tentation de Saint Antoine* as late as 1872. The key lesson Flaubert had to learn was an Oriental view of aesthetics, where silent waiting and imbibing stench and strong perfumes unleashes creativity. This is crystallised metaphorically in his rich description of the monuments in the Valley of the Kings as his journey from Cairo to Nubia moves in the return (Occidental) direction:

> A Karnac nous avons eu l'impression d'une vie de géants. J'ai passé la nuit aux pieds du colosse de Memnon, dévoré de moustiques. Le vieux gredin a une bonne balle, il est couvert d'inscriptions. Les inscriptions et les merdes d'oiseaux, voilà les deux seules choses sur les ruines d'Égypte qui indiquent la vie. La pierre la plus rongée n'a pas un brin d'herbe. Ça tombe en poudre comme une momie, voilà tout. Les inscriptions des voyageurs et les fientes des oiseaux de proie sont les deux seuls ornements de la ruine. Souvent on voit un grand obélisque tout droit avec une draperie dans toute sa longueur, plus large à partir du sommet et se rétrécissant vers le bas. Ce sont les vautours qui viennent chier là depuis des siècles. C'est d'un très bel effet, *et d'un curieux symbolisme*. La nature a dit aux monuments égyptiens: Vous ne voulez pas de moi, la graine des lichens ne pousse point sur vous? Eh bien, merde, je vous chierai sur le corps.[21]

Thus far, I have been arguing positively for a Flaubert experiencing the Orient as a continuum experience with his past, in his medical and *St Antoine* preoccupations, not as a break or disorientation. It can be argued that this is also because in spite of taking off his Occidentalism by donning native dress, his cultural postion remains quintessentially French, and actually the more authentically so.[22] Like so many travellers before him, Flaubert is more French outside France than inside as it is only in the alien and foreign context that his Frenchness has to be qualified and portrayed, or can be observed. The reality of Flaubert's travels was that he was largely in a French cultural environment throughout the whole of his visit. Contacts with Egypt were very carefully controlled and organised before he left France. The social context was largely French even if the immediate surroundings were not, as many of the Egyptian officials who invited him to stay were acculturated citizens who had direct contact with France already, that is, were travellers in the reverse direction.[23] There is no sense in which Flaubert's experience can truly be said to be a raw, Oriental, one. As French guests, Flaubert and Du Camp would simply have responded to the role allotted to them by their Oriental hosts: visits to the sights, rides on camels, visits to harems, which ramify not only classic Western Oriental experiences, but serve the host's Occidentalist understanding. This latter level of cultural interaction can then be taken as a counter-move, as Oriental protectionism against deeper colonialist imperialism.[24] In the remainder of this essay, I will read Flaubert's correspondence to the 'Voyage en Égypte' as a record of real insights into a re-orientated Occidentalism, which the refracting mirrors of current Orientalist study are beginning to demonstrate.

Flaubert was always an Egyptophile, absorbed by the Orient in his reading prior to the 'Voyage en Orient', which in turn absorbed him into an experience through which his Occidentalism could be appraised. His letters mirror the erudition of the *homme savant* position of closed Orientalist viewpoints while guarding the immediacy of the naïve Orientalist experience. The letters are interesting because they form a travel diary which is untrammelled by reworking after the event (as were his later *Notes de Voyage*), and which reflect the intimate present of emotion rather than the distant present of reason.

The letters can be categorised in several ways, but an immediately striking difference in style and volume is between those addressed to his mother and the rest. Authorial selection, variants and style of narration are determined largely by the addressee in France. It is not the case that Flaubert is more prudish with his mother.[25] On the contrary, a rare intimacy and vulnerability becomes visible, conveyed through the banalities of sightseeing and tourist experience. Flaubert's thinly veiled homesickness and fear of the unknown, of losing contact with the safe and the familiar, appear starkly. There is the constant request for his mother's own letters and repeated information on his future itinerary so that they can arrive safely, whereas the brave face of the traveller in adversity, on the edge of exciting experience and alien environments, is fed to his male addressees. Intimate in a different way from his letters to his mother, Flaubert's letters to Bouilhet voice male bravado and sexual prowess (one wonders how exaggerated) as well as deep fears about his writing abilities, with, in the same breath, sharp criticism of Bouilhet's own dramatic composition, while haranguing him for details of his friend's banal routines, local gossip and news from Paris.

Yet Flaubert's reluctant Orientalism is not merely a heightened longing for details from home. His avidity simultaneously imbibes details of the place of writing. There is a raw realism of smells and colours, descriptions and dispassionate recording which speaks of an eye for the 'petit détail qui fait vrai' regardless of cultural or social milieu. Flaubert's extraordinary sensitivity and sensibility rendering him neither culturally objective (superior) nor ironic but interculturally open should be emphasised not only for his importance as a stylist, but as a cultured critic in the best sense.[26]

Detail as technique and critique may indeed have been crystalised in the 'Voyage en Orient' experience of writing.[27] The fine line was certainly put in place between copying and noting what he saw (his government mission) and observation in a language which encapsulated both uniqueness and ordinariness into an artistic cameo. Antoine Naaman attributes to the visual/aural/olfactory descriptions of this journey what he calls Flaubert's 'acuité émotive' and 'perspicacité visionnaire'.[28] The correspondence from the 'Voyage en Orient' makes abundantly clear the immediacy of the impression and the way Flaubert's even unpolished style to his various addressees enfolds the description in an envelope of freshness.[29] The paradox is that it is the artist's work on the material which keeps it in its raw state and free of cliché. Hence the banal can be made art; Oriental and Occidental truisms become scenes latent with wonder or irony.

What perhaps has not been sufficiently highlighted and which the 'Voyage en Orient' exemplifies, is that Flaubert's search for the truth in cultural debris and clichés of all kinds has an identifiable national/racial label, while simultaneously it evokes the underlying phenomenon of the natural order of things: all civilisations degenerate and become rubble. Even at this early stage in his life and career, Flaubert has no romantic illusions or nostalgia for ancient or other civilisations as political or sociological 'better worlds'.[30] It is in the broken artefacts of Egypt, Carthage, Paris and Normandy that Flaubert can collect his archaeologies of description into a knowledge of Western culture pre-empting Foucault.

This Occidental knowing of Said's Orientalist caught up in a fictional Orientalism, is nowhere better displayed than in description of sexual exploits. Flaubert's meeting with Kuchuk Hanem (Egyptian counterpart to Marie Schlésinger in the Flaubert critical mythology of muse/*femme fatale*) is what comprises critical interest in the 'Voyage en Orient' correspondence, to the extent that the two have become almost synonymous, while the rest has been ignored. In turn, this distilled titbit has been used to place Flaubert indubitably in the nineteenth-century European male Orientalist position as exploiter.[31] Overlooked are his juvenalia, *Un Parfum à sentir* and *La Tentation de Saint Antoine* which include exotic *femme fatale* Oriental women before he ever encountered

Kuchuk. Ignored too is the context of the episode in the correspondence. The meeting comes late in the Egyptian journey and is described in a letter to Bouilhet. My contention is that Kuchuk has been set up and framed, first internally as I shall show, but more blatantly by the cultural stereotypes not of Flaubert, but his Occidental critics. Specialists both on Flaubert and on Orientalism have clearly passed on literary facts without returning to the sources. Through hasty or misinformed assumptions about Kuchuk's social position—doubly reprehensible in Orientalists—reinforcement of what can only be labelled Occidentalist mis-readings have held sway.[32] These categorise Kuchuk as a courtesan-prostitute, whereas she was an *almeh* or learned woman and therefore of *ashraf* noble class.[33] Behdad makes the very proper contextual point that the harem (that other sexually stereotyped cliché) is a European fantasy, a mythic misconstruction of Oriental sexuality, circulated principally by eighteenth-century traveller-Orientalists, but then he subjects Kuchuk to the usual treatment; she is there to satisfy male scopic desire, the position of the object.[34]

The word 'harem' (Ar. *harim*, 'forbidden place'), the part of an Oriental house reserved for wives and concubines, may have become conflated and confused with a brothel through similar pre-nineteenth-century ideas unleashed by Galland's translation of *Mille et une nuits* and the earlier travel accounts of Jean Chardin.[35] Flaubert's account, however sexist and male European, does overtly explain to Louis Bouilhet Kuchuk's *almée-savante* status, describes her complete cover—'grand tarbouch', 'immenses pantalons roses', 'gaze violette'—before then launching into the expected, possibly exaggerated, experience with this highly sexual woman. Paradoxically, Flaubert's description is closer to a Muslim feminist reading of male/female sexuality with its segregations of male/female space, public/private ritual and avoidance of intimacy because of male fear of active, female sexuality, her *fitna*.[36] This could explain some of the crudeness of Flaubert's language which reduces the act of union to a mere coupling, precisely that lack of emotional involvement the Muslim system of male/female relationships seeks to maintain.[37] Kuchuk, then, refracts Occidental powerlessness to engage her cultural reality. Her representations and silence say more about European and male gender constructs.

But Flaubert criticism's framing of Kuchuk also misfits if the letters concerning her are set in their proper context within the collection. The crucial reports of his two meetings with her appear only in his letters to Bouilhet (13 mars 1850, à bord de notre cange, à 12 lieues au-delà de Syène and 2 juin 1850, entre Girgeh et Siout) in the latter stages of his trip. Critics have inquired neither about the relationship between Flaubert and Bouilhet, nor about the place of the Kuchuk episode in the sexual exploits of the 'Voyage en Égypte' *in toto* and both are important. The second meeting is particularly surprising (if read in the vein of Flaubert's critics) for its matter-of-factness, the unexotic and ordinary, a casual encounter. Its very starkness and factuality makes any Paris brothel boudoir more Oriental and Flaubert's response callous, even cruel. Kuchuk has been ill; it is close weather; he takes her once, but regards her at length to savour an image; the overall taste is bitterness. And in the following paragraph, he describes his visit to two other women (prostitutes proper) a 'belle bougresse' and a 'grosse cochonne'.[38] This account puts the earlier, first meeting in another perspective. The details do not add up to a voluptuous, erotic, Oriental encounter. The visual description of her is mocking, a cliché, before she is judged for her negative qualities as a mediocre dancer (by the standards of a male dancer he has seen). When he eventually spends the night with her, he recalls his Paris brothel experiences as if nothing about Kuchuk is really singular.[39] Why does Flaubert recount either to his friend at all?

There is no doubt the need to brag about sexual prowess, to reassure Bouilhet of some deeper pact between them that relations with women are largely transitory and unimportant. The evidence for this is in the account of the other sexual exploits given in both these letters prior to the Kuchuk scenes and in an earlier letter of 15 January 1850 to Bouilhet. The real cause of sexual interest is male, dancers or boys in the bath-houses, and by inference of much more direct interest to Flaubert's addressee. In a rare reference to previous correspondence, Flaubert here reassures his friend:

> Ne baise pas trop, ménage tes forces une once de sperme perdu, c'est pire que dix livres de sang.—A propos, tu me demandes si j'ai consommé l'œuvre des bains. Oui, et sur un jeune gaillard gravé de la petite vérole et qui avait un énorme turban blanc. Ça ma fait rire, voilà tout. Mais, je recommencerai. Pour qu'une expérience soit bien faite, il faut qu'elle soit réitérée.[40]

The event in question has been recounted in the above-mentioned earlier letter to Bouilhet. It opens with Flaubert's open emotions of desire for his friend. Graphic and exotic description of the sensual aspects of the Egyptian experience follow: wind, heat, cold, water and then an extremely detailed and erotic description of the male dancers in female costume, their body movements and explicit lasciviousness ensues, at a length and on a level of physiological involvement quite outstripping the later descriptions of Kuchuk.[41] The dancer is Hassan-el-Bilbeis, whose *l'abeille* is the yardstick whereby Kuchuk's giratory efforts are then judged and found wanting. The account then moves to the bath-house, where attentions given to his private parts, and the description of being masturbated are obviously designed to excite the recipient of the letter.[42] The word sodomy appears quite openly in the previous paragraph about *bardaches*. There can be no other way of reading this except as an insight into the sexual proclivities and preferences of Flaubert and his closest friends.[43]

Twisting the accounts of Kuchuk, then, has served respectible criticism well to present both a laundered correspondence, a critics' Flaubert in their own cultural image, and a feminised Orientalism which is blatantly false. It is my contention that Flaubert, through his very awareness of the bigotries of Occidentalism, finds a freedom in Egypt to express his sexuality in ways which would be censurable in France, but which are part of normal sexual conduct in Mediterranean, Greek and North African, as well as Middle Eastern contexts. By implication, Flaubert's acculturation serves as a radical re-orientation of, and challenge to, French constructs of race, gender and class, what constitutes the normal and the deviant. Moreover, his 'Voyage en Orient' pre-empts Gide's experiences, for example, and demands an overhaul of European, Orientalist, classifications and assumptions.

Egypt for Flaubert goes beyond neat binaries of male/female, Orient/ Occident, a lesson his subsequent 'French' novels acknowledge. The 'Voyage en Orient' confirmed in Flaubert a precocious cynicism, a brutal realism. Flaubert's crucial visit to Egypt both in terms of his personal life and the life of his *œuvre* has an import Flaubert criticism has hitherto ignored: Flaubert is a reluctant Orientalist caught in the outsider's position not just towards this ancient culture but also towards his own. Read in the context of his return to Normandy, the visceral Egyptian and the cerebral Frenchness of his novels' style are woven together to form a liquid aridity of expression, a re-oriented Occidentalism of 'La Seine, le Nil et le voyage du rien'.[44] For Flaubert studies, my essay has explored how the 'Voyage en Orient' can be read as the crucible of his creative writing. For wider debates in Orientalism, my essay has uncovered a very different Flaubert, the Flaubert of his later *Le Dictionnaire des idées reçues*.[45] Here, he defines the Orientalist as an 'Homme qui a beaucoup voyagé'. I have shown that this journey is not an exploration of the Other land, but an archaeology of the terrifyingly known of one's own culture.

Notes

1 See e.g., Hassan al-Nouty, *Le Proche-Orient dans la littérature française de Nerval à Barrès* (Nizet, 1958); E. Said, *Orientalism* (Penguin, 1978) and more recently A. Behdad, *Belated Travelers: Orientalism in the age of colonial dissolution* (Durham, NC: Duke University Press, 1994); R. Kabbani, *Imperial Fictions: Europe's myths of Orient* (Pandora, 1994); L. Lowe, *Critical Terrains: French and British Orientalisms* (Ithaca & London: Cornell University Press, 1991); and J. M. MacKenzie, *Orientalism: history, theory and the arts* (Manchester: MUP, 1995)

2 Said, *Orientalism*, p. 169.

3 Ibid., pp. 188-90.

4 For example, ibid., pp. 113-17, 204-7.

5 Lowe, *Critical Terrains*, p. ix.

6   Kabbani, *Imperial Fictions*, pp. 72, 26, 73.

7   Behdad, *Belated Travelers*, pp. 15, 21, 59.

8   MacKenzie, *Orientalism: history.*

9   See J. Culler, *Flaubert: the uses of uncertainty* (Paul Elek, 1974) and J. Derrida, *Of Grammatology* (Baltimore: Johns Hopkins University Press, 1976).

10 See A. Dupuy, *En Marge de Salammbô: le voyage de Flaubert en Algérie-Tunisie (avril-juin 1858)* (Nizet, 1954), pp. 42–3, who makes a similar point concerning Flaubert's later 1858 trip to North Africa.

11 R. Terdiman, *Discourse/Counter-Discourse: the theory and practice of symbolic resistance in nineteenth-century France* (Ithaca & London: Cornell University Press, 1985), ch. 5, pp. 227-57.

12 See letter to his mother from Marseille (3 November 1849), pp. 520-1 even prior to his actual departure, and to Olympe Bonenfant from Cairo (5 December 1849), p. 547 seeking reassurances about his mother's health. These and all subsequent page references are to G. Flaubert, *Correspondance I*, (ed.) Jean Bruneau (NRF Gallimard, Bibliothèque de la Pléiade, 1973).

13 See e.g., his letter to his mother from Alexandria (17 October 1849), p. 530: 'J'ai engraissé depuis que je suis parti, si bien qu'à ce moment même il y a deux pantalons à moi, qui sont chez M. Chabannes, tailleur français, occupés à se faire élargir pour que mon ventre y puisse tenir sans gêne.'

14 Letter of 21 July 1850, p. 654.

15 Stated in his letter of 17 October 1849, p. 529.

16 Ibid., I, p. 557.

17 Flaubert's letter to Emmanuel Vasse de Saint-Ouen, 'A bord de notre cange, entre Kous et Keneh' (17 May 1850), p. 624.

18 Kabbani, *Imperial Fictions*, p. 72.

19 In his assessment of the 'Voyage en Égypte' section of the journey to Frédéric Baudry, au lazaret de Beyrouth [Beirut quarantine station] (21 July 1850), pp. 652–55, Flaubert begins by saying 'Savez-vous, cher ami, quel sera quant à moi le résultat de mon voyage d'Orient? ce sera de m'empêcher d'écrire jamais une seule ligne sur l'Orient' (p. 652). He then proceeds to summarise the 'État politique', the 'Économie politique', the 'Administration', the 'Beaux Arts'. Flaubert never did, in fact, write his 'Conte oriental' (see J. Bruneau, *Le 'Conte oriental' de Flaubert* (Denoël, 1973).

20 I am therefore taking a quite different line from Behdad, *Belated Travelers*, p. 66, 'Although Flaubert went to the Orient for self-dispossession, in search of a discontinuity with his European selfhood, once there, he became retentive about the Oriental referent as he witnessed its slow disappearance under the weight of European colonialism', caught as he is in the (Occidental) critical splits of Self/Other, Before/After, Anal/Erotic. al-Nouty, *Le Proche-Orient*, p. 27 also sites the journey as a break rather than my continuum reading, with 'les derniers restes de son lyrisme' in this instance.

21 Letter to Louis Bouilhet (Flaubert's closest friend and critic after the death of Alfred de Poittevin, to whom *La Tentation de Saint Antoine* was dedicated) written between Girgeh and Siout [Asyut] (2 June 1850), p. 633.

22 Again I disagree with Behdad's interesting reading of adopting national dress as 'cultural transvestism', *Belated Travellers*, p. 59. First, native dress would have been by far the more comfortable. Second, Egyptians then, as today, are

never taken in by disguised Europeans. Most important, the wearing of non-European clothes allows Flaubert to have a unique insight into the dressing-up of his own culture.

23 One of the few critics to highlight this is al-Nouty, *Le Proche-Orient*, p. 39, 'Au fonds, les voyageurs européens n'ont jamais dépassé, dans leurs investigations en pays musulmans, les frontières d'une frange sociale, contaminée par un Occident plus ou moins authentique, laquelle avait poussé en bordure de l'Orient intégral rendu hermétique par des différences de langages, de croyances et cent autres obstacles.'

24 It is only with recent critical reappraisals of Orientalism emerging from the Muslim and/or feminist perspectives that the so-called Oriental Other to the West has been permitted a voice to reply. See for example the work of F. Mernissi, *Beyond the Veil: male-female dynamics in a modern Muslim society*, (Cambridge, Mass.: Schenkman, 1975) and recent post-colonial criticism such as the work of G.C. Spivak, 'Imperialism and Sexual Difference,' in (eds) R.C. Davis & R. Schleifer, *Contemporary Literary Criticism: literary and cultural studies* (New York & London: Longman, 1989), pp. 517–29.

25 For example, his descriptions of local colour in his letter of 22 April 1850, pp. 614–18.

26 Flaubert's descriptions are so rarely moralising or loaded with value judgements as M. Salinas, *Gustave Flaubert: voyage à Carthage* (Toulouse: Mirail, 1992), p. 25, notes with reference to the much later journey to Carthage, 'Flaubert, quant à lui, s'intéressa à toutes les manifestations sans parti pris, sans indulgence'.

27 See al-Nouty, *Le Proche-Orient*, pp. 36–7, 'L'Orient donnait une autre leçon à Flaubert. Il y avait appris, en poursuivant son enquête sur le grotesque, à regarder les choses, à les scruter, et il en a gardé le pli. Mais il l'avait appris si vite qu'on ne peut nier qu'il eût depuis toujours un penchant réaliste. L'expérience orientale le mettait à nu et rendait en somme Flaubert à lui-même.'

28 A. Naaman, *Les Débuts de Gustave Flaubert et sa technique de la description* (Nizet, 1962), pp. 380, 436 repectively.

29 G. Bollème, *La Leçon de Flaubert* (Julliard 10/18, 1964), p. 185 calls this 'faire "du réel écrit"' and comments that 'La description est à la fois un approfondissement de l'analyse et un effort sur le langage' (p. 261). Letters of particular vividness are to Dr Jules Cloquet (15 January 1850), pp. 562–7 and to Louis Bouilhet (2 June [1850]), pp. 626–39, where colour is particularly rich and fresh.

30 Dupuy, *Algérie-Tunisie*, pp. 50–1, 'Reste à se demander pourquoi Flaubert éprouvait à propos de "l'Orient" ce goût instinctif, profond, invétéré, que l'on ne peut manquer de juger assez dépravé, voire morbide puisque l'écrivain s'y manifeste par une joie sadique à dénoncer la contamination fâcheuse des races, la "canaillerie immuable et inébranlable", qui, à ses yeux, en constituent le spécifique et séduisant attrait ... satisfait son incurable pessimisme et sa désillusion foncière à l'égard des civilisations ... "Tout craque ici comme chez nous".'

31 See e.g., Said, *Orientalism*, pp. 188–90, 309. Feminist critics have been particularly harsh. See, e.g., Lowe, *Critical Terrains*, pp. 76–78 and Kabbani,

Imperial Fictions, p. 73. Behdad's comments on Kuchuk have some qualifiers, but nonetheless repeat the givens of 'Orientalist eroticism' and 'scopic pleasure', *Belated Travelers*, pp. 68–9, of other critics.

32 Salinas, *Carthage*, p. 30, illustrates the obverse Occidental myth of the Oriental Woman as cipher; Kuchuk is interpreted as the 'principe féminin, le symbole troublant de la fécondité ... symbole mystique, parfaitement intégrée dans la nature. Flaubert trouvait en elle le calme et le vide du désert, la grandeur faite du sordide et de merveilleux où l'on dévine néanmoins les turbulences, la violence, la barbarie, la force, le désir de l'absolu, de néant, de mort.' This reading is perhaps even more perverse for moving farther from the actual text and because it moves Kuchuk beyond the *femme fatale* negative of the *femme vierge* to a Lilith or Pandora position.

33 Said, *Orientalism*, p. 169, discusses the *almeh* but falls for the *idée reçue* of Kuchuk as *femme fatale*. In fact, *almeh* has some of the connotations of the intellectual bluestocking, a Louise Colet figure (his poet mistress from 1846).

34 Behdad, *Belated Travelers*, p. 31.

35 See Kabbani, *Imperial Fictions*, p. 26.

36 See Mernissi, *Beyond the Veil*, pp. 3–5. *Fitna* is both a beautiful woman and what men fear in women, the disorder, chaos within, which men associate with loss of self control. Oriental and Occidental male fears are strangely mirrored in their attitudes to women and to infidels.

37 *Correspondance* I, p. viii.

38 Ibid., p. 635.

39 Ibid., pp. 605–06.

40 Ibid., p. 638.

41 *Correspondance* I, pp. 571–2. 'Comme danseurs, figure-toi deux drôles passablement laids, mais charmants de corruption, de dégradation intentionnelle dans le regard et de féminéité dans les mouvements ... et habillés en femmes [les pantalons retenus] de sorte que tout le ventre, les reins et la naissance des fesses sont à nu ... ils marchent remuant le bassin avec un mouvement court et convulsif. C'est un *trille de muscles* ... Quelquefois ils se renversent tout à fait sur le dos par terre, comme une femme qui se couche pour se faire baiser, et se relèvent avec un mouvement de reins pareil à un arbre qui se redresse une fois le vent passé ... De temps à autre pendant la danse, le cornac ou macquereau qui les a amenés folâtre autour d'eux, leur embrassant le ventre, le cul, les reins, et disant des facéties gaillards pour épicer la chose qui est déjà claire par elle-même. C'est trop beau pour que ce soit excitant.'

42 *Correspondance* I, p. 573, 'mon kellak me frottait doucement, lorsque étant arrivé aux parties nobles, il a retroussé mes boules d'amour pour me les nettoyer, puis continuant à me frotter la poitrine de la main gauche, il s'est mis de la droite à tirer sur mon vi et, le polluant par un mouvement de traction ... me répétant: *batchis, batchis.*'

43 See M. Orr, 'Reading the Other: Flaubert's Education sentimentale revisited', *French Studies* 46: 4 (October 1992), pp. 412–23 where I discuss the bisexual in Frédéric Moreau's relationship to women and Deslauriers in *L'Éducation sentimentale*.

44 P. Berthier, *Figures du fantasme* (Toulouse: Presses universitaires du Mirail, 1992) uses this subtitle to discuss *L'Éducation sentimentale*.

45 Flaubert, *Le Dictionnaire des idées reçues* (Aubier, Éditions Montaigne, 1913).

21 ∾ Egypt Imagined, Egypt Visited: Théophile Gautier

Peter Whyte

It is possible that Gautier's passion for Egypt first found expression when he was only nineteen, in a tale entitled *Un repas au désert de l'Égypte*, published anonymously in *Le Gastronome* (Thursday, 24 March 1831).[1] A French traveller, accepting hospitality from a group of Bedouins in the ruins of Thebes, discovers that the roasted gazelle has been cooked on a fire in which a mummy is the fuel. The delicacy he has consumed is 'de la gazelle à la momie!'. The story is a humorous exercise in the Romantic macabre, and the grounds for attributing the tale to Gautier are dubious,[2] but by the time he reached his mid-twenties he had developed considerable interest in ancient Egypt. This is in part accounted for by the vogue of Orientalist painting in the 1830s but there were other more direct stimuli. He published an account in 1837 of the collection of Egyptian and Greco–Roman antiquities assembled by Mimaut,[3] a former French consul general in Egypt, where he hopes that the collection will not be acquired by English buyers. He notes in particular that 'les *Tables d'Abydos*, d'un si haut intérêt pour la science, et qui constatent dix-huit siècles de rois égyptiens, ont été sciées avec précautions [*sic*] et rapportées en France'. He evokes papyrus scrolls which 'défient les Oedipes et les Champollions, et doivent contenir les plus mystérieuses et les plus singulières histoires', a notion taken up later in *Le Roman de la momie* (1858), and exclaims: 'Étrange pays que l'Égypte! on dirait que les vivants n'y ont jamais fait autre chose que d'enterrer les morts'.

The latter sentence is twice echoed in *Une nuit de Cléopâtre* (1838).[4] The narrator describes Egypt as 'cette terre, qui ne fut jamais qu'un grand tombeau, et dont les vivants semblent ne pas avoir d'autre occupation que d'embaumer les morts'.[5] Cleopatra weaves a variation on the theme, voicing her anxiety about traditional practices:

> ... dans les autres contrées de la terre on brûle les cadavres, et leur cendre se confond bientôt avec le sol. Ici l'on dirait que les vivants n'ont d'autre occupation que de conserver les morts; des baumes puissants les arrachent à la destruction; ils gardent tous leur forme et leur aspect; l'âme évaporée, la dépouille reste ...[6]

On 31 October 1856 Gautier reviewed the first volume of Ernest Feydeau's *Histoire des usages funèbres et des sépultures des peuples anciens* (Paris, 1856), which is devoted to Egypt, in *Le Moniteur universel*:

> C'est un spectacle étrange que ce peuple préparant sa tombe dès le berceau, ne voulant pas rendre sa poussière aux éléments, et luttant contre la destruction avec une invincible opiniâtreté. ... si la civilisation égyptienne eût duré dix siècles de plus, les morts eussent fini par chasser les vivants du sol natal; la nécropole eût envahi la ville, et les momies roides dans leurs bandelettes se fussent dressées contre le mur du foyer.[7]

The image is surrealistic, and indicates an enduring obsession.

Une nuit de Cléopâtre is based on the tradition, current since antiquity, that the debauched Queen of Egypt would accord a night of love to those who would accept execution the following day as the price of her favours. Gautier, who had planned a ballet scenario on Cleopatra in 1837,[8] was not the first writer of the Romantic period to tackle the subject of the Egyptian Queen or the topos of the fatal night of love. Alexandre Soumet's tragedy *Cléopâtre* had been performed in 1824. Peignot's fragment entitled *Luxe de Cléopâtre dans ses festins*, in the *Annales romantiques* of 1829 (pp. 230–2), could have provided inspiration for the scene of the banquet in Gautier's tale.[9] Pushkin's *Egyptian Nights* (1835) treats Cleopatra's nights of love,[10] although Gautier could have had no knowledge of the work at this time. Jules de Saint-Félix's *Cléopâtre, reine d'Égypte* (1836) had examined the Queen's capricious nature, but is more likely to have influenced *Le Roman de la momie* (1858).[11] Gautier was familiar with Shakespeare's *Antony and Cleopatra* (1608; printed 1623), and no doubt drew on it in his opening chapter when describing Cleopatra's barge, a celebrated evocation of which Shakespeare had put into the mouth of Enobarbus (Act II, scene 2, ll., 197–224). Gautier and Shakespeare also shared the same literary source in Plutarch's *Lives*, but Gautier's descriptions are markedly more detailed and vivid than those of his predecessors. This is explained in part by his reliance on Champollion,[12] and in part by his appreciation of paintings like Jean Gigoux's 'Cléopâtre' on which he had written in *La Presse* of 13 October 1836, when it was still incomplete, and in the same newspaper on 23 March 1838, when it was exhibited in the Salon, and Hubert Robert's 'Cléopâtre sur le Fidnus', which he mentions in *La Presse* of 15 November 1836.[13] Gautier was also indebted to John Martin,[14] whose work he had discussed in *La Presse* of 31 January 1837 and to whom he makes direct reference in the last chapter of *Une nuit de Cléopâtre*, where the description of the banqueting hall clearly evokes the celebrated picture of 'Belshazzar's Feast' (1821).

In spite of its sumptuous local colour and technical vocabulary, *Une nuit de Cléopâtre* is less a work of historical reconstruction than a highly romanticised version of antiquity, in which idealisation (the boatman in Chapter One is 'le type égyptien dans toute sa pureté') mingles with narratorial self-consciousness (the playful narrator is our contemporary and does not hesitate to create an anachronistic effect when he puts into the mouth of Cleopatra the word 'baroque' in Chapter Two). With its monumentality and its commitment to the dream of eternity, Egypt symbolizes dissatisfaction with modern life. The principal characters share the Romantic cult of the absolute. For all her cruelty and capriciousness, Cleopatra is a victim of *ennui*, and Meiamoun's restless energy and taste for danger translate into the Romantic death-wish. The link between the story and expressions of Romantic desire was evident in the original text in *La Presse*, as Gautier included in the final chapter an unattributed quotation from Hugo's *Ruy Blas*, which had first been performed on 8 November 1838. This quotation, which illustrates Meiamoun's passionate love ('Donc je marche vivant dans mon rêve étoilé'), was suppressed in all subsequent versions.

The story's final episode appeared in *La Presse* on 6 December, and Gautier began his review of current theatre on 10 December with the words 'Nous revenons d'Égypte', evoking 'le Ramasseum de Biban-el-Molouk'. He will return in imagination to that celebrated archaeological site twenty years later, in *Le Roman de la momie*, when Lord Evandale and his party discover the tomb of Tahoser; in the intervening period his growing interest in Egypt, both ancient and modern, will alternate between whimsical fantasising and a genuine longing for knowledge about a country which had become a focus of obsession.

In the summer of 1838, he had written humorously of the solitude of the obelisk from Luxor which had been erected in the Place de la Concorde on 25 October 1836, hoping that it would soon have the company of four sphinxes with whom it might converse ('Statues de la Place de la Concorde', *La Presse*, 14 August 1838), but it was not until thirteen years had elapsed that he published the poem 'Nostalgies d'obélisques' (*La Presse*, 4 August 1851), in which he lent that obelisk, stranded in a world both profane and ephemeral, the words to express its longing for its homeland, repository of the sacred and the eternal, and made its twin in Luxor, in an ironic antithesis, long for the life of Paris, on the grounds that Egypt, while a stable point in the flux of history, was the land of death. The direct inspiration for the poem came from a letter written on 13 August 1850 in Jerusalem by Maxime Du Camp,[15] sketching the subject matter of the poem and asking Gautier to dedicate it to him if he should choose to execute the plan. 'Nostalgies d'obélisques' was indeed dedicated to Du Camp in *La Presse* of 4 August 1851, but this dedication disappeared when the poem was included in *Émaux et Camées* in 1852.[16]

In 1840 Gautier began to compose a series of exotic stories and pastiches for *Le Musée des Familles*, two of which concern Egypt. *Le Pied de momie* appeared in the September 1840 issue, and is a parody of the conventions of the *conte fantastique* as it had developed in France in the 1830s. The subject matter derives from Dominique Vivant-Denon's *Voyage dans la Basse et Haute-Égypte pendant les campagnes du général Bonaparte* (Didot, 3 vols, 1802), which had been reprinted in 1829,[17] where the author recounts his discovery of a charming embalmed foot (t. II, 278; t. III. plate C). In Gautier's tale, the narrator purchases this specimen as an exotic paperweight and is led by the Princess Hermonthis, who comes to reclaim her lost extremity, into a series of dream-like adventures culminating in a descent into the tombs of the pharaohs where he is offered a reward for returning the severed foot to its rightful owner. He requests the princess's hand in marriage, opining that 'la main pour le pied me paraissait une récompense antithétique d'assez bon goût',[18] but her father rejects him on the grounds of their disproportionate ages (27 as against 3,000). Beneath the humour and the word play, there are more serious concerns. The pharaoh's reference to Isis recomposing the body of Osiris from scattered pieces reminds us of the remark made earlier by the princess about mutilation and her father's desire that her body should be buried intact.[19] The significance of such comments can be grasped only in the context of ancient Egyptian religious thought, and a passage from Gautier's review of Feydeau's *Histoire des usages funèbres et des sépultures des peuples anciens*, sixteen years later, allows us retrospectively to interpret them:

> ... l'âme n'était pas cependant déliée de toute solidarité avec le corps. Son immortalité relative dépendait en quelque sorte de l'intégrité de celui-ci. L'altération ou la privation d'un membre étaient supposées ressenties par l'âme, dont la forme eût été mutilée dans son spectre impalpable, et qui n'eût pu suivre, boiteuse ou manchote, le cycle des migrations ou des métempsycoses.[20]

The second text with an Egyptian dimension, *La Mille et deuxième nuit* (*Le Musée des Familles*, August 1842), is derived from *Les Mille et une nuits* in Galland's early eighteenth-century French translation. It combines parody of the fantastic tale with traditional fairy tale motifs (with a *péri* transforming herself into a princess and a slave to test the hero's fidelity in love), and is set in a conventional medieval Cairo. The systematic, if not always accurate, historical colour of *Le Pied de momie* contrasts with the exotic, sometimes anachronistic, local colour of *La Mille et deuxième nuit*, and references in the latter to Dauzats and Roqueplan underline the importance of Orientalist painting in Gautier's perception of Cairo. The fact that the hero lives in Esbekieh Square reminds us that Marilhat's 'La Place de l'Esbekieh' (1834) was one of Gautier's favourite paintings.[21] When Gautier used *La Mille et deuxième nuit* as the basis for the ballet *La Péri*

(1843),[22] he claimed to have had recourse to Marilhat's expertise for the costumes and décor.[23] He also requested descriptive details from Gérard de Nerval, who was in Cairo, but these were not relevant and arrived too late to be of use. The ballet is the acme of Romantic literary Orientalism, combining eroticism, in the celebrated *pas de l'abeille*,[24] opium dreams, the intervention of *péris*, initiation into ideal love and the final accession to the Muslim paradise. In the review of his own ballet which Gautier wrote in *La Presse* of 25 July 1843, which takes the form of a letter to Nerval in Cairo, he expands on the conflict between materialism and idealism which the scenario dramatises and states that he is a creature in exile, whose true home is Egypt.[25]

Having not yet travelled to Egypt, Gautier paid particular attention to the work of those who had, and wrote appreciatively of books and theatrical performances depicting the land for which he felt such longing.

Félicien David (1810–76), whom he vigorously championed in his newspaper articles and with whom he collaborated on a number of songs,[26] had travelled in the Near East and in Egypt in 1833–35. David's 'ode-symphonie', *Le Désert*, was admiringly reviewed by Gautier in *La Presse* of 16 December 1844, where he noted that the composer had studied Oriental music in Egypt and this was clear in the *Danse des Almées*, which had truly primeval charm:

> C'est pour ainsi dire un chant inné; en l'entendant, vous vous souvenez de tout ce que vous n'avez jamais su. Cette mélodie si neuve, vous croyez l'avoir trouvée vous-même et fredonnée autrefois dans une existence antérieure [...]. Certaines phrases ont cette bizarre puissance de vous transporter au-delà des univers connus, et doivent être des échos de la musique des sphères retenus par l'âme en passant d'un monde à l'autre; en entendant ce motif égyptien, sans doute contemporain des Pharaons, comme toutes les mélodies de l'Orient, où rien ne change, vous paraît démontré que vous avez été au mieux avec la reine de Saba ou avec la fameuse Rhodope qui fit bâtir la troisième Pyramide à ses frais![27]

Self-irony informs the references to the Queen of Sheba and Rhodope, but the Egyptian motif which links the present with the unchanging past of the Pharaohs, and embodies a sense of cultural continuity, is characteristic of Gautier's eclectic and syncretic cast of mind. Egypt mediates a return to the origins which transcends death itself. Gautier praises the contribution of the librettist, Auguste Colin, who also had strong Egyptian connections.[28] Gautier was to describe *Le Désert* (*La Presse*, 6 January 1845) as the culmination of an aesthetic trend, since it showed Romanticism looking beyond its traditional sources of inspiration in England and Germany to the Orient, perceived as a reservoir of archetypes.[29]

Many of Gautier's remarks on Egypt were generated by the vicissitudes of the contemporary Parisian scene and were subject to the constraints of journalism. His review of the production at the Théâtre-Français of Mme

·de Girardin's play *Cléopâtre* (*La Presse*, 15 November 1847) is long and deferential (the author was his close friend as well as the wife of the proprietor of the newspaper), but he begins with remarks which illuminate *Une nuit de Cléopâtre* (1838). Cleopatra is described as an archetype of femininity, who could have existed only in ancient Egypt:

> L'antiquité seule, où des multitudes étaient résumées par une personnalité unique, pouvait mettre au jour ces individualités énormes, ces existences colossales en dehors de toutes les proportions modernes, dont le monde attentif regardait se dérouler au-dessus de lui, dans une atmosphère étincelante, les fantaisies titaniques et démesurées.[30]

These remarks echo the beginning of the final chapter of the novella, on the grandeur of ancient civilisation, but Gautier now envisages Cleopatra not as a heroine suffering from *le mal romantique*, but as a cultural icon of the coalescence of the physical and the intellectual:

> Elle avait le don de l'universalité; elle savait tout; elle parlait toutes les langues et répondait à chacun dans son idiome; elle connaissait la poésie, la musique, tous les arts mieux que les plus habiles professeurs. Les soins d'un vaste empire, la conduite d'intrigues immenses et compliquées, les recherches d'un luxe inouï que la misère civilisée ne peut pas même concevoir, la fatigue des nuits orgiaques et de ces repas babyloniens où l'on buvait des perles fondues, rien n'altérait ce corps frêle et souple, fait d'acier et de diamant, qui semblait habité par vingt âmes ...[31]

The notion of the cultural impoverishment of the present, which can be remedied only by contact with the past, is taken up the following year in Gautier's obituary notice on the Orientalist painter Marilhat, whose importance for *La Mille et deuxième nuit* (1842) and *La Péri* (1843) has been mentioned. Gautier ascribes to Marilhat, who had travelled widely in Egypt, and signed letters 'L'Égyptien Prosper Marilhat', a kind of racial memory, as 'Le vague désir de la patrie primitive agite les âmes qui ont plus de mémoire que les autres et en qui revit le type effacé ailleurs'.[32] Marilhat is thus 'un Arabe syrien',[33] descendant of the Saracens, just as Gautier had described himself five years earlier as 'Turc, non de Constantinople, mais d'Égypte'.[34] Gautier considered in 1848 that Marilhat's 'Souvenir des bords du Nil', exhibited in the Salon of 1844, was not only his masterpiece, but one of the greatest paintings ever produced.[35] Seeing 'La Place de l'Esbekieh au Caire' for the first time in 1834 had of course been a key experience for the development of Gautier's passion for Egypt:

> *La Place de l'Esbekieh au Caire!* Aucun tableau ne fit sur moi une impression plus profonde et plus longtemps vibrante. J'aurais peur d'être taxé d'exagération en disant que la vue de cette peinture me rendit malade et m'inspira la nostalgie de l'Orient, où je n'avais jamais mis le pied. Je crus que je venais de connaître

ma véritable patrie, et, lorsque je détournais les yeux de l'ardente peinture, je me sentais exilé ...[36]

Gautier's collaboration with Ernest Reyer on *Le Sélam* (1850), a 'symphonie descriptive' on Oriental themes for which he wrote the libretto, is a good example of his vicarious re-living of the experiences of his contemporaries who had visited a country he knew only from imagination. Of the five tableaux, the last, *La dhossa*, has an exclusively Egyptian interest. Flaubert and Du Camp had witnessed the festival of Dosseh in January 1850, and the latter was to give an account of it, in the form of a letter to Gautier, in *Le Nil* (Bourdillat, 1854, pp. 63–65), but in 1850 Gautier would have had knowledge of the spectacle from Nerval, and also knew E. W. Lane's account in *The Modern Egyptians* (1836).[37] The definitive version of Nerval's *Voyage en Orient* (Charpentier, 2 vols, 1851) undoubtedly gave Gautier further inspiration.

His developing knowledge of the work of academic Egyptologists is apparent in 1851, when he reviewed, in *La Presse* of 30 December, *Bonaparte en Égypte*, 'drame militaire en cinq actes et 19 tableaux par MM. Labrousse et Albert'. He praised its spectacular qualities and the attention it paid to the scientific and military aspects of the French expeditions to Egypt. He cites Larrey, Desgenettes, Champollion, Monge, Jomard, Denon and Geoffroy Saint-Hilaire and 'les merveilleux daguerréotypes de notre camarade Maxime Du Camp'.[38] Some of the latter are found in the one hundred and fifty plates in *Égypte, Nubie, Palestine et Syrie* (Gide & J. Baudry, 1852, 2 vols in-folio). Between June and October 1852, Gautier was at last to travel to the East himself, but only to Turkey and Greece, and he was to exclaim in Constantinople: 'Je songe au Caire et à l'Égypte'.[39] Fortunately, there were opportunities on his return to sustain the dream. A revival of Rossini's *Moïse* (*Mosè in Egitto*) at the Opéra in 1852, a work he had first experienced in 1836, was enthusiastically reviewed in *La Presse* of 8 November,[40] and he will recall its subject in *Le Roman de la momie* (1858). Even a humble *panorama*, reviewed in the Spring of 1853 ('Panorama de la bataille des Pyramides', *La Presse*, 23 March 1853) could give him the sensation of being actually transported to the pyramids, 'gigantesques triangles de pierre que le temps n'a pu ébrécher et qui fatigueront peut-être l'éternité'.[41] He lavishly praises its originator, Colonel Langlois, for his thorough researches *in situ*, and the painters for the brilliance of their execution.

The publication of Du Camp's *Le Nil* (Bourdillat, 1854) brings Gautier back to his dream. In his review (*Le Moniteur universel*, 8 April 1854), he refers to his desire to travel to Egypt as 'Ce vœu resté à l'état de chimère caressée ... '.[42] In praising the accuracy of Du Camp, he recalls Marilhat's painting of one of the scenes, which had remained etched in his memory, 'un morceau d'Égypte encadré',[43] allowing him to anticipate in imagination the verbal descriptions and photographic plates. Again, artistic vision finds its corroboration in objective notation. The review of the first volume of Ernest Feydeau's *Histoire des usages funèbres et des sépultures des peuples anciens* (1856) shows how Gautier's understanding has deepened. Feydeau achieves, says Gautier, a veritable resurrection of the daily life of the past, by mingling the picturesque and the scientific. The delineation of Thebes *à vol d'oiseau* is singled out for praise, as are the plates by Prisse d'Avennes, which he considers to have set new standards for Egyptological illustration. The subject of the work naturally causes him to reflect once more on a people 'préparant son tombeau dès le berceau',[44] with its 'préoccupation d'éternité dans la mort',[45] but also on the characteristics of Egyptian art with its 'contrainte hiératique',[46] which reminds us of the aesthetic of pure form and conventional colour which Gautier was to formulate in his celebrated pre-Parnassian poem 'L'Art' the following year (*L'Artiste*, 13 September 1857). Although the poem does not mention Egypt directly, the influence is clear.

Feydeau and Prisse d'Avennes were to be a crucial influence on *Le Roman de la momie* (1858). The former made his collection of books and prints on Egypt available to Gautier, who dedicated the novel to him. It was Feydeau's erudition, he claimed, which enabled him to complete his project, and he asserted to Émile Bergerat: 'Dans *la Momie*, j'ai rendu l'Égypte amusante sans rien sacrifier de l'exactitude la plus rigoureuse des détails historiques, topographiques et archéologiques.'[47] Judith Gautier later described her father poring over the cumbersome folio volumes lent by Feydeau and transcribing his impressions directly into his manuscript.[48] He wore his erudition lightly,[49] but the list of those to whom Gautier is indebted reads like a roll of honour of nineteenth-century Egyptology: Belzoni, Champollion, Du Camp, Feydeau, Mariette, Passalacqua, Prisse d'Avennes, Wilkinson. Historical details and plates contained in works by the last three were particularly exploited in Gautier's descriptions.[50] A number of paintings of Biblical scenes, from Poussin's 'Plaies d'Égypte' to Estéban Marc's 'Passage de la mer rouge', which he mentioned in *La Presse* of 24 September 1837, probably provided general inspiration,[51] and Feydeau noted that some 'fragments de manuscrits hiéroglyphiques traduits par M. Rougé' and 'la lecture attentive de la Bible de Cahen' were instrumental in bringing the work to fruition. [52]

In the Prologue Lord Evandale mentions Champollion, Rosellini, Wilkinson, Lepsius and Belzoni. There are subsequent references to Belzoni, Champollion and Lepsius. Rumphius, the pedantic German philologist is perhaps a caricature of the latter, in this novel of time travel. A footprint, undisturbed in the dust of thirty centuries, induces in Evandale a sense of awe, which will be augmented by the 'désir rétrospectif' engendered by the discovery of the beautiful mummy (Tahoser), and culminates in a sense of the inadequacy and decadence of modern civilisation compared with the enduring qualities of Egyptian antiquity. In fact, *Le Roman de la momie* is neither an historical novel, nor an exercise in psychological analysis, but a poetic re-interpretation of the past, in which the modern Egypt of the archaeologist and the ancient Egypt of legend are confronted as emblems of the conflict of Eros and Thanatos. When Pharaoh earns the love of Tahoser, it is in a moment of despair before an invincible force which will bring about his death. When Evandale succumbs to the beauty of the same woman three thousand years later, he too is lost to the life of his own epoch.

Major international exhibitions mounted in the last two decades of Gautier's life broadened his vision. A visit to the Great Exhibition in London in 1851 rekindled a growing interest in India, but he also saw there a display of modern Egyptian manufactures, whose intrinsic merit was enhanced for him by their stylistic continuity with the artefacts of antiquity ('des gargoulettes en terre de Thèbes ... aussi pures de forme si elles eussent été tournées sur la roue du potier au temps de Rhamsès ou de Thoutmosis').[53] Similarly, the Exposition Universelle in Paris in 1867 was to deepen his fascination with China and, above all, with Egypt.[54] From replicas of mosques to live dromedaries, from scaled-down plaster models of temples and sphinxes to ancient artefacts discovered by Mariette, from John Frederick Lewis's painting of the 'maison du grand Cophte au Caire' ('The Hósh of the House of the Coptic Patriarch') to a plan in relief of the Nile valley, everything displayed in the Egyptian section was enthusiastically reported to the readers of *Le Moniteur universel* on 25 April 1867. A second article, in the same paper on 7 June, gave a detailed description of the unwrapping and dissection of a mummy carried out in the presence of various dignitaries, including Du Camp, Dumas *fils* and the Goncourt brothers, amongst the literati, and Berthelot and Mariette, from the scientific and archaeological communities. Fascinated by what he saw as the actualisation of what he had depicted from imagination in *Le Roman de la momie* (1858), Gautier was moved by the singular juxtaposition of fragility and eternity as the female form was gradually revealed, and perhaps a little disappointed that the ideal of feminine beauty, which the slim figures in the Egyptian paintings of Alma-Tadema had conveyed to him, was not realised in the angularities of bone and skin finally laid bare. A third article, on 3 August, highlighted the progress of work on the Suez canal, portrayed with such detail in relief plans and a *panorama*, that the author claimed he felt not only that he had been transported to the Isthmus but that he had already steamed through the as yet uncompleted canal.

Two years later, Gautier finally visited Egypt—as a member of the French delegation attending the opening of the Suez canal. On 9 October 1869 he left Marseilles on board the *Mœris*, bound for Alexandria. He was, he claims in the first of a series of articles published in the *Journal Officiel* from 17 February–8 May 1870,[55] riven with superstitious fears from the outset. In the event, a fall on board ship left him with a dislocated shoulder. He was unable to make the journey to Upper Egypt and, apart from a visit to Bulaq, was virtually confined to Cairo. If his visit was therefore an anti-climax, he gives no hint of it in his published work or correspondence. His account in the *Journal Officiel*, which can be supplemented by a fragment about his departure by train for Ismailia and a letter to Carlotta Grisi of 28 November 1869 describing the opening of the canal,[56] has all the qualities we expect from the mature travel writer who had already been to England, the Low Countries, Germany, Switzerland, Spain, Italy, Algeria, Turkey, Greece and Russia. Finely observed details of the sea crossing, of the arrival in Alexandria and of the departure for Cairo, picturesque details of costume, poetic evocations of the landscape of the delta viewed from the train, the emotion of seeing the Nile for the first time and in full flood, the distant view of pyramids, acrobats and snake charmers performing in Esbekieh Square, the bustle and colour of the city observed from the terrace of Shepheard's Hotel,[57] portraits of camels and donkeys, all create vibrant tableaux. As always with Gautier, the immediate vision is filtered through cultural stereotypes. People and places suggest subjects for paintings:

> Cette description, d'une scrupuleuse exactitude, ne donne pas une idée bien séduisante d'un village fellah. Eh, bien, plantez à côté de ces cubes de terre grise un bouquet de dattiers, agenouillez un ou deux chameaux devant ces portes, semblables à des ouvertures de terriers, faites-en sortir une femme drapée de sa longue chemise bleue, tenant un enfant par la main et portant une amphore sur la tête, faites glisser sur tout cela un rayon de soleil, et vous aurez un tableau plein de charme et de caractère, qui ravirait tout le monde sous le pinceau de Marilhat.[58]

A family group and a donkey are 'un tableau de la Fuite en Égypte tout fait' for a Perugino, a Raphaël or a Dürer.[59] Figures in a landscape resemble coloured bas-reliefs in ancient tombs.[60] To confirm the image of Esbekieh Square in Marilhat's painting, trees helpfully hid some of the new buildings, and 'de cette façon notre rêve n'était pas trop dérangé'.[61] Decamps' painting of the 'Patrouille turque' comes to life before his eyes.[62] A quotation from Du Camp's *Le Nil* is said perfectly to encapsulate what Gautier himself sees[63] and the visual point of reference for a description of camels is Gérôme's 'Moisson en Égypte'.[64] A group of young shepherds suggests a Biblical scene.[65] Boats on the Nile conjure up 'la forme des barris mystiques au temps des Pharaons'.[66] Sadly, only Carlotta Grisi and her entourage were to receive any account of the opening of the canal itself, which combined spectacle and emotion. The fragment of the uncompleted seventh section of the account breaks off with Gautier installed in an almost empty slow train for Ismailia, his companions having crammed themselves an hour earlier into the express in their haste to arrive at the ceremonies. His final sentence dismisses them as 'les pressés, les nerveux, les ardents, les inquiets, ceux qui ont toujours peur de ne pas arriver',[67] as if he alone had already, long since, assimilated the spirit of Egypt.

Gautier's last publication relating to Egypt was written just nine months before his death.[68] It is a book review, but is cast in fictional form, recounting a journey made by third parties with whom the writer empathises to the extent of appearing to be their actual travelling companion. Dated 'Neuilly, 29 January 1872', the piece begins with the author's overwhelming sense of dejection on the first anniversary of the surrender of Paris to the Prussians, but as he sits despondently with his cat Éponine on his knees like a 'sphinx noir', he opens Paul Lenoir's *Le Fayoum, le Sinaï, Petra. Expédition dans la Moyenne Égypte et l'Arabie Pétrée sous la direction de J.-L. Gérôme* (H. Plon, 1872) and his mood changes. First, because Lenoir, a painter who had exhibited at the Paris Salon in 1870, was also a writer of talent, and Gautier always enthused over a combination of visual and scriptural skills. Second, because the illustrations by Jean-Léon Gérôme make him nostalgic about his own jouney to Cairo in 1869, and one drawing, depicting the dancer Hasné, described by Gautier as 'le pur type égyptien antique', allows him to see the symbiosis of ancient and modern Egypt. Third, because reading affords the opportunity to journey in imagination, and, by appropriating in his own discourse the book's descriptions, to blur the distinctions between the little he had himself seen and the more extensive itinerary of Lenoir and his companions. Thus, it appears that Gautier has not only visited the pyramids of Cairo, but the Serapeum at Memphis, although this is merely a subterfuge of wish-fulfilment. Considerable pathos attaches to the conclusion of this valedictory article. As a grey mist descends on Paris, leaving the writer to his journalistic chores, it is 'comme pour baisser le rideau sur cette féerie d'Orient'.[69] No sooner conjured up, the vision fades. Gautier's dream of Egypt is finally extiguished in Neuilly on 23 October 1872. Lenoir was to pass away in 1881. Appropriately, the latter's place of death was Cairo.

Notes

1 The text is given by Charles de Spoelberch de Lovenjoul in *Histoire des Œuvres de Théophile Gautier* t. I (1887), pp. 8–11 (Slatkine Reprints, 1968) and reproduced by Paolo Tortonese in his edition of Gautier's *Voyage en Égypte* (La Boîte à Documents, 1991), pp. 87–9.

2 Lovenjoul's speculative attribution depends on a tradition in the Gautier family that the author published his first prose narrative in *Le Gastronome*.

3 'Variétés. Collection égyptienne de M. Mimaut', *La Presse* (19 December 1837). It is noted beneath the title of the article that the collection is to be sold at 22, rue d'Aguesseau, the following day. A copy of the article is to be found in the Collection Lovenjoul of the Bibliothèque de l'Institut (Paris) under C 1456 (I, 2). A truncated version was published by Paolo Tortonese in Gautier, *Voyage en Égypte* (La Boîte à Documents, 1991), pp. 168–9.

4 *Une nuit de Cléopâtre* was first published in *La Presse* of 29, 30 November and 1, 2, 4, 6 December 1838, and has been reprinted in all editions of Gautier's *Nouvelles* since 1845.

5 *Nouvelles* (Charpentier, 1923), p. 323.

6 Ibid., p. 330.

7 *L'Orient* II (Charpentier, 1877), pp. 269–70 ['Égypte ancienne'].

8 On this ballet, written for Fanny Elssler, see Charles de Spoelberch de Lovenjoul, *Les Lundis d'un chercheur* (Calmann-Lévy, 1894), pp. 18–24.

9 The parallel was established by Louise Bulkley Dillingham, *The Creative Imagination of Théophile Gautier. A Study in Literary Psychology* (Princeton: Psychological Review Company, 1927), p. 137. For further parallels, with Heine and Saint-Amant, see pp. 138, 140–1.

10 The development of Pushkin's preoccupation with the theme is traced by Leslie O'Bell, *Pushkin's 'Egyptian Nights': The Biography of a Work* (Ann Arbor: Ardis, 1984).

11 Dillingham, *Creative Imagination*, p. 138.

12 For a discussion of Gautier's indebtedness to Champollion, and historical inaccuracies, see Jean-Marie Carré, *Voyageurs et écrivains français en Égypte* t. II (Cairo: Institut français d'archéologie orientale, 2nd edition, 1956) pp. 139–41.

13 Dillingham, *Creative Imagination*, pp. 138–9.

14 *Nouvelles* (1923), pp. 355–8. For Martin's influence on Gautier, see Jean Seznec, *John Martin en France* (London: Faber & Faber, 1964).

15 Théophile Gautier, *Correspondance générale* t. IV (Droz, 1989), p. 206 [letter 1453]. Carré, *Voyageurs et écrivains* II, p. 115, believes Flaubert was the originator of the idea, which Du Camp developed later, and notes a parallel in Heine, ibid., pp. 147–8.

16 For an analysis of this poem, see Constance Gosselin-Schick, 'Nostalgies d'obélisques', *Bulletin de la Société Théophile Gautier* 12 (1990), pp. 261–71.

17 Cf. Carré, *Voyageurs et écrivains* II, pp. 145–7.

18 Théophile Gautier, *Romans et contes* (Charpentier, 1891), p. 413.

19 See ibid., pp. 414, 409.

20 *L'Orient* II, pp. 275–6. ['Égypte ancienne'].

21 Carré, *Voyageurs et écrivains* II, p. 182, note 4, considers that Gautier's topography is dependent on Marilhat's painting of the mosque of Sultan Hasan.

22 On the relationship between *La Mille et deuxième nuit* and *La Péri*, see Andrew Gann, 'La genèse de *La Péri*', in *Théophile Gautier. L'Art et l'Artiste* t. I (Montpellier, 1982), pp. 207–20.

23 Gautier's claim is made in his obituary of Marilhat (*Revue des deux mondes*, 1 July 1848), reprinted in *Portraits contemporains* (Charpentier, 1874), pp. 234–

64 [v. 240]. There is no doubt that he visited the painter on this occasion, but on the vexed question of the possible collaboration of Marilhat in this project, see Edwin Binney, *Les Ballets de Théophile Gautier* (Nizet, 1965), pp. 109–10.

24 In a letter to the dancer and choreographer Jules Perrot, written *circa* February 1842, Gautier indicates that a description of this dance, said to have been banned in Egypt, is given by Adrien Dauzats and Alexandre Dumas, *Nouvelles impressions de voyage. Quinze jours au Sinaï* (1839). Cf. Théophile Gautier, *Théâtre* (Charpentier, nouvelle édition, 1882), p. 304 [pp. 301–4] and *Correspondance générale* t. I (Geneva: Droz, 1985), pp. 299–302.

25 This 'letter' was reproduced in Gautier, *Théâtre* (Charpentier, nouvelle édition, 1882, 293–301). See also Théophile Gautier, *Correspondance générale* t. II (Geneva: Droz, 1986), pp. 40–8, for useful annotations and for Nerval's reply of 14 August 1843 (pp. 55–60).

26 On Gautier and Félicien David, see Andrew Gann, 'Lyrics by Gautier: The poet as songwriter', *Francofonia* 2 (1982), pp. 83–100, and 'Les Orients musicaux de Théophile Gautier', *Bulletin de la Société Théophile Gautier* 12 (1990), pp. 35–49.

27 Théophile Gautier, *Histoire de l'art dramatique en France depuis vingt-cinq ans* t. III (Leipzig: Hetzel, 1859), pp. 313–14.

28 Tortonese notes (*Voyage en Égypte*, p. 171) that Colin was soon to publish *Compagnie de l'Isthme de Suez* (Renouard, 1846) and *Percement de l'Isthme de Suez. Création de la première route universelle sur le globe* (Librairie Phalanstérienne, 1847).

29 'Le fait est que, depuis quelques années, l'Orient nous préoccupe comme nous préoccupait autrefois l'Angleterre ou l'Allemagne. Ne vaut-il pas mieux, après tout, se tourner vers le jour que vers la nuit?' (*Histoire de l'art dramatique en France depuis vingt-cinq ans* t. IV (Leipzig: Hetzel, 1859), p. 8).

30 *Histoire de l'art dramatique en France depuis vingt-cinq ans* t. V (Leipzig: Hetzel, 1859), pp. 167–8.

31 Ibid., pp. 168–9.

32 *Portraits contemporains* (deuxième édition, Charpentier, 1874), p. 242.

33 Ibid., p. 243.

34 *Correspondance générale* t. II (Genève: Droz, 1986), p. 41.

35 *Portraits contemporains*, p. 262.

36 Ibid., p. 239.

37 Cf. Carré, *Voyageurs et écrivains* II, pp. 31, 33, 194. A passage from Nerval's *Scènes de la vie orientale*, relating to 'la *Dhossa* ou *Dhozza*' is cited in a note to *Le Sélam* in Gautier, *Théâtre* (nouvelle édition, Charpentier, 1882), p. 243. Nerval made frequent use of E. W. Lane's *Account of the Manners and Customs of the Modern Egyptians* (2 vols, 1836) in the *Voyage en Orient* (Charpentier, 2 vols, 1851), translating extracts from Lane in appendices and incorporating elements from him in the body of the work.

38 This review is reprinted in Tortonese's edition of Gautier's *Voyage en Égypte* (La Boîte à Documents, 1991), pp. 121–2.

39 Cited by Adolphe Boschot in Théophile Gautier, *Le Roman de la momie* (Classiques Garnier, 1955), p. XXVI.

40 Théophile Gautier, *La Musique* (Charpentier, 1911), pp. 124–32.

41 Article reprinted by Tortonese in Gautier, *Voyage en Égypte* (La Boîte à

214   *Travellers in Egypt*

Documents, 1991), pp. 123–9 [v. 128].

42 *L'Orient* II, pp. 245–6.

43 Ibid., p. 250. The painting in question is undoubtedly 'Le Tombeau du sheïck Abou-Mandour, près de Rosette' (1837).

44 Reprinted in *L'Orient* II, pp. 267–79. Our quotation is from p. 269.

45 Ibid., p. 276.

46 Ibid., p. 277.

47 Émile Bergerat, *Théophile Gautier. Entretiens, Souvenirs et Correspondance* (Charpentier, 1911), p. 139.

48 Judith Gautier, *Le Collier des jours. Souvenirs de ma vie.* (Félix Juven, 1907; reprinted, Christian Pirot, 1994), chapter LVIII.

49 Carré, *Voyageurs et écrivains* II, pp. 151–80.

50 J. Passalacqua, *Catalogue raisonné et historique des antiquités découvertes en Égypte* (Paris, 1826); E. Prisse d'Avennes, *Les Monuments égyptiens* (Didot, 1857); J. G. Wilkinson, *The Manners and Customs of the Ancient Egyptians* (London, 1837 and 1854).

51 Dillingham, *Creative Imagination*, p. 117.

52 Ernest Feydeau, *Théophile Gautier, souvenirs intimes* (E. Plon, 1874), p. 93.

53 *L'Orient* I (1877), pp. 361–2.

54 Cf. 'Égypte–Vue générale', and 'L'Isthme de Suez', in *L'Orient* II.

55 These pieces were all reprinted in *L'Orient* II under the heading 'Égypte'.

56 The fragment was published by Charles de Spoelberch de Lovenjoul in his *Histoire des Œuvres de Théophile Gautier* t. II (1887), pp. 393–4 (Slatkine Reprints, 1968). The letter is in *Correspondance générale* t. X (Geneva: Droz, 1996), pp. 440–1.

57 Samuel Shepheard (1815–1866) founded his celebrated hotel on the Esbekieh Square in the mid-1840s. It was rebuilt in 1890, and finally destroyed in 1952. (Cf. Michael Bird, *Samuel Shepheard of Cairo. A Portrait* (London: Michael Joseph, 1957).) An idea of the terrace on which Gautier spent so much of his time can be gained from a Frith photograph taken about that time, reproduced in Deborah Bull and Donald Lorimer, *Up the Nile. A Photographic Excursion: Egypt 1839–1898* (New York: Clarkson N. Potter, 1979), p. 4.

58 *Voyage en Égypte* (1991), 47–8 (III).

59 Ibid., p. 50 (III).

60 Ibid., p. 56 (IV).

61 Ibid., pp. 61 (IV), 63 (V), 64 (V).

62 Ibid., p. 67 (V).

63 Ibid., p. 80 (VI).

64 Ibid., p. 82 (VI).

65 Ibid., p. 52 (III).

66 Ibid., p. 54 (III).

67 Ibid., p. 84 (VII).

68 'Une échappée dans le bleu' (Le Fayoum, le Sinaï et Petra, par Paul Lenoir), *Gazette de Paris* (30 January 1872), reprinted as 'Le Fayoum, le Sinaï et Petra' in *L'Orient* II, pp. 229–44 and in *Voyage en Égypte* (La Boîte à Documents, 1991), pp. 155–60.

69 *L'Orient* II, p. 244.

22 ∼ Juliusz Słowacki in Egypt

Jan W. Weryho

It is very difficult, indeed impossible, to discuss the Polish poet Juliusz Słowacki's visit to Egypt in 1836 except in the context of his tour of the Eastern Mediterranean through Greece, Egypt, Palestine, Syria and Lebanon. A journey through the Eastern Mediterranean (although not necessarily including Egypt) was almost a must for the Romantic authors of the early nineteenth century. We can think of Englishmen—Byron and Disraeli—and of Frenchmen—Chateaubriand, Lamartine, de Nerval and Flaubert. Słowacki's journey was part of a trend. Yet Egypt had entered his life in a sudden and tragic manner at the early age of seventeen. In this paper I shall try to be as brief as I can about Słowacki's journey through the other Middle Eastern countries and concentrate on Egypt. I must however say a few words about his life since he is virtually unknown outside Poland.

Juliusz Słowacki was born in 1809 in Krzemieniec (Kremianets' in Ukrainian) in Western Ukraine which had belonged to Poland until the Third Partition of 1795. Soon afterwards his parents moved to Wilno (Vilnius, the medieval and present capital of Lithuania) where his father, a minor poet, became a professor of Polish literature in the University. In the *Gymnasium* (secondary school) of Wilno young Juliusz's best (and only) friend was a dreamy boy four years his senior, Ludwik Szpitznagel. Szpitznagel was fascinated by the Orient. In his poem 'The Hour of Thought' Słowacki puts the following words in his mouth:

> Listen! Today I saw Oriental lands in my sleep,
> They were beautiful, charming, I often dream about them.
> I see Bedouins' faces darkened by the sun,
> I see palm groves, witnesses of ancient times.
> My thought, irresistible, flies to those lands ...

The poet continues:

> While he was dreaming thus—the cherries and flowers in the
> garden

Grew without fragrance before him, because his thought ran
    further,
And soon, with the fiery dreams of the Orient,
It shut him in a circle of flames and beleaguered him.

After finishing the *Gymnasium* in Wilno Szpitznagel studied Arabic, Persian and Turkish in the University of St Petersburg. Upon graduation, his dreams were realised: he was offered the position of dragoman in the Russian consulate in Alexandria. On the eve of departure he shot himself. I hope one day to write my speculations about his motivation. (A suicide note consisting of a short verse in Persian and Polish gives us little clue.) Whatever it was, it was a tremendous shock for his seventeen-year old friend Słowacki. Not surprisingly, Słowacki's earliest poems are set in the Orient, an imaginary Orient inspired chiefly by Byron's Turkish tales, but also by whatever Arabic poetry was available in Polish, Russian, English, French or German translation. He particularly appreciated the pre-Islamic poets, notably proto-romantic rebels against society like Shanfara and 'Antara.

Probably the best of his early Oriental (or rather Orientalist) poems is 'Lambro', set in Ottoman Greece. A Greek nationalist agitator makes this reference to Egypt:

So I shall sing, towards my aim will go;
Revive the fire, if there is a spark;
As the Egyptian in leaves of aloe
Wraps the remains of a dead man's heart;
And on the leaf he writes of rising from the dead;
And although in this leaf the heart will not revive,
At least from sad decay it shall for aye be saved,
Shall not fall into dust. The hour will arrive
When the heart's secret message it shall come to know.
Then the answer will be in the heart—below.
[Translated by J. W. W.]

During the Polish Uprising of 1830 Słowacki was sent to London to seek support. English intellectuals, especially the literary circles, were very sympathetic towards the Polish cause, but the British Government had no intention of entering into a quarrel with Russia. One result of Słowacki's visit to Britain was the drama 'Maria Stuart'. After the fall of the Uprising Słowacki settled in Paris, the capital of the Polish political émigrés. King Louis Philippe, brought into power by a revolution which had inspired the ill-fated Polish uprising, granted him a French passport, which later proved very useful during his Oriental journey. From this time dates the poem 'Paryń', also rich in Oriental imagery, this time from the Bible: the city on the Seine is compared to Babylon on the Euphrates, place of exile. Soon afterwards the poet moved to Geneva. In February 1836 he went to Italy.

In Naples he met three Poles, Zenon Brzozowski and two brothers, Stefan and Alexander Hońyński who invited him to accompany them on a trip to Greece and Egypt. When he pleaded lack of money they offered to lend him 1,000 roubles, to be returned without interest within four years. Thus began his Oriental journey. Our chief sources of information are not only the poems he wrote on the way, but, more factually, the letters to his mother to whom he felt very close.

In August 1836 he took ship in Otranto, arriving in Patras on 10 September. Slowly, taking almost a month, he crossed the Peloponnesus on horseback. Yet, unlike most tourists in Greece, he showed little interest in classical antiquities with the exception of the tomb of King Agamemnon in Mycenae. What he wanted to see most of all were the battlefields of the recent War of Independence against the Turks: the Greeks had succeeded where the Poles had failed! And besides, he had written his short epic, 'Lambro', about the Greek struggle for independence before he had seen Greece.

On 12 October he took a ship in Athens for Alexandria. His mood was sad, for Alexandria had been the destination of his Orientalist friend Szpitznagel who had committed suicide. On 20 October, shortly before arrival in Alexandria, he wrote the poem 'Hymn', wishing he were sailing to Poland instead of Egypt (or anywhere else for that matter)

> I know that my ship is not sailing to Poland,
> While sailing about the world.

It is interesting to note that this poem is in the form of an Arabic *mukhammas* with the fifth verse of each stanza ending in the same rhyme repeated through the length of the poem. Słowacki could read Arabic poetry only in translation. The excitement of arrival in Alexandria and the sight of a real Oriental city after semi-Oriental Greece quickly dissipated the poet's gloomy mood. Anxious to see more of the country he travels by Nile boat to Cairo. Visiting the slave market he was very impressed by the beauty of the Ethiopian slave girls. As a good revolutionary he should have denounced the institution of slavery, but instead he played with the idea of buying himself a slave girl. He would teach her Polish and she would come to appreciate his poetry, a Pygmalion-like dream.

More seriously and more urgently he wanted to see the pyramids. Three years before, he had written a drama, 'Kordian', in which an old soldier from Napoleon's Polish corps tells the young hero about their amazing height: 'they could be seen from Poland if the Carpathians did not block the view'. On 29 October, the day after his arrival in Cairo, he set out to see the pyramids, a three-hour journey on donkey back. Untired, he climbed to the top of the pyramid of Cheops where, to his tremendous excitement, he found, among numerous other graffiti, an inscription in Polish: 'Pass on to the centuries the memorable day of 29 November 1830' (the date of the outbreak of the Polish uprising).

On 6 November Słowacki and his companion Brzozowski rented a Nile boat with eight sailors and began a trip in Upper Egypt which lasted a month. The French Consul obtained for Słowacki a *firman* from Ibrahim Pasha, the son of Muhammad 'Ali, the viceroy of Egypt, which was read with great respect by all local dignitaries. A Polish physician practising in Cairo, Dr Hermanowicz, had given him some medicines, but he did not need them. The traveller was charmed by the Egyptian landscape:

> A lovely journey! I drew a lot because words were insufficient to express everything which had hit me in the eyes. Lots of cranes flying in the blue sky, lots of other water birds, clouds of pigeons flying over the villages; little villages built of clay, most often standing in palm groves, sometimes huge rocks, and vultures as big as a man sitting at sunset on the hills.[1]

In Asyut he saw his first crocodile. Although he was slightly disappointed that the pyramids were not as high as he had expected he found other Egyptian antiquities much more impressive than anything which he had seen in Italy or Greece: 'Egypt has blocked Greece from my mind—nothing is more marvellous than the ruins which are on the bank of the Nile.'

From Asyut he sailed on to Dendera where he met the Hońyński brothers who had travelled ahead. He describes the temple in Dendera:

> That building, the largest after the pyramids, plunged us into ecstasy. We walked among the pillars as if stunned, we sat on the ground admiring, talking with pity about those voyagers who cannot imagine such marvels. In short, we have fed our eyes, our heart and we have locked in our heart a day of memories—so marvellous that it even augmented our friendship between us.[2]

The trip to Upper Egypt ended with a visit to Thebes and to the temple of Isis on the island of Philae. In Thebes Słowacki was most impressed by the huge statue, supposedly of the Homeric hero Memnon, but really of the Pharaoh Amenhotep III.

After five days in Cairo Słowacki began on 10 December his desert journey by camel towards the Holy Land, the ostensible goal of his pilgrimage. His interpreter-guide, Soliman, had been the guide of Champollion and told Słowacki many anecdotes about the great French scholar. Unfortunately Słowacki does not repeat any of them. In the evenings Soliman used to chant long Arabic poems. Słowacki did not understand the words, but appreciated the beauty of the language.

Having crossed the Sinai the caravan was stopped at the Egyptian–Ottoman border near al-'Arish. The government of Muhammad 'Ali had ordered all travellers between Egypt and Palestine to undergo twelve days quarantine. Słowacki was most indignant. He did not see much sense in the quarantine and felt the ruler of Egypt was a tyrant imposing his will upon free Bedouins. Like most romantics he admired the Bedouins as representatives of a natural free life. Nevertheless he became friendly with the Italian physician in charge of the quarantine station, Dr Steble. Dr Steble told him the story of one Bedouin Arab, originally from Lebanon, who had lost his wife and seven children in the plague. Słowacki was much shaken by the tragic story and wrote one of his most moving poems, 'Ojciec Zadńumionych' ('Father of the Plague-Ridden'). The dignified resignation of the suffering protagonist reminds us of the Book of Job, the action of which had taken place not very far from al-'Arish.

Dr Steble had recently married Miss Malagamba, a half Italian, half Cypriot-Greek girl, sister of the Sardinian Vice-Consul in Haifa, whose beauty and charm had been enthusiastically praised by Lamartine in his *Voyage en Orient*. Słowacki, who had read Lamartine's book published in 1835, was hoping to meet her. His step-sister, Hersylia Bécu, was urging him to marry her. He came too late! On the last day of the quarantine, towards the end of December 1836, Dr Steble invited Słowacki to his home to meet his wife. But Słowacki's caravan was waiting to proceed, the camels already loaded, and he politely declined the invitation.

We have now left Egypt. I shall try to describe the continuation of the poet's journey as briefly as possible. He arrived in Jerusalem on 13 January 1837. He spent the night 14/15 January in the Church of the Holy Sepulchre where he underwent some kind of mystical experience. Słowacki, until now a free-thinker and a strong anti-clerical, became a mystic, although he continued to denounce Church dignitaries, even the Pope, when he felt they were being subservient to unjust political régimes. No doubt Dr Steble's story about the Father of the Plague-Ridden had contributed to his conversion, bringing home to him the fragility of human life. His own health had never been very strong.

After visiting all the Biblical places in Palestine he arrived in Damascus. He was not impressed. Having seen Cairo he apparently felt about the great Middle Eastern cities that, having seen one, he had seen them all. He was more impressed by the ruins of Ba'albek. Perhaps the huge columns reminded him of the temples of Egypt. He spent six weeks in the Armenian monastery of Betcheszban near Ghazir meditating about his experiences and writing. Besides the 'Father of the Plague-Ridden' he wrote here the allegorical tale 'Anhelli', also set in the East, but a very different East, namely Siberia, place of forcible exile of so many Poles, which, luckily for him, he had not seen. He introduces there the prophetic figure of a Mongol shaman, the personification of wisdom. 'Anhelli' is the only work of Słowacki which, as far as I am aware, has been translated into Arabic.

Zenon Brzozowski was proceeding by land to Istanbul, but Słowacki was not interested, which is strange because Istanbul had been one of the centres of Polish émigré political activity, although it did not reach its full importance until the time of the Crimean War. Besides, of all Islamic countries, Turkey had had the greatest cultural influence on Poland, even if the relations consisted most often of warfare. Słowacki remained in Beirut waiting for a ship to take him back to Italy.

In Beirut he was joined by Stefan Hońyński who had just arrived from Egypt. His younger brother Alexander had refused to leave Cairo, having fallen in love with an Arab girl. Słowacki always refers to the modern Egyptians as Arabs. The young lady may have been a Copt, more easily accessible to a Christian visitor from Europe. I do not know whether the romance had a happy outcome.

After forty days in Beirut Słowacki boarded ship for Italy arriving in Livorno early in July 1837. He settled in Florence, moving to Paris in December 1838. For some time he felt a nostalgia for the Orient:

> It is true what the Orientals say that whoever had tasted the air over there, then, if he can, returns there again, in spite of all the discomforts of a continuous journey. Life there is so strange and light that now Europe seems dark to me. Houses have become black, the air has thickened, someone has breathed upon the glass and clouded the mirror of dreams.[3]

He did not learn much Arabic: by his own estimate 200 words without any understanding of grammar. Unlike his late friend Szpitznagel, his Orientalism was not in the least scholarly. He gave up cigars in favour of a *narghile*. I wonder whether this slowed down a little the progress of the consumption which would eventually claim his life. Contrary to what he claimed in the letter quoted above he never returned to the East. It is strange that, having written so many poems about Egypt, he did not write a single poem about Palestine or Lebanon. Palestine had been the scene of his religious conversion, and he had enjoyed his stay in Lebanon and liked the people, judging from his letters.

How far did the Oriental journey influence Słowacki's later writings? He planned a drama about Ramesses II being reincarnated as a modern Egyptian peasant, but apparently never started it. In 1841 he published a long epic, 'Beniowski', set in eighteenth-century Ukraine, partly in the Crimea—then an Islamic country, inhabited by Muslim Tatars. Słowacki had never been to the Crimea, although he had as a teenager made a trip to Odessa. His description of the Crimea and its Islamic local colour is based entirely on his observations of the Middle East, so much so that three Tatar women are by a slip of the pen called *Arabki* instead of *Tatarki*.

But that is all. Why did he not make a greater use of his Oriental experience? Maybe he felt he had exorcised Szpitznagel's ghost. Besides, in an atmosphere overcharged with nationalism, ambitious to wrest the politico-literary leadership of the Polish émigrés from his rival Adam Mickiewicz, Słowacki felt forced to give all his attention and talent to Polish themes. Later in the century another Polish exile, a certain Józef Konrad Korzeniowski, tried to escape his Polish burden on British ships and in an Orient more distant than Słowacki's Middle East. To do so he felt he had to use the English language.

From December 1838 Słowacki lived in Paris which he had compared to Babylon in his 1832 poem. In 1848, the year of revolutions, Słowacki went to Poznań, the chief city of the Prussian-occupied part of Poland, to join the revolution which had broken out there. Hounded by the Prussian police he was forced to return to Paris. He died there on 4 April 1849, aged forty. In 1927 his remains were entombed in the crypt of the Cathedral in Cracow, next to Adam Mickiewicz, among the tombs of the old Kings of Poland.

Notes

1 Letter to his mother dated 17 February 1837.
2 Letter dated 27 November 1837.
3 Letter to his mother dated 24 November 1837.

23 ∾ French Women Travellers in Egypt: A Discourse Marginal to Orientalism?

John David Ragan

This paper describes a group of French women travellers in Egypt whose accounts are relatively unknown and are often absent from traditional Orientalist bibliographies. They have been marginalised over the years, and their accounts either dismissed as unimportant *petite histoire*,[1] or simply not republished or cited. However, their perceptions and their experiences in Egypt make a fascinating historical contribution which sometimes differs fundamentally from the dominant Orientalist discourse. They challenge existing paradigms of Orientalism and they also offer very promising opportunities for further original research. These and other 'marginalised' French travellers' accounts of Egypt were found during a recent exhaustive study of primary source material in relatively large and 'unweeded' collections of French travel literature about Egypt. A number of such collections exist in Cairo, the most remarkable being the Bibliothèque of the Jesuit Collège de la Sainte Famille (BSF), to whose conservator, Father Maurice Martin S.J., I owe my most sincere thanks.

The essential problem in conducting research on marginal travellers in Egypt is that if one works from bibliographies one is inevitably led to reinforce the Orientalist canon of recognised travellers, from Chateaubriand to Flaubert, who have already been cited by other historians and literary critics. This procedure merely reinforces the image the research consensus already presents of the 'typical' European traveller. Working one's way through relatively large and 'unweeded' collections of French travel literature on Egypt like that of the BSF, however, one discovers accounts which have been ignored over the years, like these by French women travellers in Egypt.

Suzanne Voilquin is one of the most interesting of these travellers. Her trip to Egypt in 1834 was her first great adventure overseas, a voyage of self-realisation, a utopian dream mixed with the terrible reality of the black plague. She describes her experiences in a fascinating travel account published in 1866, *Les Souvenirs d'une fille du peuple ou la Saint-Simonienne en Égypte, 1834 à 1836*.[2] Born in a working-class artisan family of the Saint Merry parish in Paris, Suzanne Voilquin grew up working long

222

hours as a seamstress. She learned to read at convent school and from her brother, who for a time had studied to be a priest. Dedicated and liberated, she was a member of the Saint-Simonians, an early utopian socialist group which advocated the emancipation of women and their equality with men, racial equality, the abolition of inheritance and greater freedom in relationships between men and women. The Saint-Simonians created a religion of progress; they prayed to God the Mother as well as to God the Father; they argued for the possibility of divorce and remarriage (illegal in France at that time), and they began to set up communal houses all over Paris. When the government jailed the movement's leaders and broke up the communal houses, the Saint-Simonians took up contributions and sent a group of members to Egypt, where they offered their services for the modernisation of the country to its ruler, Muhammad 'Ali.[3]

The story of the Saint-Simonians in Egypt is fascinating. A number of them were engineers from the École Polytechnique, one of the best schools in France. They undertook one of the early surveys for a canal at Suez and were closely connected to Ferdinand de Lesseps, the French consul in Alexandria who was later instrumental in the construction of the canal. They worked on an early dam on the Nile and some of them stayed in Egypt, like Charles Lambert, who became director of the Egyptian School of Mining Engineering and of the Egyptian École Polytechnique.[4] Although the Saint-Simonian movement is fairly well known, little work has been done on the women who participated in this movement and particularly those who went to Egypt, such as Suzanne Voilquin, Clorinde Tajan-Rojé,[5] Cécile Fournel,[6] Clara Charbonnel, Caroline Carbonnel,[7] Judith Grégoire,[8] Angelique Jarry[9] and Delphine Martin.[10]

In Cairo, Suzanne Voilquin worked in the clinic of a Frenchman, Dr Dussap. She tutored his teenage daughter Hanem in French, and both she and Hanem received medical training in Dussap's clinic. Suzanne Voilquin had always wanted to be a doctor, and had argued that there should be women doctors with whom women could discuss problems which they would be too embarrassed to reveal to a man. Suzanne Voilquin's own mother had died of a cancer whose early symptoms she had been too embarrassed to discuss with her doctor. Dussap intended to train both Hanem and Suzanne Voilquin to be women doctors in Egyptian families. However, in 1835 a terrible epidemic of the black plague hit Cairo. Instead of taking refuge in Upper Egypt with many of the Saint-Simonians, Dussap, Hanem and Suzanne Voilquin remained in Cairo and kept the clinic open, treating plague victims. Suzanne Voilquin caught the plague and survived, but nearly everyone else in the household caught the disease and died— first Hanem, then Dussap who was broken-hearted at his daughter's death, then in a rush, many of the other household members.

In the Saint-Simonian archives at the Bibliothèque de l'Arsenal in Paris there are boxes full of hundreds of letters to and from Saint-Simonians in Egypt, both men and women. Some of them literally breathe panic as the plague stalks Cairo and they report up to 1,200 deaths a day.[11] There is one letter in which a young Saint-Simonian named Ismayl Urbain,[12] who arrived in Egypt at the age of twenty-one, tells a friend that he is love with Hanem and has asked her to marry him. Both Urbain and Hanem were of mixed African and French ancestry, Hanem's mother being Sudanese, and had worked together in Dussap's clinic. Urbain, then working as a French teacher in Damietta, asked Suzanne Voilquin to intercede for him with Hanem's family.[13] In another box is a letter from Suzanne Voilquin to Urbain in Damietta, gently telling him that Hanem has died of the plague.[14]

Suzanne Voilquin describes the deaths of the people she loved in heart-breaking detail but she nevertheless speaks of her youth and her trip to Egypt with a passionate intensity. She continued her medical studies at the Egyptian School of Medicine where she supervised the first class of young women in the School of Maternity. Amira el Azhary Sonbol has praise for the tradition begun at this school of combining European techniques with customary Egyptian medical structures and practices in the training of *hakima*s, or Egyptian women doctors in public health services.[15] Suzanne Voilquin eventually returned to France, where she studied at the University of Paris and obtained a qualification as a midwife. She led a restless life, spending seven years in Russia, and more than ten years in New Orleans. She was one of the early advocates of homeopathic medicine, and she always remained an activist, a feminist and a traveller.

Suzanne Voilquin's book was re-published by Maspero in 1978, but unfortunately in an edited version whose character is fundamentally changed by a number of cuts made in the original text.[16] A collection of her letters from Russia found in the archives of the Marguerite Durand Women's Library in Paris has also been published,[17] and Provost Laura Strumingher of Hunter College has found traces of Suzanne Voilquin in New Orleans, with the help of the University of New Orleans History Department chairman, Dr Joseph Logsdon and archivist D. C. Hardy.[18]

Suzanne Voilquin wrote a series of articles about Egypt for *Le Siècle*[19] to help pay for her studies at the University of Paris, and these can be consulted at the Bibliothèque nationale in Paris, as can *La Tribune des femmes ou la femme nouvelle*,[20] a feminist journal of which she was the editor.

Jehan d'Ivray was the pen-name of another interesting French woman traveller in Egypt, whose real name was Jeanne Puech (d'Alissac), Mme Fahmy-Bey. Jean-Jacques Luthi suggests that she used a pen-name because editors were reluctant to publish works by women.[21] She was born on 17 April 1861, the daughter of the railway stationmaster in Bessèges, in the

Gard department of southern France. In 1879 she married Sélim Fahmy, an Egyptian medical student in France, and the same year, after he had obtained his degree, she returned with him to Egypt. They lived there for about forty years and raised a family of three children.

Jehan d'Ivray became a well-known novelist, publishing about twenty books and a variety of articles. *Au Cœur du harem*,[22] published as a novel, is in fact an autobiographical travel account of her trip to Egypt as a young teenage wife and of the first two years which she spent in Cairo in the house of her husband's extended family. In an historical work on Napoleon Bonaparte[23] and the French occupation of Egypt, she used Arabic sources to give a more balanced account, including Egyptian points of view and accounts of French massacres of Egyptians. She was well known in literary circles in Cairo, Alexandria and Paris, and she collaborated with Mme Hoda Chaarawi Pasha and Mme Céza Nabarawi in their famous Egyptian feminist journal, *L'Egyptienne*.[24]

Jehan d'Ivray was very interested in other French women travellers who had preceded her to Egypt. *L'Aventure Saint-Simonienne et les femmes*[25] focuses primarily on the story of Suzanne Voilquin, and is critical of the Saint-Simonians. She argues that the men who espoused these liberated morals and radical ideas in their youth went on to be reintegrated into influential positions in French society, whereas the women were destroyed by the experience. Among other things, she cites a series of letters in the 'Arsenal' from Suzanne Voilquin to Prosper Enfantin, the leader of the Saint-Simonians in Egypt,[26] which shows Suzanne Voilquin slowly sinking back into working-class poverty as she desperately tries to care for her ageing father and niece, begging for help from Enfantin, who was by then in an influential position on the Board of Directors of the Lyon–Paris Railway.

Jehan d'Ivray also wrote about another French woman traveller and writer who had preceded her to Egypt: 'La Contemporaine', alias Ida Saint-Elme, alias Elzelina Van Aylde Jonge, alias Maria Elzelina Johanna Versfelt.[27] She was a former member of Napoleon's secret police and a courtesan. As a mature woman and a successful freelance writer she published a fascinating and extremely well-written account of her adventurous, low-budget travels through Egypt and the Eastern Mediterranean in 1829 and 1830.[28]

Pseudonyms were not a problem with the more aristocratic French women travellers, such as the Countess Agénor de Gasparin,[29] the Countess Juliette de Robersart,[30] the Countess Mornière de la Rochecantin,[31] Adelaïde Sargenton-Galichon[32] or Mme Lee Childe.[33] The Countess de Gasparin, who was in Egypt in 1847 and 1848, is an interesting traveller who is one of many analysed by Dr Sarga Moussa.[34] Another French woman writer and poet who visited Egypt, and who was well-known in French literary circles, was Louise Colet,[35] a friend of Flaubert. For scandalous muck-raking on the Egyptian court in 1865, we can turn to Olympe Audouard.[36] However, we must look elsewhere than in the accounts of these more moneyed or aristocratic French woman travellers in Egypt if we are seeking opinions which vary from the norms of the Orientalist discourse.

I would like to end with three basic conclusions. First, the possibility exists for a major work of original research on French women in the Middle East. French travel literature on the Middle East includes a number of relatively forgotten accounts of women and an analysis of their perceptions and experiences would be a valuable historical study. An equivalent work has already been published by Billie Melman on English women and the Middle East,[37] and it could serve as an excellent point of comparison on gender and methodology. A number of bibliographies of French travel literature about Egypt and the Middle East which already exist including works by Carré,[38] Lichtenberger,[39] Kalfatovic,[40] Luthi,[41] Monicat,[42] Régnier[43] and Clément[44] would provide an excellent starting-point.

Secondly, these women's accounts are in some ways fundamentally different from those written by French men during the same period. The experience of a French woman could be different if only because she could be admitted to the women and children's part of the house in an Egyptian family. This was the part of the house which European men never saw and which became for them the exotic and forbidden harem. A woman's experience could be like that of Jehan d'Ivray, who spent two years in the house of her Egyptian husband's extended family before she and her husband set up their own house as a couple. Her time was devoted to family matters and to visits and relations with the women and children of a multitude of other Egyptian families in Cairo.[45] A significant part of Suzanne Voilquin's account of Cairo is centred upon her friendships and experiences with Hanem and other Egyptian women in Cairo.

If, on the other hand, we take Flaubert's account of his trip to Egypt[46] as an example in counterpoint, we see that practically the only Egyptian women whom he meets are prostitutes, and we also see that his journal is almost empty of any concept of what life might be like in an Egyptian family. Some of the French women's accounts of Egypt make the blunt sexual vulgarity of Flaubert seem almost superficial. Nor do the women's accounts seem to have the erotic imagery of the Orient as a sexually appealing woman. However, some of the women's accounts do contain romantically inclined references to Egyptian men and in a few cases, veiled references to the beauty of their bodies.[47] In any case, the experiences of family life in some of the French women's accounts seem to represent a much more profound and human look at Egyptian society than that provided by many of the more well-known accounts of the Orientalist canon.

Nevertheless, it is very important to realise that although gender is a significant factor in these accounts, it is by no means the only one. For many of the countesses and other rich and aristocratic French women travellers the Egyptians remain for the most part the servants who bring them their meals or who retrieve lost croquet balls for them in the garden of the British consulate.[48] On the other hand, travellers such as Suzanne Voilquin or Ida Saint-Elme are travelling on such limited budgets that they come into direct and sometimes disastrous contact with a much more 'concrete' reality of life in Egypt than the more famous travellers do. Their financial status and their class force them into a much greater integration into Egyptian life and in the end give them a very different view of Egypt. Other factors in addition to gender, class and financial situation which may influence a traveller's view of Egypt include race, philosophical, religious or political background, personal character, sensibility and experience.

This leads to my third and final conclusion, which is that the Orientalism described by Edward Said[49] does not exist as a 'discourse' in the Foucauldian sense, that is, as an internalised *language* or system of thought which *prevented* people from thinking otherwise. My research on women travellers and marginal travellers shows that there were plenty of people around who were 'thinking otherwise', who were speaking 'ungrammatically'. Instead, I would argue that Orientalism was a *consensus of acceptable opinion*, very much like a modern research consensus. It did not prevent people from thinking or speaking otherwise, but it ensured that people who did so were less likely to be published, republished and cited, and less likely to have funding for their travels.

I would further emphasise the importance of *selection* in the construction of the Orientalist 'discourse'. It is very possible today to look at the Orientalist canon from Chateaubriand to Flaubert, to see the uniformity of this 'discourse' and to conclude that there must have been a language, a system of thought, which kept these people from thinking otherwise. Instead, my research indicates that the uniformity which we see today was produced by a long process of peer review which weeded out over the years all other points of view which were simply not cited, not republished, and not collected by libraries and which as a result did not become part of the Orientalist canon.

I would argue that this peer review, this research consensus, was closely connected to the structures of power in European society and that the ideas which it favoured were those which the European colonial enterprise needed to maintain its power structure. Nevertheless, the surprising variety of material which has come down to us in spite of this process indicates that the Orientalist discourse was not hermetically closed but rather permeable and porous, and under constant challenge and discussion. I believe that it is precisely this dynamic process which we should study if we are ever to understand or to change the Orientalist discourse.

One of the most stimulating arguments which I have found with respect to discourse and Orientalism is in the book *Critical Terrains* by Lisa Lowe.[50] In this brilliant work of theoretical analysis Lowe points out that there are other discourses based, for example, on gender, which intersect with the Orientalist discourse, creating 'moments of instability'[51] at which this dominant discourse is subject to challenge. I would argue that there are a multiplicity of such discourses and such moments.

It is important to realise that we are dealing with a complex cultural interface in Egypt and not just a simple binary opposition. This is not intended as an apology for colonialism. What I am arguing for is an appreciation of the thickly textured nature, the variety and the diversity of forms, motives and nuances in the historical record which the texts I am studying represent. We need to beware of the over-simplification, the abstract conceptualisation represented by what Billie Melman calls 'binary models'.[52] I would favour a more empirical approach based upon the primary sources which argues from an extensive knowledge of the material rather than from a textual analysis of a few examples. I would also argue that we need to be more specific in our definition of exactly what is exploitative and what is not, a specificity which the vague notion of discourse simply does not allow.

I would like to see a little more appreciation for the liberating aspects of the travelling experience, which offers the opportunity to contrast the abstract structure of the Orientalist discourse with the concrete reality represented by Egypt itself. As a traveller myself, I cannot help but empathise with these French women travellers in Egypt. I am not so interested in rich or aristocratic travellers like Chateaubriand and Flaubert, who make up the bulk of the Orientalist canon. Instead I am interested in the ones with small budgets and lots of dreams, in the ones who tried very hard to reach out, to experience and to understand another culture, in the marginal travellers like these women. The nineteenth century was full of them. They are less likely to leave an historical record, but I think that if you go back to the primary sources and dig, you can still find them.

Notes

1   Jean-Marie Carré, *Voyageurs et écrivains français en Égypte*, 2e edition (Cairo: Institut français d'archéologie orientale du Caire, 1988, first published 1932), pp. 251–64.

2   Suzanne V [Voilquin], *Souvenirs d'une fille du peuple ou la Saint-Simonienne en Égypte, 1834 à 1836* (Sauzet, 1866).

3   For further information on the Saint-Simonians, see their archives at the Bibliothèque de l'Arsenal, Paris (hereafter 'Arsenal'). The Fonds Enfantin,

Fonds Eichthal, etc. contain extensive documentation of their efforts to construct a new society and a new relationshiop between men and women.

4 Philippe Régnier, *Les Saint-Simoniens en Égypte, 1833–51* (hereafter *Saint-Simoniens*). Preface by Amin Fakhry Abdelnour (Cairo: Banque de l'Union Européene, 1989) (available at the Arsenal).

5 Régnier, *Saint-Simoniens*, p. 182 cites Rojé and her husband as does Suzanne Voilquin, *Mémoires d'une Saint-Simonienne en Russie* (Éditions des Femmes, 1977), p. 115.

6 Jehan d'Ivray, *L'Aventure Saint-Simonienne et les femmes* (Felix Alcan, 1930), p. 125 and Régnier, *Saint-Simoniens*, p. 180 both mention Cécile Fournel.

7 Régnier, *Saint-Simoniens*, p. 179, cites Clara Charbonnel and Caroline Carbonnel.

8 Régnier, *Saint-Simoniens*, pp. 112–14, 180 and Ivray, *L'Aventure*, p. 150 both cite Judith Grégoire.

9 Régnier, *Saint-Simoniens*, p. 181.

10 Ivray, *L'Aventure*, p. 160 cites Delphine Martin.

11 Arsenal, Fonds Eichthal, Ms. 13 739 No. 15, 'Letter from Cognat to Urbain, at Damiette, April 12, 1835'.

12 Ismayl Urbain, *Voyages d'Orient suivi de poèmes de Ménilmontant et d'Égypte* (ed.) Philippe Régnier (L'Harmattan, 1993). He later converted to Islam and took the name Ismayl, spending much of his life in North Africa.

13 Arsenal, Fons Enfantin 7789/37, 'Letter from Urbain to Ollivier April 21, 1835'.

14 Arsenal, Fonds Eichthal, Ms. 13 739 No. 233, 'Letter from Suzanne Voilquin to Ismayl Urbain, April 18, 1835'.

15 Amira el Azhary Sonbol, *The Creation of a Medical Profession in Egypt, 1800–1922* (Syracuse, N.Y.: Syracuse University Press, 1991), pp. 45–7.

16 Suzanne Voilquin, *Souvenirs d'une fille du peuple ou la Saint-Simonienne en Égypte* (Maspero, 1978). A comparison of page 167 of the modern edition with pages 152–5 of the original 1866 Sauzet edition demonstrates the extent of the cuts, which diminish Voilquin's strongly individual and independent character, eliminate her passionate links with 19th-century Romanticism, and make for a dryer and more academic work.

17 Voilquin, *Russie*.

18 The New Orleans city directories for the 1850s list a Mrs S. Monnier as a midwife in 1850 at Gravier and St John Streets; in 1851 at 157 St Peter Street and from 1852 to 1854 at 159 Dauphine Street. Suzanne Voilquin frequently used her maiden name, Monnier, and practised as a midwife for most of her adult life.

19 Suzanne V. [Voilquin], 'Lettres sur l'Égypte', *Le Siècle* (Paris, 1937), 16 and 24 February, 23 and 25 March, 11 and 21 April, 3 May, 2, 29 and 30 August, 20 September and 30 November. Bibliothèque nationale, Paris (Per Micr. D 108).

20 'La Tribune des femmes ou la femme nouvelle', incomplete collection at the Arsenal, complete collection at the Bibliothèque nationale, Paris.

21 Jean-Jacques Luthi, *Introduction à la littérature d'expression française en Égypte* (1798–1945) (Éditions de l'École, 1974), pp. 278–9.

22 Jehan d'Ivray, *Au Cœur du harem* (Juven, 1914), consulted in BSF (205/3).

23 Jehan d'Ivray, *Bonaparte et l'Égypte* (A. Lemerre, 1914).
24 *L'Égyptienne* (Cairo), 1/1, Feb 1925, to 16/164, April 1940, consulted at the Marguerite Durand Library, Paris.
25 Ivray, *L'Aventure*.
26 Arsenal, FE 7791 Nos. 133–45, 'Letters from Suzanne Voilquin to Prosper Enfantin'.
27 Jehan d'Ivray, 'Une aventurière sous l'Empire; variété inédite', *Les Œuvres libres* (1936), 18e v. pp. 184, 175–206.
28 La Contemporaine (Ida Saint-Elme), *La Contemporaine en Égypte* (Ladvocat, 1831).
29 La comtesse (*née* Valérie Boissier) Agénor de Gasparin, *Journal d'un voyage au Levant: Grèce, Égypte, Syrie* (Ducloux, 1848).
30 Juliette de Robersart, *Égypte: Journal de voyage* (Victor Palmé, 1867).
31 La comtesse Mornière de la Rochecantin, *Du Caire à Assouân* (Jouve, 1913).
32 Adelaïde Sargenton-Galichon, *Sinai, Ma'ân, Petra: Sur les traces d'Israel et chez les Nabatéens* (Le Coffre, 1904), with an introduction by the marquis de Vogüe.
33 Mme Lee Childe, *Un hiver au Caire* (Calmann Levy, 1890) (hereafter *Hiver*).
34 Sarga Moussa, *La Relation orientale. Enquête sur la communication dans les récits de voyage en Orient (1811–1861)* (Klincksieck, 1995).
35 Louise Colet, *Les Pays lumineux, voyage en Orient* (Dentu, 1879).
36 Olympe Audouard, *Les Mystères d'Égypte dévoilés* (Dentu, 1865).
37 Billie Melman, *Women's Orients: English Women and the Middle East, 1718–1918. Sexuality, Religion and Work* (Ann Arbor: University of Michigan Press, 1992).
38 Carré, *Voyageurs*.
39 Marguerite Lichtenberger, *Écrivains français en Égypte contemporaine (de 1870 à nos jours)* (Ernest Leroux, 1934).
40 Martin R. Kalfatovic, *Nile Notes of a Howadji: a bibliography of travelers' tales from Egypt, from the earliest time to 1918* (Metuchen, New Jersey, and London: The Scarecrow Press, 1992).
41 Luthi, *Expression*, and *Le Français en Égypte* (Beirut: Naaman, 1981).
42 Benedicte Monicat, 'Pour une bibliographie des récits de voyages au féminin (XIXe siècle)', *Romantisme* 77: 3 (1992), pp. 95–100.
43 Régnier, *Saint-Simoniens*.
44 R. Clément, *Les Français d'Égypte aux XVIIe et XVIIIe siècles* (Cairo: Institut français d'archéologie orientale du Caire, 1960).
45 Lichtenberger, *Écrivains*, 153–5 and 165.
46 Gustave Flaubert, *Voyage en Égypte*, (ed.) Pierre-Marc de Biasi (Grasset, 1991).
47 Childe, *Hiver*, p. 271.
48 Ibid.
49 Edward W. Said, *Orientalism* (1978) and his *Culture and Imperialism* (New York: Alfred A. Knopf, 1993).
50 Lisa Lowe, *Critical Terrains: French and British Imperialisms* (Ithaca, New York: Cornell University Press, 1992).
51 Ibid., p. X.
52 Melman, *Women*, p. 316.

Part Six

E. W. Lane and Scholarly Perceptions

24 ∾ Edward Said and Edward William Lane

John Rodenbeck

Since its publication in 1978, Edward Said's book *Orientalism* has become one of the most celebrated and influential academic studies in the English-speaking world. It has not been without its critics, however, from the beginning; and its least satisfactory pages have been recognized as the six (159–64)[1] in which Said passes sentence on Edward William Lane (1801–76), the great ethnographer, translator, and lexicographer,[2] best known to non-Arabists as the author of the *Account of the Manners and Customs of the Modern Egyptians* (1836).[3] It is not only Lane's ethnographic work that is discredited by Said, but also his personal character, which Said presents as the real subject of *Manners*.

A grudging compliment to *Manners* in the Introduction to *Orientalism* (p. 15) was certainly composed well after the main text had been completed. Allowing readers who have never read Lane's book to leap to the naïve conclusion that Said admires it, this Introduction appears to be his attempt to reconcile the universal esteem in which *Manners* continues to be held with the denunciation of it he had just written. This denunciation ignores altogether the one issue that is fundamental in judging any ethnographic text: was what Lane wrote really true at the time he wrote it? Evading this problem, Said ascribes the book's status to its 'style'; and commends its author, in effect, as a minor belle-lettrist.

No such faint praise can disguise the intention to discredit Lane and his work that emerges in later pages. Said cites biographical material, but his construction of Lane's character seems to have been formed *a priori*, in response to neo-Marxian political presumptions and to the strategic rhetorical requirements of *Orientalism* as a whole, itself a paradigm of the kind offered by 'discourse theory', according to which everything written is some form of collectively composed *Tendenzliteratur*.[4] Citations of the text of *Manners* refer only to the Author's Preface (1836), its Table of Contents, and two pages of Chapter VI.

Said's introductory paragraph opens the attack with an odd declaration to the effect that the impression Lane wished to give was that his study was a work of immediate and direct, unadorned and neutral description, whereas it was in fact the product of considerable editing (the work he wrote was not the one he finally published) (p. 159).

Only a small portion of what Lane wrote about Egypt has ever been published. *Manners* was conceived, researched and written for its own sake, however, not edited out of any larger work; and the text Lane published as *Manners* certainly consisted of what he had written as *Manners*.[5] Said's rhetoric, however, has an obfuscating effect: by setting up 'editing' as the opposite of positive qualities such as *immediacy, directness, straightforwardness*, and *neutrality*, he equates it with negative qualities such as *alienation, deviousness, slyness*, and *prejudice*; it thus becomes *calculation, duplicity*, even *conspiracy*. What Said seems to imply is that the more careful Lane's writing is, the more it becomes suspect, even perverse.

Said then fires off (pp. 159–60) a salvo of sarcastic comments that are, unhappily, as ignorant as they are ill-intentioned:

> While Lane dallies in his preface with a Dr Russell's 'account of the people of Aleppo' (a forgotten work), it is obvious that the *Description de l'Égypte* is his main antecedent competition.[6] But this work, confined by Lane to a long footnote [*sic*], is mentioned in contemptuous quotation marks as 'the great French work' on Egypt. That work was at once too philosophically general and too careless, Lane says; and Jacob Burckhardt's famous study was merely a collection of proverbial wisdom, 'bad tests of the morality of a people'. Unlike the French and Burckhardt, Lane was able to submerge himself amongst the natives, to live as they did, to conform to their habits, and 'to escape exciting, in strangers, any suspicion of ... being a person who had no right to intrude among them.' Lest that imply Lane's having lost his objectivity, he goes on to say that he always conformed only to the *words* (his italics) of the Koran, and that he was always aware of his difference from an essentially alien culture. Thus while one portion of Lane's identity floats easily in the unsuspecting Muslim sea, a submergent part retains its secret European power, to comment on, acquire, possess everything around it.

The barrage of dishonest quotations, mixed metaphors, anachronisms, errors of fact, innuendo, and *ad-hominem* slurs that gives this paragraph such a hostile character opens with the third word of the first sentence: the 'forgotten work' by 'a Dr Russell' that Lane 'dallies' with is the two-volume second edition of Alexander Russell's *The Natural History of Aleppo*. It has not been 'forgotten' in our own time—no less a figure than the late Albert Hourani cited this standard account in his *History of the Arab Peoples* as recently as 1991—and it was certainly well known in Lane's.[7]

To declare, next, that the 'main antecedent competition' for Lane's little book, written for cheap distribution by the Society for the Dissemination of Useful Knowledge, could be either the two or three dozen massive volumes of the *DE* or Chabrol de Volvic's long-outdated 'Essai sur les mœurs des habitants modernes de l'Égypte' contained within it is to be guilty either of misunderstanding Lane's aims and audience or of a malicious intention to misrepresent them.[8] Chabrol de Volvic's essay accounts for less than five per cent of the *DE*'s text, and fewer than five per cent of its 907 engravings had any bearing on the early nineteenth-century Egyptians' daily lives. Contrary to what Said suggests, moreover, Lane's Preface expresses 'high admiration' for portions of the 'great French work'. The 'contempt' ascribed to Lane's quotation marks is the invention of Said himself.

Said's own attitude toward the *DE* is far more questionable. Like some of the 'Orientalists' he describes, he seems to suppose that nineteenth-century Egypt was 'eternal' and 'unchanging' and that therefore the survey begun by the French in 1798 would still be valid in all respects nearly forty years later. That idea is particularly inaccurate if applied to the period of Egyptian history in question. Lane's audience were well aware of the radical transformations already effected under Muhammad 'Ali. Lane's major motive for writing *Manners*, indeed, apart from love of Egypt, was his desire to record traditional ways of living that he and his audience knew were likely to disappear.

That the scholarship deployed in these pages is as dubious as the attitudes it is meant to justify is betrayed by such items as 'Jacob Burckhardt's famous study', to which Said insinuates in his third sentence that Lane does less than justice by regarding it as 'merely a collection of proverbial wisdom'. This 'famous study' does not exist except as a phantasm of Said's own; in fact, when Lane was writing his Preface, Jacob Burckhardt (1818–97) was still no more than a schoolboy.

To suppose this mistake of identity arose from ignorance is to adopt the most charitable explanation. The Swiss historian's monumental renown would have made him a potent cultural icon, if indeed he had ever written any book, 'philosophical' or otherwise, remotely like the one invented by Said. The Burckhardt in question, however, as the readers to whom Lane addressed his Preface were well aware, is John Lewis Burckhardt (1784–1817), the Anglo–Swiss explorer, and the book Lane comments on is Burckhardt's *Arab Proverbs; or the Manners and Customs of the Modern Egyptians Illustrated from their Proverbial Sayings current at Cairo*, completed seven months before Burckhardt's death in 1817, but not published until 1830.[9]

'These sayings are useful,' Burckhardt remarks in his Preface, 'as they serve to show us how Arabs judge of men and things, and in this respect it must be acknowledged that many are dictated by wisdom and sagacity.' They demonstrate, he adds, that 'the principles of virtue and honour, of friendship and true charity, of independence and generosity, are perfectly well known to the modern inhabitants of Egypt, although very few among them take the trouble of regulating their conduct accordingly.'[10] The fullest of Burckhardt's annotations offer information about Cairene ways as they had been before 1817. They do not constitute a 'study' and they are in no sense 'philosophical', though they do indeed display Burckhardt's personal revulsion at Arab ways; and Lane's remark should certainly be understood in part as a defence of Egyptian manners and morals against Burckhardt's censorious animosity.[11]

Said suggests that Lane felt himself superior to Jacob Burckhardt because he could 'submerge himself amongst the natives' and Jacob Burckhardt could not. Pointless except as an attempt at disparagement, this insinuation underlines the fact that Said has seized upon the wrong Burckhardt.

Known in Cairo as Shaykh Ibrahim ibn 'Abd Allah, John Lewis Burckhardt was sent by his employers in London, the African Association, to learn the Arabs' language, manners and customs from the Arabs themselves. Arriving in the Middle East in 1809 already disguised as an Indian Muslim, he spent the next three years in Aleppo, where he had perfected his Arabic and converted to Islam, an act by no means incompatible either with Enlightenment Deism or with anti-Arab sentiments. After rediscovering Petra and carving his name on the cheek of Ramesses II at Abu Simbel, he made the pilgrimage to Mecca and Madina, then returned to Cairo. There he died in 1817 at the age of 33, leaving 2,000 piastres, his slaves, the contents of his house, and his wife to his friend, the Scottish-born convert 'Uthman Effendi.[12] Living and dying as an Arab, the man buried in Cairo as 'Shaykh Hajj Ibrahim ibn 'Abd Allah of Lausanne' had taken far more trouble than Lane ever would to 'submerge himself amongst the natives, to live as they did, to conform to their habits, and "to escape exciting, in strangers, any suspicion of ... being a person who had no right to intrude among them".'

In a less than scrupulous effort to suggest that Lane slunk through the alley-ways of Cairo like a spy in disguise, Said quotes from Lane's Preface, but excises the final clause of Lane's sentence: '*whenever it was necessary for me to witness any Muslim rite or festival*' [Author's italics].[13] There is, of course, nothing in the least extraordinary about how Lane clothed himself. Virtually all European travellers and sojourners in Egypt between 1810 and 1850 routinely dressed in Eastern clothes for their own comfort and safety.[14] What Lane wore was the costume worn by millions of Christian or Muslim townsmen throughout the European portions of the Ottoman empire—not only in Constantinople, Smyrna or Trebizond, for example, but also in Saloniki, Sofia, Belgrade, Bucharest and Jassy—as well as by most European males, Turkish or otherwise, in Cairo. It was unobtrusive. Unobtrusiveness was its whole point.

Unlike Burckhardt, Lane never pretended to be an Arab or an Egyptian. And he differed in other ways from Burckhardt, who 'always associated reluctantly with the Arabs' and wrote of 'the utter depravity of manners and morals and of the decline of laws and civil institutions throughout the Mohammedan world.'[15] He differed from Burckhardt in his intimacy with Egyptians, his gusto for Egyptian life, his sympathy with it, and the pleasure he derived from it. While Burckhardt hated Egypt and lived there reluctantly, Lane declared it a 'paradise' and remarked that 'it will always be the country for me'.[16]

Said's next sentence claims (p. 160) that Lane 'goes on to say that he always conformed only to the *words* (his [i.e., Lane's] italics) of the Koran, and that he was always aware of his difference from an essentially alien culture.' What Lane actually wrote is as follows:

> While from the dress which I have found most convenient to wear, I am generally mistaken, in public, for a Turk, my acquaintances of course, know me as an Englishman: but I constrain them to treat me as a Muslim, by my freely acknowledging the hand of Providence in the introduction and diffusion of the religion of El-Islám, and when interrogated, avowing my belief in the Messiah, in accordance with the *words* of the Kor-án, as the Word of God infused into the womb of the Virgin Mary, and a Spirit proceeding from Him.[17]

The word *words* is italicised here by Lane because he is in fact referring *literatim* to specific words, in such Qur'anic passages as Suras III: 45, IV: 171, and XIX: 17, by which God Himself, as Muslims believe, has defined forever the nature of Jesus. As the utterance of God Himself, these words— of which Lane's English is a perfectly accurate paraphrase—also indicate what should be the formal attitudes of any orthodox Muslim. The Qur'anic definitions of the nature of Christ that Lane specifically points to were likewise true for an educated nineteenth-century Evangelical Christian like himself, not of course because he regarded them as the revealed Word of God, but because they coincided with what his own theological traditions also taught as truth. The Qur'an thus provided an area within which religious attitudes, rather than diverging, could meet without hypocrisy.[18] In later life, Arberry tells us, 'Lane never began his day's work without uttering the Arab dedication Bismi-llah—"in the name of God".'[19]

Up to this point (p. 160) only charity could absolve Said of breathtaking impudence. His persistent misconstruction and misquotation of Lane's words are so clearly willful that they suggest precisely the 'bad faith' of which he accuses Lane (p. 161). In the remaining pages of his treatment, however, Said contrives nothing less than the wholesale replacement of both Lane's work and Lane himself with invented figments of his own. Supplanting *Manners* with a fictional substitute—a 'narrative' that 'follows the routine of an eighteenth-century novel, say one by Fielding' (p. 161)—he displaces the real Edward William Lane with a grotesque imposture, 'subduing his animal appetite in the interest of disseminating [*sic*] information' (p. 164).

In terms of mature critical judgment, Said's statements are often amusingly malapropos. He complains (p. 162), for example, that Lane does not provide 'smooth transitions', but gets his reader 'bogged down in descriptions, complete with charts and line drawings, of Cairene architecture, decorations, fountains, and locks. When a narrative strain re-emerges, it is clearly only a formality' (p. 162). Looking at the first two pages of Lane's Chapter VI, he grumbles that 'we have here a typical Lane-esque interruption of the main narrative with untidy detail' (p. 163).

These comments are equivalent to a declaration that Evans-Pritchard and Lévi-Strauss, let us say, ruined good stories by putting in ethnographic observations, or that Malinowski, Benedict, Mead, or Dubois spoiled what would otherwise have been charming narratives of adventure in the South Seas by obtruding facts and paying insufficient attention to 'smoothness' in their transitions, while allowing themselves to get 'bogged down in descriptions.'[20] Said apparently fails to understand that 'descriptions, complete with charts and line drawings, of Cairene architecture, decorations, fountains, and locks' are precisely the point of the book.

It is tempting to presume that although Said had looked into a copy of *Manners*, he had not actually read it at all. How else can one explain such obliviousness to the chief purpose of the whole book? Said's censure of Lane for putting in 'detail' sits badly, moreover, with his own assertion that Lane's 'main antecedent competition' was the *DE*, that enormous compendium of multitudinous detail and is totally incompatible with his own Introduction, where he praises Lane precisely for his 'intelligent and brilliant details' (p. 15).

Unless one concludes that when Said wrote his attack on Lane he had not read *Manners*, such incompatibilities are inexplicable. This conclusion is confirmed a few pages later in the discussion of Flaubert, when Said ascribes to *Manners* a piece of popular misinformation that Lane himself took a great deal of trouble, in one of the most famous passages in the book, to refute explicitly and absolutely.

The version of Lane himself that Said offers us has even less verisimilitude than his version of *Manners*. Using Lane's droll confession that when his neighbours tendered him a Muslim widow, only slightly used, as a wife on liberal terms, he declined the offer, Said invents a Puritan fanatic who refuses in general to have sexual relations with 'Oriental' women (p. 163). The character Said thus concocts to replace the real Lane belongs to a perennial comœdic type. He describes his 'Lane', for example, as a man who not only gave up 'the sensual enjoyments of domestic life' while he was resident in Cairo, but also avoided 'entering the human life-cycle' (p. 163). Making 'a firm [*sic*] and literal [*sic*] disengagement ... from the productive processes [*sic*] of Oriental society,' Said says, shifting dramatically to the historical present tense, this creature 'literally [*sic*] abolishes himself as a human subject by refusing to marry into human society' (p. 163).

The lexical butchery in such statements—particularly the perversion of the word *literal* to mean precisely its opposite[21]—suggests both semantic and epistemological strains. Either as the cause or the effect of such stress, Said's circumlocutions eventuate in the accusation that Lane was guilty of 'disengaging himself from the generation of Egyptian–Oriental life' (p. 164). This wonderfully neo-Victorian euphemism would seem to mean that the 'Lane' of Said's invention not only withheld his sexual favours from his Cairene neighbours' mothers, wives, sisters, and daughters, but did so to their universal chagrin.

The argument that Said is attempting to make is that since his 'Lane' gave no time to what the old calypso calls 'pitching woo with native peach' he must have been a wicked hypocrite racked by sexual repression, unworthy of anyone's trust. Implicitly contrasted with poor 'Lane' in this familiarly pop-Freudian scenario is one of the very few (and most of them French) heroes of Orientalism—Gustave Flaubert, the bookworm-tourist who whored his way through the Middle East with such assiduity that he inevitably repatriated an even more durable souvenir than all his most orchidaceous memories of 'Kuchuk Hanem': venereal disease.[22] Flaubert's status as a late-twentieth-century heavyweight culture-hero—a parallel in literature to Jacob Burckhardt in history—allows him likewise to be used in *Orientalism* as an icon of what is approved. Said's 'Lane', on the other hand, 'antiseptically and asexually lexicographical', disengaged 'from the generation of Egyptian–Oriental life', is dismissed as guilty of 'the subordination of genetic ego to scholarly authority' (p. 164).

In formulating this portion of his attack on Lane, Said seems unaware of the provisions of Islamic law governing marriage, conversion and apostasy. In order to wed any Muslim woman, even for a contractual term— not currently customary in Sunni Islam, though permissible in Shi'i Islam and perhaps not unusual in Sunni Egypt in Lane's day or earlier—Lane would have had to take the formal step of becoming a Muslim. Since Muslim law prescribes death as the penalty for apostasy, this step would have been irrevocable.[23] Nor does Said seem to have known that during the first of his three sojourns in Cairo Lane had been presented by his friend and patron Robert Hay with a young Greek slave girl, Anastavoula Georgiou, otherwise known as 'Nafeeseh'.

The purpose of the gift was not to provide Lane with intellectual companionship.[24] Lane took Nafeeseh home with him to England, then brought her back to live with him in Egypt during his second sojourn, from December 1833 to October 1835, when he actually wrote *Manners*. Five years later he married her. In 1844, while Lane was working on the *Lexicon*—i.e., during precisely the time that Said must be referring to when he claims that Lane was 'antiseptically and asexually lexicographical'—she suffered a miscarriage in the ninth month of a pregnancy. 'She has a disorder', Lane wrote to Hay.

> You need not now wonder why she has never borne me a living child, nor hope that I may ever have such a blessing. … All I can hope for … is that she may continue many years without more pain than she now suffers. Should she do so, I shall be sufficiently blessed in her; for never … has there existed a more affectionate wife.[25]

That Lane's marital life should have to be adduced in his defence is testimony to the unhappy style of the argument contained in these few pages of *Orientalism*. The fact that Said does not resort to such calumny elsewhere in the book is very odd. Why should Lane—of all people—have been so singled out for an attack? He created no 'Orientalist Structures and Restructures' (to use Said's own term) and founded no identifiable orthodoxy. Said's insinuations about him and his work thus not only lack a perceptible basis in anything resembling fact, but are also irrelevant to the logic of *Orientalism* as a whole.[26] If they serve its merely polemical ends, they simultaneously raise serious questions about its scholarship, rationality, taste, and bona fides.

The 1995 reprint of *Orientalism* presented an opportunity for emendation, but it contains no changes from the original text. Jacob Burckhardt continues his hitherto unknown career as an Orientalist, writing famous studies of Egypt that have mysteriously disappeared. The Nile still rises a thousand miles or so northward of its real source and 'awalim are still identified as dancing prostitutes. Lane still labours on as an egomaniacal drudge, pursuing Arabic lexicography by sexual sublimation, while *Manners* remains the fictional history of a hero like Joseph Andrews or Tom Jones, but with too many details disrupting the narrative flow. Said's claim in the Afterword appended to this reprint, that he himself 'genuinely admires' Lane (p. 336), therefore strikes one not only as irrelevant, but as hypocritical—even if all he means is that he thinks Lane was a good second-rate 'stylist'.[27]

Notes

1   Page numbers in parentheses refer to Edward W. Said, *Orientalism* (New York: Vintage Books, 1979). Identical in pagination and every other respect is the body of the text in the 1995 Penguin reprint of *Orientalism* (Harmondsworth: Penguin, 1995), hereinafter 'the 1995 reprint'. New numbers have had to be given to the pages of notes, however, because a new 26-page Afterword was inserted immediately before them. But the old index was simply reprinted: there are no references to this Afterword in it and all references to pages after 328 are 26 pages short.

2 Said refers to Lane's monumental *Arabic–English Lexicon* merely as 'unfinished', leaving it to be inferred that Lane's greatest work was never even published. It is in fact a standard reference; and critics with a better command of Arabic than Said have naturally had more to say about it. For a fuller discussion, see pp. 244 ff. below.

3 *An Account of the Manners and Customs of the Modern Egyptians, written during the years 1833, 34, and 35,* hereinafter *Manners.* Page references are to the text of the fifth revised edition, edited by Edward Stanley Poole (London: John Murray, 1860), as published in the Everyman Library (London: J. M. Dent & Sons, 1908, reprinted 1914, 1917, 1963), cited as 'Lane'.

4 Among materials Said could not have seen is the standard biography, Leila Ahmed, *Edward W. Lane: A Study of his Life and Work and of British Ideas of the Middle East in the Nineteenth Century* (London and New York: Longman and Librairie du Liban, 1978). For an analysis of Said's critical method, see Dennis Porter, *Haunted Journeys: Desire and Transgression in European Travel Writing* (Princeton: Princeton University Press, 1991), pp. 3–4.

5 See Jason Thompson, 'Edward William Lane's "Description of Egypt", *IJMES* 28 (November 1996), pp. 565–83; and "OF THE OSMA'NLEES, OR TURKS" An Unpublished Chapter from Edward William Lane's *Manners and Customs of the Modern Egyptians'*, *Turkish Studies Association Bulletin* 19 (Autumn 1995), pp. 19–39. Said's oddly phrased parenthetical observation appears to accuse Lane of not having written *Manners* at all.

6 Commission des sciences et des arts, *Description de l'Égypte, ou recueil des observations et des recherches qui ont été faites en Égypte pendant l'expédition de l'armée française.* First edition (Imprimerie Impériale/ Imprimerie Royale, 1809–22), twenty volumes. Second edition (C. F. L. Panckoucke, 1821–29), thirty-seven volumes, hereinafter *DE.*

7 For a full citation of Russell, see bibliography. Albert Hourani, *A History of the Arab Peoples* (London: Faber and Faber, 1991), p. 516. See Ralph Davis, *Aleppo and Devonshire Square* (London: Macmillan, 1967) and Anita Damiani, *Enlightened Observers: British travellers to the Near East 1715–1855* (Beirut: American University of Beirut, 1979), pp. 133–70.

8 Chabrol de Volvic's article is *DE*, no. 109, *État moderne*, Sixième partie, II [first edition], 2 (suite), pp. 361–526. An engineer, he was only 25 when Bonaparte appointed him to the Commission, nearly 50 by the time this piece was first published. When Lane returned from Egypt in 1828 he found that the *DE* was finally about to be completed, but he could not afford to buy a set. In *Colonising Egypt* (Cambridge, 1988), Timothy Mitchell follows Said's lead to assert (p. 29) that 'both [David] Roberts [the artist] and Lane were also inspired to visit Egypt by the famous *DE*, ... And both of them set off declaring that their purpose was to correct the "inaccuracies" of the *DE*, which somehow they knew to exist even before seeing the "original" it claimed to represent.' The published reference Mitchell cites for this remark (Ahmed, *Edward W. Lane*, p. 9) fails to mention the *DE* at all. For a definitive discussion, see Thompson, 'Lane's "Description of Egypt"'.

9 John Lewis Burckhardt, *Arab Proverbs; or the Manners and Customs of the Modern Egyptians Illustrated from their Proverbial Sayings current at Cairo, Translated and Explained,* (ed.) Sir William Ousely (London: H. Colburn,

1830), reprinted with an introduction by C. E. Bosworth (London: Curzon Press, 1984) (see Ahmed, *Edward W. Lane*, pp. 89–96). The standard biography—not cited in *Orientalism*—is Katherine Sims, *Desert Traveller: The Life of John Lewis Burckhardt* (London: Gollancz, 1969).

10 Burckhardt, 'Translator's Preface', *Arab Proverbs*, pp. v–vi.

11 Lane, p. xx: 'Burckhardt's "Arabic Proverbs" and their illustrations, convey many notions of remarkable customs and traits of character of the modern Egyptians; but are very far from composing a complete exposition or, in every case, a true one; for national proverbs are bad tests of the morality of a people.'

12 See Jason Thompson, 'Osman Effendi: A Scottish Convert to Islam in Early Nineteenth-Century Egypt', *Journal of World History* 5:1 (1994), pp. 99–123.

13 Said's suggestion that Lane wore a 'disguise' is elaborated by Mitchell in *Colonising Egypt* (p. 27) and is equated with espionage, schizophrenia, or megalomania by Rana Kabbani in *Imperial Fictions: Europe's Myths of Orient* (London: Pandora, 1994), pp. 47, 50, 89–92, 110, 117. Notwithstanding her own earlier remark that donning local costume was 'almost a routine practice', Leila Ahmed declares that virtually all Europeans who ever wore local clothing in the Middle East thus expressed 'enmity, aggression and rivalry'—and must have been spies: see Ahmed, *Edward W. Lane*, pp. 95–6. Such charges ignore well-documented realities. Emanating from Arabs who habitually wear Western clothes, they suggest either double-think or accidental confession. Logically, the accusers themselves might be held to be spies, planted in the West by some malign Arab power.

14 See Ahmed, *Edward W. Lane*, pp. 88–9, Sarah Searight, *The British in the Middle East* (New York: Atheneum, 1970), plates and captions pp. 128–9, 168–9; and Jason Thompson, *Sir Gardner Wilkinson and His Circle* (Austin: University of Texas Press, 1992), pp. 38–9, 44–7, with plates showing Lane's friends Gardner Wilkinson and Robert Hay and two of Hay's artists in Turkish dress. Well-known travellers in Egypt during the years immediately before or during Lane's first sojourn (1825–28) who recorded themselves as wearing Turkish dress include Irby and Mangles, William Rae Wilson, Dr Robert Richardson, James Webster and the Marquis de Laborde. Notable long-term sojourners in Egypt who habitually wore Turkish dress included Dr Madden of Alexandria, Prisse d'Avennes, Linant de Bellefonds, and J. F. Lewis.

15 Quoted in Ahmed, *Edward W. Lane*, p. 94.

16 See ibid., pp. 33, 89–95. Lane wrote, as he says, with Burckhardt's 'book before me' and was fully aware that his own attitudes were far less censorious than Burckhardt's. The contrast is clearest in their parallel descriptions of Cairene weddings. Compare, for example, Burckhardt, p. 139 with Lane, p. 177. The latter passage is also the only valid gloss on Lane's famous declaration in his unpublished 'Draft of the Description of Egypt' that as he landed in Alexandria in 1825 he felt 'like an Eastern bridegroom, about to lift the veil of his bride'. Quoted in Ahmed, *Edward W. Lane*, p. 1; Arberry, *Oriental Essays*, p. 89; Thompson, 'Lane's "Description of Egypt"', p. 566. The subject of this passage is not eroticism, but the drama of decisions made for life.

17 Lane, p. xxi. Every Muslim scholar to whom I have shown Said's phrase 'conformed only to the *words* of the Koran' has found it completely meaningless.

18 Sura IV.171 goes on, of course, to enunciate a unitarianism with which Lane might not have agreed.

19 Arberry, *Oriental Essays*, p. 120.

20 *Manners*, however, has a far more unassailable epistemological validity than the classic ethnographic works on the South Seas. Mead's account of 'coming of age' in Samoa, for example, the fruit of a sojourn only twelve weeks long, has been shown to be based upon a playful hoax perpetrated by her adolescent informants.

21 Cf. 'Quite literally, the [French] occupation [of Egypt] gave birth to the entire modern experience of the Orient' (87). The word *structural* is likewise used (e.g., 164, 187) to hypostatise what is in fact merely metaphorical.

22 See Francis Steegmuller, *Flaubert in Egypt: A Sensibility on Tour: A Narrative drawn from Gustave Flaubert's Travel Notes and Letters, translated from the French and edited by Francis Steegmuller* (Chicago: Academy, 1979), p. 215, quoting a letter of 14 November 1850, more than a year after Flaubert had left France.

23 Lane describes the infliction of such a penalty for apostasy: the condemned woman was paraded through the streets before being strangled and thrown into the Nile. In an earlier case Muhammad 'Ali had intervened to pardon the prisoner (see Lane, pp. 111–12).

24 See Ahmed, *Edward W. Lane*, pp. 38–40, 48. Hardly more than an infant, 'Nafeeseh' had been among the non-Muslim captives acquired during Ibrahim's Morea campaign (1824–28). In the circle around Lane in Cairo in the 1820s several Englishmen assured themselves of 'the sensual enjoyment of domestic life' by keeping slave-concubines. Salt and Bonomi both participated in the 'generation of Oriental–Egyptian life' by fathering children on theirs. Robert Hay married Kalitza Psaraki, the Greek girl he had purchased in Alexandria, four years after he bought her (1824). See Thompson, *Gardner Wilkinson and His Circle*, pp. 95–8.

25 Letter of 17 December 1844, quoted in Ahmed, *Edward W. Lane*,

26 Said does not show Lane's influence in any of the subsequent scholarship he stigmatizes as 'Orientalist', suggesting only that *Manners* was read by Nerval and Flaubert. The pages on Flaubert (pp. 185–90) contain curious errors. It was not in Wadi Halfa but in Esna that Flaubert and Maxime Du Camp hired the famous Syrian prostitute–dancer they called 'Kuchuk Hanem' (p. 186). Nor is either Esna or Wadi Halfa within a thousand miles of 'the upper reaches of the Nile'. Thus neither place can symbolically occupy 'a position structurally similar to the place where the veil of Tanit—the Goddess described as *Omniféconde*—is concealed in *Salammbô*' (p. 187). Nor are '*awalim* to be identified with Egypt's dancing prostitutes, an error that E. W. Lane demolishes on pp. 361–2, 384. The fact that Said actually cites Lane as its source (p. 186) suggests once again that when he wrote *Orientalism* he had not read *Manners*.

27 1995 reprint, p. 336.

25 ∾ Texts from Nineteenth-Century Egypt: The Role of E. W. Lane

Geoffrey Roper

Edward William Lane was born in Hereford in 1801.[1] His father died when he was young, and he was educated at local schools, where he mastered classics and mathematics. He had it in mind to read for a degree in mathematics at Cambridge, but after a brief visit there he abandoned the idea, apparently because he took a dislike to the place and its life-style. Instead he went to London in 1819, and learnt the craft of engraving with his elder brother Richard, later a noted artist and lithographer. There he developed an interest in Egypt, possibly stimulated by Belzoni's spectacular exhibition of Egyptian antiquities at the Egyptian Hall in Piccadilly in 1821. But he was also already becoming interested in linguistic matters, and he seems to have shared in the excitement aroused about that time by the decipherment of the hieroglyphs by Champollion and Young. Lane's name is in the list of subscribers to Young's *Hieroglyphics*, the first part of which was published by the Egyptian Society in 1823.

So fascinated was he by things Egyptian that he determined to go to Egypt himself. One of Lane's predominant characteristics throughout his life was a meticulous, even obsessive, thoroughness in everything he undertook. He was not content, as most other travellers and Egyptologists were, to spend time in Egypt without a good knowledge of the language and culture of its inhabitants. At an early stage, therefore, he started to learn Arabic, and by 1822 he had, it seems, compiled or copied a grammar of the colloquial language. He devoted so much time and energy to his studies, while still working as an engraver, that his health was impaired; and in 1825 he decided that the time had come, for that reason especially, to carry out his intention of visiting Egypt.

This is not the place to examine in detail Lane's travels and residence in Egypt, but rather to discuss his role as a scholar in the field of texts in and from Egypt, and as a purveyor of literary and linguistic knowledge from Egypt to Europe. His first such interest, as we have seen, was in the ancient Egyptian language and its writing system. The fruits of that interest are to be found in his unpublished manuscript entitled 'Notes and Views in Egypt and Nubia', also known as the 'Description of Egypt'. This he wrote during

244

and after his first stay in Egypt, 1825–29; the final version is in the British Library in London, which purchased it from his widow in 1891.[2] The detailed 'Supplement on the Ancient Egyptians' contains much on the language and history of ancient Egypt, and in the main body of the work are also detailed descriptions of sites and monuments, whose value has been attested by Egyptologists.[3] It is tempting to speculate that, had matters taken a different turn, Lane's name might have gone down, like that of his colleague at that time, John Gardner Wilkinson, among the household names of early Egyptology.

Lane's interests, however, developed along different lines. He became more and more interested in the contemporary inhabitants of Egypt and their Arab culture and heritage, and determined to make an original study of them. Already a significant part of the 'Description' was given over to this: the section on the history of Muhammad 'Ali and his period, for instance, is based mainly on the work of the Egyptian historian 'Abd al-Rahman al-Jabarti, who died in 1825, the year of Lane's arrival in Egypt. His celebrated history did not become well-known among Western scholars until it was published more than half a century later, and it is indicative of Lane's rapid immersion in Egyptian Arab intellectual culture that he should have realised its importance at such an early stage. In fact he acquired his own manuscript copy, written in 1829, which is now in the British Library.[4]

The sections of Lane's 'Description' which relate to the earlier history and topography of Cairo are drawn largely from another important Arabic source, the *Khitat* of Maqrizi, together with his own observations, which he carefully compared with Maqrizi. This section was subsequently revised by Lane's nephew Reginald Stuart Poole in 1847, and was eventually published in 1896 under the title *Cairo Fifty Years Ago*.

Lane's second book, and his first to be published, was his best-known work, the *Manners and Customs of the Modern Egyptians*,[5] consisting partly of revisions to sections of his 'Description', and partly of new material gathered during his second residence in Cairo, from 1833 to 1835. A detailed examination of the descriptive and ethnographic material, which occupies the greater part of the book, is beyond the scope of this paper; what needs to be mentioned, briefly, is its significance as a source for the study of Arabic literature. Classical literature is treated quite cursorily; of much greater importance are the sections dealing with the popular legends and romances related by the professional story-tellers and reciters in the cafés of Cairo. Lane gives extensive translated extracts from the romances of Abu Zayd, Al-Zahir Baybars and Dalhama, and these, together with some manuscripts of them which he acquired in Cairo, and which are now in the British Library,[6] have helped scholars to sort out the different recensions.[7] They have also cast light on the background and antecedents of more recent

performance and recitations of such material.[8] However, it has been pointed
out that Lane's attitude to this *sira* literature was influenced by the educated
literati with whom he associated in Cairo, and who tended to disparage
such semi-classical literature.[9]

After Lane had returned to England in 1835, and published *Manners
and Customs* the following year, he turned his attention to translating
another corpus of popular literature, the *Alf Layla wa-Layla*, the Thousand
and One Nights or Arabian Nights. He hoped to produce a version which
would supersede the popular but inadequate renderings of the French
translation by Galland. His translation, replete with scholarly notes, was
first published in parts from 1838 onwards, and achieved great popularity,
which it retained for nearly a century: at least twenty-two editions or
impressions were published between 1838 and 1930, and partial reprints
were still appearing as late as the 1970s.[10]

On the literary merits of Lane's translation, opinions have differed
sharply: while many Victorian middle-class readers clearly found it to their
taste, others have agreed with Burton, who condemned its 'stiff and stilted
style'.[11] Robert Irwin, in his recent *The Arabian Nights: a companion*
(1994),[12] considers it 'grandiose and mock-Biblical'; he concludes that Lane
was 'not a literary man'. This is fair criticism: Lane was primarily a scholar,
not a *littérateur*, and his almost complete withdrawal from English society
probably did impair his capacity to render a text such as the Arabian Nights
into a suitable contemporary English literary style—although Burton
considered it characteristic of a period 'when our prose was, perhaps, the
worst in Europe'. Burton, of course, had a vested interest in attacking Lane,
since he was anxious to maximise sales of his own translation. His
accusations that Lane's knowledge of Arabic was inadequate are, however,
more serious. 'He had,' says Burton, 'small store of Arabic at the time—
Lane of the Arabian Nights is not Lane of the dictionary.' It is difficult to
sustain this accusation in the light of what we know about Lane's career
and achievements up to that time. He had already made extensive use of
Arabic authors such as Maqrizi and al-Jabarti when writing his 'Description
of Egypt'; his *Manners and Customs* also contains extensive translations of
other Arabic texts, as well as many scholarly insights which could only have
come from a deep study of Arabic language and literature. Furthermore
several later Arabists, whose scholarship was of a much higher order than
Burton's, have testified that Lane's renderings are accurate and of scholarly
value.[13]

Another charge levelled by Burton, and others, was that Lane's version
was seriously incomplete. To this Lane himself pleaded guilty: 'I have
thought it right,' he wrote, 'to omit such tales, anecdotes, &c. as are
comparatively uninteresting or on any account objectionable.' He also

confessed that he had left out about a half of the poetry contained in the text. By modern standards these omissions are indefensible, and the reader who wishes to savour the full erotic and poetic flavour of the Arabian Nights must turn to the later versions of Payne, Burton, Mardrus and others. In Lane's time, however, such material was indeed unpublishable, and if he wished to provide the general public with a new version, he had no choice but to adapt it to what was acceptable in early Victorian drawing-rooms.

But Lane's version is also partial and incomplete in another respect. He based his translation primarily on the edition of the text by 'Abd al-Rahman al-Sharqawi, printed and published at the Egyptian state press at Bulaq in 1835.[14] But this text was based on a single Egyptian manuscript of a version which represented a specifically Egyptian, indeed a Cairene, version of the tales, and excluded much of the material from the Syrian and Iraqi recensions.[15]

Lane's reliance on the Egyptian recension both resulted from and reinforced his view that Cairo was the true setting of all the tales, and that the tales themselves shed light on contemporary Egyptian urban life. Indeed he regarded his rendering of the Arabian Nights as an extension of, and companion to, his *Manners and Customs*. Both books became popular among the Victorian middle classes, and their conjunction may have had an effect which the author did not intend. He wanted, probably, to give a solid factual account of Egyptian life, and a scientific rendering of the Arabian Nights, which would de-romanticise both, and help to educate the British public about Egyptian and Arab culture. To some extent he may have succeeded—indeed, Robert Irwin in his *Companion* traces the subsequent decline in the grip of the Arabian Nights on the English literary imagination and points out that Lane's presentation of 'fuller and more accurate knowledge ... led to a closing of the gates of imagination'.[16]

However, as far as contemporary British travellers to Egypt were concerned, its immediate effect seems to have been rather the opposite. The Egyptian scholar Rashad Rushdi, in his perceptive account of English travel literature relating to Egypt in the time of Muhammad 'Ali, pointed out that the period from the late 1830s to *ca.* 1850 was characterised by a growth in the subjective, romantic, Orientalising kind of reaction,[17] which may well have been stimulated by the new association of Cairo with the world of the Arabian Nights. It is worth quoting, for example, the words of Emma Roberts, whose *Notes of an Overland Journey* appeared in 1841. She reacted against the increased ease and speed afforded by the recently opened 'overland route' through Egypt, writing: 'I disliked the idea of hurrying through a scene replete with so many interesting recollections. I had commenced reading the "Arabian Nights Entertainment" at the age of five years: since which period, I had read them over and over again at every opportunity, finishing with the last published number of the translation by Mr Lane. This study has given me a strong taste for everything relating to the East.'[18] Roberts, and other travellers of her time, wanted to find in Egypt the Arabian Orient of their imagination, and Lane's works stimulated that imagination, just as the scholarly efforts of the early Egyptologists had stimulated imaginative interest in the world of the Pharaohs.

After *The Thousand and One Nights*, Lane next turned his attention to translating the Qur'an. His version was first published in 1843. It was not complete, being merely selections interpolated with a commentary based on the famous Jalalayn. As a later translator of the Qur'an A. J. Arberry observed, it 'is not a great book',[19] and was soon eclipsed by the complete versions of Rodwell (1861) and Palmer (1880).

Meanwhile, Lane had made up his mind to embark on a project of a vastly more ambitious nature, which was to occupy him for most of the rest of his life, and which, along with the *Manners and Customs*, constitutes his chief claim to gratitude among scholars. This was his great Arabic lexicon, the *Madd al-Qamus*. To gather materials for this, he made his third, last and longest visit to Egypt, from 1842 to 1849. There he again immersed himself in Egyptian life and society, and worked unceasingly in gathering and transcribing lexicographical materials with the aid of Egyptian helpers, and especially of his friend and principal colleague Shaykh Ibrahim al-Dasuqi. The latter wrote an interesting account of his association with Lane, which appeared in 'Ali Mubarak's celebrated topographical and historical encyclopaedia *al-Khitat al-Tawfiqiyya*.[20] It starts as follows:

> Among those who came to us from the distant country, ... to find some of the books of lexicography and translate them into English, was the sagacious, expert and quick-witted littérateur, a man of gracious character linked with sweet virtue, distinguished among his own kind for his brilliant intellect, the outstanding Mansur Effendi, of the gentle temperament, known in his home town, London, as Mr Lane.'[21]

Dasuqi was amazed at Lane's knowledge of Arabic: 'on his tongue there was no solecism (lukna) nor defect ('ayb) ... [he was] eloquent as though he were an 'Adnani or a Qahtani ... that he had achieved such eloquence, in spite of being a foreigner, aroused the utmost admiration.' He goes on to describe Lane's household and way of life, his generosity, his religious beliefs, and how they worked together on the lexicographical texts. Dasuqi copied out for Lane the whole of al-Zabidi's great *Taj al-'Arus*, in 24 volumes, which Lane took back to England. It is now preserved in the British Library,[22] along with the first draft of Lane's own work, which has only recently been discovered.[23] The relationship between Dasuqi and Lane may also have formed the basis of a later fictional work by 'Ali Mubarak, entitled '*Alam al-Din* (Alexandria, 1299/1882), which has been shown to illuminate the attitude of Egyptian scholars towards Orientalists.[24]

Dasuqi was not the only contemporary Arab scholar to praise Lane. The Lebanese author and journalist Faris (later Ahmad Faris) al-Shidyaq, who lived in Cairo between 1828 and 1835, also mentioned him in one of his books about Europe and European scholars, first published in 1863. He noted approvingly his role as a translator of the 1001 Nights and his association with scholars and writers in Egypt.[25]

According to Lane's own account, during these seven years in Cairo in the 1840s he worked uninterruptedly for six days a week from dawn to midnight, except for a few minutes for meals and half an hour for exercise. He received visitors only on Fridays.[26] However, he found time to correspond with other European scholars, and especially with the Deutsche Morgenländische Gesellschaft, to whose *Zeitschrift* he contributed.[27] In fact the German scholars Lepsius and Bunsen wanted the Lexicon to be published in Berlin, at the expense of the Prussian government. Lane, however, declined this offer, because, he said, 'conditions were proposed to me to which I could not willingly accede'.[28] What these were remains unknown.

In 1849 Lane left Egypt for the last time and returned to England, where he settled permanently in the seaside resort of Worthing. His biographers all state that he then worked on his Lexicon continuously until the end of his life. However, it seems that this is not entirely true. In 1854 there appeared an anonymous work entitled *The Genesis of the Earth and of Man*, printed first as a pamphlet for private distribution, and then expanded into a book which went into two editions, still anonymous.[29] This was not included by Lane-Poole in his list of Lane's works, appended to his biography of him.[30] It appeared under the name of Lane's nephew Reginald Stuart Poole, who, however, was designated on the title-page only as 'Editor', and presents himself merely as such in his preface. It is in fact attributed by two standard bibliographical reference works to Lane himself, albeit without any authority being cited.[31] No other external bibliographical evidence of its authorship seems to be available, but internal evidence does corroborate the attribution. The work is a close philological examination of the Hebrew text of the 'Book of Genesis' in the Bible, combined with an ethnological study of the origins of human races, with especial reference to Egypt. In numerous places there are philological comparisons between Hebrew and Arabic, and the author cites De Sacy and also Arab historians. This was just five years before the first publication of Darwin's *Origin of Species*, and the conflict between science and religion was already in the air. Lane-Poole mentions that this was something which much interested Lane, and also that he made a close study of the Hebrew Bible.[32]

If, as seems likely, this work was by Lane, it partly explains why it took so long to get out the first volume of the Lexicon, which did not appear until 1863. But there was another reason, namely that he was working through the Arabic roots in the order in which they appear in the famous *Qamus* of Firuzabadi, which formed the basis of al-Zabidi's *Taj al-ʿArus*, Lane's principal source. This dictionary arranges the roots in alphabetical order of the final, not the initial radicals. As Lane's Arabic–English dictionary was to be arranged in normal alphabetical root order, this would logically mean that nothing could be published until the whole work was complete. It was, however, eventually decided to bring it out in parts, and Lane got round the problem by completing those roots beginning with the letters required, ahead of the point which he had reached in his original plan. Five parts were published in the 1860s and 1870s, but in 1876, Lane died, having completed the entries only as far as the root *q-d*.

Incomplete as it was, the Lexicon was a remarkable achievement. As mentioned above, Lane based it principally on al-Zabidi's *Taj al-ʿArus*, which, he said, 'would of itself alone suffice to supply the means of composing an Arabic lexicon far more accurate and perspicuous, and incomparably more copious, than any hitherto published in Europe'.[33] But the work is certainly not, as some have said, simply a translation of Zabidi. Lane considered it necessary to collate it and supplement it with as many other sources, lexicographical and otherwise, as he could lay his hands on. No less than 112 such sources are cited in the Lexicon. Not only that, but Lane also brought to the work a large store of knowledge which he had acquired personally, through reading and from his Arab teachers and colleagues in Cairo.[34]

Every serious classical Arabic scholar, for the last hundred years and more, has been indebted to Lane's work, and many tributes have been paid to it. Just three examples must suffice here. Reinhart Dozy, in the Preface to his own later Arabic dictionary, described it as 'ce chef-d'œuvre de patience, d'érudition, d'exactitude, de saine critique'.[35] In 1915 J. G. Hava wrote in the Preface to his Arabic–English dictionary, *al-Faraʾid al-Durriyya* that he had followed 'the standard work of Mr Lane, as it is by far the best work ever published in this line'.[36] Later, in 1947, Henri Fleisch, in his classic survey of Semitic studies, opined that, as far as Arabic was concerned 'notre meilleur dictionnaire européen est celui de E. W. Lane ... l'auteur a compilé, judicieusement critiqué et traduit avec sureté les anciens lexiques arabes'.[37]

A few adverse criticisms have also been made. The German scholar Erich Bräunlich discovered that Lane had been led astray by errors in his manuscript copy of the *Taj al-ʿArus* in one or two places.[38] More seriously, the Lexicon has been seen as too exclusively early classical, because of its reliance on traditional Arabic philological sources. Although this criticism may be exaggerated, it is true that his Lexicon does concentrate on strictly classical vocabulary, and that is why later European lexicographers, such as Dozy (1881; 2nd ed., 1927) and Fagnan (1923), found it necessary to compile further dictionaries of post-classical usage.

The other major drawback of Lane's Lexicon is its incompleteness. He made it clear before his death that he wanted his great-nephew Stanley Lane-Poole to finish the task. Lane-Poole, however, almost completely failed in this assignment, confining himself to publishing in two further volumes the remainder of Lane's incomplete notes, with unsatisfactory results: the entries in these last two parts are sketchy and full of lacunæ. His lame excuse was that by then the Arabic text of the *Taj al-'Arus* had been published in Cairo, and scholars could consult that—as though his great-uncle's life-work had been no more than an abortive attempt at an edition of Zabidi. In fact it is clear that Lane-Poole had lost interest in the project,[39] and preferred to move on to less demanding tasks.

Two later attempts have been made, in this century, to carry on where Lane left off. An English scholar called Carlyle Macartney started at *q-d*, but although he filled some 62 school exercise-books, did not reach the end of the letter *qaf*. His efforts now languish in three boxes in the Library of the School of Oriental and African Studies (SOAS) in London.[40]

Much more important is the massive Arabic–German–English dictionary, the *Wörterbuch der klassischen arabischen Sprache* (Wiesbaden, 1970–), being published under the auspices of the Deutsche Morgenländische Gesellschaft. This represents the fruits of many decades of work by a series of German scholars. It is compiled on different principles from those of Lane, drawing its material directly from Arabic literary texts, rather than relying mainly on lexicographical sources. But it is of great significance that the compilers decided to start publication at the letter *kaf*, so that, for the time being, this major reference work serves as a supplement to Lane, rather than superseding him.

Lane's reputation among contemporary and later scholars was always very high. Although he was never a member of any university or institution, he received academic honours from the Deutsche Morgenländische Gesellschaft, the Academie des Belles-Lettres in France, the Royal Society of Literature and the Royal Asiatic Society in Britain, and from the University of Leiden.

Arab scholars too, have, in general, been favourable towards Lane, and have not regarded him with that mistrust which many other European Orientalists have attracted. Najib al-'Aqiqi called him an Imam among Orientalists.[41] Ahmad Amin drew on his work, and even his illustrations, for his own dictionary of Egyptian customs and traditions;[42] likewise 'Abd al-Hamid Yunus in his study of the Hilaliyya epic.[43] 'Abd al-Rahman Zaki gives him a special entry in his Encyclopaedia of the City of Cairo.[44] Even Tibawi, otherwise a scourge of Orientalists, has a good word for him: through the tangle of missionaries and shallow-minded travel-writers, he writes, 'the figure of the disinterested scholar is discernible ... in the indefatigable E. W. Lane'.[45] More recently, Edward Said, in his highly influential study of Orientalists, has taken a more jaundiced view of Lane,[46] which is discussed elsewhere in this volume.

There is still room, and indeed a need, for a full biography of Lane. Of the two books about him which have been published, neither really satisfies the need. The *Life* written by his great-nephew Lane-Poole soon after his death is both sketchy and hagiographic in tone. It presents Lane not as he was, but as Lane-Poole wished him to be seen by high Victorian society. Many facts which Lane-Poole must have known, such as those relating to Lane's slave-wife, and to his authorship of the work on 'Genesis', are suppressed. The other book, published in 1978 by the Egyptian scholar Leila Ahmed, is more interesting and valuable; but it approaches the subject mainly from the point of view of English literary criticism and the history of English images and conceptions of the Middle East up to Lane's time. It lacks, however, any extensive biographical research. Much still remains to be investigated about Lane's early life, for instance, and the formative influences upon him, which produced such an assiduous scholar and interpreter of the people, culture and language of Arab Egypt.

Notes

1 This and other biographical information which follows is taken mainly from Stanley Lane-Poole, *Life of Edward William Lane* (London, 1877), A. J. Arberry, *Oriental Essays* (London, 1960) and Leila Ahmed, *Edward W. Lane: A Study of His Life and Works and of British Ideas of the Middle East in the Nineteenth Century* (London, 1978).

2 BM Add. Mss 34,080–88. See *Catalogue of Additions to the Manuscripts in the British Museum*, MDCCCLXXXVIII–MDCCCXCIII (London, 1894), pp. 193–5, which summarises the contents.

3 See W. R. Dawson and E. P. Uphill, *Who was Who in Egyptology*. 3rd edition by M. L. Bierbrier (London, 1995), p. 235.

4 BM Mss Or. 4628–4630. See C. Rieu, *Supplement to the Catalogue of the Arabic Manuscripts in the British Museum* (London, 1894), p. 827.

5 E. W. Lane, *An Account of the Manners and Customs of the Modern Egyptians, Written in Egypt during the years 1833, 34 and 35*, 5th edition, (ed.) E. W. S. Poole (London, 1860).

6 BM Mss Or. 4618–4657. See Rieu, *Supplement*, vii–viii; M. Galley, 'Manuscrits et documents relatifs à la Geste hilalienne dans les bibliothèques anglaises', *Littérature orale arabo-berbère* 12 (1981), pp. 183–4, 191–2.

7 For example, C. Huart, *A History of Arabic Literature* (London, 1903), p. 405; 'Abd al-Hamid Yunus, *Al-Hilaliyya fi al-tarikh wa-al-adab al-sha'bi*. 2nd

edition (Cairo, 1968); H. T. Norris, *The Adventures of Antar* (Warminster, 1980), pp. 42–3, 68, 196 n. 61; Galley, 'Geste'.; B. Connelly, *Arab Folk Epic and Identity* (Berkeley & Los Angeles, 1986), pp. 31–2, etc.

8   S. Slyomovics, *The Merchant of Art: An Egyptian Hilali Oral Epic Poet in Performance* (Berkeley and Los Angeles, 1987), p. 3 and various footnotes.

9   Connelly, *Epic*, pp. 10, 31–2.

10 For example, *Best Selections from the Arabian Nights Entertainments* (New York, 1976).

11 The *Book of the Thousand Nights and a Night*, (tr.) Sir R. F. Burton. Library edition (London, 1894), vol. I, p. xxii.

12 Robert Irwin, *The Arabian Nights: A Companion* (London, 1994).

13 For example, J. Oestrup, 'Alf Laila wa-Laila', *Encyclopaedia of Islam*. First edition, vol. I (Leiden and London 1913), pp. 252–6 and E. Littmann, 'Alf Layla wa-Layla', *Encyclopaedia of Islam*. New edition, vol. I (Leiden & London 1960), pp. 358–64.

14 [*Alf Layla wa-Layla*] (Bulaq, 1835). Lane's copy, sumptuously bound in full morocco, with extensive marginal annotations by Muhammad 'Iyad al-Tantawi, is in Cambridge University Library (Adv.b.88.78–9).

15 For accounts of the complex textual bibliography of the *Arabian Nights*, cf. [*Alf Layla wa-Layla.*] *The Thousand and One Nights (Alf Layla wa-Layla) from the earliest known sources*. Arabic text edited with introduction and notes by Muhsin Mahdi. *Kitab Alf Layla wa-Layla min usulihi al-'Arabiyya al-ula, haqqaqahu wa-qaddama lahu wa-'allaqa 'alayhi Muhsin Mahdi* (Leiden, 1984–94); Irwin, *Companion*.

16 Irwin, *Companion*, p. 274.

17 Rashad Rushdi, 'English travellers in Egypt during the reign of Mohamed Ali', *Bulletin of the Faculty of Arts*, Jami'at Fu'ad al-Awwal [Cairo University], 14 February (1952), p. 40.'.

18 E. Roberts, *Notes of an Overland Journey Through France and Egypt to Bombay* (London, 1841), p. 133, cited by Rushdi, 'English Travellers', p. 40.

19 Arberry, *Oriental Essays*, p. 107.

20 'Ali Mubarak, *al-Khitat al-Tawfiqiyya al-jadida li-Misr al-Qahira wa-muduniha wa-biladiha al-qadima wa-al-shahira* (Bulaq, 1306 [1889]). 20 parts.)

21 'Ali Mubarak, *al-Khitat*, vol. 11, p. 10. There is a pun here: the word translated above as 'gentle' is, in the Arabic, 'layyin'. The seemingly akward rhetoricism of this passage, as it emerges in my literal translation, is attributable to Dasuqi's use of *saj* (rhymed prose).

22 BM Mss Or. 4154–4177. See Rieu, *Supplement*, pp. 592–4, for a detailed description.

23 Described and analysed by P. Stocks, 'Edward William Lane and his Arabic–English "Thesaurus"', *British Library Journal* 15 (1989), pp. 23–34.

24 See G. Alleaume, 'L'Orientaliste dans le miroir de la littérature arabe', *British Society for Middle Eastern Studies Bulletin* 9 i (1982), pp. 5–9, 12 n.3.

25 Ahmad Faris al-Shidyaq, *Kitab al-rihla al-mawsuma bi-al-Wasita ila ma'rifat Malita wa-Kashf al-mukhabba' 'an funun Urubba* (Tunis, 1280 [1863/64]), p. 125.

26 E. W. Lane, *Madd al-Qamus. An Arabic–English Lexicon, Derived from the Best*

and the Most Copious Eastern Sources (London, 1863–93). 8 vols, see vol. I (1863), p. xxii.

27 E. W. Lane, 'Ueber die Lexicographie der arabischen Sprache', *Zeitschrift der Deutschen Morgenländischen Gesellschaft* 3 (1849), pp. 90–108 and his 'Ueber die Aussprache der arabischen Vocale', *Zeitschrift der Deutschen Morgenländischen Gesellschaft* 4 (1850), pp. 187–97.

28 Lane, *Madd al-Qamus* (1863), vol. I, p. xxiii.

29 Edinburgh (1856) and London (1860).

30 Lane-Poole, *Life of Edward William Lane*, pp. 141–2.

31 S. Halkett and J. Laing, *Dictionary of Anonymous and Pseudonymous English Literature*. New & Enlarged, (eds) J. Kennedy, W. A. Smith & A. F. Johnson. Vol. 2 (Edinburgh, 1926), p. 365; *National Union Catalogue: pre-1956 imprints*, vol. 314, London (1974), p. 353.

32 Lane-Poole, *Life of Edward William Lane*, pp. 132–3.

33 Lane, *Madd al-Qamus* (1863), vol. I, p. 6.

34 Much of this material, it seems, he recorded in his own interleaved copy of Freytag's *Lexicon Arabico–Latinum* (Halle, 1830–37). See Lane-Poole's Preface to Lane (1863–93), vol. VII, p. i; M. Krek, 'E. W. Lane's working copy of his lexicon', *Journal of the American Oriental Society* 89 (1969), pp. 419–20.

35 R. Dozy, *Supplément aux dictionnaires arabes*. 2e edition (Leiden & Paris, 1927), t. I, p. VI.

36 J. G. Hava, *Al-Fara'id al-durriyya fi al-lughatayn al-'Arabiyya wa-al-Inkiliziyya*; *Arabic–English dictionary* (Beirut, 1915), [p. i].

37 H. Fleisch, *Introduction à l'étude des langues sémitiques* (Paris, 1947), p. 106 n.1.

38 E. Bräunlich, 'Zu Lane Sp. 371A und 414b', *Islamica* 3 (1927), pp. 273–4.

39 See J. A. Haywood, *Arabic Lexicography*. 2nd edition (Leiden, 1965), p. 125.

40 Ms. Arabic 216773. See A. Gacek, *Catalogue of the Arabic Manuscripts in the Library of the School of Oriental and African Studies, University of London* (London, 1981), p. 14, No. 23.

41 Najib al-'Aqiqi, *Al-Mustashriqun* (Beirut, 1937), p. 88.

42 Ahmad Amin, *Qamus al-'adat wa-al-taqalid wa-al-ta'abir al-Misriyya* (Cairo, 1953), *passim*. Most of the plates at the end of the book are reproduced from Lane's *Manners and Customs*.

43 Yunus, *Al-Hilaliyya* (1968).

44 'Abd al-Rahman Zaki, *Mawsu'at madinat al-Qahira fi alf 'am* (Cairo, 1969), p. 238.

45 A. L. Tibawi, 'English-speaking Orientalists: a critique of their approach to Islam and Arab nationalism', *Muslim World* 53 (1963), p. 188.

46 Edward W. Said, *Orientalism* (London: Routledge & Kegan Paul, 1978), pp. 158–65.

Part 7

European Influences on Egypt

Philip Sadgrove

In the first half of the nineteenth century the Orient attracted the attention
of the 'civilised world', not only because of the grave questions it posed for
European politics, but also because it was led by the force of events to make
all sorts of ameliorations to improve the way of life of its inhabitants. Egypt
had particularly been the focus of attention, as the classical land *par
excellence*, the land of enigmas from the time of Herodotus, offering the
interested foreigner a vast field for scientific investigation. The interest that
it inspired amongst Europeans increased each year. By the 1830s the
Europeans that inhabited the country, the visitors or those *en route* to British
India felt the need for a literary society to act as a focal point for their
activities, bringing together or publishing important documents and
interesting memoires on the country. An institution was needed that could
offer to all specialisms new information on Egypt and its neighbours and
that could also serve as a centre in which residents and travellers could meet.[1]
Several abortive attempts were made to establish such a body in the last
decades of Muhammad 'Ali Pasha's reign (1805–49). The European
community to be thus served was small: in 1836 it was reckoned to be
3,000; in 1840 this figure was broken down into 2,000 Italians, 7–800
French and some 80–100 British.

During the brief but traumatic occupation of Egypt by the French
(1798–1801), they had established the first such learned society in Cairo,
the Institut d'Égypte, in August 1798. The Institut had grandiose aims: it
was to be the counterpart of the Institut National in Paris, with its own
review, *La Décade égyptienne*. It had sections devoted to the main areas of
scholarship: mathematics, physics, political economy and literature and the
arts. The Institut formed its own library, open to the public, stocked with
books brought to Egypt on board Bonaparte's flagship *l'Orient*.[2] When the
French forces evacuated in 1801, the Institut and its library went too,
leaving no vestige of its presence in the country. The immediate significance
of the Institut's activities for the intellectual life of the Egyptians was
minimal.[3] The members of the Institut were almost entirely French; the
only outsider was the Arab interpreter and Syrian priest Dom Raphaël de

Monachis. Those that visited the French body went primarily out of curiosity; the Egyptian chronicler al-Jabarti records an account of visits he made to the library.[4] The Institut was a totally foreign institution founded by an occupying power that did not need to seek the consent, consult, or involve the local authorities. In the autonomous Egypt of Muhammad 'Ali's reign the European founders of the successor institutions sought the support and involvement of the Egyptian authorities for their undertakings; these foreigners owed their continued presence in the country to the favour of the ruler.

Until the arrival of the French Egypt possessed no public libraries of modern European works. The small indigenous literate section of the population could avail themselves of the many famous ancient mosque libraries, containing rich collections of Arabic manuscripts; unfortunately these had suffered years of neglect and access to these collections was often difficult.[5] Muhammad 'Ali had lavished no attention on these collections, since he 'was perfectly indifferent as to old Arabic literature. He wished to create a new epoch in Egypt, both as a soldier and revolutionist, and it was the modern science of Europe that was more likely to suit his purpose than any amount of the curious theology and literature of the earlier Arabic period.'[6]

With the development by the Pasha of education to build an effective military and civil structure, amongst the first European libraries established were those in Muhammad 'Ali's new schools, clearly intended for the staff and student body. One such library, described by Heyworth-Dunne as 'the first of its kind to be owned by any non-European community in Egypt', was to be found from *circa* 1820 in the Bulaq school, Madrasat al-Handasa (School of Engineering), in the palace of Isma'il Pasha.[7] It had mainly French and Italian books; most of these books had been ordered by Muhammad 'Ali through the first student sent on an educational mission to Europe, 'Uthman Nur al-Din.[8] Although British visitors might belittle the collection, it was admitted that 'an establishment of this sort reflects credit on the pasha, and must be productive of great good, for if the boys were to read all the trash, and the worst trash which France could send them, they would be every way, even in morality, gainers'.[9] In the 1830s the Bulaq school and its library became part of the Qasr al-'Ayni school, the military school Madrasat al-Jihadiyya.

The viceroy, though illiterate, had himself built up a European library, in its infancy in January 1822, full of books relating in one way or another to Egypt, with some twenty-five thousand volumes in several languages. This library, in the charge of the Scottish convert to Islam, Osman Effendi, was open to travellers 'of any degree', who were loaned books to read in their lodgings. A public reading room was opened in 1822 adjoining the library.[10] In 1251 (1835–36) Muhammad 'Ali opened a library in the Citadel, called al-Maktaba al-Khidiwiyya (The Khedivial Library),[11] perhaps formed from this earlier collection, which may be the library known from 1827–1832/1243–1248 as the Khaznat al-Kutub al-'Amira (The Royal Library).[12] In the late 1830s there were other significant libraries in the capital: according to Paton the largest library in Egypt was that of the son of Muhammad 'Ali, Ibrahim Pasha, with 8,000 volumes, which contained Arabic and Turkish books and manuscripts.[13] The books of the mosques of the Morea and Greece, brought to Egypt by Ibrahim Pasha after his campaign, numbering 1,500 volumes, were deposited in the Citadel. The largest library of a private individual, with some 5,000 volumes, was that of Habib Effendi, a Turk, who had been municipal governor of Cairo.[14]

The first cultural institution founded by foreigners was on a modest scale. All the cultural societies of the Pasha's reign received their strongest support from the small British colony. In Alexandria *circa* 1828 there existed an English Reading Society that provided a library primarily for the British community.[15] Precisely when it was active is not known; de Cadalvène reported that in 1829 there had been no library in Alexandria.[16] In 1843 there was still a reading room and library in the city in the corner of the 'Frank' square.[17]

A few years later another society, with more scholarly pretensions, attempted to offer similar facilities to the European residents of Cairo; the Société Égyptienne/Egyptian Society, 'open to gentlemen of all nations', was founded in 1836[18] on the initiative of the principal European residents of Cairo.[19] It included members from the British, French and German communities.[20] The objects of the association were:

1. To form a rendezvous for travellers, with the view of associating literary and scientific men, who may from time to time visit Egypt.

2. To collect and record information relative to Egypt, and to those parts of Africa and Asia which are connected with, or tributary to, this country.

3. To facilitate research, by enabling travellers to avail themselves of such information as it may be in the power of the society to obtain, and by offering them the advantage of a library of reference containing the most valuable works on the East.[21]

Amongst the founders were the British vice-consul Dr Alfred S. Walne and the US vice-consul in Cairo George R. Gliddon, son of John Gliddon.[22] It had originally been called the Société Orientale, but a little after its creation changed its name to the Société Égyptienne.[23] The Armenian Yusuf Hekekyan Bey seems to have been one of the few active local members; born in Istanbul and educated extensively in England, he became the Nazir of the Muhandiskhana and the School of Arts and Crafts [Madrasat al-'Amaliyyat]. The statutes of September 1836 fixed the number of members at twenty-one.[24] The Fifth Report for 1841 speaks of the 'flourishing condition of the Society's interests'. It had in that year some 149 members.[25]

Many prominent Europeans renowned for their studies of Egypt were associated with the society; amongst the honorary members were the director of the Mission égyptienne in Paris Edme-François Jomard, Lane, the Italian Egyptologist Niccolo Rosellini, the Coptic scholar the Reverend Dr Henry Tattam and the Egyptologist Sir John Gardner Wilkinson. The members included diplomats, merchants, archaeologists, doctors, missionaries, educationalists and others.[26]

This first Egyptian scholarly society was endowed and encouraged by the Pasha; understanding the importance of the historic monuments of the Nile valley and of investigations in the arts and sciences, the Egyptian government generously supported its efforts.[27] As promised the Society provided, by renting rooms, a place where members of the foreign communities could meet, and a rendezvous for travellers.[28] The society held a monthly general meeting, at which papers were read on archaeology and scientific matters; the principal scholarly concerns of the society were 'linguistic matters', presumably a reference to hieroglyphics and archaeology.[29] These preoccupations were a reflection of the frenzy of activity up and down the Nile that the country had witnessed, investigating, recording and sometimes acquiring Egypt's ancient monuments from the time of the French occupation.

One of the chief functions of the society was to provide a library for members and for the use of visitors to Egypt:

> Quant à la Société Égyptienne, elle est fondée depuis six ans et avait pour but, dans son principe, de rassembler, par le moyen des souscriptions annuelles des membres (la souscription est de 105 piastres) le plus de livres possibles, mais surtout de livres ayant trait à l'Orient sous quelque rapport que se soit, histoire, géographie, religions, mœurs, etc., etc.[30]

The Society created in Cairo one of the most complete reference libraries that existed in Egypt. It provided a source for information and 'improvement' that facilitated literary and scientific investigation and research.[31] The Statutes of the society expressed the hope that the 'collection of valuable notices' by foreigners, i.e. the carrying out of research would be made easier, not only by the use of the printed and manuscript sections of the library, but also through the personal help of members who lived in Egypt.[32] There had been a lack of such facilities in general for foreigners in Egypt. By January 1838 the society's rooms had been fitted out, a collection of the best works on Egypt procured and a museum was in the process of collection.[33] It was built up through money and other contributions from members, and through gifts from honorary members and travellers; in 1842 Hekekyan Bey gave some valuable works to the library.[34] This library had its premises in the Coptic quarter of Cairo in 1843.[35]

The society published its annual reports and Laws and Regulations in Cairo and Alexandria at the small European presses that had started to operate.[36] In 1842 the Society declared that it would henceforth publish its annual reports in both English and French. Early in 1842 the society decided to consecrate a third of its funds to meeting the expenses of publishing memoirs or papers relative to the Orient, written by members. Several 'gentlemen' had promised contributions:[37] Linant, Lambert, Perron, Pruner and Dr A. Figari.[38] Only the paper of Linant's was to see the light of day. The President of the Society, Linant de Bellefonds, had a paper he had read at the society on 5 July 1842, his *Mémoire sur le lac Moeris* published by the society and printed at A. E. Ozanne's press in Alexandria in 1843. It was a description of Fayoum, Bahr Yousef and Lake Keiroun. The Egyptian Society's Report of 1845 published Heinrich Abeken's sketch of some recent discoveries in Ethiopia made by a Prussian mission under Professor Lepsius.[39]

By 1842 the society had started to dissolve and some of its members formed a new body, the Association Littéraire. It dissolved because of internecine quarrels amongst the members.[40] It may be that, despite these events, the society lingered on in some form or another, for in 1864 Walmass spoke of its members, saying 'some have died, and many others have left, the society has remained impoverished and now has barely kept its name.'[41]

The first scholarly journal of Muhammad 'Ali's reign appeared in 1842, the *Miscellanea Ægyptiaca*, published in Alexandria, 'ex typographia P. R. Wilkinson' by the Association Littéraire d'Égypte.[42] With over one hundred and forty pages this was the most substantial work in a European language printed in Egypt in the Pasha's reign. The introduction was written in French with articles in both French and English. It included a 'Compte-rendu des fondateurs de l'Association Littéraire d'Égypte' by H. Abbot [*sic*].[43] All the articles were written by members:

Sir Gardner Wilkinson 'A Tour to Bubastis, Sebennytus and Menzaleh';

E. Prisse d'Avennes 'Excursion dans la partie orientale du Delta', 'Légendes royales de Skhai', 'Lois du Tar et du Dyeh' and 'Culte du soleil chez les anciens Égyptiens';

A. D. R., 'Notes sur le Sennar';

J. T. Bell, 'Extract from a Journal of Travels in Abyssinia, in 1840–42', and 'Range of the Thermometer';

Dr Verdot,[44] 'Du climat de l'Égypte' and 'Miscellanées. Alphabet hymiarite, Antiquités, etc.'

It had appointed distributors in London, Paris, Calcutta and Madras. In 1845 a new edition of *Miscellanea Ægyptiaca* appeared in Cairo 'ex typographia ægyptiaca' at the expense of the association.[45]

After the partial disbandment of the earlier Société Égyptienne, the Association Littéraire d'Égypte, another predominantly European society based in Cairo, had been founded on 15 February 1842 to serve as a meeting place for travellers and residents. It was founded by Abbott, an English doctor in the service of the Pasha, and Prisse d'Avennes. More than its predecessor it seems to have courted and won the patronage of prominent government figures: it was under the presidency of Boghos Youssouf-Bey, Minister of Foreign Affairs, with Prisse d'Avennes and Johnstone as the vice-presidents.[46] It counted amongst its patrons Ibrahim Pasha and Sulayman Pasha.[47] The dismembering of the Society was a consequence of discord between Abbott, its former secretary general, and Walne, its former president.[48] The society's aims were to:

1. De recueiller et de publier au moins chaque année un recueil d'observations et de recherches sur les sciences naturelles, l'histoire, l'archéologie, la linguistique de l'Égypte et des pays voisins, de publier également aux frais de l'Association et au moyen de la lithographie quelques ouvrages spéciaux de littérature orientale.

2. De faciliter les recherches des voyageurs et de ses colloborateurs en leur offrant dans un pays dénué de collections littéraires et scienifiques [sic] l'inappréciable ressource d'une Bibliothèque composée des meilleurs ouvrages anciens et modernes sur l'Orient, et l'entrée d'un Cabinet d'histoire naturelle et d'antiquités, ses compléments indispensables.[49]

The new society had about 60 members after about three months. By February 1843 the membership had increased to a hundred, most of whom were British.[50] Many of the same individuals were associated with both societies. The members included the Director of the School of Medicine Clot-Bey, F. Mengin, Dr Cuny, the East India Company's agent Lieutenant Waghorn, R. N. and the Greek merchant and consul of Belgium Etienne Zizinia. The honorary members included the following distinguished savants and Orientalists: Jean and Jacques Champollion-Figeac, Frédéric Cailliaud, Charles Lenormant, Jean-Antoine Letronne, Rosellini, Jomard, Lane, Dr Richard Lepsius, L'Abbé Amadeo Peyron, Joseph-Toussaint Reinaud, the Reverend Tattam and Sir Gardner Wilkinson.[51] The library was on a more modest scale than that of the Egyptian Society; it had about 200 books given by the British, with a few offered by members, such as Prisse d'Avennes.[52]

It had not been easy for the Association to produce its *Miscellanea Ægyptiaca*. In 1842, since the first general meeting, the publication committee of the new society had been negotiating with the Imprimerie du Commerce in Alexandria to publish its journal.[53] They were finally able to have it published when the new press of P. R. Wilkinson in Alexandria was founded.[54] This was perhaps the lithographic press given by Sir Gardner Wilkinson to the society. The society's statutes were also printed in 1843 in Alexandria.[55] The society's lithographic press was used in February 1843 to print the first part of *Miscellanea Hieroglyphica ou Études sur l'histoire, la religion et la langue des anciens égyptiens* by Prisse d'Avennes.[56]

While these institutions may not have survived Muhammad 'Ali's reign, they prepared the way for more concrete and abiding efforts in the reign of his successors. This was the pattern in many areas of cultural activity; the seeds sown by Muhammad 'Ali were often reaped in the reign of his grandson the Khedive Isma'il. This was the case with the development of printing, the expansion of the Bulaq press, the growth of Arabic and foreign-language journalism and the development of educational institutions. The reign of Muhammad 'Ali's successor, 'Abbas (1849–54), witnessed the destruction of much that his grandfather had achieved in these areas. His successor Muhammad Sa'id (1854–63) was, however, much more encouraging to such developments; under his patronage in 1859 the grander concept of the Institut d'Égypte was revived with the foundation in Alexandria of the still extant Institut Égyptien with its own bulletin and rich library;[57] again this was brought about at the initiative of foreign residents, mainly Frenchmen, with the support of the Egyptian government.[58]

Jomard, the last survivor of Napoleon's Institut and member of both the societies of Muhammad 'Ali's reign, provided the impulse for the Institute's creation.[59] Many of those involved in the earlier societies, Walmass, Lambert, Prisse d'Avennes, and Figari, joined the Institut. Though the Institut was open to all, it was still primarily a European institution and could not be described as an indigenous society of savants. However, for the first time there were a limited number of Arab members involved, such as the Egyptian educationalist Rifa'a Bey al-Tahtawi, the Egyptian lawyer Qadri Bey and the Lebanese publisher Khalil al-Khuri and contributions on Arabic subjects were published in its Bulletin, including poetry by Rifa'a Bey, Khalil al-Khuri and Père Michel. Though the library of the Association disappeared without trace,[60] in 1873/1874 the last survivors of the earlier Egyptian Society, Youssef Bey Hekekyan, Linant Pacha de Bellefonds and Monsieur Cany deposited that society's books at the newly founded Bibliothèque Khédiviale (1870) in Cairo,[61] the first national library in Egypt. The short-lived cultural societies of Muhammad 'Ali's reign had in a modest, but concrete, form begun the process that was to lead to the creation of a milieu in which more permanent indigenous institutions could be established.

Notes

1 These were the views expressed by the founders of the Association Littéraire d'Égypte in *Miscellanea Ægyptiaca de l'Association Littéraire d'Égypte. Anno 1842*, vol. 1 (Alexandria, 1842), p. v.

2 R. G. Canivet, 'La bibliothèque de l'expédition', *Revue internationale d'Égypte* 4, nos 4–5 (Aug–Sept 1906), pp. 122–3.

3 J. Heyworth-Dunne, *An Introduction to the History of Education in Modern Egypt* (London, 1968), p. 96.

4 'Abd al-Rahman al-Jabarti's *Chronicle of the First Seven Months of the French Occupation of Egypt* (ed. and tr. S. Moreh) (Leiden, 1975), pp. 116–7 and his *al-Ta'rikh al-Musamma 'Aja'ib al-Athar fi al-Tarajim wa-al-Akhbar* (Cairo, 1322), vol. 3, pp. 35–6.

5 E. W. Lane, *The Manners and Customs of the Modern Egyptians* (London, 1963), hereinafter *Manners and Customs*, p. 214.

6 A. A. Paton, *A History of the Egyptian Revolution* (London, 1870), hereinafter *Egyptian Revolution*, vol. 2, pp. 247–8.

7 Heyworth-Dunne, *Education*, p. 110.

8 Ibid., and G. Forni, *Viaggio nell'Egitto e nell'Alta Nubia* (Milan, 1859), vol. 1, p. 140.

9 Anon. [J. M. Sherer], *Scenes and Impressions in Egypt and in Italy* (London, 1824), p. 197.

10 A Field Officer of Cavalry [D. Mackworth], *Diary of a Tour Through Southern India, Egypt and Palestine in the Years 1821 and 1822* (London, 1823), p. 246 and R. R. Madden, *Travels in Turkey, Egypt, Nubia and Palestine in 1824–1827* (London, 1829), vol. 1, p. 320.

11 Heyworth-Dunne, *Education*, p. 206 and Amin Sami, *Taqwim al-Nil wa-'Asr Muhammad 'Ali Basha* (Cairo, 1923), vol. 2, p. 464.

12 *al-Waqa'i' al-Misriyya*, no. 401, 9 Safar 1248 (8 July 1832) in ibid., 2, p. 398.

13 Paton, *Egyptian Revolution*, vol. 2, p. 247; J. A. St John, *Egypt and Mohammed Ali* (London, 1834), vol. 2, p. 397 and Sir John G. Wilkinson, *Modern Egypt and Thebes* (London, 1843), hereinafter *Modern Egypt*, vol. 2, pp. 263–4.

14 Paton, *Egyptian Revolution*, vol. 2, p. 247.

15 *The Regulations of the English Reading Society* in the James Burton Collection, *Collectanea Ægyptiaca-Miscellaneous Subjects*, BL Add. Ms. 25, 663, f. 149 in the British Library.

16 E. de Cadalvène, *L'Égypte et la Turquie* (Paris, 1836), vol. 1, p. 11.

17 Wilkinson, *Modern Egypt*, vol. 2, p. 173.

18 'Die beiden ägyptischen Gesellschaften', *Zeitschrift der deutschen Morgenländischen Gesellschaft* [ZDMG] i (1847), p. 206. Yacoub Artin, 'Lettres inédites du Dr Perron à M. J. Mohl', *Bulletin de l'Institut Égyptien*, 5th ser., iii, 2nd fasc. (Cairo, 1909), hereinafter 'Lettres inédites', p. 145, n.1. Artin gives 1835 as the year of its foundation. It was to call itself by both its English and French names.

19 C. Rochfort Scott, *Rambles in Egypt and Candia with Details of the Military Power and Resources of Those Countries* (London, 1837), vol. 1, p. 217, n.*.

20 ZDMG *i* (1847), p. 206.

21 *Laws and Regulations of the Egyptian Society* (Alexandria, n.d. [1840?]), p. 1.

22 Sir William Wilde, *Narrative of a Voyage to Madeira, Teneriffe and Along the*

27 ∾ Views of al-Azhar in the Nineteenth Century: Gabriel Charmes and 'Ali Pasha Mubarak

Michael J. Reimer

Introduction

The nineteenth century witnessed a vastly increased flow of European travellers to Egypt. Nearly all of these travellers spent some time in Cairo. At the heart of old Cairo lay *al-Jami' al-Azhar*, the most important mosque in the city and 'the principal university of the East'.[1] Paradoxically, few European observers say anything of significance about al-Azhar. The poverty of European descriptions of al-Azhar is demonstrated in the two most respected studies of Egypt published in the nineteenth century, i.e., the *Description de l'Égypte*[2] and E.W. Lane's *Manners and Customs of the Modern Egyptians*.

The *Description* contains two articles (by M. M. Jomard and De Chabrol) which discuss al-Azhar. Jomard recognises the centrality of al-Azhar, but his description of it is short and superficial.[3] Jomard mentions the mosque's size, but there is neither a ground plan nor a description of the mosque's form. He notes its Fatimid origins and subsequent history, though he is apparently ignorant of the mosque's expansion in the eighteenth century.[4] Al-Azhar is accurately described as the most popular and richly endowed of Cairo's mosques. De Chabrol adds that teaching is centered on the Qur'an, prophetic traditions, and law, with each 'sect' (*madhhab*) possessing its set of texts and jurisconsults (*muftis*); he also remarks the prevailing ignorance of science and philosophy. Jomard observes that students—about 1,500—have come from all over the Islamic world to receive instruction at al-Azhar, and are housed in apartments (*riwaqs*), allocated according to their nationality; and he notes that there are many poor and blind students at al-Azhar, the latter group possessing their own *riwaq*. De Chabrol gives the annual quantity of grain supplied to the Azharis by the government (5,600 *ardabbs*), which is distributed by the shaykhs who head the university's various subdivisions. He also mentions that of the forty to fifty teaching shaykhs, only five or six have a significant following. The shaykhs are distinguished only by their age, knowledge and virtue, their small income deriving from allowances, gifts and fees. However, Shaykh al-Azhar has a certain primacy, holding the authority to fill vacant positions in the 'faculty'. De Chabrol adds important details about the method of instruction and of promotion to the rank of 'professor' (discussed below).

This is all the *Description* has to say about al-Azhar. This is strange, since the French had named leading shaykhs of al-Azhar as representatives on the governing council they established after capturing Cairo in 1798. Moreover, they knew of the institution's socio-political influence, since it became the centre of uprisings against their rule. Such information probably remained unpublished since Jomard's treatment of al-Azhar is so meagre and De Chabrol's, while somewhat more detailed, is also brief.

Similarly, Edward Lane, whose works abound in insights into Egyptian culture, has little to say of al-Azhar. He corrects Jomard's erroneous interpretation of the mosque's name (not 'la Mosquée des Fleurs', but rather 'the Splendid Mosque'). He is also more conscious than the French savants of the eighteenth-century growth of the institution, having consulted the chronicle of 'Abd al-Rahman al-Jabarti.[5] He supplies a few details concerning the ground plan of the mosque; the diverse activities carried on in the forecourt; the state of the sanctuary; the arrangement, internal organisation, and relative sizes of the *riwaqs*; the curricula and career paths followed by the students; and the mosque's place as a refuge for the poor and homeless.[6] Lane, writing over three decades after the French expedition, explains the losses which al-Azhar has sustained since that time, since al-Azhar lost much revenue when Muhammad 'Ali confiscated agricultural lands which had been part of the mosque's endowment. Also, unlike the *Description*, Lane names some of the leading personalities at al-Azhar (Hasan al-'Attar, Muhammad Shihab, 'Abd al-Rahman al-Jabarti and Hasan al-Quwaysini), and notes the ascendancy of the Shafi'i *madhhab* at al-Azhar. Like De Chabrol, he comments regarding the scholars of al-Azhar that ' ... their studies in the present age are confined within very narrow limits'. In all, his discussion is historically informed and wisely nuanced, but—in the light of al-Azhar's enormous influence—quite short.[7]

The remarks of most other travellers are less illuminating than even the brief comments in the *Description* and *Manners and Customs*. Three reasons may be offered for the general neglect of al-Azhar by travel writers: their preoccupation with Egypt's ancient monuments, the unattractive appearance of al-Azhar, and the undeveloped state of al-Azhar as a tourist sight.

First, for most travellers before the French invasion of Egypt, the fascination of Egypt was its association with biblical history and classical antiquity. To these was added in the nineteenth century a new interest in the civilisation of ancient Egypt.[8] So great was the excitement about ancient Egypt amongst early nineteenth-century travellers that ' ... the early travel-works often read as if Egypt were merely a desolate field of monuments.'[9] By contrast, the sights and sounds of Islamic Cairo were the alien backdrop to this much older civilisation the European traveller was seeking to encounter.

Secondly, even for those with an interest in Arab–Islamic civilisation al-Azhar was a disappointment. Connoisseurs of Islamic architecture rhapsodised about the grandeur of the mosque of Sultan Hasan and the austere beauty of the mosque of Ibn Tulun. But al-Azhar exhibits neither charm nor originality. Moreover, it was obscured by other buildings and in very bad repair. In the 1830s, Lane wrote: 'It is not remarkable in point of architecture, and is so surrounded by houses that very little of it is seen externally.' As late as 1896, a guidebook commented in the same vein: 'Little of the exterior is visible, except a portion of the wall on the E. side, the W. and S. gates, decorated in the Turkish florid style, and the 6 minarets, built at different periods, and not remarkable.'[10] The structure was in such a dilapidated condition, an 1883 report of the Comité de conservation des monuments de l'art arabe commented: 'Des travaux considérables ont été exécutés dans cette mosquée, mais ils passent presque inaperçus, par suite de l'extension de ce monument. Les principaux corps de cet édifice sont étayés et demandent une reconstruction entière.'[11]

Thirdly, al-Azhar had not attained the status of a tourist attraction. In analytical terms, such an 'attraction' comprises sightseers, a sight, and a 'marker' (i.e., an interpretative agent which supplies information about the sight and vouches for its authenticity).[12] As mentioned above, there was nothing intrinsically interesting in al-Azhar's buildings; and guidebooks (the most common 'markers' for tourists) pointed out that little or none of the original building remains, thus precluding a claim to attention on the basis of 'authenticity'.[13] As an 1896 handbook suggested, al-Azhar's significance derives from ' ... the interest it awakens, and the scene it presents, as the principal university of the Mohammedan world.'[14] However, such an interest was not easily kindled. Al-Azhar represented an alien cultural tradition, and it was difficult for the ordinary sightseer to 'see' or appreciate the learning which occurred at al-Azhar, without considerable effort, imagination, and assistance.[15]

This essay compares travellers' comments regarding al-Azhar with those of the Egyptian author-technocrat, 'Ali Mubarak Pasha, which appear in part 4 of his encyclopedia of Egypt (the *Khitat*).[16] However, there is a problem of commensurability. The *Khitat*'s description of this mosque runs to some 34 densely-written pages. Because travel books' remarks on al-Azhar are generally brief, few works can stand comparison with the *Khitat*.

This in itself bespeaks the difference in foreign and indigenous perspectives on the monuments of Egypt.[17]

For this reason the present essay will focus its attention upon a single travel text: Gabriel Charmes' *Cinq mois au Caire et dans la Basse-Égypte*, the only book by a bona fide traveller, and contemporary with the *Khitat*, in which a full chapter is devoted to a description of the mosque of al-Azhar.[18] As we shall see, Gabriel Charmes, though little known today, was a prolific writer on political affairs, whose works enjoyed a wide circulation in France and beyond. His description of al-Azhar is worthy of consideration, both because of his personal influence and because he recognized the significance of al-Azhar for Egypt and Islam. Although his book casts light on the history of al-Azhar, our main interest is in his perception and presentation of al-Azhar. We will therefore consider the construction of his travel narrative, the motifs and misapprehensions in his description of Muslim religious and educational institutions, and his use of al-Azhar as a symbol of Islam. Along the way, we will compare Charmes' text with that of 'Ali Mubarak's *Khitat*, in terms of the latter's discursive organisation, motifs, and treatment of the relationship between al-Azhar and Islam.

Gabriel Charmes and 'Ali Mubarak on al-Azhar

Gabriel Charmes was a political journalist who first attracted notice for his articles in the prestigious *Journal des Débats*. His family hailed from Aurillac where he was born in 1850. Though his father was only a provincial notary, his maternal grandfather had served as a general in Bonaparte's Grande Armée.[19]

Gabriel was the youngest of three brothers, who all attained high positions in Paris. His oldest brother, Francis, joined the French Foreign Ministry in 1880, was elected to the Chamber of Deputies in 1881 and to the Senate in 1900. His older brother, Xavier, held the post of 'Directeur au Service des Missions' at the Ministry of Public Instruction. Gabriel and Xavier Charmes helped to create the Institut français d'archéologie orientale in Cairo in 1880, and worked for the conservation of Islamic art.[20] In politics, the Charmes brothers seem to have inclined toward the conservative republicanism of Adolphe Thiers. Gabriel, in particular, supported a vigorous colonial policy which he believed ought to be concerted with that of Great Britain.[21]

In certain respects, Gabriel Charmes' biography is similar to that of 'Ali Mubarak Pasha. Both were boys from the provinces who, at an early age, achieved success in their respective capitals. Both men advanced their careers through their experiences abroad: Charmes visited Egypt and other

Mediterranean countries, 'Ali Mubarak trained as a military engineer in France. Though differing in their occupations ('Ali Mubarak was an administrator, Charmes a publicist), both directed their writings to the education of their countrymen: 'Ali Mubarak sought to awaken Egyptian interest in the attainments of European civilisation and an awareness of Egypt's own great history, while Gabriel Charmes strove to enlighten the French public concerning the cultures of the Middle East and to expose errors in French policy toward the region.

Charmes was encouraged to travel to Egypt by a colleague at the *Journal des Débats*; he was also seeking a healthful climate, since he had tuberculosis.[22] He also aimed to enhance his reputation as a specialist in international affairs: hence his book on Egypt (1880) was followed by *L'Avenir de la Turquie, le panislamisme* (1883), Voyage en Palestine (1884), *La Tunisie et la Tripolitaine* (1885), and *Politique extérieure et coloniale* (1885).[23]

Charmes set out for Egypt in December 1878. The date is important, since Egypt was nearing a political crossroads: only six months later the reigning Khedive, Isma'il Pasha, was deposed. During the voyage from France to Egypt Charmes conversed with Europeans who had lived for years in Cairo or Alexandria. Also among his fellow passengers was Prince Hasan, son of Isma'il,—whose presence did not deter Charmes' European interlocutors from pronouncing Isma'il the chief obstacle to Egypt's progress.

Though better informed than most travellers, Charmes arrived with expectations formed by his reading and his acquaintance with persons who had been to Egypt. He did not arrive in Egypt as a *tabula rasa*. Neither, of course, does today's tourist. One important difference, however, is that after 1850 the traveller ordinarily arrived by sea in Alexandria, with its large European colony. Cairo too had a growing European community. Although touristic services existed, these European colonists were still the people most likely to mould the traveller's opinions, since his short sojourn and lack of facility in the local languages made it impossible for the ordinary traveller to formulate an independent assessment of complex Egyptian institutions—such as al-Azhar.

Gabriel Charmes' commentary on al-Azhar is no exception to this rule. As he indicates in a footnote, he has borrowed from the book of Edouard Dor (also known as Dor Bey), the Swiss Inspector General of Schools under Khedive Isma'il, in composing his own description of al-Azhar. Charmes certainly visited al-Azhar, made his own observations, and omitted certain points from Dor's text. However, the core of his description is from Dor's *L'Instruction publique en Égypte*, and there are numerous details about the history, student life, pedagogical methods, curriculum, and system of promotion at al-Azhar, which merely recapitulate Dor's work.

Gabriel Charmes begins his discussion of al-Azhar—which the traveller 'must' visit before leaving Cairo—by noting the college's position as a survivor amongst the schools of medieval Islam. He recalls specifically the resistance of al-Azhar during the 1798 insurrection against Bonaparte. This incident of course really happened, although it is not true, as Charmes suggests, that al-Azhar was never subdued by the French troops.[24] But it is a useful fiction, since it allows him to employ the metaphor of bombardment and resistance in describing al-Azhar:

> Like the cannon balls of Bonaparte, contemporary ideas, the principles of European civilisation, fell impotently against the walls of El-Azhar, without making a breach there, without succeeding in overthrowing the invincible ramparts behind which had taken refuge this last relic of the Middle Ages.[25]

Herein the first *leitmotiv* in European travel-writing: the Orient is a museum of changeless artifacts, 'a phenomenon of arrested development'.[26] Gabriel Charmes repeats here the absurd statement of Edouard Dor (who is usually better informed) that al-Azhar is exactly as it was when it was founded some nine centuries before. This false claim ignores a multitude of changes in al-Azhar of which at least two should be mentioned: the change from a centre for Isma'ili propaganda to a centre of Sunni learning; and the eighteenth-century enlargement of the mosque by the Mamluk Beys, who doubled the size of the sanctuary and built the imposing gate which became the principal entrance to the mosque. Charmes seeks to make al-Azhar a vehicle for returning through history to Islam's remote past; but the proposition is itself ahistorical, and the past to which we return is nothing more than a retrojection of the present.

By contrast, 'Ali Mubarak's *Khitat* lays out an objective architectural history of al-Azhar. 'Ali Mubarak, like Gabriel Charmes, borrows almost verbatim from previous writers, but his sources are superior. This in itself is no surprise: what is surprising is that 'Ali Mubarak, in recounting the Isma'ili origins of the mosque-college, also fails to mention the heretical character of Isma'ili doctrine. He does not, however, leap in ignorance from the distant origins of al-Azhar to the present, to claim that al-Azhar has not changed in nine hundred years.

Having summarily disposed of al-Azhar's history, Charmes' description proceeds by means of physical movement, in which we are invited to participate, a common mode of presentation for the travel writer. We enter the mosque through Bab al-Muzayyinin (Gate of the Barbers), busy with its fruit and vegetable sellers, the smells of *ful madammas*, and the sight of barbers cutting hair. Passing into the great court, we see hundreds of schoolchildren reciting the Qur'an; only a few paces away, older students, grouped in compact masses, assuming diverse postures—sitting cross-legged, crouching, reclining, lying down—listen attentively to their master seated before his customary pillar within the mosque.

In these passages, the second *leitmotiv* of the travel writer appears: the astonishing diversity of the Orient. In fact, the kaleidoscopic effect is first felt upon arrival in Alexandria where, as Charmes says, one glimpses the types of races and dress to be observed in the interior: Bedouin Arabs, Egyptian fellahs, Greeks, Albanians, Nubians, and Negroes of all sorts.[27] This observation is an essential element in the Orient's strangeness to the Western traveller.

For Charmes, as for other European observers, particularly striking is the spectrum of activity, much of it unconnected with worship or learning, yet occurring in an institution of religious education: people are seen napping, sewing, chatting, eating, hawking food and drink, or just loitering. It is especially unusual to see the very young and the very old juxtaposed in an educational setting. For Charmes, the scene at the mosque's vestibule is already 'fort original', but the spectacle within is 'bien plus étrange, bien plus varié, bien plus pittoresque encore'.

This brings us to a sharp contrast between the European observer and his Egyptian counterpart, both in mode of presentation and in substance: after setting forth the architectural history of al-Azhar, 'Ali Mubarak proceeds analytically, locating and cataloguing the physical accoutrements of al-Azhar. He then moves to a discussion of living and learning at al-Azhar, turning finally to a history of the institution since the seventeenth century. His is the work of an 'encyclopedist' who seeks to map al-Azhar historically and spacially.[28] For 'Ali Mubarak, the picturesque aspects of the courtyard scene simply do not exist. Besides, no Egyptian reader of the *Khitat* would be interested in the scene Charmes has described.

This is not to say that 'Ali Mubarak does not recognise the diversity which exists at al-Azhar, but his appreciation of it is that of an administrator, not an artist. His description includes a list of the *riwaq*s at al-Azhar and the nationalities they represent, as well as precise details concerning each *riwaq*'s location, size, facilities, leadership, organisation and financial condition.[29] In one of the *Khitat*'s few lyrical passages, 'Ali Mubarak pronounces a roll call of nations, from Java to Morocco, who come to al-Azhar in search of knowledge. However, the voice of the administrator soon returns, as he criticises the tendency of the students from different regions to clash with one another over trivialities.[30]

Having passed through the courtyard and arrived at the scene of actual instruction, Gabriel Charmes digresses into a discussion of student life and scholarly attainment at al-Azhar. He knows something of the arrangement of *riwaq*s, though he depends on Dor Bey for the details he gives and is far less informative than 'Ali Mubarak. Like 'Ali Mubarak, he gives a sampling of the geographic range covered by the *riwaq*s. This collection of Muslim students is important in forming an image of al-Azhar as the symbol not just of Egypt but of the whole of Islam, to which he will later refer. He also remarks approvingly on the *laisser faire* accorded to the students. Everything depends upon their own initiative. He sees in this freedom great, but alas unrealised, potential: 'Les étudiants possèdent de leur coté une liberté qui pourrait être d'une fécondité merveilleuse.'[31]

. Similarly, Charmes admires the unregulated competition for recognition amongst the shaykhs of al-Azhar. He is especially enchanted by the informal way in which a student becomes a shaykh, and his description of this process is even longer and more detailed, and more entertaining and imaginative, than that of 'Ali Mubarak.[32] He envisions a little drama (which he certainly never witnessed) wherein the ambitious student tutors his comrades until they, impressed by his eloquence and knowledge, say to him (though presumably not in French): 'Mais pourquoi donc ne serais-tu pas un maître, toi aussi?' From this moment he assumes his place at the foot of a pillar in the mosque and begins to gather disciples. The ulema trust to the common judgment in the beginning: if his reputation grows, the shaykhs engage him in a kind of verbal joust which takes place in the presence of a crowd of students. It is this duel, or series of duels, which settles the fate of the newcomer, who if successful is welcomed into the fraternity of Azhari ulema.

Charmes thinks this an excellent system, were it not for one thing:

> Combien de pareil procédés de recrutement pour les professeurs rendraient fertile l'enseignement de la mosquée de El Azhar, si, par sa nature même, il n'était condamné à la plus complète, la plus irrémédiable stérilité![33]

In his opinion with regard to the liberty of students and the recruitment of new teachers at al-Azhar, Gabriel Charmes is unusual. He would appear to concur with Timothy Mitchell, who has sought to establish in a recent book that the traditional style of learning at al-Azhar was 'remarkably flexible and free of coercion ... ' and that the institution possessed 'an order without recourse to regulation and structure ... '[34] In contrast, most European observers, including Charmes' authority for his description, Dor Bey, saw this system of pedagogy and promotion as defective. Charmes locates the defect in the 'nature' of al-Azhar but Dor Bey finds the institution's conservatism to be the consequence of its being an autonomous corporation seeking to defend itself against the state. In addition, indulgence and weakness have caused some shaykhs to support unworthy candidates, and intramural intrigues and cronyism have similarly contributed to a decline in standards.[35]

However, Dor suggests that a milestone has been passed since the old system has been replaced by a reform project, in which the candidates for the position of teaching shaykh had to state the texts they would teach and be examined in them by a board of examiners. He believes that this project augurs great changes at al-Azhar—a prediction which was, however, erroneous.[36]

'Ali Mubarak also describes this informal system of promotion to the position of teaching shaykh (*al-tasaddur lil-tadris*).[37] In his words:

> It used to be the case that no one presented himself to teach except those who had undertaken those disciplines taught in the Azhar, had studied them from the mouths of the *shuyukh*, and had become qualified to come forth with solutions to problems and difficult issues, thus needing no higher permission unless *de politesse* and to have the blessing (of the senior staff) ... But later they became lax in this, until it got to the point where hardly anyone would object to a new teacher, and so their number increased, including among them those who were unqualified.[38]

The essential point is that, under the old regime, students were promoted to teaching positions without any formal accreditation. With al-Azhar's expansion in the latter half of the nineteenth century, this system broke down. Many of the new teachers were incompetent, hence the 1872 examination reform.

'Ali Mubarak gives the details of another of the reforms (which is also mentioned by Dor Bey but omitted by Gabriel Charmes, for whom the unreformed system is a vestige of the 'changeless' Islamic past). Under the new regime, individual shaykhs kept their right to teach at their customary pillar, but collective rights of the madhhabs—which had engendered ugly turf battles—were revoked.[39]

Nevertheless, 'Ali Mubarak does not applaud the changes which have occurred at al-Azhar because very significant problems remain. Students continue to quarrel over places to sit because of overcrowding. Worse still, many Azharis are unaware of the most basic principles of hygiene.[40]

With regard to the system of examination, the *Khitat* mentions that limiting the number admitted to examination has increased students' dedication to their studies. He thus agrees with Gabriel Charmes and Dor Bey, who insist that Europeans who claim that Azhari students are lazy and inattentive are wrong. Dor emphasises this point, saying that Europeans who remark the inattention of Azharis are only observing the results of their own disruptive presence in the mosque. The proof of this is that the students could not possibly memorise the prodigious quantity of texts in which they are trained without consistent attention to their instructors. On the other hand, the European critics opine that the rational faculties are sacrificed in the process: the hypertrophy of the memory has caused the atrophy of reason amongst the scholars and students of al-Azhar.[41]

'Ali Mubarak, on the other hand, moves beyond the issue of the attention or inattention of students, to a criticism of student motivation. He suggests that many students put social advancement ahead of the pursuit of knowledge. Also, al-Azhar's students are so absorbed with esoterica that they are unable to answer the questions of outsiders. Thus, 'Ali Mubarak's remarks stand in sharp contrast to Gabriel Charmes' comments. Unlike Charmes, he does not believe that there is anything praiseworthy about the extraordinary liberty permitted to students at al-Azhar. For 'Ali Mubarak, al-Azhar was an inverted image of the kind of disciplined education he had attempted to establish as a government administrator.[42]

Contrasts, Conclusions, and a Final Question

There are important differences in the views of Gabriel Charmes and 'Ali Mubarak with regard to al-Azhar. To a great extent, these reflect the differences between the writers and their audiences.

For Gabriel Charmes, a political journalist and traveller writing for a European audience, al-Azhar's appeal is located in its picturesque qualities, and in a mythic immutability which makes the visitor feel that he is being transported back to the origins of Islam. Like other Europeans writing about the Middle East, Charmes argues that the main thing lacking is an openness to new ideas of science and social progress. This is the reason for the stagnation of al-Azhar and Islam, contradicting his earlier assertion that al-Azhar is changeless. Charmes ends his discussion of al-Azhar by acknowledging that Islam had at one time possessed a vital force, but that it had ceased to develop and was stagnant. He thus admits to the reality of change in the religion, albeit of a regressive kind. Al-Azhar, representing a petrified Islam, has become an obstacle to the progress of Muslim peoples. Al-Azhar, like Egypt, like Islam, cannot regenerate itself and must be revitalised by the 'mature' powers of Europe. It is the Orientalist position in a nutshell.[43]

For 'Ali Mubarak, an educator and administrator writing for an Egyptian audience, al-Azhar also possesses historical depth. It is, however, a real and documented history. This difference stands out in the treatment of al-Azhar's architecture. For Gabriel Charmes, as for almost all European observers, al-Azhar's architecture holds little interest. For 'Ali Mubarak, on the other hand, its architecture is the nexus which links al-Azhar to the broader history of Egypt. Thus the *Khitat* parades before the reader the great men who built al-Azhar and who devoted their lives and fortunes to its people.[44] The mosque is thus related implicitly, not to Islam as a religion, but to Egypt as a national community—and not indeed to its future, but to its past. Al-Azhar's glory, in the *Khitat*, is the glory of a nation's heritage, and constitutes a title to fame for Egypt throughout the Islamic world.[45]

Unlike Gabriel Charmes, 'Ali Mubarak does not see in al-Azhar a symbol of Islam itself, important as it is for the Islamic world. Al-Azhar is simply an old, tradition-encrusted institution, and its criticism in no way implies criticism of the religion it espouses. 'Ali Mubarak is firmly convinced of the essential rationality of Islam. Like other Islamic modernists, he sees no inherent conflict between the modern sciences developed in Europe and an Islam purged of corrupting accretions.[46] If al-Azhar stands in the way of these adjustments, then it must be replaced. 'Ali Mubarak's life was dedicated to educational projects which were destined to do precisely that.[47]

There is a telling similarity in the views of Charmes and Mubarak, in spite of their other differences. Both are 'outsiders' to al-Azhar, and both conclude that al-Azhar is intellectually static. Is this assessment valid? The question is sharpened if we recall that our authors were writing in the 1870s, a period of significant political and social change in Egypt. Did these currents leave al-Azhar's educational priorities untouched? It is a question which awaits investigation using other sources.

Notes

1 E. W. Lane, *Manners and Customs of the Modern Egyptians* (London, 1836), p. 211.
2 *Description de l'Égypte* , hereinafter *Description*, 22 vols. (Paris, 1809–22).
3 See M. Jomard, 'Description abregée de la ville et de la citadelle du Kaire', *Description: État Moderne*, t. 2, Pt. 2, pp. 579–778 (see esp. pp. 665–8); and M. De Chabrol, 'Essai sur les mœurs des habitans modernes de l'Egypte', *Description Etat Moderne*, t. 2, Pt. 2, pp. 361–526 (see esp. pp. 393–5).
4 Noted by Dr Ayman Fu'ad Sayyid in his Arabic translation of Jomard's article in *Description* entitled *Wasf madinat al-Qahira wa Qal'at al-Jabal* (Cairo, 1988), p. 176, n. 1.
5 'Notes and Views of Egypt and Nubia' (British Museum Library, Add. 34080, vol. I, 39, 173, 215).
6 Lane, *Manners and Customs*, p. 89; more data on al-Azhar as a refuge is given in James Augustus St John, *Egypt and Nubia* (London, 1845), pp. 245–8.
7 Lane, *Manners and Customs*, pp. 88–9, 211–20. Lane's manuscripts in the British Museum Library ('Notes and Views of Egypt and Nubia', Add. 34,080–34,088) contain some additional material on al-Azhar. It should be emphasised that the works of M. Jomard, M. De Chabrol, and E. W. Lane were the product of years of residence in Egypt. Their comments inspired other travel writers; their neglect of al-Azhar was *a fortiori* true of less observant visitors.
8 Peter Clayton, *The Rediscovery of Ancient Egypt* (New York, 1990), pp. 14–50.
9 Leila Ahmed, *Edward W. Lane* (London, 1978), p. 51.
10 Lane, *Manners and Customs*, p. 213; Mary Brodrick (ed.), *A Handbook for Travellers in Lower and Upper Egypt* (London: Murray, 1896), p. 349.
11 Comité de conservation des monuments de l'art arabe, Procès-verbaux, 23 November 1883.
12 Based on Dean MacCannell, *The Tourist: A New Theory of the Leisure Class*

(New York, 1976), pp. 41ff.

13 Seeing the original artefact is an essential part of tourism: 'The rhetoric of tourism is full of manifestations of the importance of the authenticity of the relationship between tourists and what they see' MacCannell, *The Tourist*, p. 14. The 'inauthentic' character of al-Azhar's structure thus detracted from its touristic appeal.

14 Brodrick (ed.), *Handbook* (1896), 349.

15 Assistance from, for example, a local contact familiar with al-Azhar or an analytical study of the institution. Murray's 1896 *Handbook* recommends Edouard Dor Bey's *L'Instruction publique en Égypte* (Paris, 1872), precisely the 'marker' used by Gabriel Charmes, whose work is analysed below.

16 *Al-Khitat al-Tawfiqiyya al-Jadida*, 20 pts., (Bulaq, 1887–88).

17 Donald M. Reid, 'Cultural Imperialism and Nationalism: the Struggle to Define and Control the Heritage of Arab Art in Egypt', *International Journal of Middle East Studies* 24 (February 1992), pp. 57–76. Contrasting the European 'preservationist' approach to monuments with the indigenous attitude, Reid says: 'Egyptians from many walks of life were devoted to the shrines of al-Azhar, Sayyidna Husayn, Sayyida Zaynab ... Such mosques were living centers of worship and study, not museums to represent a dead past for Western tourists.'

18 Gabriel Charmes, *Cinq mois au Caire et dans la Basse-Egypte* (Cairo, 1880), hereinafter *Cinq mois*; his chapter, 'La Mosquée d'El Azhar', is pp. 343–56; an authorised translation into English (with additional notes by the author) was done by William Conn and appeared as *Five Months at Cairo and in Lower Egypt* (London, 1883).

19 Jules Lermina (ed.), *Dictionnaire biographique et bibliographique de la France contemporaine*, 2 vols. (Paris, n.d.), s.v. 'Charmes, Marie-Julien-Joseph-Françise dit Francis'.

20 M. Prevost and Roman d'Amat, *Dictionnaire de biographie française* (Paris, 1956), vol. 8, pp. 599–602 (cited below as *DBF*); J. Vercoutter (ed.), *Livre du centenaire, 1880–1980* (Cairo: I.F.A.O., 1980), pp. vii–viii; Charmes' connection with the preservation of Arab art is in Reid, 'Cultural Imperialism and Nationalism', pp. 60–1.

21 A somewhat unusual stand for a Frenchman in the wake of Britain's occupation of Egypt in 1882: see his *Politique extérieure et coloniale* (Paris, 1885), pp. xiv–xvii.

22 *Cinq mois*, p. 5; *DBF*, 8, p. 601.

23 A full list of his books is in *DBF*, 8, p. 601. Charmes died in 1886.

24 The insurrection was put down by a rain of bombs, after which the mosque was ransacked by French troops. See Christopher Herold, *Bonaparte in Egypt* (London, 1963), pp. 192–7.

25 *Five Months*, pp. 334–5.

26 Edward W. Said, *Orientalism* (New York, 1978), pp. 145, 206, 208.

27 *Cinq mois*, p. 29.

28 Jack Crabbs, *The Writing of History in Nineteenth-Century Egypt* (Cairo, 1984), pp. 109ff.

29 *Khitat* 4, pp. 20–5.

30 *Khitat* 4, pp. 13, 30.

31 *Cinq mois*, p. 350.

32 Ibid., pp. 348–50.
33 Ibid., p. 350.
34 Timothy Mitchell, *Colonising Egypt* (Cambridge, 1988), pp.84–5. Dr Mitchell cites Dor Bey as an example of European criticism of al-Azhar, as discussed below.
35 Dor, *L'Instruction publique*, 153–4.
36 Ibid., 155–6; A. Chris Eccel, *Egypt, Islam, and Social Change: al-Azhar in conflict and accommodation* (Berlin, 1984), 159–62.
37 Cf. the present writer's 'Contradiction and Consciousness in 'Ali Mubarak's Description of al-Azhar', *International Journal of Middle East Studies*, 29 (February 1997), pp. 53–69.
38 *Khitat* 4, p. 41; cited and translated by A. Chris Eccel, *Egypt, Islam, and Social Change*, p. 159.
39 *Khitat* 4, p. 27.
40 *Khitat* 4, pp. 27, 29.
41 *Five Months*, pp. 351–2; Dor, *L'Instruction publique*, p. 164.
42 Gilbert Delanoue, *Moralistes et politiques musulmans dans l'Egypte du XIXe siècle*, 2 vols. (Cairo, 1982), 2, pp. 497–8.
43 *Cinq mois*, pp. 355–6.
44 *Khitat* 4, pp. 10–14.
45 Cf. Reimer, 'Contradiction and Consciousness' pp. 57f.
46 Delanoue, *Moralistes et politiques*, 2, pp. 528–40.
47 Ibid., 2, pp. 507–14.

28 ∾ Some Egyptian Travellers in Europe

Paul Starkey

The inclusion of a paper on Egyptian travellers to Europe in a volume entitled 'Travellers in Egypt' may seem slightly odd. It seems worthwhile, however, both to remind ourselves that travel across the Mediterranean in the nineteenth century (the period on which this volume has concentrated) was not all from West to East, and to make the point that the routes by which cross-cultural influences took effect during this period were more complex than might be apparent from a study of European travellers alone. For the sequence of events given momentum by Napoleon's invasion of Egypt in 1798—with its cultural ramifications in projects such as the Institut d'Égypte and the attendant rise in Western enthusiasm for, and travel to, the country—had a profound effect also both on the development of indigenous Egyptian institutions and on the growth and direction of modern Arabic literature in that country.

The reforms of Muhammad 'Ali, who was able to establish himself as ruler of Egypt in 1805 following the departure of Napoleon's troops, were of course subservient to his political ambitions, and his own interest in Western ideas was largely limited to what they could teach him about government and warfare. But his policies had important cultural side-effects. About fifty primary schools were set up during his reign, together with some higher educational institutions. A printing press was established in 1822, and an official newspaper (*al-Waqa'i' al-Misriyya*) founded six years later. Western books began to be translated into Arabic and Turkish. Foreign instructors, at first mainly Italian but later mostly French, were imported to train the officers, engineers, doctors, administrators and others needed to revitalise the country. Finally—and most importantly from the point of view of the present subject—Egyptian students were dispatched to study in France and Italy, often being required on their return to translate the books from which they had studied.[1] The encounter between East and West embodied in these early educational missions is a perennial theme in modern Arabic literature, and one which has by no means exhausted its potential for development.[2]

It is, therefore, not simply through happy coincidence, but rather a complex set of historical circumstances, that the second half of the 1820s, which saw the great Orientalist Edward Lane in Cairo, also saw the Azharite

280

Rifa'a Rafi' al-Tahtawi (sometimes regarded as the father of modern Arab thought) in Paris, as *imam* to an Egyptian educational mission. In this paper, I propose to look briefly at al-Tahtawi's account of his visit to France, and at those of two later—and rather different—travellers to Paris, 'Ali Mubarak and Muhammad al-Muwaylihi; I shall conclude with some brief observations on how the theme of the 'Egyptian in Paris' (or elsewhere in the West) has been subsequently developed by modern Arabic writers.

Rifa'a Rafi' al-Tahtawi (1801–73) was one of Egypt's most prominent nineteenth-century *'ulama'* (religious officials).[3] Sent to Paris by Muhammad 'Ali for five years from 1826, he developed a deep appreciation of Western and particularly French culture, returning in 1831 to Egypt to begin a distinguished career in public service. Under Muhammad 'Ali he headed both the School of Languages and the Translation Department, whose function was both to teach European languages to Egyptian students, and to translate European works into Arabic. He was also for a time editor of Egypt's first Arabic-language newspaper *al-Waqa'i' al-Misriyya*. His career suffered setbacks at different times, and for some years he was exiled to the Sudan; but he later served as director of no less than five government agencies: the War School, the Translation Department, the School of Accounting, the School of Civil Engineering, and the Buildings Department.

Al-Tahtawi's most lasting service to Egypt was probably as an educator and translator. He and his students spent much time editing and translating into Arabic European works on history, biography, geography, science and engineering. In addition to all this, al-Tahtawi himself composed a number of original literary works in Arabic, including (most important for our present purpose) a work published in 1834 called *Takhlis al-ibriz ila talkhis Bariz* ('The refining of gold for the summary of Paris'—a typical nineteenth-century title), in which he gives an account—perceptive, and often surprisingly sympathetic—of his encounter with French culture.[4] In keeping with al-Tahtawi's primary role as an educator, the work is written for the most part in a straightforward Arabic prose style, its main purpose clearly being to give his fellow-countrymen as much information as possible about European society. After giving a description of the journey from Cairo to Paris, he describes the topography of Paris (with detailed comments on how to pronounce the city's name), the Parisian character, and the system of government in France.[5] Parisians in al-Tahtawi's eyes are distinguished from other Christians by their keen intelligence, and quickness of understanding—in this respect being quite unlike the ignorant and uncurious Copts whom the author had known in Egypt.[6] The French are hospitable, and curious to find out about strangers, though many of their women are distinguished by their lack of faithfulness, and adultery and fornication among them are reckoned only minor faults, especially in the unmarried. In short, 'Paris is a paradise for women, purgatory for men, and hell for horses: the women enjoy good fortune either through their wealth or beauty; the men, caught between the two groups, are slaves to their women, while the horses have to pull the carriages day and night along the paved streets.'[7] After a short description of the French system of government, al-Tahtawi moves on to describe European styles of dress and eating, his intellectual curiosity manifesting itself in his inclusion of not only the French restaurant but also the Parisian system of slaughterhouses, from which his Egyptian servant returned thanking God that he was not a French cow![8] Further chapters deal with the recreations available to the people of Paris—theatres, balls and public parks; with Parisian health care, and with the Catholic religion. A further section of the book details the punishing régime of study which the Egyptian educational mission followed while in Paris, listing the books which al-Tahtawi read on the French language, history, philosophy, mathematics, geography and the like, and including for good measure a selection of correspondence between the author and various learned Frenchmen, among them Silvestre de Sacy.[9] A later section of the work gives a brief account of French political developments since the revolution; after a final section providing some fragments of information on various arts and sciences of the West, the work concludes with al-Tahtawi's return from France to Egypt.[10]

Al-Tahtawi's work is a crucial landmark in the development of modern Arabic literature, for although writers such as the historian al-Jabarti had discussed European ideas on the basis of what he had seen during the French invasion, al-Tahtawi's book is almost certainly the first attempt to describe modern Western civilisation on the basis of an extended period of residence in Europe itself.[11] Although not an uncritical admirer of French society, he is happy to give credit where he believes it is due—comparing Western education, in particular, favourably with that of al-Azhar and other Egyptian institutions, with their emphasis on traditional learning.

Although undistinguished from a literary point of view, al-Tahtawi's work paved the way for other works in similar vein, the most imaginative of which is undoubtedly Faris (later, Ahmad Faris) al-Shidyaq's *al-Saq 'ala al-Saq* ('Leg over leg'), a fictionalised autobiography revolving around the author's travels from Lebanon to Egypt, Malta, France and England.[12] A flamboyant character who is thought to have aspired to the Chairs of Arabic in both Oxford and Cambridge, al-Shidyaq strictly speaking falls outside the scope of this paper, being Lebanese rather than Egyptian. From a literary point of view, however, his work is both unique and ahead of its time; moreover, the fact that the work was itself published in Paris (in 1855), with financial assistance from other members of the Arab community in

France and England, is an interesting indication of the extent to which such communities had by this date become established in both Paris and London.

One of the next significant 'travel books' to Europe by an Egyptian author belongs to 'Ali Mubarak (1823–93) who, like al-Tahtawi, had a distinguished career as an official, serving at various times as Minister of Public Works, Education and Charitable Foundations (Awqaf). Lasting monuments to his energy and influence may be found in the two major institutions which he founded, the Egyptian National Library (Dar al-Kutub) and the Egyptian Teachers' College (Dar al-'Ulum), now a branch of the University of Cairo.

Mubarak's most important literary work is undoubtedly the encyclopedia *al-Khitat al-Tawfiqiyya*, a detailed description of Egypt's topography that runs to twenty volumes. Arranged on the lines of the traditional Islamic *khitat* genre, Mubarak's comprehensive account of the streets, buildings and monuments of contemporary Egypt is a mine of information for nineteenth-century historians. Unfortunately, it has tended to overshadow his other main literary production, *'Alam al-Din*, a four-volume pseudo-fictional work, in which he traces the adventures of an Azharite shaykh (possibly al-Tahtawi himself) who has gone abroad to learn of Europe's ways.[14] In writing this massive work of some 1,400 pages Mubarak was drawing largely on his own experience, having been sent to Europe in 1844 to study for some five years at the Military Academy in Metz as a military engineer. In his introduction, 'Ali Mubarak makes clear that the work is intended to be an educational work, one of its purposes being to compare conditions in the East with those in the West:[15] he has written it as a story, he says, in order to make it more attractive to his readers.

In the book,[16] 'Alam al-Din accompanies an English orientalist (probably modelled on Lane) to Europe, and the work includes an elaborate description of their journey via Alexandria and Marseilles to Paris—a feature which itself recalls al-Tahtawi's earlier work. At each juncture, there is an opportunity to give information about local customs and points of interest: for example, on stopping at Tanta in the Egyptian Delta (famous for its *mawlid*), they discuss different types of festivals in East and West.[17] At times, Mubarak's explanations lapse into the trivial: as this is the first time the shaykh has been in a train, for example, we have an elaborate description of why the bell sounds when the train is about to leave![18] At other times, however, his professional interests show through, and we are treated to weighty expositions—for example, on the development of the steam engine or the building of the pyramids. In Paris itself, the two travellers visit various institutions of social and cultural significance, including the Bourse, banks, a theatre, a public library, a hospital and so on.[19] Although the aim is primarily an educational one, the work is also interesting from a literary point of view, as being arguably the first modern Arabic work in which the action is advanced largely by means of dialogue; moreover, although the technique is rather crude, the use of fictional characters within a narrative framework for the purpose of social criticism undoubtedly pointed the way for many later writers. If when reading the *Khitat* we occasionally have the impression that we are faced with a relic from an older literary tradition, with *'Alam al-Din* we have certainly entered a more modern world.

Unlike al-Tahtawi and 'Ali Mubarak—public figures of some eminence as well as writers—the importance of the third author to be discussed is almost entirely literary. Muhammad al-Muwaylihi was born in Cairo, probably in 1858, and was educated privately there. Banished from Egypt in 1882 for distributing political pamphlets at the time of the Urabi rebellion, he joined his father in Italy, and later travelled with him to France and England. After spending several years in Istanbul, he returned to Cairo in 1887, where he resumed his career as a journalist. He died in 1930, after a long period in semi-retirement.[20]

Al-Muwaylihi's reputation today rests mainly on the composition of one of the pioneering works of modern Arabic fiction, *Hadith 'Isa ibn Hisham* (a title that evokes one of the most famous works of classical Arabic literature, the *Maqamat* of al-Hamadhani), which originally appeared in article form over a number of years from 1898 onwards under the title 'Fatra min al-zaman' ('A Period of Time'). Appearing for the first time in book form in 1907, the work is structured around a Minister of War from the time of Muhammad 'Ali, Ahmad Pasha al-Manikali, who is resurrected from the grave and who makes the acquaintance of the narrator, 'Isa ibn Hisham, a contemporary Egyptian, who serves as his guide to a Cairo which is rapidly becoming transformed into a cosmopolitan metropolis with an administration heavily indebted to French and British influence.

Al-Muwaylihi's work thus serves both as a work of social criticism and as a pivotal literary creation, standing as it does between the classical Arabic tradition of the *maqamat*, and the modern Arabic tradition heavily indebted to Western forms of the novel, short story etc. For present purposes its most interesting feature is not only that the work as a whole functions as a *critique* of the influence of Western culture on traditional Egyptian society, but also that the final part of the book, as it appeared in later editions, contains a sort of appendix entitled *al-Rihla al-thaniya* ('the second journey'), in which the author describes the visit made by himself to the Great Paris Exhibition of 1900, following a visit to England in the same year when he covered the Khedive's state visit.[21] We find here little about Paris itself, and much of what there is is rather conventional: crowds, bright lights, houses which reach the skies, a comparison of the Eiffel Tower with the Tower of Babel, and a Frenchman sitting at a café table with a glass of wine in one hand and an evening newspaper in the other. Much of the description is devoted to the Exhibition itself (for which a French Orientalist serves as a guide), and in particular to the Egyptian exhibit, where, in a chapter entitled 'Slandering the homeland', al-Muwaylihi describes the shame of seeing a lewd collection of belly-dancers, followed by a tableau depicting a traditional school, with a schoolmaster drumming Qur'anic verses into the pupils while beating them with palm leaves, while the visitors to the Exhibition mock and jeer at the state of education in Egypt. When the group moves on to an exhibit of an armless girl spinning with her feet, they can stand it no longer, and leave the Egyptian exhibit, which has brought their nation into such disgrace: questioning one of their countrymen about the reasons for this shameful display, they are told that, since the Egyptian government declined to respond to the official invitation, the exhibition has been organised for profit by a group of European 'Orientalists' resident in Egypt in conjunction with some worthless Egyptians.[22]

In devoting such a large proportion of his 'Second Journey' to a description of the Great Exhibition, al-Muwaylihi was following a well-trodden path, for, as Timothy Mitchell points out in his book *Colonising Egypt*, 'of the eight works published in Cairo during the last ten years of the nineteenth century describing the countries and ideas of Europe, five were accounts of a trip to an Orientalist congress or a world exhibition'.[23] In this respect, perhaps, *Hadith 'Isa ibn Hisham* stands at the end of an era. In other respects, however, the work stands at the beginning of a new period in the development of modern Arabic literature—for the themes of the impact of Western culture on traditional society, and the clash between Eastern and Western values, have proved to be among the most fertile in the history of the twentieth-century Arabic novel and short story. The Egyptian, or Arab, student who goes to the West to pursue his studies, and whose life is thereby both challenged and changed, is a recurrent figure in the works of later twentieth-century writers, not only from Egypt but from other parts of the Arab world: the Egyptian Tawfiq al-Hakim, the Lebanese Suhayl Idris, or the Sudanese al-Tayyib Salih. In this respect, the cultural shock-waves of the enterprise which forms the main subject of this volume have had effects that none of the participants could have foreseen: not only has the West's perception of the East been changed, but the East's perception both of the West and of itself.

Notes

1 On the general background, see A. Hourani, *Arabic Thought in the Liberal Age 1798–1939* (London: Oxford University Press, 1970), especially chapter 3; M. Daly (ed.), *Cambridge History of Egypt*, vol. 2 (Cambridge: Cambridge University Press, 1998) (forthcoming).

2 On this general theme, cf. Issa J. Boullata, 'Encounter between East and West: a theme in contemporary Arabic novels', *Middle East Journal* 30: 1 (1976), pp. 49–62; Nedal M. Al-Mousa, 'The Arabic *Bildungsroman*: a generic appraisal', *IJMES* 25 (1993), pp. 223–40.

3 On al-Tahtawi generally, see Hourani, *Arabic Thought*, pp. 67–83; Jack A. Crabbs, Jr., *The Writing of History in Nineteenth-Century Egypt* (Detroit: Wayne State University Press, 1984), pp. 67–86; Israel Altman, 'The Political Thought of Rifa'ah Rafi' al-Tahtawi, a Nineteenth Century Egyptian Reformer', unpublished Ph.D. thesis, University of California, Los Angeles, 1976.

4 References in the present paper are to the Cairo: Dar al-Taqaddum ed., 1323/ 1905. A French translation by A. Louca, entitled *L'Or de Paris*, was published in Paris in 1988.

5 Tahtawi, *Takhlis*, pp. 25–95.

6 Ibid., p. 60.

7 Ibid., p. 66.

8 Ibid., pp. 102–5.

9 Ibid., pp. 178–84.

10 Ibid., pp. 245–63.

11 For al-Jabarti (1753–1825) and his account of the French invasion, see *al-Jabarti's Chronicle of the First Seven Months of the French Occupation of Egypt* ..., ed. and tr. by S. Moreh (Leiden: Brill, 1975).

12 The full title is *al-Saq 'ala al-Saq fi ma huwa al-Firyaq* (Paris: Benjamin Duprat, 1855). On this work, see Mattityahu Peled, '*al-Saq 'ala al-Saq*: a Generic Definition', *Arabica* XXXII (1985), pp. 31–46; Paul Starkey, 'Fact and Fiction in *al-Saq 'ala al-Saq*', in R. Ostle, E. de Moor & S. Wild (eds), *Writing the Self in Modern Arabic Literature* (London: Saqi, 1998) (forthcoming).

13 *al-Khitat al-Tawfiqiyya al-Jadida*, 20 pts (Bulaq, 1887–88). For Mubarak generally, and the *Khitat* in particular, see Crabbs, *History*, pp. 109–19; S. Fliedner, *'Ali Mubarak und seine Hitat* (Islamkundliche Untersuchungen, 140) (Berlin: Schwarz, 1990).

14 *Kitab 'Alam al-Din*, 4 vols (Alexandria, 1882). An indication of the extent to which it has been eclipsed by Mubarak's other work is that it receives not a single mention in the *Encyclopaedia of Islam* entry for Mubarak.

15 *'Alam al-Din*, vol. 1, pp. 5–8.

16 For a general discussion, see Ghislaine Alleaume, 'L'Orientaliste dans le miroir de la littérature arabe', *British Society for Middle Eastern Studies Bulletin* 9:1 (1982), pp. 5–13.

17 *'Alam al-Din*, pp. 132–63.

18 Ibid., pp. 88–132.

19 Ibid., vol. 4, pp. 1253 ff.

20 For al-Muwaylihi generally, see Roger Allen, *A Period of Time* (Exeter: Ithaca Press, 1992).

21 These chapters were added from the 4th edition onwards (Cairo: Matba'at Misr, 1927), after *Hadith 'Isa ibn Hisham* had been adopted as a school textbook. See Allen, *Period*, pp. 41–4.

22 al-Muwaylihi, *Hadith*, p. 325ff.

23 Timothy Mitchell, *Colonising Egypt* (Berkeley: University of California Press, 1991), p. 180.

∾ Select Bibliography

Where appropriate, Paris and London have been omitted as places of publication for French and English publications respectively.

Abbadie, Jeanne Vandier *d'Nestor L'Hôte (1804–1842)* (Leiden, 1963).
— 'Lettre inédite de Nestor L'Hôte' in *Bulletin de la Société française d'égyptologie* (Dec. 1962).
Abu-Lughod, Janet. *Cairo: 1001 Years of the City Victorious* (Princeton: Princeton University Press, 1971).
Ackerman, Gerald. *The Life and Work of Jean-Léon Gérôme, with a Catalogue raisonné* (London & Paris, 1986).
Adams, W. Y. *Nubia: Corridor to Africa* (Princeton: Princeton University Press, 1977).
Ahmed, Leila. *Edward W. Lane: A Study of His Life and Works and of British Ideas of the Middle East in the Nineteenth Century* (London & New York: Longman & Librairie du Liban, 1978).
Alf Layla wa-Layla. (ed.) 'Abd al-Rahman al-Sharqawi (Bulaq, 1251 [1835]).
[*Alf Layla wa-Layla.*] *The Thousand and One Nights, Commonly Called, in England, The Arabian Nights' Entertainments. A New Translation from the Arabic, With Copious Notes, by E. W. Lane* (1839–41), 3 vols, a new edition, (ed.) Edward Stanley Poole (1882).
[*Alf Layla wa-Layla.*] *The Book of the Thousand Nights and a Night.* Translated from the Arabic by Sir R. F. Burton. (ed.) L. C. Smithers. Library edition (1894), 12 vols.
[*Alf Layla wa-Layla.*] *The Thousand and One Nights (Alf Layla wa-Layla) from the Earliest Known Sources.* Arabic text edited with introduction & notes by Muhsin Mahdi. *Kitab Alf Layla wa-Layla min usulihi al-'Arabiyya al-ula, haqqaqahu wa-qaddama lahu wa-'allaqa 'alayhi Muhsin Mahdi* (Leiden, 1984–).
'Ali, Muhsin Jassim. *Scheherazade in England: A Study of Nineteenth-Century English Criticism of the Arabian Nights* (Washington, 1981).
Allen, Roger. *A Period of Time* (Exeter: Ithaca Press, 1992).
Alleaume, Ghislaine. 'L'Orientaliste dans le miroir de la littérature arabe', *British Society for Middle Eastern Studies Bulletin* 9:1 (1982), 5–13.

Altman, Israel. 'The Political Thought of Rifa'ah Rafi' al-Tahtawi, a Nineteenth Century Egyptian Reformer', unpublished Ph. D. thesis, University of California, Los Angeles, 1976.

Amin, Ahmad. *Qamus al-'adat wa-al-taqalid wa-al-ta'abir al-Misriyya* (Cairo, 1953).

'Ancient buildings at Cairo', *The Saturday Review* (3 Sept. 1892), 277–78.

Anderson, Robert & Ibrahim Fawzy (eds). *Egypt in 1800: Scenes from Napoleon's Description de l'Égypte* (London: a. privately published & b. Barrie & Jenkins; Cairo: AUC Press [as *Egypt Revealed: Scenes from Napoleon's Description de l'Égypte*], 1987).

al-'Aqiqi, Najib. *Al-Mustashriqun* (Beirut, 1937).

Arberry, A. J. *British Orientalists* (William Collins, 1943).

— 'The Lexicographer: Edward William Lane' in his *Oriental Essays: Portraits of Seven Scholars* (George Allen & Unwin, 1960), 87–121.

Artin, Yacoub. 'Lettres inédites du Dr Perron à M. J. Mohl', *Bulletin de l'Institut Égyptien*, 5th ser. , iii, 2nd fasc. (Cairo, 1909).

Arundale, Francis. *Illustrations of Jerusalem and Mt. Sinai, Including the Most Interesting Sites between Grand Cairo and Beyrout* (Henry Colburn, 1837).

al-Asad, Mohammed. 'The Mosque of al-Rifa'i in Cairo', *Muqarnas* 10 (1993),108–24.

Asad, Talal. *Anthropology and the Colonial Encounter* (New York: Humanities Press, 1975).

Asfour, Khaled. 'The Domestication of Knowledge: Cairo at the Turn of the Century', *Muqarnas* 10 (1993), 125–37.

Audouard, Olympe *Les Mystères de l'Egypte dévoilés* (Dentu, 1867).

Avennes, E. Prisse d'. *Miscellanea Hieroglyphica ou Études sur l'histoire, la religion et la langue des anciens égyptiens* (Alexandria: P. R. Wilkinson, 1843).

Baedeker, Karl. *Egypt and the Sûdan: A Handbook for Travellers*, 7th Remodelled Edition (Leipzig: Karl Baedeker; London: T. Fisher Unwin; New York: Charles Scribner's Sons, 1914).

Balboni, L. A. *Gli Italiani nella Civiltà Egiziana del Secolo XIX* (Alexandria, 1906).

Baldwin, George. *Political Recollections Relative to Egypt, Containing Observations on its Government under the Mamlukes* (1802).

— *Speculations on the Situation and Resources of Egypt*, a pamphlet. *Published in Two Editions in 1801 and 1802 under the title of Political Recollections Relative to Egypt containing Observations on its Government Under the Mamlukes.*

Bankes, W. J. (ed.). *Narrative of the Life and Adventures of Giovanni Finati* (1830).

Bartlett, William H. *The Nile Boat* (1850).

Baudson, Émile & Henri Labaste. *Un artiste ardennais: le peintre J. B. Couvelet et son temps (1772–1830)* (Mézières-Charleville, 1934).

Bellori, G. P. in *Viaggi di Pietro Della Valle il Pellegrino, Parte Prima* (Rome: 1662).

Belzoni, Giovanni B. *Narrative of the Operations and Recent Discoveries within the Pyramids, Temples, Tombs, and Excavations, in Egypt and Nubia, etc.* (1820).

— *Forty-four Plates Illustrative of the Research and Operations of G. Belzoni in Egypt and Nubia* (1820).

— *Six New Plates* (1822).

Belzoni, Sarah. *Mrs Belzoni's Trifling Account in Giovanni Belzoni's Narrative* (1820).

Bendiner, Kenneth P. 'The portrayal of the Middle East in British Painting, 1825–1860' Ph. D. thesis, Columbia University (1979).

Behdad, A. *Belated Travelers: Orientalism in the Age of Colonial Dissolution* (Durham: Duke University Press, 1994).

Bierbrier, M. L. (ed.), *Who Was Who in Egyptology*, 3rd revised edition (EES, 1995).

Bird, Michael. *Samuel Shepheard of Cairo. A Portrait* (Michael Joseph, 1957).

Bonomi, Joseph & Sharpe, Samuel. *The Alabaster Sarcophagus of Oinemepthah I, King of Egypt, now in Sir John Soane's Museum* (1864).

Borruso, A. 'Viaggi e scritti sull'Egitto di Edward William Lane', *Islam: Storia e Civiltà* 6 (1987), 41–47.

Boullata, Issa J. 'Encounter Between East and West: A Theme in Contemporary Arabic novels', *Middle East Journal* 30: 1 (1976), 49–62.

Braunlich, E. 'Zu Lane Sp. 371A und 414b', *Islamica* 3 (1927), 273–74.

Brodrick, Mary (ed.). *A Handbook for Travellers in Lower and Upper Egypt* (Murray, 1896).

Bruneau, J. *Le 'Conte oriental' de Flaubert* (Denoël, 1973).

Bull, Deborah & Lorimer, Donald. *Up the Nile: A Photographic Excursion: Egypt 1839–1898* (New York: Clarkson N. Potter, 1979).

Burckhardt, John Lewis. *Arab Proverbs; or the Manners and Customs of the Modern Egyptians Illustrated from their Proverbial Sayings current at Cairo, translated and explained*, (ed.) Sir William Ousely (H. Colburn, 1830). Reprinted with an introduction by C. E. Bosworth (Curzon Press, 1984).

Burford, Robert. *Description of a View of the Great Temple of Karnak, and the Surrounding City of Thebes, Now Exhibiting at the Panorama, Broadway, Corner of Prince and Mercer Streets, New York. Painted by Robert Burford, from Drawings Taken in 1834, by F. Catherwood* (1839; reprinted at San Antonio: Van Siclen Books, 1988).

Burton, Sir Richard *Personal Narrative of a Pilgrimage to al-Madinah and Meccah*, 2 vols (New York: Dover, 1855/1964).

Buttet, Xavier de. 'Nestor L'Hôte' in *Bulletin de la Société historique de Haute Picardie*, XII (1934).

Bystroń, Jan St. *Polacy w Ziemi Świvtej, Syrti i Egipcie* (Kraków: 1930).

Cadalvène, E. de. *L'Égypte et la Turquie* (1836).

Camp, Maxime Du. *Égypte, Nubie, Palestine et Syrie* (1852).

— *Le Nil* (Bourdillat, 1854).

Canivet, R. G. 'La bibliothèque de l'expédition', *Revue internationale d'Égypte* 4: 4–5 (Aug–Sept 1906), 122–23.

Carré, Jean-Marie. *Voyageurs et écrivains français en Égypte*, 2ᵉ edition (Cairo: IFAO, 1988, first published 1932; 2nd edition, 1956).

Černý, J. *Egyptian Stelae in the Bankes Collection* (Oxford: 1958).

Charbol de Volvic, Gilbert-Joseph-Gaspard de, comte. 'Essai sur les mœurs des habitans modernes de l'Égypte', *Description de l'Égypte*, no. 109, *État Moderne*, sixième partie, II [first edition], 2 (suite) (Imprimerie nationale, 1822), 361–526.

Champollion, J.-F. *Lettres écrites d'Égypte et de Nubie en 1828 et 1829* (1833).

Charmes, Gabriel. *Cinq mois au Caire et dans la Basse-Égypte* (Cairo, 1880), tr. by William Conn, *Five Months at Cairo and in Lower Egypt* (1883).

Chevedden, P. 'Making Light of Everything: Early Photography of the Middle East and Current Photomania', *MESA Bulletin* 18 (1984), 151–74.

Childe, Blanche de Triqueti. *Un Hiver au Caire. Journal de voyage en Egypte par Mme. Lee Childe* (Calmann Levy, 1883).

Clayton, Peter A. *The Rediscovery of Ancient Egypt: Artists and Travellers in the Nineteenth Century* (1982, repr. 1985, 1990, 1996).

Clément, R. *Les Français en Egypte aux XVIIe et XVIIIe siècles* (Cairo: IFAO, 1960).

Colet, Louise. *Les Pays lumineux. Voyage en Orient* (Dentu, 1879).

Colin, Auguste. *Compagnie de l'Isthme de Suez* (Renouard, 1846).

— *Percement de l'Isthme de Suez. Création de la première route universelle sur le globe* (Librairie Phalanstérienne, 1847).

Conner, P. (ed.), *The Inspiration of Egypt* (Brighton, exhibition catalogue, 1983).

Contemporaine, La (pseud. of Ida Saint-Elme, *aka* Maria Elzelina Johanna Versfelt & as Elzelina Van Aylde Jonge). *La Contemporaine en Egypte* (Ladvocat, 1831).

Crabbs, Jr. Jack A. *The Writing of History in Nineteenth-Century Egypt* (Detroit: Wayne State University Press, 1984).

Cumming, Constance Gordon. *Via Cornwall to Egypt* (1885).

Daly, M. (ed.), *Cambridge History of Egypt*, vol. 2 (Cambridge: Cambridge University Press, 1998) (forthcoming).

Damer, Georgina. *Diary of a Tour in Greece, Turkey, Egypt and the Holy Land* (1841).

Damiani, Anita. *Enlightened Observers: British Travellers to the Near East 1715–1855* (Beirut: AUB, 1979).

Daniel, Norman. 'Orientalism Again' [The Antonius Lecture for 1987], in (ed.) Hopwood, 175–89.

Dauzats, Adrien & Alexandre Dumas. *Nouvelles impressions de voyage. Quinze jours au Sinaï* (1839).

Dawson, Warren R. & Uphill, Eric P. *Who Was Who in Egyptology: A Biographical Index of Egyptologists, of Travellers, Explorers, and Excavators in Egypt, of Collectors of and Dealers in Egyptian Antiquities; of Consuls, Officials, Authors, Benefactors, and Others Whose Names Occur in the Literature of Egyptology, from the Year 1500 to the Present Day, But Excluding Persons Now Living* 2nd edition (EES, 1972).

Delanoue, Gilbert. *Moralistes et politiques musulmans dans l'Egypte du XIXe siècle*, 2 vols (Cairo, 1982).

Denny, Walter B. 'Quotations In and Out of Context: Ottoman Turkish Art and European Orientalist Painting' in *Muqarnas* 10 (1993), 220–30.

Denon, Baron Dominique Vivant (-). *Voyage dans la Basse et Haute-Égypte pendant les campagnes du général Bonaparte* (Didot, 3 vols, 1802), tr. *Travel in Upper and Lower Egypt* (1902).

'Die beiden ägyptischen Gesellschaften', *Zeitschrift der deutschen Morgenländischen Gesellschaft* i (1847), 206.

Dodwell, H. H. *The Founder of Modern Egypt* (Cambridge, 1931).

Dor Bey, Edouard. *L'Instruction publique en Egypte* (1872).

Eccel, A. Chris. *Egypt, Islam, and Social Change: al-Azhar in Conflict and Accommodation* (Berlin, 1984).

Edwards, Amelia. *One Thousand Miles up the Nile* (1877) (reissued by Virago).

Edwards, I. E. S. 'The Bankes Papyri I and II', *The Journal of Egyptian Archaeology* 68 (1982), 126ff.

Elwood, Anne Katherine (Mrs Colonel). *Narrative of a Journey Overland by the Continent of Europe, Egypt and the Red Sea to India, Including a Residence There and a Voyage Home, 1825–1828* (1830).

— *Memoirs of the Literary Ladies of England from the Commencement of the Last Century* (1841).

Enkiri, Gabriel. *Ibrahim Pacha (1789–1848)* (Cairo, 1948).

Fagan, Brian. *The Rape of the Nile: Tomb Robbers, Tourists, and Archaeologists in Egypt* (1977).

Fahim, Hussein. *Travel Literature: An Ethnographic Perspective* (in Arabic) (Kuwait: National Council for Culture, Arts, and Letters, 1989).

Fathy, Hassan. *Architecture for the Poor* (Chicago, 1973).

Fay, Eliza. *Original Letters from India Containing a Narrative of a Journey Through Egypt, 1779–1815*, ed. E. M. Forster (reissued: Hogarth Press, 1986).

Felix, Orlando. *Notes on Hieroglyphs* (1830).

Feydeau, Ernest. *Histoire des usages funèbres et des sépultures des peuples anciens* (1856).

Flaubert, Gustave. *Correspondance* I, (ed.) Jean Bruneau (NRF Gallimard, Bibliothèque de la Pléiade, 1973).

— *Voyage en Egypte* (ed.) Pierre-Marc de Biasi (Grasset, 1991).

Fliedner, S. *'Ali Mubarak und seine Hitat* (Islamkundliche Untersuchungen, 140) (Berlin: Schwarz, 1990).

Forni, G. *Viaggio nell'Egitto e nell'Alta Nubia* (Milan, 1859).

Frith, Francis. *Egypt and Palestine Photographed and Described by Francis Frith*, 2 vols (1858–60). Issued in 25 parts; 76 albumen prints, 225 x 165 mm.

— 'The Art of Photography', *The Art Journal* 21 (1 Mar 1859), 71–72.

— *Cairo, Sinai, Jerusalem, and the Pyramids of Egypt: A Series of Sixty Photographic Views by Francis Frith. With Descriptions by Mrs. Poole and Reginald Stuart Poole* (1860, 1861). Issued in 20 parts; 60 albumen prints, approx. 225 x 165 mm.

— *Egypt, Sinai, and Jerusalem: A Series of Twenty Photographic Views by Francis Frith. With Descriptions by Mrs. Poole and Reginald Stuart Poole* (1860). 20 albumen prints, approx. 380 x 480 mm. Republished (1862). Issued in 10 parts.

— *The Holy Bible: Illustrated with Photographic Views of Biblical Scenery from Nature by Frith* (1862). 20 albumen prints, 225 x 165 mm.

— *Egypt, Nubia, and Ethiopia: Illustrated by One Hundred Stereoscopic Photographs, Taken by Francis Frith for Messrs. Negretti and Zambra. With Descriptions and Numerous Wood Engravings, by Joseph Bonomi and Notes by Samuel Sharpe* (1862). 100 albumen stereo pairs.

— *The Holy Bible: Containing the Old and New Testaments Illustrated with Photographs by Frith* (Glasgow, 1862–63). 56 albumen prints, 225 x 165 mm.

— *Egypt, Sinai and Palestine, Supplementary Volume* (1862). Vol. 1, *Sinai and Palestine*. Vol. 2, *Lower Egypt, Thebes and the Pyramids*. Vol. 3, *Upper Egypt and Ethiopia*. Four-volume series; total of 148 albumen prints, 225 x 165 mm; text by Frith.

— *Egypt and the Holy Land in Historic Photographs: 77 Views by Francis Frith*, Introduction & Bibliography by Julia van Haaften; Selection & Commentary by Jon E. Manchip White (New York, 1980).

Gann, Andrew. 'Les Orients musicaux de Théophile Gautier', *Bulletin de la Société Théophile Gautier* 12 (1990), 35–49.

[Gautier, Théophile]. 'Un Repas au désert de l'Égypte', *Le Gastronome* (Thursday, 24 Mar 1831).

Gautier, Théophile. 'Variétés. Collection égyptienne de M. Mimaut', *La Presse* (19 Dec. 1837).

—— 'Statues de la Place de la Concorde', *La Presse* (14 Aug. 1838).

—— 'Une Nuit de Cléopâtre', *La Presse* (29, 30 Nov. & 1, 2, 4, 6 Dec. 1838).

—— 'Le Pied de momie', *Le Musée des Familles* (Sept. 1840).

—— 'La Mille et deuxième nuit', *Le Musée des Familles* (Aug. 1842).

—— Obituary of Marilhat, *Revue des Deux mondes* (1 July 1848).

—— 'Nostalgies d'obélisques', *La Presse* (4 Aug. 1851).

—— *Égypte, Nubie, Palestine et Syrie* (Gide & J. Baudry, 1852, 2 vols in-folio).

—— 'Panorama de la bataille des Pyramides', *La Presse* (23 Mar 1853).

—— *Le Roman de la momie* (1858).

—— 'Une échappée dans le bleu' (Le Fayoum, le Sinaï et Petra, par Paul Lenoir), *Gazette de Paris* (30 Jan. 1872), reprinted as 'Le Fayoum, le Sinaï et Petra', *L'Orient* II, 229–44.

—— *L'Orient* II (Charpentier, 1877).

—— *Correspondance générale* t. I–X (Geneva: Droz, 1985–96)[continuing].

—— *Voyage en Égypte* (La Boîte à Documents, 1991).

Glinel, C. *Alexandre Dumas et son oeuvre; notes biographiques et bibliographiques* (Geneva: Sladkine, 1967).

Goldziher, I. 'Al-Dasuki, al-Sayyid Ibrahim b. Ibrahim', *Encyclopaedia of Islam*. New edition, vol. II (Leiden & London, 1965), 167.

Gordon, Lucie Duff. *Letters from Egypt and Last Letters from Egypt* (1865) (re-issued by Virago).

Gosselin-Schick, Constance. 'Nostalgies d'obélisques', *Bulletin de la Société Théophile Gautier* 12 (1990), 261–71.

Grossier, Claudine. *L'Islam des Romantiques: 1811–1840* (Éditions Maisonneuve et Larose, 1984).

Haaften, Julia Van. 'Introduction and Bibliography' in *Egypt and the Holy Land in Historic Photographs. 77 Views by Francis Frith*, selection & commentary by Jon D. Mandchip White (New York, 1980).

—— 'Francis Frith's Grand Tour', *Portfolio* 2 (1980), 56–61.

Hagen, Victor W. von. *Frederick Catherwood Arch!* (New York: OUP, 1950).

—— *F. Catherwood: Architect-Explorer of Two Worlds* (Barre, Massachussetts: Barre Publishers, 1968).

[Hali] Burton, James. *Excerpta Hieroglyphica*, in four parts (Cairo, 1825–28).

Hall, Richard. *Lovers on the Nile* (Collins, 1980).

Halliday, Fred. '"Orientalism" and its Critics', *British Journal of Middle Eastern Studies* 20 ii (1993), 145–63.

Halls, J. J. *The Life and Correspondence of Henry Salt, Esq.* (1830).

Harlé, Diane. 'Nestor L'Hôte, dessinateur de Champollion: deux albums inédits d'aquarelles et de dessins', *La Revue du Louvre et des Musées de France* 4 (Oct 1990).

—— 'Le Ramesseum de Nestor L'Hôte', *Memnonia* I (Cairo, 1990–91).

—— 'Aquarelles et dessins inédits de Nestor L'Hôte, dessinateur et campagnon de Champollion' , *Actes du Colloque international célébrant le bicentenaire de la naissance de Jean-François Champollion, «l'Egyptologie et Champollion»*, Grenoble, 29 Nov.–1ᵉʳ Dec. 1990 (Grenoble, 1994).

— 'Nestor L'Hôte, ami et compagnon de Champollion', *Atti VI Congresso internazionale di eggitologia* (Turin, 1993).

Harlé, Diane & Jean Lefebvre. 'Nestor L'Hôte', *Souvenirs de voyage. Autographes et dessins français du XIXe siècle* (27 Feb–18 May 1992).

— *Sur le Nil avec Champollion. Lettres, journaux et dessins inédits de Nestor L'Hôte. Premier voyage en Egypte 1828–1830*. Preface by Christiane Ziegler (Caen-Orléans: Éditions Paradigme, 1993).

Hay, Robert. *Illustrations of Cairo* (Tilt & Bogue, 1840).

Herold, J. Christopher. *Bonaparte in Egypt* (Hamish Hamilton, 1963).

Heyworth-Dunne, J. *An Introduction to the History of Education in Modern Egypt* (1968).

Hopwood, Derek. *Studies in Arab History: the Antonius lectures, 1978–87* (London: Macmillan in association with St Antony's College and World of Islam Festival Trust, 1990).

Horeau, Hector. 'Nestor L'Hôte', *La Revue de l'Orient*, Notices biographiques (1843–46).

Hoskins, G. A. *Visit to the Great Oasis of the Libyan Desert* (Longman, Rees, Orme, Brown, Green, & Longman, 1837).

——— *A Winter in Upper and Lower Egypt* (Hurst & Blackett, 1863).

Hoskins, H. *British Routes to India* (1928).

Hourani, A. *Arabic Thought in the Liberal Age 1798–1939* (London: OUP, 1970).

Ilbert, Robert. 'Heliopolis: Colonial enterprise and Town Planning Success?', *The Expanding Metropolis Coping with the Urban Grown of Cairo*, Proceedings of Seminar 9, 'Architectural Transformations in the Islamic World', held in Cairo, 11–15 Nov. 1984, Aga Khan Award for Architecture (Singapore, 1985), 36–42.

Ilbert, Robert & Mercedes Volait, 'Neo-Arabic Renaissance in Egypt, 1870–1930', *Mimar* 13 (1984), 26–34.

Irby, Charles Leonard & Mangles, James. *Travels in Egypt, Nubia, Syria, and Asia Minor in 1817 and 1818* (London: Privately printed, 1821).

— *Travels in Egypt, Nubia, Syria, and Asia Minor during the years 1817 and 1818* (T. White & Co., Printers, 1823).

— *Travels in Egypt, Nubia, Syria and the Holy Land*. Popular edition (John Murray, 1844).

— *Travels in Egypt, Syria and the Holy Land* (John Murray, 1845. Reprint Darf Publishers Ltd., n. d.).

Ivray, Jehan d'. (pseud. for Mlle. Jeanne Puech-d'Alissac, married name Mme. Sélim Fahmy-Bey, husband's title 'Bey'). *Au Cœur du harem* (F. Juven, 1911).

— *Bonaparte et l'Egypte* (A. Lemerre, 1914).

— *L'Aventure Saint-Simonienne et les femmes* (Alcan, 1928).

Jabarti, 'Abd al-Rahman al-. *'Aja'ib al-athar fi al tarajim wa-al-akhbar*, in 4 vols (Bulaq, 1297/1879–1880), vol. 2. Tr. as *Merveilles biographiques et historiques* …tr. Chefik Mansour Bey, Abdulaziz Khalil Bey, Gabriel Nicolas Khalil Bey & Iskender Ammoun Effendi (Cairo: Imprimerie nationale, 1888).

— *al-Ta'rikh al-Musamma 'Aja'ib al-Athar fi al-Tarajim wa-al-Akhbar* (Cairo, 1322).

— *al-Jabarti's Chronicle of the First Seven Months of the French Occupation of Egypt* ..., ed. & tr. S. Moreh (Leiden: Brill, 1975).

James, T. G. H. 'Egyptian Antiquities at Kingston Lacy, Dorset', *KMT. A Modern Journal of Ancient Egypt* 4: 4 (San Francisco: Winter 1993–94).

Jomard, Edmé-François. *Voyage à l'Oasis de Syouah* (1823).

Jomard, Edmé-François et al. Commission des sciences et des arts. *Description de l'Égypte, ou recueil des observations et des recherches qui ont été faites en Égypte pendant l'expédition de l'armée française.* First edition (Imprimerie impériale/Imprimerie royale, 1809–1822), 20 vols [plus full-folio plates]. Second edition (C. F. L. Panckoucke, 1821–1829), 37 vols [plus full-folio plates & Atlas].

— "Observations sur plusieurs usages du Kaire", in 'Description de la ville et de la citadelle du Kaire, accompagné de l'explication des plans de cette ville et de ses environs, et des renseignements, sur sa distribution, ses monuments, sa population, son commerce et son industrie. ' *Description de l'Égypte* 112, Chapitre III, §VIII, *État moderne*, sixième partie, II [first edition], 2 (suite) (Imprimerie nationale, 1822), 731–40.

— 'Description abregée de la ville et de la citadelle du Kaire', *Description: État Moderne*, t. 2, Pt. 2, 579–778, translated into Arabic by Ayman Fu'ad Sayyid, *Wasf madinat al-Qahira wa Qal'at al-Jabal* (Cairo, 1988).

Jorrand, Caroline & Jean Lefebvre. *Nestor L'Hôte. Voyages sur le Nil avec Champollion,* Catalogue de l'exposition réalisé par la Bibliothèque municipale et le Musée de Laon (13 Oct 1990–5 Jan 1991).

Jourda, P. *Exotisme dans la littérature française depuis Chateaubriand* (Boivin, 1938).

Kabbani, Rana. *Europe's Myths of Orient* (Bloomington: Indiana University Press, 1986).

— *Imperial Fictions: Europe's Myths of Orient* (Pandora, 1994).

Kákosy, L. *Dzsehutimesz sírja Thébában* (Budapest, 1989).

Kalfatovic, Martin R. *Nile Notes of a Howadji: A Bibliography of Travellers' Tales from Egypt, from the Earliest Time to 1918* (Metuchen, New Jersey & London: The Scarecrow Press, 1992).

Karig, J. S. & R. Leive, *Auf der Suche nach der »Gottfried« und der Sammlung Minutoli* (Jahrbuch Preußischer Kulturbesitz XXX, Berlin, 1993), 133–53.

Koppelkamm, Stefan. *Der imaginaire Orient: Exotische Bauten des achtezehneten und neuzehnten Jahrhunderts in Europa* (Berlin, 1987).

Krek, M. 'E. W. Lane's working copy of his lexicon', *Journal of the American Oriental Society* 89 (1969), 419–20.

Laborde, Léon Emmanuel Simon Joseph, marquis de. *Voyage de l'Arabie Pétrée par Léon de Laborde et Linant* (Girard, 1830), with 69 drawings. Translated into English as *Journey through Arabia Petraea, in Mount Sinai, and the Excavated City of Petra, the Edom of the Prophecies* (John Murray, 1836), second edition (1838).

Lamartine, Alphonse de. *Voyage en Orient.* t. 2ᵉ (Firmin Didot, 1849, first edition, 1835), 23–43. (Œuvres de M. de Lamartine).

Lane, Edward W. *An Account of the Manners and Customs of the Modern Egyptians, Written in Egypt during the years 1833, 34 and 35* (2 vols, 1836). 5th rev. edition, (ed.) Edward Stanley Poole (John Murray, 1860). (1963).

— *Selections from the Kur'an: with an Interwoven Commentary* (1843).

— 'Ueber die Lexicographie der arabischen Sprache', *Zeitschrift der Deutschen Morgendländischen Gesellschaft* 3 (1849), 90–108.

— *Madd al-Qamus. An Arabic-English Lexicon, Derived from the Best and the Most Copious Eastern Sources* (1863–93), 8 vols. Parts 6–8 ed. Stanley Lane Poole.

Leclant, Jean. 'Le Voyage de Nicholas Huyot en Egypte (1818–1819) et les manuscrits de Nestor L'Hôte', *Bulletin de la Société française d'égyptologie* (Dec. 1961).

Lenoir, Paul. *Le Fayoum, le Sinaï, Petra. Expédition dans la Moyenne Égypte et l'Arabie Pétrée sous la direction de J. -L. Gérôme* (H. Plon, 1872).

Lenormant, Charles & Nestor L'Hôte. *Musée des antiquités ou recueil des monuments égyptiens, architecture, statuaire, glyptique et peinture* (1841).

Leon, Edwin De. *The Khedive's Egypt* (Sampson Low & Co., 1877).

Lerebours, N. P. *Excursions daguérriennes: vues et monuments les plus remarquables du globe*, 2 vols (1842).

Lewis, J. M. *John Frederick Lewis, R. A. , 1805–1876* (Leigh-on-Sea, 1978).

L'Hôte, Edouard. 'Nestor L'Hôte ses travaux, ses voyages', *Revue de Paris* (Sept 1842).

L'Hôte, Nestor. *Notice historique sur les obélisques égyptiens et en particulier sur l'obélisque de Louqsor* (1836).

— *Lettres écrites d'Egypte en 1838 et 1839* (1840).

— 'Lettres écrites d'Egypte en 1840–1841', *Le Moniteur universel* (June 1841).

Lichtenberger, Marguerite. *Écrivains français en Égypte contemporaine (de 1870 à nos jours)* (Ernest Leroux, 1934).

Linant de Bellefonds Bey, *Mémoire sur le lac Moeris* (Alexandria: A. E. Ozanne's Press, 1843).

— *L'Etbaye. Pays habité par les Arabes Bicharieh. Géographie, Ethnologie, Mines d'or* (1868).

— *Mémoires sur les principaux travaux d'utilité publique exécutés en Égypte depuis la plus haute antiquité jusqu'à nos jours* (1872–1873).

Llewellyn, B. 'Frank Dillon and Victorian Pictures of Old Cairo houses', *Ur: The International Magazine of Arab Culture* 3 (1984), 2–10.

— 'Eastern Light', *FMR* (Aug 1984), 131–53.

— *The Orient Observed* (1990).

Lott, Emmeline. *The English Governess in Egypt: Harem Life in Egypt and Constantinople* (1866).

Lovenjoul, Charles de Spoelberch de. *Histoire des Œuvres de Théophile Gautier* t. II (1887), (Slatkine Reprints, 1968).

Lowe, Lisa. *Critical Terrains: French and British Imperialisms* (Ithaca, New York: Cornell University Press, 1992).

Luthi, Jean-Jacques. *Introduction à la littérature d'expression française en Egypte (1798–1945)* (Editions de l'École, 1974).

— *Le Français en Egypte* (Beirut: Naaman, 1981).

MacKenzie, J. M. *Orientalism: History, Theory and the Arts* (Manchester: MUP, 1995).

Madden, Richard Robert. *Travels in Turkey, Egypt, Nubia, and Palestine, in 1824, 1825, 1826, and 1827* (H. Colburn, 1829; Whitaker, Teacher, 1833), 2 vols.

— *Egypt and Muhammad Ali* (1841).

Mahdy, Hossam M. 'Attitudes Towards Architectural Conservation, The Case of Cairo', unpublished Ph. D. thesis, Glasgow (1992).

Malti-Douglas, Fedwa. 'Discussions of New Books: Re-orienting Orientalism', *The Virginia Quarterly Review* 55 iv (Autumn 1979), 724–33.

Manniche, Lisa. *City of the Dead, Thebes in Egypt* (BMP, 1987).

Manzalaoui, Mahmoud. 'Mouths of the Sevenfold Nile: English Fiction and Modern Egypt' in (ed.) Hopwood, 139–40.

Maunier, René. *Bibliographie économique, juridique et sociale de l'Égypte moderne (1798–1916)* (Cairo, 1918).

Mayes, Stanley. *The Great Belzoni* (1959).

Mazuel, J. *L'Œuvre géographique de Linant de Bellefonds* (1937).

Melman, Billie. *Women's Orients: English Women and the Middle East 1718–1918. Sexuality, Religion and Work* (Ann Arbor: The University of Michigan Press, 1992).

Mernissi, F. *Beyond the Veil: Male-Female Dynamics in a Modern Muselim Society*, (Cambridge, Mass.: Schenkman, 1975).

Międzyrzecki, Artur. *Kombatanci i podróżnicy*, z 16 rysunkami z Podróżya Wschód Juliusza Słowackiego (Warszawa: Czytelnik, 1960).

Minutoli, C. von. *Gesellschaftliche Spiele und gymnastische Uebungen bei den alten Aegyptern* ([Leipziger] Illustrirte Zeitung, XIX. Band, Nr. 490, 331; Leipzig, 1852).

Minutoli, Johann Heinrich Menu von. *Reise zum Pempel des Jupiter Ammon etc* (1824).

— *Abhandlungen vermischten Inhalts, zweiter Cyclus* (Berlin und Stettin, 1831).

Minutoli, Wolfradine Menu von. *Recollections of Egypt 1820–21* (1827), tr. from the French.

— *Reise der Frau Generalin von Minutoli nach Egypten. Deutsch herausgegeben von Wilhelmine von Gersdorf* (Leipzig, 1841).

Mitchell, Timothy. *Colonising Egypt* (Cambridge: CUP, 1988; Berkeley: University of California Press, 1991).

— 'The World as Exhibition', *Journal for Comparative Study of Society and History* (Ann Arbor: University of Michigan, 1989).

Monicat, Benedicte, 'Pour une bibliographie des récits de voyages au féminin (XIXᵉ siècle), *Romanticisme* 77: iii (1992), 95–100.

Moritz, Bernhard. *Catalogue de la section européenne (de la Bibliothèque Khédiviale)*. 1. *L'Égypte* (Cairo, 1901, 2nd edition).

Mousa, Nedal M. Al-. 'The Arabic *Bildungsroman*: A Generic Appraisal', *IJMES* 25 (1993), 223–40.

Moussa, Sarga. 'La Rencontre de l'autre. Enquête sur la communication dans les récits de voyage en Orient (1811–1861)'. Thèse en littérature française, sous la direction du professeur Michel Jeanneret (University of Geneva), Geneva, Feb. 1993. Unpublished Ph. D. thesis.

Moussa-Mahmoud, Fatma. 'English Travellers and the Arabian Nights', *The Arabian Nights in English Literature*, (ed.) P. L. Carraciolo (Basingstoke, 1988), 95–110.

Mubarak, 'Ali. *Kitab 'Alam al-Din* 4 vols (Alexandria, 1882), 4 vols.

— *Al-Khitat al-Tawfiqiyya al-jadida li-Misr al-Qahira wa-muduniha wa-biladiha al-qadima wa-al-shahira* (Bulaq, 1306 [1889]). 20 parts.

Munier, Henri. *Tables de la Description de l'Egypte suivies d'une bibliographie de l'expédition française de Bonaparte* (Cairo: IFAO, 1943).

al-Muwaylihi. *Hadith 'Isa ibn Hisham.* 4th edition (Cairo: Matba'at Misr, 1927).

Nehls, H. *Zwischen Dilettantismus und Wissenschaftlichkeit. Der Berliner Antikensammler Johann Heinrich Carl Freiherr Menu von Minutoli (1772–1846)* (Berlin: Freie Universität).

Neil, Rev William (ed.), *The Cleghorn Papers: A Footnote to History* (1927).

Nerval, de G. *Voyage en Orient* (Charpentier, 2 vols, 1851).

Nightingale, Florence. *Letters from Egypt* (Barrie & Jenkins, 1987).

Nikitin, V. 'Puteshestviya real'nye i voobrazhaemye' in (ed.) A. Dyuma, A. Doza. *Puteshestvie v Egipet*, tr. M. Taymanova (Moscow: Nauka, 1988), 3–15.

Noakes, V. *The Life of Edward Lear* (1968).

Nouty, Hassan al-. *Le Proche-Orient dans la littérature française de Nerval à Barrès* (Nizet, 1958).

O'Bell, Leslie. *Pushkin's 'Egyptian Nights': The Biography of a Work* (Ann Arbor: Ardis, 1984).

Orr, M. 'Reading the Other: Flaubert's Education Sentimentale Revisited', *French Studies* 46: 4 (Oct. 1992), 412–23.

Passalacqua, J. *Catalogue raisonné et historique des antiquités découvertes en Égypte* (1826).

Paton, A. A. *A History of the Egyptian Revolution* (1870).

Peet, T. Eric. *The Inscriptions of Sinai* (EEF, 1917).

Peled, Mattityahu. '*al-Saq 'ala al-Saq*: a Generic Definition', *Arabica* XXXII (1985), 31–46.

Pertek, Jerzy. *Polacy na szlakach morskich świata* (Gdańsk: Gdańskie Towarzystwo Naukowe, 1957), 456–59.

Piotrovsky, M. 'Posleslovie' in (ed.) A. Dyuma, A. Doza. *Puteshestvie v Egipet*, tr. M. Taymanova (Moscow: Nauka, 1988) 274–86.

Pitts, Joseph. *A Faithful Account of the Religion and Manners of the Mohametans*, 3rd edn. (1731).

Poole, Sophia Lane, *The Englishwoman in Egypt: Letters from Cairo, Written During a Residence There in 1842, 3, & 4*, 3 vols (Charles Knight & Co., 1844–1846).

Poole, Stanley Lane. 'Arab Art Monuments', *The Academy* 6 (1874).

—— *Life of Edward William Lane* (Williams & Norgate, 1877). Also published in Lane 1863–93 (see above), vol. 6, v–xxxix.

Porter, Dennis. 'The Perverse Traveler: Flaubert in the Orient', *Haunted Journeys: Desire and Transgression in European Travel Writing* (Princeton: Princeton University Press, 1991), 164–83.

Prangey, Joseph-Philibert Girault de. *Monuments arabes d'Égypte, de Syrie et d'Asie Mineure* (1842).

'The Preservation of mediaeval Cairo', *The Architect & Contract Reporter* (6 Mar 1896), 153.

[Prussian Expedition to Egypt], *Denkmaeler aus Aegypten und Aethiopien* (Leipzig, 1849–59).

Ragan, John David. 'Interesting Sources on French Travel Literature', *Travellers in Egypt: Notes and Queries* 3 (Dec. 1996), pp. 10-14.

Raymond, André. *Grandes villes arabes à l'époque ottomane* (Sindbad, 1985).

Régnier, Philippe. *Les Saint-Simoniens en Egypte, 1833–1851.* Preface by Amin Fakhry Abdelnour (Cairo: Banque de l'Union Européene, 1989).

— *Saint-Simoniens. le Livre nouveau des Saint-Simoniens* (Tusson, Charente: Éditions du Lerot, 1991).

— 'Les Femmes Saint-Simoniennes: De l'égalité octroyée à l'autonomie forcée, puis revindiquée'. Communication au colloque 'Femmes dans la cité', organisé par la Société de la révolution de 1848 en novembre 1993, forthcoming.

Reid, Donald M. 'Cultural Imperialism and Nationalism: The Struggle to Define and Control the Heritage of Arab Art in Egypt', *International Journal of Middle East Studies* 24 (Feb 1992), 57–76.

Reimer, Michael J. 'Contradiction and Consciousness in 'Ali Mubarak's Description of al-Azhar', *International Journal of Middle East Studies*, forthcoming (1997).

Reychman, Jan. *Podróżicy polsey na Bliskim Wschodzie w XIX w.* (Warszawa: Wiedza Powszechna, 1972), 114–23.

Richardson, Robert. *Travels Around the Mediterranean, and Parts Adjacent: In Company with the Earl of Belmont, during the years 1816, 1817, and 1818, extending as far as the Second Cataract of the Nile, Jerusalem, Damascus, Balbec, etc* (Printed for E. Cadell, 1822), 2 vols.

al-Rifa'i, 'Abd al-Rahman. *'Asr Isma'il* (Cairo, 1932, reprinted 1972).

Roberts, David. *The Holy Land, Syria, Idumea, Arabia, Egypt & Nubia* (1842–49), including *Egypt and Nubia*, vol. III (1849).

Roberts, Emma. *Notes of an Overland Journey Through France and Egypt to Bombay* (1841).

Robinson, Jane. *Wayward Women: A Guide to Women Travellers* (Oxford & New York: OUP, 1993).

Rochecantin, La Comtesse Mornière de la. *Du Caire à Assouân* (Jouve 1913).

Romer, Isabella. *A Pilgrimage to the Temples and Tombs of Egypt* (1846).

Rowley-Conwy, P. 'Nubia AD 0–550 and the "Islamic" Agricultural Revolution: Preliminary Botanical Evidence from Qasr Ibrim, Egyptian Nubia', *Archéologie du Nil moyen* 3 (1989), 131–38.

Royal Academy of Arts, London & National Gallery of Art, Washington, *The Orientalists: Delacroix to Matisse*, (ed.) Mary Anne Stevens (1984), cat. no. 73.

Rushdi, Rashad. 'English Travellers in Egypt During the Reign of Mohamed Ali', *Bulletin of the Faculty of Arts*, Jami'at Fu'ad al-Awwal [Cairo University], 14 ii (1952), 1–61.

Said, Edward W. 'East isn't West: The Impending End of the Age of Orientalism', *TLS* 4792 (3 Feb 1995), 1–2.

— *Orientalism* (London: Routledge & Kegan Paul, 1978; New York: Pantheon, 1978; Vintage Books, 1979; Harmondsworth: Penguin, 1995).

— *Culture and Imperialism* (New York: Alfred A. Knopft, 1993).

Sami, Amin. *Taqwim al-Nil wa-'Asr Muhammad 'Ali Basha* (Cairo, 1923).

Sammarco, Angelo. *Précis de l'histoire d'Égypte*, vol. IV. *Les Règnes de 'Abbas, de Sa'id, et d'Isma'il (1848–79)* (Rome, 1935).

Sammarco, Angelo (ed.) *Alessandro Ricci e il suo giornale dei viaggi* (Cairo: Soc. Royale Géogr, 1933), 2 vols.

Sargenton-Galichon, Adelaïde. *Sinai, Ma'ân, Petra: Sur les traces d'Israel et chez les Nabatéens* (Le Coffre, 1904).

Scott, C. Rochfort. *Rambles in Egypt and Candia with Details of the Military Power and Resources of Those Countries* (1837).

Searight, Sarah. *The British in the Middle East* (London, 1969; New York, Atheneum, 1970; reprinted 1979).

— *Steaming East* (1991).

Shafiq, Munir. *Qadaya al-tanmiya wa al-istiqlal wa al-sira' al-hadari* (Tunis, 1989).

[Sherer, J. M.] Anon. *Scenes and Impressions in Egypt and in Italy* (1824).

al-Shidyaq, Faris (later, Ahmad Faris). *al-Saq 'ala al-Saq fi ma huwa al-Faryaq* (Paris: Benjamin Duprat, 1855).

— *Kitab al-rihla al-mawsuma bi-al-Wasita ila ma'rifat Malita wa-Kashf al-mukhabba 'an funun Awruba* (Tunis, 1280 [1863/64]).

Shinnie, M. (ed.). *Linant de Bellefonds. Journal d'un voyage à Méroé dans les années 1821 et 1822*, Occasional Papers 4 (Khartoum: Sudan Antiquities Service, 1958).

Sidebottom J. *The Overland Mail* (1948).

Sims, Katherine. *Desert Traveller: the life of John Lewis Burckhardt* (Gollancz, 1969).

Słowacki, Juliusz. *Podróżna Wschód*, (ed.) Łukasz Kurdybacha. (Jerozolima: Ministerstwo Wyznań Religijnych i Oświecenia Publicznego, 1944). (Szkolna biblioteczka na Wschodzie, t. 50). Introduction by Ł. Kurdybacha.

— *Dzieła wybrane* (Warszawa: Panstwowy Instytut Wydawniczy, 1954),4 v.

— *Wybór pism: wiersze różne* (Londyn: Swiatpol, 1947). (Biblioteka arcydzieł polskich, t. 2).

— *The Father of the Plague-Stricken at El Arish*, tr. from the Polish by M. B. Peacock & G. R. Noyes (1930).

— *La Peste au désert à El-Arish*, tr. to French by Venceslas Gasztowtt (1879).

— *Anhalli: nashid ramzi qawmi*, tarjamaha wa-'arrabaha Yusuf As'ad Daghir (Bayrut: 1948).

Sotheby's, *Important Orientalist Paintings from the Collection of Coral Petroleum*, sale catalogue (22 May 1985).

— *Important Nineteenth-Century Pictures from a European Private Collection* (20 Nov 1996).

Saint John, James Augustus. *Egypt and Mohammed Ali* (1834).

— *Egypt and Nubia* (1845).

Starke, Marianna. *Travels on the Continent Written for the Use and Particular Information of Travellers* (1820).

Starkey, Paul. 'Fact and Fiction in *al-Saq 'ala al-Saq*', in R. Ostle, E. de Moor & S. Wild (eds), *Writing the Self in Modern Arabic Literature* (London: Saqi, 1998) (forthcoming).

Steegmuller, Francis (ed.). *Flaubert in Egypt: A Sensibility on Tour: A Narrative Drawn from Gustave Flaubert's Travel Notes and Letters, translated from the French and edited by Francis Steegmuller* (Boston, 1972; Chicago: Academy, 1979).

Stephens, John Lloyd. *Incidents of Travel in Egypt, Arabia Petraea, and the Holy Land*, 2 vols (New York: Harper and Brothers, 1837).

Stevens, M. A. *The Orientalists: Delacroix to Matisse* (National Gallery of Art, Washington, exhibition catalogue, 1984).

Stocks, P. 'Edward William Lane and his Arabic-English "Thesaurus"', *British Library Journal* 15 (1989), 23–34.

— *The Blue Guide to Egypt* (1994).

300   *Travellers in Egypt*

al-Tahtawi, *Takhlis al-ibriz ila talkhis Bariz* (1834; Cairo: Dar al-Taqqadum ed. , 1323/1905). A French tr. by A. Louca, *L'Or de Paris* (Paris, 1988).

Terterian, I. 'Romantism kak celostnoe yavlenie', *Voprosy literatury* (1983/84), 151–83.

Teynard, Félix. *Calotypes of Egypt, A Catalogue raisonné with an essay by Kathleen Stewart Howe* (New York, 1992).

Thompson, Jason. *Sir Gardner Wilkinson and His Circle* (Austin: University of Texas Press, 1992).

— '"I Felt Like an Eastern Bridegroom": Edward William Lane's First Trip to Egypt, 1825–1828', *Turkish Studies Association Bulletin* 17 (1993), 138–41.

— 'Edward William Lane as an Artist', *Gainsborough's House Review* (1993/94), 33–42.

— 'Osman Effendi: A Scottish Convert to Islam in Early Nineteenth-Century Egypt', *Journal of World History* 5 i (1994), 99–123.

— 'A reassessment of Edward William Lane', *ARCE Newsletter* 166 (Fall/Winter 1994–95), 1–5.

— 'Edward William Lane as Egyptologist', *Minerva* 6 (Fall 1995), 12–17.

— '"OF THE OSMANA'NLEES, OR TURKS" An Unpublished Chapter from Edward William Lane's *Manners and Customs of the Modern Egyptians*', *Turkish Studies Association Bulletin* 19 (Autumn 1995), 19–39.

Tibawi, A. L. 'English-Speaking Orientalists: A Critique of Their Approach to Islam and Arab Nationalism', *Muslim World* 53 (1963), 185–204 & 298–313. Also in *Islamic Quarterly*, 8 (1964), 25–45 & 73–88.

Tillett, Selwyn. *Egypt Itself: The Career of Robert Hay, Esquire of Linplum and Nunraw, 1799–1863* (SD Books, 1984).

Titmarsh, W. A. [W. M. Thackeray], *Notes of a Journey from Cornhill to Grand Cairo* (1846); reprinted with new introduction by S. Searight & illustrations compiled by B. Llewellyn (Heathfield: Cockbird Press, 1991).

Tolmacheva, Marina. 'The Medieval Arab Geographers and the Beginnings of Modern Orientalism', *IJMES* 27 ii (May 1995), 141–56.

Tortonese, Paolo (ed.), *Gautier's Voyage en Égypte* (La Boîte à Documents, 1991).

Treugutt, Stefan. Juliusz Słowacki, romantic poet (Warsaw: Polonia Publishing House, 1959).

— 'Słowacki Juliusz' in *Wielka Encyklopedia Powszechna PWN* (Warszawa: Pałswowe Wydawnictwo Naukowe, 1967), vol. 10, 596–98.

Tucker, Judith E. *Women in Nineteenth-Century Egypt* (Cambridge: CUP, 1985; Cairo: AUC Press, 1986).

Urbain, Ismayl. *Voyages d'Orient suivi de poèmes de Ménilmontant et d'Égypte* (ed.) Philippe Régnier (L'Harmattan, 1993).

Vercoutter, Jean. *The Search for Ancient Egypt* (Thames & Hudson Publications, Series of New Horizons, 1992).

Vercoutter, J. (ed.). *Livre du centenaire, 1880–1980* (Cairo: IFAO, 1980).

Villoteau, Guillaume-André. "Des *a'ouâlem*, des *ghaouâzy* ou danseuses publiques, des diverses espèces de ménétriers, jongleurs, saltimbanques, farceurs, etc. , qui font usages de quelques instruments de la musique" in 'De l'état actuel de l'art musicale en Égypte', *Description de l'Égypte* 82, Chapitre II, Article v, *État moderne*, Première Partie, I [first edition], 1 (Imprimerie nationale, 1809), 694–700.

Voilquin, Suzanne. *Souvenirs d'une fille du peuple ou la Saint-Simonienne en Egypte, 1834 à 1836* (Sauzet, 1866).
— *Mémoires d'une Saint-Simonienne en Russie* (ed.) Maité Albistur & Daniel Armogathe (Editions des Femmes, 1977).
— *Souvenirs d'une fille du peuple ou la Saint-Simonienne en Egypte, 1834 à 1836* (Maspero, 1978), abridged version.
— 'Lettres sur l'Egypte', *Le Siècle* (1837).
Webster, James. *Travels Through the Crimea, Turkey, and Egypt; Performed during the years 1825-28. Including Particulars of the Last Illness and Death of the Emperor Alexander, and of the Russian Conspiracy in 1825* (H. Colburn, 1830), 2 vols.
Whyte, Peter. *Théophile Gautier, conteur fantastique et merveilleux* (Durham: DMLS, 1996).
Wilde, Sir William. *Narrative of a Voyage to Madeira, Teneriffe and along the Shores of the Mediterranean, Including a Visit to Algiers, Egypt, Palestine ...Cyprus and Greece* (Dublin, 1840).
Wilkinson, Sir John Gardner. *The Manners and Customs of the Ancient Egyptians* (1837 and 1854).
— *Modern Egypt and Thebes* (1843).
— *Handbook for Travellers in Egypt* (John Murray, 1847; 1896).
— *The Architecture of the Ancient Egyptians* (1850).
Williams, C. 'Jean-Léon Gérôme: a case study of an Orientalist painter' in Sabra Webber (ed.), 'Fantasy or Ethnography?', *Papers in Comparative Studies* 8 (Ohio State University, 1995).
Wilson, William Rae. *Travels in Egypt and the Holy Land* (Printed for Longman, Hurst, Reese, Orme, & Browne, 1823).
Wood, A. *Thomas Young* (Cambridge, 1954).
Wood, Alfred C. *A History of the Levant Company* (1964).
Zajączkowski, Ananiasz. *Orient jako źródło inspiracji w literaturze romantycznej doby mickiewiczowskiej* (Warszawa: Państwowy Instytut Wydawniczy, 1955).
Zaki, 'Abd al-Rahman. *Mawsu'at madinat al-Qahira fi alf 'am* (Cairo, 1969).

Archival Sources

Les Archives Nationales, Archives des Affaires Etrangères, Paris

B I, Alexandria, Mure (French consul), n. d.; Correspondance Politique, Turquie, t. 162. 'Conventions preliminaires d'un traite de commerce et navigation de l'Inde par Suez, arretées et conclues au Caire le 10 Janvier 1785. '; t. 166. 'Memoire contenant les details de ce que les anglois viennent s'eprouver en Egypte et de la traine odieuse dont les sujets du Roy été la victime'. Enclosed in a letter to Hennin, 3 Feb 1780.

302   *Travellers in Egypt*

Ashmolean Museum, Archives of the Griffith Institute Archives, Oxford

Joseph Bonomi's unpublished diary (transcript). Lane, Edward William. 'Accounts and Memoranda Cairo. 1825', f. 50v; Manuscript second draft of 'Description of Egypt', unfoliated; Small notebook diaries from Lane's first trip to Egypt, 1:7.

Bibliothèque de l'Arsenal, Paris

Voilquin, Suzanne. Correspondance (unpublished). Fonds Enfantin 7791/133–45, 7613/214, 7627/58–64, 7791/123–29, 7861/Br. 4, 9, 11, 12, 18 & Fonds Eichthal MS 13 739/233.

Bibliothèque Nationale, Paris.

Manuscrits. Nouvelles acquisitions françaises. 20. 377, 20. 396–20. 404. L'Hôte, Nestor.

Bodleian Library, Department of Western Manuscripts, Oxford

Ms Eng. lett d 165, ff. 77–8 Edward William Lane to Robert Hay (Cairo, 9 January 1834); lett d 165, ff. 141–2. Lane to Robert Hay (Cairo, 15 Oct 1842); misc. d. 234f. 5. Lane.

British Library, Department of Manuscripts at the British Museum, London

Additional Manuscripts 35118 f. 37, Baldwin to Edward Monckton; Fortesque Mss, vol. II, Appendix V, Grenville to Dundas, 25 Jan 1793; 25651, ff. 2, James Burton, Orlando Felix & papers of J. Bonomi, including visit to Jabal Barkal; 25658, ff. 79–83, James Burton, Orlando Felix & papers of J. Bonomi; 25663, ff. 42–1070. Felix papers; f. 149, The Regulations of the English Reading Society in the James Burton Collection, Collectanea Ægyptiaca-Miscellaneous Subjects; 29812–60, especially 29831, ff. 25 *et seq*. Robert Hay's unpublished collection of sketches & notes; 31054, f. 41. Manuscript diary of Robert Hay; 34080–8. Edward William Lane's papers, including 'Notes and Views of Egypt and Nubia'; 38094, ff. 81–2. Frederick Catherwood to Robert Hay (2 May 1835); 41463. H. B. Martin Mss. Warren R. Dawson papers, including Westcar diary.

British Library, Oriental Collections, London

Or. MSS 4154–4219 & 4618–4657 Edward William Lane's collection of Arabic manuscripts.

German Institute of Archaeology Library, Cairo

Westcar diary.

India Office Records, London

Factory Records, Egypt and the Red Sea, vol. 5, O'Donnell to Ibrahim Bey, 8 July 1779; vol. 5a, Dundas *et al.* to Carmarthen, 19 May 1786; 17 Sept 1791; 9 Nov 1793.

Public Record Office, Kew

FO 24/1, Heads of Instructions to Baldwin from the India Board, 19 May 1786; Baldwin to Carmarthen, 2 Apr 1788; Baldwin to Grenville, 17 Sept 1791; Grenville to Dundas, 8 Feb 1793; Baldwin to Grenville, 10 Apr 1793; Baldwin to Grenville, 29 Mar 1796; Baldwin to Dundas, 21 Apr 1796; FO 78/1, 'Copy of a bond drawn up in Arabic by order of the Government of Egypt, obtained by violence from those who signed' (translation), n. d.; Ainslie to Hillsborough, 17 Apr 1780; FO 78/7, Ainslie to Carmarthen, 10 Oct 1786; Ainslie to Carmarthen, 25 Oct 1786; Carmarthen to Ainslie, 1 Sept 1786.

State Papers (SP) 97/53, Baldwin to Ainslie (copy), 24 June 1777; SP 97/54, Translation of *Hatti Sherif* to the Government of Egypt; SP 97/55, Baldwin to Ainslie (copy), 31 Aug 1779; Ainslie's Memorial to the Porte (translation), 24 Sept 1779.

Treasury, T. 1 /759, Board Paper, 16 Jan 1796; T. 1 /760, 29 Jan 1796.

WO 1/361 (Ceylon), Cleghorn to Dundas, 10 June 1795.

Thomas Cook Archive, London

Riggs, Miss. 'Dairy of the First Cook's Tour in Egypt and Palestine', unpublished diary (1869).

'Thomas Cook in Egypt', a draft paper (1995).

Victoria and Albert Museum, London

Searight collection

∽ Index of People and Places